Kazakhstan's Emerging Economy

Emerging Markets Studies

Edited by Joachim Ahrens, Alexander Ebner, Herman W. Hoen,
Bernhard Seliger and Ralph Michael Wrobel

Vol. 5

PL ACADEMIC RESEARCH

Roman Vakulchuk

Kazakhstan's Emerging Economy

Between State and Market

PL ACADEMIC RESEARCH

Bibliographic Information published by the Deutsche Nationalbibliothek
The Deutsche Nationalbibliothek lists this publication in the Deutsche Nationalbibliografie; detailed bibliographic data is available in the internet at http://dnb.d-nb.de.

Zugl.: Bremen, Jacobs University, Diss., 2013

Library of Congress Cataloging-in-Publication Data
Vakulchuk, Roman, 1984-
Kazakhstan's emerging economy : between state and market / Roman Vakulchuk.
pages cm
Includes bibliographical references
ISBN 978-3-631-65095-0 — ISBN 978-3-653-04328-0 (ebook)
1. Kazakhstan—Economic policy—1991- 2. Kazakhstan—Economic conditions—1991- I. Title.
HC420.5.V35 2014
338.95845—dc23

2014031260

D 579
ISSN 2190-099X
ISBN 978-3-631-65095-0 (Print)
E-ISBN 978-3-653-04328-0 (E-Book)
DOI 10.3726/978-3-653-04328-0

PL Academic Research is an Imprint of Peter Lang GmbH.

Peter Lang – Frankfurt am Main · Bern · Bruxelles · New York · Oxford · Warszawa · Wien

This publication has been peer reviewed.

www.peterlang.com

Acknowledgements

I would like to take this opportunity to express my deepest gratitude to my academic advisors, Prof. Dr Joachim Ahrens, Prof. Dr Margrit Schreier, Prof. Dr Welf Werner, for exemplary guidance and advice, understanding, patience and continuous encouragement throughout the course of my studies. I have been unbelievably fortunate to have these three academic advisors who have motivated me, while also setting high academic standards.

I wish to thank Dr Joachim Ahrens, who was always there to listen and give insightful advice and inspiration. He showed me the importance of being able and willing to listen to advice and also think independently.

I am deeply grateful to Dr Margrit Schreier for invaluable advice, constructive criticisms, thorough and very helpful revisions of my methodological chapter throughout my studies.

And to Dr Welf Werner I am truly indebted and grateful for his encouragement, practical advice and thought-provoking criticisms, helpful insights and enriching research ideas.

This work would not have been possible without the love and patience of my family. I wish to express my warm gratitude to my parents, Ludmila and Anatoliy, for their understanding, encouragement, motivation, support and patience. To them I dedicate this work. Further I wish to thank my wife Kateryna, for her constant encouragement, support and motivation, as well as my grandmother, brother, and sister for their support.

I am also very pleased to acknowledge and thank Dr Indra Øverland, Farrukh Irnazarov, Dr Alexander Libman, Dr Martin Spechler, Dr Manuel Stark, Alibek Tusupbekov, Zafar Salmanov and Susan Höivik for their constructive criticisms and contributions to my work. Further, I am truly indebted to Gulnura Zhazylbekova for her invaluable support and motivation.

It is my great pleasure to thank friends and colleagues at the KIMEP University in Almaty, the Private University of Applied Sciences in Göttingen, and Jacobs University Bremen in Bremen, for assistance with data collection and research. I am thankful to my colleagues at the Norwegian Institute of International Affairs (NUPI) for their support and encouragement.

I am also grateful to the Norwegian Institute of International Affairs (NUPI) for the support in the publication of this book.

Finally, I deeply appreciate the financial support of the Volkswagen Foundation, which provided a scholarship for my doctoral studies, for the research project described here as well as for the publication of this book.

Roman Vakulchuk Oslo (Norway), August 2014

Abstract

Kazakhstan has become a successful market reformer under the leadership of President Nursultan Nazarbayev. This book focuses on Kazakhstan's distinct transition path, describing in depth the type of market economy that has evolved in the country since 1991. The main research question is: what type of a market economy is emerging in Kazakhstan? To address this question, this work studies the role of the state in steering economic processes, and analyses the interaction between the state and private business.

The research design is based on qualitative cross-sectional interview study. The Varieties of Capitalism approach and a 'core–periphery' analytical framework are applied to classify the evolving model of capitalist economy in Kazakhstan. The findings indicate that application of the Varieties of Capitalism approach to the post-communist transition economy of Kazakhstan has its limits. This is due to the massive role of the state in the transition context and the fact that this approach is poorly suited for explaining sudden institutional changes in the economy. Therefore, the Varieties of Capitalism approach is complemented by the 'core–periphery' analytical framework, as developed in this study and proven useful in accounting for the large role of the state in the economy. The results indicate that the economy of Kazakhstan represents a hybrid 'core–periphery' model, in which the 'core' part is more state-led, whereas the 'periphery' part is more market-oriented. Each economic part has elements of both state and market coordination. Importantly, the rules of the game for economic players differ in the 'core' and in the 'periphery'; likewise with coordination mechanisms.

Qualitative data collection and analysis were employed in order to provide an in-depth description of a distinct type of Kazakhstan's economy. The study involves the analysis of secondary and primary sources. For primary data collection 159 semi-structured interviews were conducted in Kazakhstan in 2009–2010 with public officials, experts, representatives of international organizations, representatives of private domestic companies, foreign enterprises and state-owned companies, and representatives of employer associations and labour unions.

In addition to making an important contribution to the body of knowledge on interviewing elites in Kazakhstan and Central Asia, this research makes an innovative contribution to the broader scholarly literature on economic and institutional transition of Kazakhstan. Moreover, this study adds to the processes of cumulative knowledge-building on emerging economies in post-Soviet Central Asia and similar countries in transition.

Table of contents

List of figures

List of tables

List of Cases in Point

List of acronyms and abbreviations

ADB	Asian Development Bank
AFN	Committee for the Control and Supervision of the Financial Market and Financial Organizations of the National Bank of the Republic of Kazakhstan
AmCham	American Chamber of Commerce
AMFOK	Association of Microfinance Organizations of Kazakhstan
AMME	Association of Mining and Metallurgical Enterprises
BEEPS	Business Environment and Enterprise Performance Survey
BP	British Petroleum
CEO	Chief Executive Officer
CIS	Commonwealth of Independent States
CME	Coordinated Market Economy
CSR	Corporate Social Responsibility
DAMU	Entrepreneurship Development Fund
EBRD	European Bank for Reconstruction and Development
EFA	Education for All
EITI	Extractive Industries Transparency Initiative
ENI	Ente Nazionale Idrocarburi
ENRC	Eurasian Natural Resources Corporation
ETF	European Training Foundation
EU	European Union
EUROBAK	European Business Association of Kazakhstan
FDI	Foreign Direct Investment
FIAK	Financial Institutions' Association of Kazakhstan
FIC	Foreign Investors' Council
FSA	Financial Supervision Agency
GDP	Gross Domestic Product
GIZ	Deutsche Gesellschaft für Internationale Zusammenarbeit
HHI	Herfindahl Hirschman Index
HR	Human Resources
IBRD	International Bank for Reconstruction and Development
IF	Interview Form

IFK	Investment Fund of Kazakhstan
IMF	International Monetary Fund
IT	Information Technology
ISSA	International Social Security Association
JSC	Joint-Stock Company
KASE	Kazakhstan Stock Exchange
KTJ	National Railway Company 'Kazakhstan Temir Joly'
LME	Liberal Market Economy
M&A	Mergers and Acquisitions
MCO	Microfinance Organization
NBF	National Business Forum
NBK	National Bank of Kazakhstan
NFRK	National Fund of the Republic of Kazakhstan
NGO	Non-Governmental Organization
NIF	National Innovation Fund
NPVET	National Programme of VET Development
OECD	Organization for Economic Cooperation and Development
PR	Public Relations
PSA	Production Sharing Agreement
R&D	Research and Development
REPO	Repurchase Agreement
SME	Small and Medium-Sized Enterprises
UNCTAD	United Nations Conference on Trade and Development
UNDP	United Nations Development Program
UNECE	United Nations Economic Commission for Europe
UNESCO	United Nations Educational, Scientific and Cultural Organization
UNICEF	United Nations International Children's Emergency Fund
USAID	United States Agency for International Development
USD	United States Dollar
VAT	Value-Added Tax
VET	Vocational Education and Training
VoC	Varieties of Capitalism

Chapter 1. Introduction: Kazakhstan's distinct model of economic transition

We put our faith in a radical market reform of our economy, introduced expedited market reforms, and passed the necessary legislation. Kazakhstan today has a functioning market economy.
From the Address of the President of Kazakhstan to the People of Kazakhstan, 'Kazakhstan on the Way to Accelerated Economic, Social and Political Modernization' (2005)

After gaining independence in 1991, Kazakhstan embarked on a strategy of introducing market economic principles into the economic reform processes (Pomfret 2005; Charman 2007; Spechler 2008; Knox 2008). Since independence the country has been open for market capitalism (Spechler 2003). Today, it is a country with an officially recognized market economy (US Department of State 2002; Eicher 2004a) and, according to the classification of the International Monetary Fund (2011a: 122); Kazakhstan belongs to the group of 'Emerging and Developing Economies'. As Teal et al. (2011) argue, in 20 years of statehood Kazakhstan has made remarkable progress in terms of shifting from a command to a market-oriented economy. According to the Bertelsmann Foundation (2010), the country ranks as one of the most advanced countries of the former Soviet Union in terms of implementing market reforms. However, economists and other scholars continue to debate whether the country has really completed the transition from a planned to a market economy. For instance, whereas Agrawal (2008: 90) holds that the main transition phase is already over, the European Bank for Reconstruction and Development has maintained that the current reform and transition process in Kazakhstan is not yet complete (EBRD 2010a).

Among the post-Soviet states, Kazakhstan's economy was one of the hardest hit by the disintegration of the USSR (Alshanov 2011). Inflation was rampant, unemployment was high and the entire economy was almost in ruins in the early 1990s (Alshanov 2011; Laurens 2004). However, the economic reforms of the 1990s helped the country recover quickly from the economic downturn (Alshanov 2011; Pomfret 2009). Indeed, since independence, the economic performance of Kazakhstan has been remarkable, with high economic growth especially during the second decade of independence (Knox 2008).

Kazakhstan's model of economic reform is distinct in many respects. For one thing, the economic success of the country has been associated with the personality of President Nursultan Nazarbayev (Aitken 2009). His widely used slogan 'the economy first, then politics!' is associated with the country's progressive economic reforms.[1] Since independence President Nazarbayev has expressed his vision of making Kazakhstan an economically successful and prosperous country, and achieving the development heights of the Western world (Dave 2007: 1). Economic reform has been prioritized above political reform, with Nazarbayev using his power to promote market-oriented reforms (Zarakhovich 2006). According to Simon (2009: 68), many scholars support the idea that the first stage of transition should prepare the ground for the emergence of a market economy.

Economic development has also been heavily influenced by the country's political regime and by the state. Charman (2007) agrees that the state has played an important role in the economic reform processes in the country. The role of the state is seen as to promote the creation of a socially-oriented mixed market economy, based on a combination of the competitive self-regulation of production and the state regulation of economic processes (Nazarbayev 2003). As the country's political leader and reformer, President Nazarbayev, has repeatedly stressed the importance of active state participation in the economy as a model for Kazakhstan's market economy. From the early years of independence, he has emphasized this principle of state regulation: 'Our strategy of healthy economic growth is based upon strong market economy, active state's role and attraction of significant foreign investments' (Nazarbayev 2003: 41). Thus, three major pillars of the economy have been prioritized: market economy, an active role for the state and foreign direct investment (FDI). As regards the third, although FDI in Kazakhstan has been mainly directed towards its energy resources (Waikar et al. 2011), it has had positive effect on economic growth after 2000 and has helped to develop the economy (Waikar et al. 2009). Peyrouse (2008) notes that liberalization reforms of the 1990s paved the way for attracting FDI.

After the dissolution of the USSR, both Kazakhstan and Russia chose to pursue a 'shock therapy' approach in their development strategies (Hall and Elliott, 1999). This approach entails the rapid implementation of liberalization reforms, privatization, and macroeconomic stabilization (Lipton and Sachs 1990). Similar to Russia (Åslund 2007), Kazakhstan has managed, with partial success, to implement liberal economic reforms (see Chapter 2). Here we should note one puzzling observation regarding privatization. Newly independent states are generally expected to emphasize protection of their sovereignty, and thus be unwilling to share state ownership of oil and gas resources with foreign companies (Thomson 1995; Birnie and Boyle 1992, referred in Luong and Weinthal 2001). In case of Kazakhstan, however, the government was willing to privatize its energy industry, and foreign companies purchased the majority of

1 Interview with President Nazarbayev, *Euronews*, January 15, 2010, available at: http://ru.euronews.com/2010/01/15/nazarbayev-economy-first-then-politics/, accessed 5 January 2014.

state-owned corporations in the oil and gas sector in the early 1990s (Luong and Weinthal 2001). In its economic policy model, the country oriented itself towards the West by offering its natural resources in return. As argued by Dorofeyev, public relations director at KazMunaiGas (the national oil and gas company), 'we offered oil to the West in exchange for technology, know-how and money' (in Zarakhovich 2006; see also subsection 2.2.1 on privatization in Kazakhstan). Even though contrary trends emerged and the state increased the shares of the national oil companies in production-sharing agreements with foreign investors after 2000 (Pomfret 2011: 16–17; Palazuelos and Fernandes 2012), still the initial country's openness and willingness to engage with international actors seems puzzling and requires closer scrutiny.

In contrast to Kazakhstan, Uzbekistan has chosen a gradual transition model of 'stability at any cost' (Spechler 2000: 102). This proved effective in terms of economic growth during the first decade of independence, but has failed to provide strong and competitive market institutions in the long run (Akimov and Dollery 2006). Many other countries of the former Soviet Union faced similar difficulties after gaining independence; however, not all of them managed to implement progressive liberalization reforms as Kazakhstan did. Due to the liberalization reforms of the early 1990s, Kazakhstan's financial system is today considered to be the most advanced of the CIS countries (Tumenbayeva 2012; Pomfret 2009; Seitkasimov 2009; Akimov and Dollery 2007; AmCham 2004; Merrill and Whiteley 2003).

Charman (2007: 180) defines Kazakhstan as 'a state-led liberal market economy' and Spechler (2008: 33) as 'state-led' capitalist economy, pointing to the key role of the state in the economic realm. As Hall and Soskice (2001: 49) note, the political regime may play a large role in shaping the formation of a particular type of economy. Similarly, according to Mendelski (2008), the role of the state is crucial in the formation of institutions in a transition economy. Treacher (2007) defines Kazakhstan as a 'soft authoritarian' state, and Simon (2009: 68) notes that economic liberalization has been conducted 'under the conditions of a limited democracy'. All the same, prudent reform measures during the first years of independence paved the way for subsequent high economic growth and the transition to a market economy (Olcott 2008; Simon 2009). Today Kazakhstan has the most advanced economy in Central Asia (Pasadilla 2010: 4).

The country was severely hit by the world economic crisis of 2008; however, it managed to recover faster than any other country in the West or Asia, thanks not least to an appropriate government economic policy (Aitken 2012). The emerging market-oriented model of economy made it possible to achieve high economic growth (Knox 2008) and rapidly overcome the economic crisis of 2008 (Aitken 2012; Pomfret 2009). However, today the economy is heavily dependent on the export of natural resources, oil and gas in particular (Cutler

2012; Smirnova et al. 2012), and economic growth has remained unsustainable due to weak economic diversification, poor energy infrastructure and the dependence on energy exports (Gumppenberg 2007; Spence 2009; Aidarkhanova 2010; Heinrich and Pleines 2012). That said, the economy of Kazakhstan is the most diversified of the Central Asian countries (Amin and Ainekova 2012: 46) and economic growth has led to higher standards of living (Gumppenberg 2007).

The main challenge for the country has been to ensure optimal use of the ever-expanding petroleum industry and distribute petroleum revenue in the best interests of the whole nation (Chapman 2011; Najman et al. 2005). Although oil production is forecast to provide petroleum revenues until the 2050s (Lücke 2010), the government has taken numerous measures to diversify the economy and optimally distribute the petroleum revenue (OECD 2011a; OECD 2011b; Wandel 2010: 7). The National Fund of the Republic of Kazakhstan (NFRK) was established in 2000 to take charge of excess petroleum revenues, avoid the 'resource curse' and maintain fiscal stability (Kalyuzhnova 2006; Dzharkinbayev 2011: 51). From 2000 to 2010 the Fund's accumulated assets grew from USD 1.2 billion to USD 33.7 billion (Dzharkinbayev 2011: 51), and there was no evidence of the 'resource curse' affecting the economy (CASE 2008: 6). Moreover, after 2000 the government has launched various development programmes aimed at diversifying the economy, including 'Diversification of Kazakhstan's Economy through Cluster Development in Non-Extracting Sectors of Economy' adopted in 2004, and 'The State Programme on Accelerated Industrial Innovative Development' for the period 2010–2014. However, these programmes have not met the set objectives, largely because scientific research institutes pursue technological activities 'on behalf of industrial firms' (Islamic Development Bank 2011: xvii), which do not have proper infrastructure and knowledge for implementing technology-driven diversification programmes. A further problem is the lack of qualified human resources, especially skilled senior managers and engineers (Mashuri 2010: 34). Serious challenges for technological and economic development remain (Pomfret 2011; Sinicina 2006).

Kazakhstan's development path has become distinct in many respects. There are three empirical puzzles that make its development strategy particularly interesting and distinct from other similar countries in transition. First, in the early 1990s the economy was nearly ruined: inflation reached four-digit figures, economic stagnation was pervasive with high unemployment rates, and future economic prospects were unclear. Then, after 2000 the country witnessed a period of high economic growth, with lessening income inequality and lower unemployment. True, the export of energy resources helped the country to recover from the economic collapse of the 1990s. On the other hand, we should bear in mind that, without appropriate market-oriented political and economic institutions formed in the country after 1991, the management of energy resources would hardly have proven sustainable and successful.

The second puzzling observation relates to privatization processes. What drove the government to open the economy to foreign actors? As discussed above, newly-independent resource-rich countries are generally expected to seek to protect their sovereignty and tend not to open their economies to foreign capital. Kazakhstan is amply endowed with natural resources, oil and gas in particular. Nevertheless, the country largely privatized its energy sector and has been open to FDI in natural resources ever since independence in 1991.

Third, why Kazakhstan was not trapped by the 'resource curse'? Many scholars have held that it is vulnerable to the 'Dutch disease' (Kalyuzhnova 2011; Ustyantseva 2010; Kalyuzhnova 2006; Cohen 2003; Wakeman-Linn et al. 2003; Kuralbayeva et al. 2001). The economy is indeed dependent and relies heavily on energy revenues. And yet, the government managed to avoid the negative impact of excessive oil revenues on the economy by establishing the NFRK. Kazakhstan is seen as an authoritarian state with limited democratic rule (Simon 2009: 68) – and yet, the government has established a market-oriented environment in which progressive economic reforms have been implemented, institutions developed and the impacts of the 'resource curse' avoided.

These three puzzling observations regarding the distinct market reform path the country has followed since independence lead to the main research question of this book: *what type of a market economy is emerging in Kazakhstan?* Answering this question will also shed light on why Kazakhstan has become a more successful market reformer than other former Soviet republics.

I assume that the economy of the country has been gravitating towards a distinct type of a market economy which has elements of two different types of economies: Liberal Market Economy (LME) and Coordinated Market Economy (CME). These two types are embedded in the Varieties of Capitalism (VoC) approach, the theoretical framework put forward by Hall and Soskice (2001); this firm-centred approach distinguishes between the LME and CME-type of countries according to the differences in coordination mechanisms that govern relations between private firms (see Chapter 3 on the VoC approach). I argue that the structure of the economy of Kazakhstan reflects the elements of these two different market models of economy. Thus, I examine the role and the contribution of each economic model to the formation of a market economy in the country. I use qualitative data collection and analysis to provide an in-depth description of a distinct type of Kazakhstan's economy.

To understand the essence of the evolving market economy in the country, it is necessary to account for the role of the state in the reform process. Answering the main research question will help to explain how and to what extent the state has shaped the emergence of market economy in Kazakhstan.

Consequently, the main research question has been refined as follows:

1. What is the role of the state in steering economic processes in Kazakhstan, and how does the interaction between the state and private business take place?
2. How do relations between private economic actors shape the emerging economy in Kazakhstan?
3. What is the role of other market players, such as labour unions and employer associations, in influencing state–business interaction and in shaping economic relations in the country?

The relations between the state and business are at the core of this analysis (see research question 1). I analyse how the objectives of the state and business interact, with special attention to the scope of state involvement in economic processes over time. I examine how and why the shift in various degrees of state involvement has occurred, identifying its specific stages. I analyse interaction between the state and business at various levels, assess state attitudes towards different parts of private business as well as business attitudes towards the state and its economic policy. Further, I identify the major problems encountered by foreign and domestic business, with the mechanisms employed to overcome these difficulties. I also shed light on the growth opportunities for private firms in key industries of the economy.

Even so, analysing the state–business nexus is not sufficient to fully reveal the nature of the emerging market economy; we also need to understand how private companies interact with each other. Given the paucity of the literature on inter-firm relations (see subsection 3.3.6), it is important to augment what is already known, examining how private firms from different industries interact and what implications this interaction has for the country's economy. Thus, the second research question is: how do relations between private economic actors shape the emerging economy in Kazakhstan? Here the interaction between private firms will be analysed by looking at the type of interaction (cooperation or competition), the regulation of competition within key industries of the economy as well as merger and acquisitions policies of private firms. I also identify the key requirements – size of business, type of activity, state regulation, type of industry – for cooperation/non-cooperation between private firms.

Finally, this book examines how other market players such as labour unions and employer associations influence state–business relations and contribute to the formation of the economy (see research question 3). Although state–business relations are the major indicator of market-economic relations, the increasing but also ambiguous role of other market players should be taken into account as well. Analysing the role of other market players can help to explain the peculiarities of the economy, and thereby the motives and incentives that drive various economic actors.

This study has formed part of a larger research project, 'Emerging Market Economies in Central Asia: The Role of Institutional Complementarities in the Reform Processes',[2] where an international team of researchers has studied the emerging market economies and the economic reforms pursued in Kazakhstan and Uzbekistan. In 2009/2010, my colleagues and I conducted 159 semi-structured interviews with key political decision-makers and economic players in Kazakhstan who are directly and indirectly involved in economic processes and shape the formation of the economy in the country. Respondents were public officials, experts, representatives of private domestic and foreign companies, state-owned companies, representatives of international organizations and labour unions/employer associations. I acted as the leading interviewer in 135 interviews, and as second interviewer in 9 interviews, while my colleagues conducted the remaining 15. The first sub-period of the field trip lasted four months in Almaty (from August to November 2009); after three months spent in Germany, the research team went to the field for a further nine months in 2010 (March–November) travelling between Almaty and Astana. All categories of respondents were addressed simultaneously, except for public officials, whom I first started to interview in early 2010 in Astana.

My own work has been a smaller part of this comprehensive research project. In this book I draw on my own experience from 159 interviews, as well as observations from the field and prior knowledge of Kazakhstan's economy. However, for data analysis I focused on a smaller sub-set of the research project and selected 48 interviews out of 159.

In the interviews I was concerned with the unofficial stances taken by respondents: their subjective perceptions of how the economy and economic institutions function in the country, how the state coordinates the economy and how the interaction between various economic players is shaped. Gaining insights from economic actors and political decision-makers into the country's market-oriented reform path was important for two reasons. First, it was necessary to provide an overview of market reforms from a perspective of those who directly observed and participated in economic reform and decision-making processes since independence, as they are aware of the underlying reasons for dynamic changes in economic policy-making. They can provide essential information on how the economy has evolved, what have been the main development challenges and how the country has dealt with them. Moreover, it is important to account for the dynamic nature of economic changes in the context of Kazakhstan, as discussed in subsection 3.3.7.

---

2 This project was funded by the Volkswagen Foundation and based at the Private University of Applied Sciences, Göttingen, Germany.

Second, it was important due to concerns about data reliability (as discussed in section on 4.2 on doing fieldwork in Central Asia). In fact, one reason which prompted me to collect primary data was the lack of reliable economic data on Central Asia (European Community 2007; World Bank 2008; Wilkinson 2008; Smith 2012).

The Varieties of Capitalism approach serves as a starting point; further, a 'core–periphery' framework, developed within this research project, has subsequently been applied for analysis. First, the VoC approach is used for classifying institutions in Kazakhstan. It also facilitates the descriptive analysis of various parts of the economy. In general, the VoC approach has been widely and successfully applied to assess the market economies in the post-Communist states of Eastern Europe (Martin 2002; Cernat 2002; Knell and Srholec 2007; Buchen 2007; Mykhnenko 2007; Crowley and Stanojevic 2011; Luly 2012). Applying the VoC approach to institutional subsystems in Kazakhstan also helped identify existing institutions in key domains: the financial system, corporate governance, industrial relations, the social security system, vocational education and training and inter-firms relations (Hall and Soskice 2001). I also took care to account for the role of foreign economic players operating in Kazakhstan within each subsystem, since foreign firms may exert an influence on institutional development and change in a transition context (King 2007: 186, in Mendelski 2008: 9).

However, preliminary analysis of conducted interviews revealed that the VoC approach has its limitations. It cannot help to explain the large and often key role of the state in the economic reform processes. Therefore, I decided to complement the VoC approach with a 'core–periphery' analytical framework, which became the data-driven part of my analysis. The VoC framework was applied during the first phase of the project and served as an important starting point for the analysis. During the second phase of the research project – the analysis of primary data – the VoC approach was complemented by the 'core–periphery' framework, with the latter classification used as the main framework for my analysis and the VoC playing the supplementary role. In the end, the application of these two frameworks helped shed light on the type of market economy that has been emerging in Kazakhstan.

Schematically, the overall theoretical approach can be presented in three steps (Figure 1.1). In the first step, I identified and classified the institutional structure of the economy according to the VoC approach.

Figure 1.1. Theoretical approach

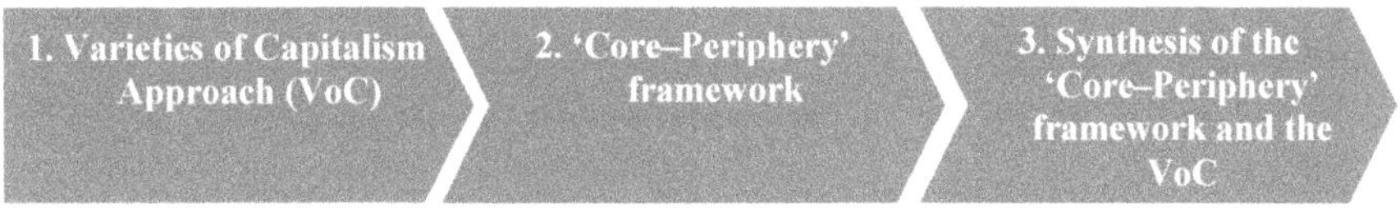

In the second step, based on the preliminary analysis of the interviews, I identified the 'core–periphery' structure of the economy, later used as the analytical framework for data analysis. The first two steps represented two general frameworks that were used to classify institutional subsystems in Kazakhstan. In the third step, I applied the combination of the 'core–periphery' framework and the VoC approach to provide an in-depth analysis of the institutional structure of the economy and identify the type of the emerging market economy.

The major strength of this research project and its approach lie in the fact that both secondary and primary sources have been employed to identify the type of economy emerging in Kazakhstan. The literature review and interviews have helped to reveal the nature of the interaction between private players and the state sector. The research results show that the economy has been gravitating towards a distinctly state-dominated model, in which some parts of the economy are partly or entirely state-led but based on market principles, whereas other parts are market-driven. Importantly, the state-dominated model is based on market principles in the sense that the state participates in the economy by utilizing market mechanisms in the regulation and coordination of the economy. I argue that the interaction between the private sector and the state is a key factor behind the coordination between various institutional domains, which in turn means that state–business interaction is crucial for understanding how the market-oriented economy is formed. Analysis of the interviews showed that the economy of Kazakhstan is divided into two main parts: a dominant 'core' economy, consisting of capital-intensive industries (e.g. natural resources) and with mainly the state and large foreign and domestic business; and a 'periphery', consisting of less capital-intensive industries (e.g. manufacturing), with mainly private small and medium-sized businesses (SMEs). Viewed from an institutional perspective, Kazakhstan has in fact two economic systems in the country. To identify which parts of the economy are market-driven and which are state-led I analysed the major components of state–business interaction by conducting a qualitative content analysis of the interviews.

In terms of *structure,* this book consists of four main analytical chapters, plus a final concluding chapter. Chapter 2 provides an overview of the economic development of Kazakhstan since independence, together with remarks on the role of the government in steering economic processes, micro- and macroeconomic adjustment, shaping the state–business interaction and cooperating with foreign investors. It shows the key role the state has played in coordinating economic processes and provides essential background for understanding the nature of institutional reforms and Kazakhstan's economic model.

Chapter 3 then applies the VoC framework to classify the key economic institutions in the country, on the basis of the literature consulted.

Chapter 4 outlines the research design and methodology, with details on the sampling strategies used for conducting the interviews, as well as the actual composition of the sample, levels of sampling, the interviewees and the selection criteria. It explains the data collection and the issues involved in the substantial fieldwork conducted for this study, and outlines the methods used in analysing the interview data. The 'core' and 'periphery' parts of the economy were analysed with the help of content analysis, a method which helps to systematize and make clear the results of qualitative data collection. Chapters 3 and 4 build on various academic sources which represent a range of disciplines and methodological approaches: economics, international political economy, political science, area studies, and qualitative methods.

Chapter 5 presents the results of the qualitative data analysis. The overall findings of this research are summarized in terms of the distinction between the 'core' and 'periphery' parts of the economy. The 'core' and 'periphery' characteristics are then described in detail, based upon the results of the content analysis. The identification of the 'core' and 'periphery' parts of the economy and their associated characteristics represents the main result of the data analysis and the major research contribution of this study.

Finally, in the Conclusion (Chapter 6) I discuss how my results and the major finding – the existence of 'core' and 'periphery' economies in Kazakhstan – can contribute to the literature as well as to cumulative knowledge-building on economic transition in the post-Soviet space and in similar countries in transition. The results of this work should be seen as complementary to studies conducted by other scholars and international organizations.

Chapter 2. Kazakhstan's economy since independence

2.1. Stabilization, economic reform and macroeconomic performance

2.1.1. Economic growth and the structure of the economy

We begin with a review of the literature on economic reform, macroeconomic performance and economic policy measures in Kazakhstan since 1991, to show how the economy has evolved since independence.

The economy has faced a range of challenges, passing through phases of recession, stagnation and then strong economic growth (Pomfret 2003: 9; Agrawal 2008: 90; Bhuiyan 2010: 34). Today, Kazakhstan's economy is considered to be the most advanced of the former Soviet Central Asian states (Agrawal 2008: 92; Emerging Markets Monitor 2007: 4; Nichol 2012: 10). In addition, the country has pursued several radical economic reform measures since gaining independence in 1991 (McKee et al. 2002: 6; OECD 2005a: 16), and these market reforms are widely seen as the most successful among the countries of Central Asia (Gleason 2003; Agrawal 2008: 92; Ursulenko 2010), and even in the CIS (Schäfer et al. 2010: 704). By 2006, the economy of Kazakhstan accounted for 60 per cent of regional GDP (Zarakhovich 2006). However, at the beginning of the 1990s, few observers could say where the country's development strategy would lead to or what the results of its economic reform would be. It took almost a decade before Kazakhstan's economy was recognized as a market economy (Cummings and Nørgaard 2004: 691). The EU recognized Kazakhstan as a country with a market economy in 2000 (Daly 2008: 7); this was followed by the USA in 2002 (US Department of State 2002).

The first ten years of independence were extremely difficult. Alshanov (2011), who is considered the mastermind of liberal economic reforms in Kazakhstan in the 1990s (Zarakhovich 2006), argues that the economy was in ruins during the first years of independence. In 1995, GDP dropped to 61.4 per cent of the 1990 level (Hare and Naumov 2008: 1). In fact, the economy was most vulnerable immediately after the collapse of the USSR in 1991 because it remained tightly integrated in the larger Soviet economy (Alshanov 2011; Raiskhanova 2000), retaining the distinctive feature of a country where the major cities are located far apart (Gaggiotti et al. 2008: 117).

One reason why the national economy was on the verge of collapse was because of the 'painful' rupture in its economic relations with other former Soviet republics (Simon 2009: 80). With the dissolution of the Soviet Union, Kazakhstan lost a major outlet for its agricultural and mining production, and thus an economic downturn was inevitable (Brown 1998). To a considerable extent, Kazakhstan had been a periphery, its main function being to ensure food security for the former USSR (Alshanov 2011; Belaya and Mykhaylenko 2010).

Agriculture had accounted for 42 per cent of the economy, followed by industry (mining and energy) (21 per cent), construction (16 per cent), and transport and communication (10 per cent) (Pomfret 1995). As of 1990, the oil and gas reserves of the country remained generally underdeveloped (Ostrowski 2009: 349); and, as Pomfret (2005: 859) notes, resources were 'poorly utilised' throughout the first decade of independence. Oil production grew rapidly only after 1999 in the oil-producing Aktobe, Atyrau, Kyzylorda and Mangistau regions (Najman et al. 2005).

Since independence, the government has persistently sought to restore economic cooperation with other former Soviet republics, regularly stressing the importance of centre–periphery economic relations in Central Asia (Alshanov 2011; Olcott 2008; Vielmini 2013). Dragneva (2004: 281) calls Kazakhstan a 'CIS-enthusiast', as it has regularly called for various forms of integration – not only in Central Asia, but in the CIS as well. This indicates the overall significance of the country's economic and institutional path-dependency, which in turn can largely explain the development of the present institutional frameworks in Kazakhstan as a whole (Alshanov 2011).

However, despite this institutional path-dependency, the economic indicators and GDP components have changed drastically (see Figure 2.1, GDP concentration by industry). By 2008, the composition of GDP had been transformed, with oil and gas accounting for 51 per cent of GDP and agriculture only 5 per cent, compared to 21 per cent and 42 per cent respectively in 1991 (Picker 2010; Alshanov 2011). Oil and gas have become the main component of GDP due to Kazakhstan's abundance of natural resources, with oil reserves forecast for the next 65 years and coal reserves for 308 years (OECD 2011a: 12). The country is currently 10th with respect to global proven oil reserves and may well become one of the biggest oil producers in the world (CASE 2008).

The World Bank uses a more aggregate approach in assessing the composition of GDP. Accordingly, in 2009, the services sector accounted for 53.3 per cent of GDP, followed by industry (40.3 per cent), manufacturing (11.4 per cent) and agriculture (6.4 per cent) (World Bank 2011b). Wheat exports are the main element of the agricultural sector, making the country the dominant exporter of wheat in the region (OECD 2011a: 12). Kazakhstan is also one of the biggest grain exporters in the world (Meyers and Goychuk 2012: 77). Moreover, its agricultural potential is enormous: it has the second highest ratio of arable land per person in the world – 2.04 hectares on average (see World Bank 2000: in Fergus 2003: 109).

Figure 2.1. GDP concentration by industry in 2008

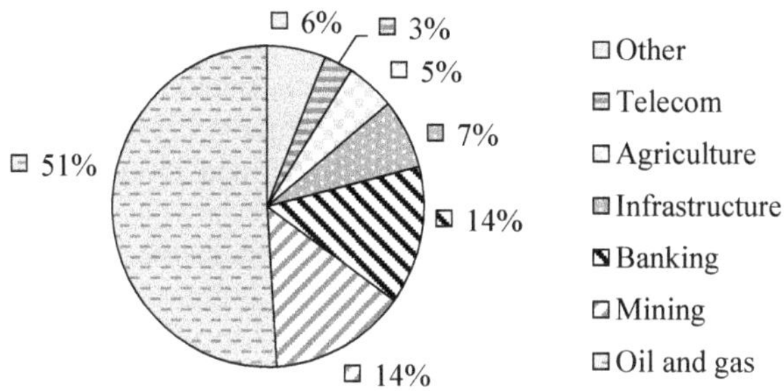

Source: Author's illustration based on UCG and McKinsey (in Picker 2010).

In the period 1999–2010, the country experienced significant economic growth (see Figure 2.2, where the 1989 GDP level is taken as 100 per cent) – largely because of revenues from energy resources due to high energy prices worldwide (Alshanov 2011), and the boom in the construction sector stimulated by building a new capital in Astana (Hare and Naumov 2008: 1).

Oil resources are the main driver of Kazakhstan's economic development, as Pomfret (2003: 18) has noted. Oil revenues allowed the country to fully meet its debt obligations to the International Monetary Fund (IMF) already in 2000, before 2007, which had been set as the final year for debt repayment (Amagoh and Markus 2010: 16).

Figure 2.2. GDP development in Kazakhstan

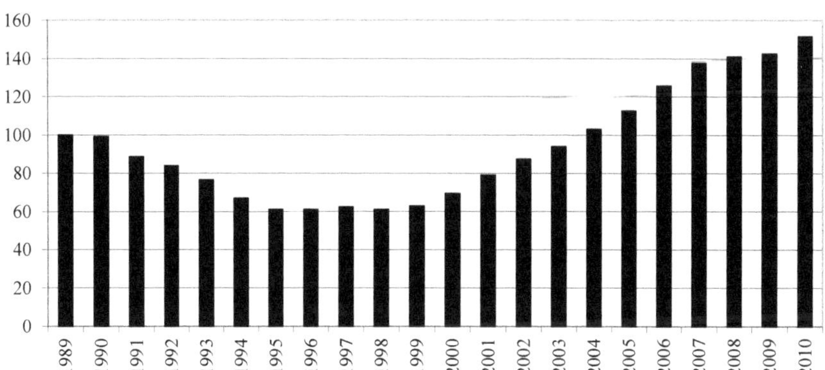

Source: Author's illustration based on EBRD (2010a).

The major economic objective to emerge as a result of some two decades of independence has been to diversify the economy away from its dependence on natural resources and to modernize major industries by implementing industrialization programmes (Toxanova 2008; Abusseitov 2011). These development programmes are as follows: 'Diversification of Kazakhstan's Economy through Cluster Development in Non-Extracting Sectors of Economy' launched in 2004; 'The State Programme on Accelerated Industrial Innovative Development' for the period 2010–2014.

The country set itself the target of joining the 50 industrialized countries in the world based on the World Bank's 'ease of doing business' indicator (Abusseitov 2011; *The Economist* 2008b); by 2011, Kazakhstan ranked 59 out of 183 countries and 50 out of 189 countries in 2013 on this indicator (World Bank 2011a: 2; World Bank 2013: 3). To achieve this ambitious goal, the government introduced the major national development programme 'Kazakhstan 2030: Prosperity, Security and Improvement of Welfare of the Citizens of Kazakhstan' in October 1997 (OECD 2005a: 17), which set seven key long-term priorities:

- national security;
- domestic political stability and consolidation of society;
- economic growth based on an open market economy with high level of foreign investments and internal savings;
- health, education and well-being of citizens;
- energy resources;
- infrastructure, in particular transport and communication;
- professional state (Akorda 2012).

To realize its overall economic objectives, the government has formulated the following official stages of development:

- the Development Plan for the period 1998–2000 aimed at promoting effective and successful reforms in the political, economic and social realms;
- the Strategic Plan of Development of the Republic of Kazakhstan until the Year 2020 aimed at meeting development objectives 2000–2010;
- the State Program of Accelerated Industrial and Innovative Development for the period 2010–2015, aimed at diversifying the economy away from oil (Akorda 2012).

In 2012, President Nazarbayev announced the adoption of a new development programme 'Kazakhstan 2050: New Political Course of the Established State', which set new strategic goals for the country until 2050:

- a strong and successful state;
- sustainable process of democratization and liberalization;
- harmony and peace among social, ethnic, and religious groups;
- national economy and Kazakhstan's role in international division of labour;
- strong social policy to ensure social stability and harmony;
- globally recognized country;
- proactive role in promoting nuclear non-proliferation regime (Akorda 2014).

The key role for implementing the overall economic strategy is assigned to Samruk-Kazyna (International Monetary Fund 2011b), the biggest investment holding corporation, which focuses on the modernization and diversification of the economy (Samruk-Kazyna 2012). According to the IMF country report (2011: 4), Samruk-Kazyna has been delegated the leading role regarding the development of key sectors in the economy through lending and external financing. In 2010, Samruk-Kazyna controlled assets in major industries of the economy equivalent to 50 per cent of the country's GDP and around 45 per cent in 2013 (EBRD 2010a: 121; Samruk-Kazyna 2013). However, the academic literature has tended to neglect questions of the effectiveness of these programmes and the role of Samruk-Kazyna. Similarly, realization of these programmes has been poorly researched by local think-tanks and academic centres, and by international organizations as well, and only a few scholars and international organizations have studied this area.

So far these development and diversification programmes have failed to meet fully the objectives set, due mainly to the lack of proper institutional infrastructure for innovative activities and the lack of qualified professionals and engineers in this area (Islamic Development Bank 2011: xvii; Mashuri 2010: 34). Further, Sitenko (2011: 114) argues that development programmes in the country, and innovative technologies as part of them, are poorly implemented because of the weak ties between industry and R&D, and a poorly developed market of technology transfer. To boost innovative technological development in the country she proposes further integration with Russia and Belarus within the currently functioning Customs Union of these three countries.[3] Vielmini

3 The Customs Union between Belarus, Kazakhstan and Russia, established in 2010, aims at promoting economic integration between three countries and building integrated energy and transport markets (Vinokurov 2010).

notes (2013), however, that technological advances for Kazakhstan as a result of its participation in the Customs Union have yet to be seen.

According to a report from the United Nations Economic Commission for Europe (UNECE 2012a), as a result of government attempts to foster innovation and modernization in various areas, the R&D system has been structured around vertical axes (state enterprises–ministries–design bureaux and intermediaries), horizontal axes (key institutions to promote R&D, such as the National Innovation Fund and DAMU) and regional axes (municipalities and local enterprises). The main barrier to effective development of the R&D system is seen in the weak horizontal coordination of R&D initiatives and projects (ibid). The overall share of enterprises producing innovative products and technologies in the economy reached only 4.0 per cent in 2008; still, that was a slight increase over 2003, when it was only 2.1 per cent (Imanberdiev 2011). By comparison, this figure was 13 per cent in Russia, 28 per cent in Romania, 32 per cent in Slovenia, and 38 per cent in Poland in 2008 (ibid). In her study of the telecommunications sector, Smirnova (2014) found that the main problem that hinders innovation is weak collaboration between universities and private firms; only big companies view positively and develop partner relations with universities. Among the major obstacles to developing university–industry collaboration are the lack of fiscal incentives and the lack of traditions of such interaction on the part of local companies (ibid: 642, 643).

Table 2.1 presents local companies in terms of the size of their capital. The production output of 10 companies stands for altogether 47 per cent of the country's GDP. These companies represent mainly natural resource industries (oil and gas, metals mining) but also the financial and transportation sector, and are state-owned to varying degrees. Seven companies out of ten were involved in the production of mineral resources. The remaining three are KTJ, the BTA Bank and Kazkommercbank: KTJ is a national railway corporation and the latter two provide financial services.

In 2005, SMEs contributed to only 14 per cent of GDP (ADB 2005). Six years later, according to the Agency of Statistics (2011), the share of SMEs in country's GDP had grown to 20.2 per cent. This ratio is close to the average level of low-income countries, and points to the existing problems of small and medium entrepreneurship (Smirnova et al. 2012). Pasadilla (2010: 8) notes that SMEs employ only 25 per cent of the working population, whereas the average employment level for upper-middle income group of countries to which Kazakhstan otherwise belongs is 40 per cent. Thus SMEs have been lagging behind the international standard levels in terms of their contribution to total economic output and employment.

Since independence, President Nazarbayev has initiated a range of large-scale reforms to support and develop SMEs (ADB 2005; Spence 2009; Ostrowski 2010; Luly 2012). In the view of Özcan (2011), the market structure provides appropriate conditions for the growth of SMEs. However, as Spence (2009) notes, resource-dependence and weak economic diversification of the country as well as its burdensome bureaucratic administration of business represent obstacles to the internationalization of SMEs and limit their potential for making a larger contribution to the economy. According to the 2010 report of the Bertelsmann Foundation, even though SMEs in Kazakhstan benefit from constantly decreasing tax levels, their activities are constrained by complex bureaucratic requirements. Moreover, as the 2012 report of Standard and Poor's indicates, unlike SMEs, large companies – especially in the resource industries – tend to enjoy better opportunities for receiving loans and credits, both domestically and internationally (see subsection 3.3.2.3 for overview of other problems in the corporate sector).

Table 2.1. Companies by size of capital (2008)

No. of companies	Company	Industry	Revenue, USD bln
10	KazMunayGas	Oil and gas	21
	Tengizshevroil	Oil and gas	14.3
	ENRC	Metals mining	6.8
	Kazakhmys	Metals mining	5.2
	Mangistaumunaigaz	Oil and gas	4.0
	KTJ	Transportation	4.0
	PetroKazakhstan	Oil and gas	3.8
	BTA Bank	Banking	3.5
	CNPC	Oil and gas	3.5
	Kazkommercbank	Banking	3.2
47	**Industry**	**No. of companies**	**Revenue, USD bln**
	Oil and gas	8	49.6
	Banking	9	13.2
	Mining	4	13.2
	Construction/infrastructure	13	9.5
	Telecom	3	2.9
	Agriculture	4	1.5
	Other	6	3.6
More than 50,000	**Industry**	**No. of companies**	**Revenue, USD bln**
	Trade	18,181	2.0
	Construction/infrastructure	7,915	2.0
	Real estate	7,395	1.2
	Manufacturing	353	1.0
	Oil, gas and mining	6,248	0.5
	Other	10,520	1.5

Source: Author's presentation based on Expert Russia and McKinsey (in Picker 2010).

2.1.2. Inflation

The break-up of the USSR disrupted the enterprise–industry ties that had been an integral part of the Soviet economic system (Agrawal 2008: 100). In Kazakhstan, the entire economy, including the financial sector, was on the verge of collapse (Alshanov 2011). In 1992, a price liberalization programme was initiated (De Broeck et al. 1997) to adjust domestic price levels to the standards adopted in other market economies. By 1997 price liberalization processes were completed; however, these processes were accompanied by high levels of inflation (ibid). Hyperinflation of the first years of independence worsened the economic situation in the country (Brown 1998). Until the Central Bank was assigned an independent role as regards monetary policies and the regulation of the financial system, the country passed through several stages of hyperinflation (Laurens 2004), with the inflation rate soaring to 1662.2 per cent in 1993 (see Table 2.2). In 1995, the government, with the help of the Central Bank, cut inflation to 176.3 per cent and laid the foundations for the subsequent development of the financial sector (Laurens 2004; Hare and Naumov 2008). Kazakhstan adopted a successful inflation target policy that must be seen as successful compared to other Central Asian states (Dufrenot and Sand-Zantman 2004), and since 1997 the inflation rate has remained relatively stable. In 1998 it was reduced to 7.3 per cent; in 2005 it reached 7.6 per cent; in 2011 it was down to 7.4 per cent; in 2013 it reached 4.8 per cent.

Table 2.2. Inflation rate (consumer prices), percentage figures

Year	1993	1994	1995	1996	1997	1998	1999	2000	2001	2002
Inflation	1662.3	1401.9	176.3	39.1	17.4	7.3	8.4	13.3	8.4	6
Year	**2003**	**2004**	**2005**	**2006**	**2007**	**2008**	**2009**	**2010**	**2011**	**2012**
Inflation	6.6	6.9	7.6	8.6	10.8	17.0	7.3	7.4	7.4	6

Source: Author's presentation based on International Monetary Fund (2011b), Index Mundi (2012d) and Agency of Statistics (2012a; 2014a).

Laurens (2004) notes that the hyperinflation in the 1990s became 'a blessing in disguise' for the Kazakhstan, as it forced the state to take effective measures to accumulate more capital. This was achieved through a prudent monetary policy and and significant inflows of FDI (see subsection 2.1.7).

2.1.3. Unemployment

Before independence the unemployment rate was only 0.6 per cent of the total labour force (UNICEF 2002: 5). However, immediately after the collapse of the USSR, unemployment increased dramatically, by 1998 comprising 13.7 per cent of the labour force (Index Mundi 2012c). Moreover, it was acknowledged that the real unemployment rate could be substantially higher than officially declared figures (Verme 1998: 23). Verme notes that discrepancies between official and real figures are explained by general lack of belief that the government could provide any support in finding job opportunities or getting unemployment benefits. During the first years of independence, few in the unemployed population received benefits from the state: in 1996, only 3.8 per cent were officially registered as unemployed, whereas unofficially the rate reached 12 per cent, again according to Verme (1998). This latter figure was calculated from labour force surveys. Unemployment peaked in 1998 (Figure 2.3), and by 2001 had fallen to 10 per cent. In the period from 2001 to 2008, it decreased further, to 7 per cent (Klaveren et al. 2010). Finally, in 2011, unemployment stood at a mere 5.4 per cent. In 2012, the unemployment rate was among the lowest in the entire CIS (*Zakon.kz* 2012a). Importantly, due to state efforts from 2001 onwards, labour relations have become more 'formalized' than before, in the sense that the state began controlling the formalization of labour relations more strictly (Klaveren et al. 2010).

Figure 2.3. Unemployment as percentage of total labour force

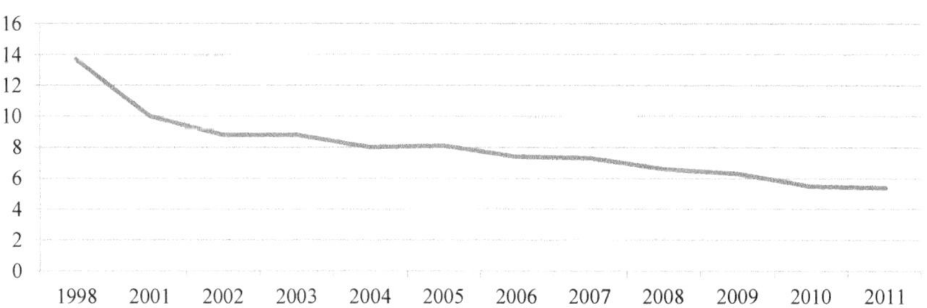

Source: Author's illustration based on Index Mundi (2012c).

As noted by the Islamic Development Bank (2011: 11), economic growth in the second period of independence helped to lower the unemployment rate. Industries like construction, services, finance and education were the main drivers of increased employment, whereas sectors like agriculture, manufacturing and mining accommodated only an insignificant share of the unemployed population. Further, according to the Islamic Development Bank, the state is seen as the key actor, forcing local governments and employers to limit the number of dismissals in exchange for tax benefits. However, recent official figures on employment still do not always reflect the real situation (*Zakon.kz* 2012a), for two reasons: first, the maximum unemployment benefit is currently 18,000 Tenge (USD 120 by the exchange rate of 2 June 2013) per month, which is extremely low for people living in big cities. Second, it is difficult for people who have lost their jobs to register as 'unemployed' due to complicated and time-consuming registration procedures; and as a result, dismissed employees prefer not to register as 'unemployed' (*Zakon.kz* 2012a), but are officially categorized as 'self-employed' (Agency of Statistics 2012b). According to the definition of the World Bank (2012a), 'self-employed workers are those workers who, working on their own account or with one or a few partners or in cooperative, hold the type of jobs defined as a "self-employment jobs" (i.e. jobs where the remuneration is directly dependent upon the profits derived from the goods and services produced).' Overall, the relative success in keeping the unemployment rate low has been credited to the prudent policies of the government (*Zakon.kz* 2012a).

2.1.4. Income distribution

Kazakhstan belongs to the group of upper middle-income countries (World Bank 2012b). Hare and Naumov (2008) note that, despite the traditional wisdom that holds that resource-rich countries grow slowly and have more significant income inequality compared to countries without resources, the economy of Kazakhstan has grown rapidly; moreover, its Gini coefficient has decreased after 2000 (Figure 2.4). This index shows the scale of income distribution or consumption spending within a given country: a Gini coefficient of 0 indicates absolute equality and an index of 100 absolute inequality (World Bank 2012b). In 2001, the country's index was equal to 41.11 per cent, the worst in its history. However, in parallel to rapid GDP growth after 2001, the Gini index fell to 33.85 per cent in 2003, to 30.76 per cent in 2006 and to 29.04 per cent by 2009 (World Bank 2012b).

Among the republics of the former Soviet Union, Kazakhstan is placed along with Kyrgyzstan and Tajikistan in the group of 'least unequal' countries (Figure 2.5), ahead of Russia and Azerbaijan, two other resource-rich countries. Compared to the first period from 1990 to 1996, the Gini coefficient rose slightly in Kazakhstan, while it decreased in Russia.

Figure 2.4. Gini coefficient, Kazakhstan

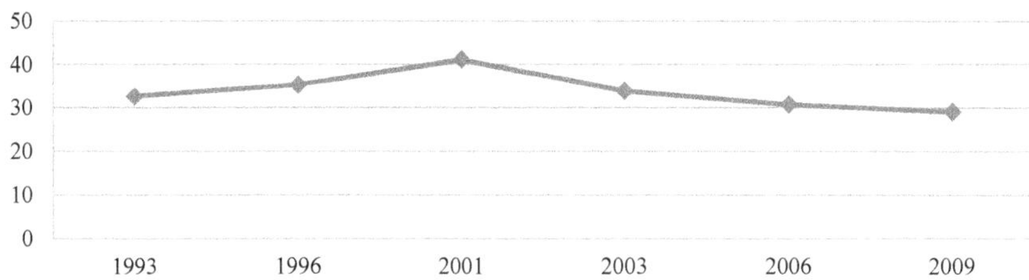

Source: Author's illustration based on World Bank (2012b).

Figure 2.5. Gini coefficient, former Soviet Union

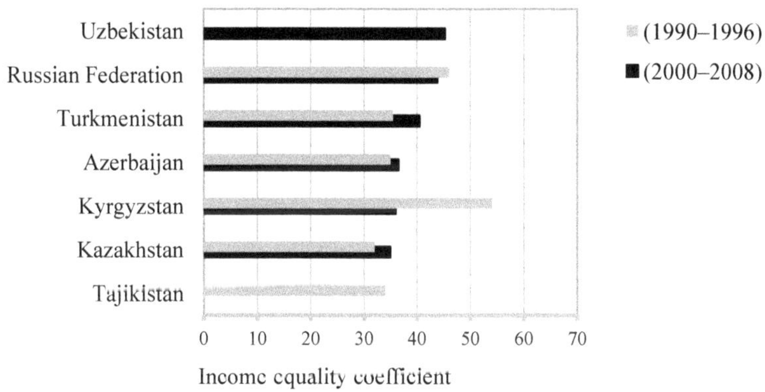

Source: Author's illustration based on United Nations (2011).

Fergus (2003) points to the problem of significant poverty and social gaps between urban areas and oil-producing regions during the first decade of independence and the early 2000s. Overall, the problems of unequal income distribution after 2000 were evident. According to Pomfret (2006a) in his study of household expenditures in Kazakhstan, the country's economic performance during the second decade of independence was driven largely by the oil boom. However, Pomfret finds that oil revenues had a positive impact on income growth in the cities in non-oil producing regions, but yielded hardly any significant benefits for the population in oil-producing regions. This paradox can be explained by the fact that petroleum revenue coming from oil-producing regions has benefited two main big cities – Almaty and Astana, which are two main economic centres in the country (ibid).

2.1.5. Current account balance development

Alam and Banerji (2000: 3–4) argue that during the first decade of independence the market-oriented policy of the government helped to stabilize the country's balance of payments, defined by the International Monetary Fund (Ghosh and Ramakrishnan 2006: 1) as 'the difference between the value of exports of goods and services and the value of imports of goods and services.' As Figure 2.6 shows, the current account balance in Kazakhstan has undergone various fluctuations since 1995 (World Bank 2012b). From 1991 to 2000, the balance was negative and macroeconomic performance vulnerable, given the country's dependence on exports of natural resources (Alam and Banerji 2000). The current account balance reached its lowest point in 2007, when it was negative and equalled 8 per cent of GDP. There was a sharp decline in 2007 due to the world economic crisis, but in 2008 it experienced rapid positive growth and accounted for 4.8 per cent of GDP (Figure 2.6). By 2011, the current account balance had achieved the highest surplus level in Kazakhstan's history, accounting for 7.6 per cent of GDP.

Figure 2.6. Current account balance development as percentage of GDP

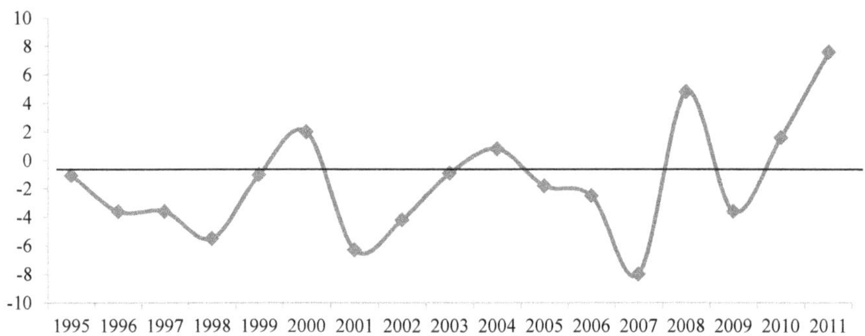

Source: Author's illustration based on World Bank (2012b).

Relatively high volatility levels in Kazakhstan's current account balance can be explained by the country's dependence on energy resources and high exposure to external conditions (e.g. the world economic crisis of 2008 and fluctuations in the global oil price after 2000). This should be borne in mind in light of the dynamic nature of economic reform processes and changing state attitudes toward various economic actors in the country.

2.1.6. Public and private sector debt

Strong economic growth and intensive development of the oil industry helped Kazakhstan to fulfil its external debt obligations to the IMF in 2000, as noted – well ahead of 2007, set as the final year for debt repayment (Amagoh and Markus 2010: 16; International Finance Corporation 2009).

Dzharkinbayev (2011) notes that since independence the government has sought to reduce the government debt gradually in relation to GDP. In 2001, the ratio of government debt-to-GDP was 20.4 per cent; in 2006 it decreased to 6.7 per cent. However, in 2009 it rose to 10.2 per cent and to 10.7 per cent in 2010, due not least to the impact of the economic crisis (Dzharkinbayev 2011: 55). Given the implementation of anti-crisis measures during and after the economic crisis of 2008, the government borrowed from internal sources and from abroad, which led to the overall increase in government debt during this period (ibid: 55–56). Overall, as Uzagalieva (2006: 409) notes, the significant contribution towards reducing the public debt after 2000 should be attributed to the accumulation and effective use of petroleum revenues by the National Fund of the Republic of Kazakhstan (NFRK) and the National Bank of Kazakhstan (see also subsection 2.2.2 on fiscal policy in Kazakhstan).

Regarding the private sector debt, during the period 1991–2000, external borrowing by private companies peaked in 1997; the total amount of private debt reached USD 3.7 billion in 1994–1997 (Kazkommerts Securities 1998: 8). In the period from 2000 to 2011, the share of private sector debt increased dramatically, reaching USD 86.977 billion early 2007 (*Interfax* 2007). Intensive external borrowing during the period of rapid economic growth (60 per cent of credits for the corporate sector were externally borrowed funds) triggered an overheating of the economy; as a result, the world economic crisis of 2008 hit Kazakhstan especially hard (Spechler 2010: 3).

According to the International Finance Corporation (2009), private sector debt in Kazakhstan is relatively low by international standards. Similarly, Standard and Poor's (2012) also emphasize that private sector debt in Kazakhstan is low, with the main credit actors being domestic banks, pension funds and various insurance firms. In 2011, the share of domestic credit by the private sector accounted for 39 per cent of GDP; household debt to GDP did not exceed 10 per cent; and mortgage loans were only 4 per cent of GDP (ibid).

According to the International Finance Corporation report (2009), the low level of public and private sector debt, coupled with abundant natural resources, should make Kazakhstan less vulnerable to economic crisis in the future.

2.1.7. Foreign direct investment and trade

In order to comprehend the nature of economic reform processes in the country and the type of economy which is emerging, it is also necessary to account for the role of foreign investors in the post-independence period. As explained in Chapter 1, President Nazarbayev assigned a special role to foreign investors in forming Kazakhstan's market economy. Because foreign firms exert an influence on institutional development and change in a transition context (King 2007: 186, in Mendelski 2008: 9), the role of foreign capital and foreign companies in shaping market development in the country should be examined.

Since independence, Kazakhstan has offered attractive operating conditions for foreign investors (Libman 2008), with the government creating an investment regime that targeted domestic and foreign investors equally (Tasmagambetov 2005: 34; Zarakhovich 2006; UNCTAD 2010). Since 1991, Kazakhstan has been more reliant on FDI than the other Central Asian states (Kalyuzhnova and Nygaard 2008). FDI reached 33 per cent of GDP in 2011 (Figure 2.7), putting Kazakhstan number 22 in the world as regards the FDI/GDP ratio; the current global average was 21.70 per cent (Economy Watch 2012a). This also shows the country's high economic openness to international economic actors and capital as well as its intensive integration into the world economy. In 2012, President Nazarbayev declared that since 1991 USD 170 billion had been invested by foreign investors; this, he added, had clearly helped to develop the economy: 'without FDI, there would be no today's Kazakhstan!'[4]

Figure 2.7. FDI in Kazakhstan as percentage of GDP

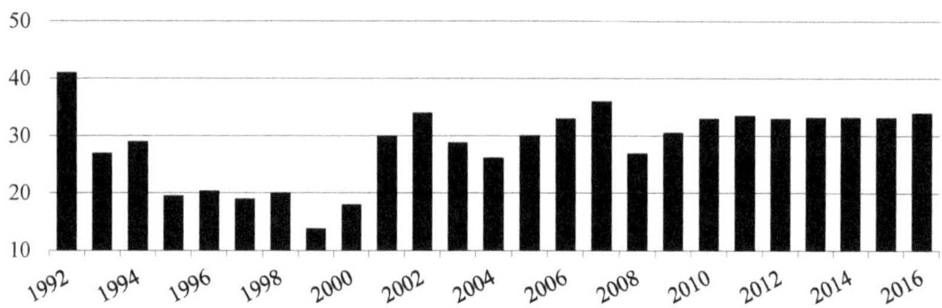

Source: Author's illustration based on Economy Watch (2012a).

4 From the dialogue of President Nazarbayev with the local community in Karaganda, *Headline.kz*, 2 December 2012, available at: http://news.headline.kz/chto_v_strane/nazarbaev_schitaet_chto_nujno_tschatelnee_razbiratsya_s_povyisheniem_zarplat.html, accessed 20 January 2014.

In 2008, Kazakhstan became the second-largest recipient of FDI (after the Russian Federation) among the CIS countries (UNCTAD 2008). Figure 2.8 shows the dynamics of foreign direct investment starting from 1993. The overall dynamic became positive after 2001, when global oil prices rose considerably, allowing FDI to increase exponentially until 2009 (Gabdullin et al. 2012: 482). Then, the global economic crisis hit the country's major industries and FDI levels fell slightly.

Figure 2.8. Dynamics of FDI (USD million)

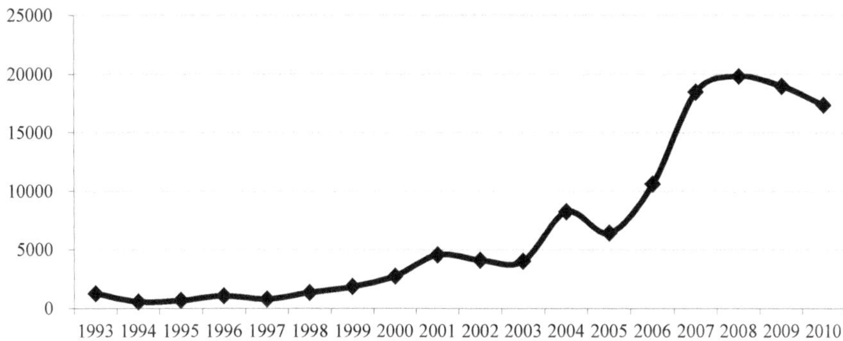

Source: Author's illustration based on Alshanov (2011).

FDI has centred on the oil and gas sector, construction, finance and banking, heavy industry and agriculture in Kazakhstan (OECD 2011a: 12). For instance, in 2009, the lion's share of FDI – 70 per cent in total – was channelled into the energy sector and related geological work (ibid: 18). Energy resources, mainly oil and gas, have been an important target for FDI in Kazakhstan (Waikar et al. 2011). Figure 2.9 shows the historical trend in the distribution of FDI by industry. FDI in the energy sector (mining and quarrying) has been the highest since 1991. The financial sector experienced greater FDI during the economic boom in the country 2006–2008, before the economic crisis set in. Further, most FDI in construction can be classified as part of FDI in energy, as foreign investors invested largely in building energy infrastructure in the country.

As Figure 2.7 shows, FDI in Kazakhstan accounted for 33 per cent of GDP in 2011. As seen from Figure 2.10 the most important countries of FDI origin since 1991 have been the Netherlands, the USA, the UK, France, British Virgin Islands, China and Russia. They have provided investments in the areas which needed reform and for which the state did not have enough financial resources. Their contributions have related primarily to the energy industry; however, FDI in this industry were also used to develop other sectors in the economy.

Figure 2.9. FDI per industries, in millions of USD

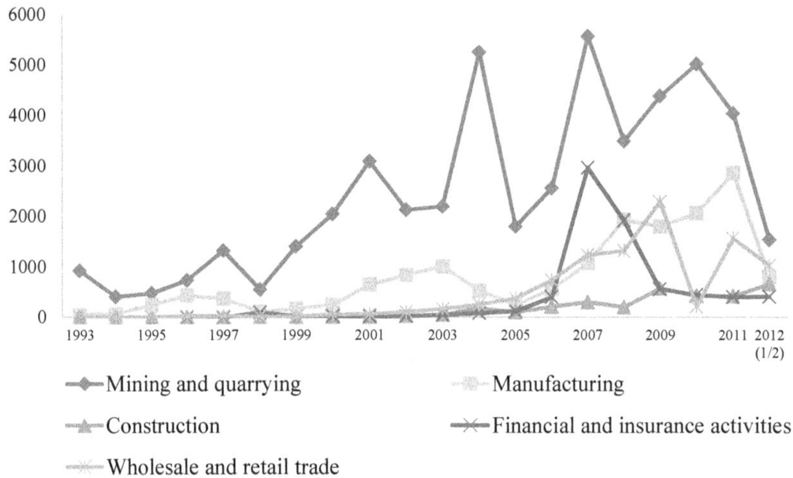

Source: Author's illustration based on Government of the Republic of Kazakhstan (2013).

Figure 2.10. FDI in Kazakhstan since independence, by country

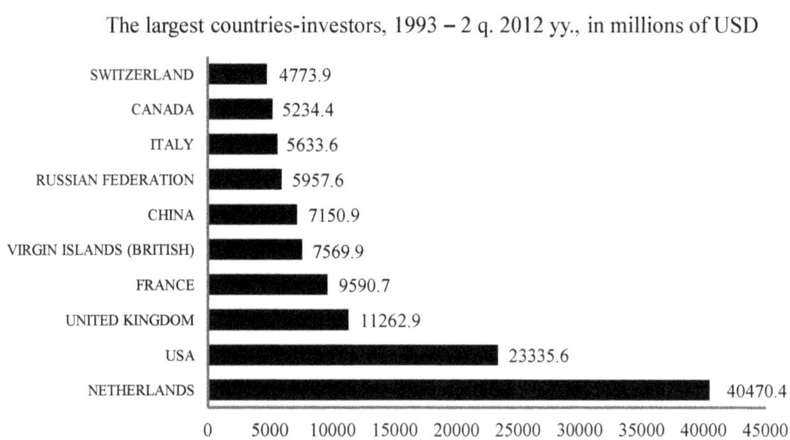

Source: Author's illustration based on Government of the Republic of Kazakhstan (2013).

Officially, investment is welcome in any industry in Kazakhstan (UNCTAD 2010); according to Article 3 of the Law on Investments (2003), investors have the right to invest in any types of business activity and no limitations exist, except when 'required by the necessity of protection of the national security'. The state pays special attention to fostering investment conditions for foreign companies (Tekenov 2006). In 1996, the 'State Committee on Investments' was formed (UNCTAD 2010) – now part of the Ministry of Industry and Trade (Foreign Investors' Council 2012) – serving as the executive body of the Foreign Investors' Council, which was established in 1998 and chaired by the President. The Council coordinates the relations between large foreign businesses and the state (Foreign Investors' Council 2012).

Kazakhstan stands out from other post-Soviet countries in that it has established a predictable business environment for foreign investors (Libman 2008); its success in attracting FDI (Libman and Ushkalova 2009) confirms this. However, this is by no means the only important factor. As Koch and Chaudhary (2002) argue, Kazakhstan was able to attract FDI in the 1990s by implementing liberalization reforms. Similarly, Alam and Banerji (2000: 3–4) note that during the first decade of independence the market-oriented policy of the government triggered a massive inflow of FDI. Since 1991, an attractive feature for foreign companies has been the fact that the foreign investors could enjoy 'unique guarantees', the result of the adoption of the production-sharing agreement (PSA), which became the first of its kind in the CIS (Libman 2008). Further, as Libman (2008) notes, being treated in a privileged way, foreign corporations exerted a conspicuous influence on the government until the early 2000s – at which point, Kazakhstan's oil boom changed the situation. In 2001, GDP growth reached 13.5 per cent; in the course of one year, FDI grew substantially, from USD 2.78 billion in 2000 to 4.56 billion by 2001; and it has increased year on year ever since (OECD 2005a: 16). In 2003, a new Law on Investment was adopted; before then relations with foreign investors had been shaped within the framework of the 1994 Law on Foreign Investment and the 1977 Law on State Support of Direct Investment (UNCTAD 2010). Under this new law, the government guarantees legal protection to foreign investors against expropriation and repatriation of capital (ibid). Overall, in the period 2000–2008, the investment climate was seen as favourable by foreign investors, and FDI increased significantly between 2005 and 2008 as a result (Figure 2.8).

In 2010, the Law on Subsoil Use became the next landmark in the investment regime evolution for foreign corporations, changing the rules of the game between the state and large foreign businesses (Satpaev 2010). As Satpaev notes, overall there were two investment periods in the country. The first period, from 1991 to 2002, is seen as the period affording 'the most favourable treatment' to foreign investors. The second period, from 2002 and until the present, has been characterized by 'the policy of investment parity introduction' and the elaboration of the 'Kazakh Content'[5] concept, which is part of the Law on Subsoil Use passed on 24 June 2010 (Law on Subsoil Use 2010), under which the government tightened conditions for big foreign investors (Satpaev 2010: 38–40; Voloshin 2011: 16–17), and overall investment conditions for foreign investors worsened somewhat (Toft and Duero 2011). Within the second decade of independence (2000–2010), the scope of state involvement in the energy sector increased gradually (ibid). This was due not least to the fact that the government reconsidered and renegotiated several oil contracts with large foreign investors after 2007 (Pomfret 2011; Toft and Duero 2011; Partlett 2008; Kalyuzhnova and Nygaard 2008).

Some scholars see the introduction of the Law on Subsoil Use as part of the rise of Kazakhstan's *resource nationalism* policy (Sarsenbayev 2011; Toft and Duero 2011). Resource nationalism refers to a situation when the government seeks to gain better national control over natural resources and obtains more bargaining power over foreign investors; this occurs when the basic development period of a country is almost over and the government has accumulated sufficient economic resources and knowledge to manage the country's natural resources (Sarsenbayev 2011; Hosman 2009). Several scholars have studied relations between the government and foreign investors in the petroleum industry in Kazakhstan. Hosman (2009) applies game theory to decision-making in Kazakhstan's energy sector, and argues that the state was able to learn new lessons from managing its energy industry, thus strengthening its bargaining position vis-à-vis foreign energy actors over time. Similarly, Ciarreta and Nasirov (2012) note that, due to high oil prices in the world since 2000, the government has become stronger, accumulating enough financial resources, and has started to exercise stricter control over the use of its oil and gas resources.

Partlett (2008) holds that Kazakhstan, similarly to Russia, was driven by cost–benefit calculations when it started renegotiation of its biggest oil contracts. Thus, it was not so much resource nationalism based on ideology: it was economic cost-benefit logic which drove the country to renegotiate some long-term contracts with foreign investors. Partlett further notes that short-term reputational losses were less important for Kazakhstan than the expected long-term economic gains as a result of renegotiations. This view is supported by Kalyuzhnova and Nygaard (2008), who argue that the reason for the government to intervene in the energy sector was based on economic considerations and the

---

5 This concept was aimed at 'unifying the conceptual apparatus of laws on Subsoil, Subsoil Use and Public Procurement on issues affecting the Kazakhstan (local) content; strengthening state control over the activities of mining companies in their acquisition of goods, works and services of Kazakh origin; automating the calculations of Kazakhstan content in the procurement of subsoil users; introducing a register of goods and services produced by Kazakh producers' (GRATA 2010).

understanding that the contracts of the early 1990s did not fully reflect the interests of the country. In particular, they note that the participation terms of the national oil and gas company KazMunayGas in the Kashagan project were renegotiated and its share was increased from 8.33 per cent to 16.81 per cent as a result of government demands in 2008 (KazMunayGas 2011; Haritonova 2008). Similarly, Palazuelos and Fernandes (2012) underscore that the government revised the major oil contracts concluded with foreign companies in the 1990s, whereby the national oil companies have raised their stake. However, despite stricter regulations on foreign actors, national oil companies do not fully control the upstream and downstream chain of oil production and revenue generation: it remains largely in the hands of foreign companies, which have retained strong bargaining positions in relation to the government.

A comprehensive survey conducted by Ernst and Young (2010) found foreign investors satisfied with their investment decisions. Many of them reported that the business environment was challenging, but that there were opportunities nonetheless; and many investors still saw Kazakhstan as an important and strategic market.

It is also important to touch upon trade relations of Kazakhstan with other countries in order to better understand the scope of influence of foreign investors and individual countries on Kazakhstan's economy. Table 2.3 shows main export and import partners in 2009 (this year was taken when the sample design was developed in 2009–2010; see subsection 4.4.5 on selected countries).

Since independence, the main economic partners of Kazakhstan have been China, Russia, the USA and the EU member states (Yesdauletova 2009; Schmitz 2009; Peyrouse 2008; Gumppenberg 2007; Bohr 2004), in terms of FDI and trade. Economically, Russia's role is viewed as dominant (Yesdauletova 2009); however, Kazakhstan's largest trade partner today is the European Union (Delegation of the European Union to Kazakhstan 2012).

In 2011, the EU's share in Kazakhstan's total external trade amounted to 49 per cent (Delegation of the European Union to Kazakhstan 2012). Relations with China in the 1990s were mainly diplomatic; however, during the second decade of Kazakhstan's independence, economic relations intensified significantly; today Kazakhstan has become an attractive market for Chinese investments and capital (Peyrouse 2008; Kaukenow 2009).

Table 2.3. Main export and import partners of Kazakhstan (2009)

Exports – partners	Imports – partners
1. China 16.34 per cent	1. Russia 28.5 per cent
2. France 9.23 per cent	2. China 26.72 per cent
3. Germany 8.32 per cent	3. Germany 6.59 per cent
4. Russia 6.9 per cent	4. Italy 5.58 per cent
5. Ukraine 5.52 per cent	5. Ukraine 4.8 per cent

Source: Author's illustration based on Economy Watch (2012b).

2.1.8. Summary of economic development since independence

Since independence, the economy of Kazakhstan has been challenged by disintegration and the rupture of its economic ties with other republics of the former Soviet Union. Hyperinflation, high unemployment rates, recession, stagnated growth were widely used terms to describe the economic situation in the early 1990s. By the turn of the millennium, the country had made significant progress in terms of dealing with the economic challenges of the 1990s.

Economic growth has been largely dependent on export of energy resources. The most significant rise in GDP levels took place after 2000 when the country began to develop its energy resources more actively. Export of oil and gas has become the main GDP item. The internal structure of the economy indicates the dominance of large companies, as the share contributed by small and medium-sized enterprises (SMEs) in the national GDP was only 20.2 per cent in 2011.

In the early 1990s, *inflation* rates soared – reaching 1662.3 per cent measured in terms of consumer prices. Government measures and active involvement of the National Bank of Kazakhstan to reduce inflation were effective, and by 1998 the inflation rate fell to 7.3 per cent. The hyperinflation of 1990s gave an important impetus to the government to accumulate capital by active increase of hard-currency reserves and attracting FDI.

Unemployment peaked in 1998 when it accounted for 13.7 per cent of the labour force. After 2000, unemployment has decreased gradually, standing at 5.4 per cent in 2011. During the same period, the government forced employers to formalize labour relations, thereby reducing the share of illegal employment in the economy. Currently, Kazakhstan's unemployment rate is among the lowest in the CIS.

According to the World Bank classification, Kazakhstan in its *income distribution* belongs to the group of upper middle-income countries. After 2000, the Gini coefficient fell from 41.11 per cent in 2001 to 29.04 per cent in 2009. Despite its endowment with natural resources, the country is placed along with Kyrgyzstan and Tajikistan in the group of 'least unequal countries', ahead of Russia and Azerbaijan, which are also resource-rich countries.

Current account development indicates high dependence of the economy on export of natural resources and overall vulnerability to external shocks, such as the world economic crisis of 2008 when Kazakhstan experienced a negative balance, accounting for minus 8 per cent of GDP.

Analysis of *public and private sector debt* shows interesting tendencies. The country was able to repay its external debt to the IMF already in 2000, thanks to the active development of the oil industry and significant exports of energy products. Moreover, the ratio of government debt to GDP has decreased over time, despite a slight increase due to the consequences of the economic crisis in 2009 and 2010. Kazakhstan was severely hit by the global economic crisis of 2008, due not least to the active external borrowing of local banks that resulted in an increase in private sector debt.

Finally, we have seen that foreign investors from different countries have played a prominent role in the formation of a market economy in the country. Foreign investors have indeed made a significant contribution to shaping Kazakhstan's economy since independence, and their role and influence are taken up in greater depth in Chapters 4 and 5.

2.2. Economic reform measures

2.2.1. Privatization

Major milestones of economic reform included early privatization, and then nationalization within many industrial sectors of the economy. As Troschke and Zeitler argue (2006: 53), privatization in Kazakhstan 'was more profound' than in Uzbekistan, its main regional economic counterpart. According to the 2006 report of Bertelsmann Foundation, mass privatization in the 1990s helped the country overcome the economic decline as it allowed inflows of foreign capital into the economy. Charman (2007) identifies three major stages in privatization:

1) *First privatization phase (1991–1993)*

During this first phase 'a mass privatization' system based on 'privatization vouchers' was launched (Charman 2007: 167). In January 1991, the Kazakh State Property Committee was established to privatize public enterprises (Pomfret 1995: 90). Big state corporations were privatized in telecommunications, energy and other major industries (Perlman 2007: 1335). By the end of this period, enterprises from trade, consumer services and agriculture had been effectively privatized (Kalyuzhnova 1998, in Charman 2007: 167). Importantly, the energy sector was largely privatized; foreign investors purchased the majority of shares (more than 50 per cent) in state-owned oil and gas companies through competitive tenders and auctions

(Koshanov 1995; Weinthal and Luong 2001; Luong and Weinthal 2010). These investors were represented by big oil corporations such as BP (UK), ChevronTexaco and ExxonMobil (USA), ENI (Italy), Shell (Netherlands); and PSAs and concessions were introduced (Kalyuzhnova and Nygaard 2008; Luong and Weinthal 2010). FDI was necessary for the country's economic development, so the government placed special legislative conditions, supported by the constitution, to guarantee the security of private ownership to foreign investors (Luong and Weinthal 2010: 263).

2) *Second privatization phase (1993–1995)*

The second phase involved the further selling-off of most state corporations (Pomfret 2005); however, the state failed to establish a competitive environment for the private sector, as there was no appropriate legal framework in place (Charman 2007). More than 10,000 firms in various industries were privatized (Zarakhovich 2006). In 1992, the government had announced its plan to privatize 80 per cent of small- and medium-sized companies in services; by 1995, 63 per cent of small-sized companies had been privatized (Jermakowicz et al. 1996).

3) *Third privatization phase (1995–1998)*

The third phase saw the completion of ownership transfer (Charman 2007). By 1996, 93 per cent of firms in the industrial and agricultural sectors had been privatized (Simon 2009: 71). As noted by Alam and Banerji (2000), this large-scale privatization was driven by the government's fiscal needs; they also indicate that, compared to Uzbekistan and other countries in transition, Kazakhstan is far ahead in terms of gaining revenues from privatization (see Table 2.4). In 1998, revenues from privatization as a share of GDP largely exceeded the average indicator of transition countries (4.3 per cent in Kazakhstan, as against 1 per cent in Uzbekistan, and 0.7 per cent in transition countries on average). Alam and Banerji conclude that high privatization revenues were the result of selling big oil concessions during the period 1995–2000, which largely helped the government to offset the budget deficit.

Table 2.4. Revenues from privatization, 1993–1998 (percentage of GDP)

	1993	1994	1995	1996	1997	1998
Kazakhstan	4.5	1.7	3.1	3.8	3.1	4.3
Uzbekistan	0.2	0.7	0.8	0.8	0.5	1.0
Transition average	0.6	0.5	0.5	0.6	0.9	0.7

Source: Tanzi and Tsibouris (1999, in Alam and Banerji 2000: 7).

There is, however, a *fourth phase* which has begun after 2000, during which a reverse trend occurred in the form of re-nationalization (Libman 2008). By 2005, the state had taken full control over 15 joint-stock companies (Charman 2007). After 2000, the share of state assets in the economy rose (Pomfret 2006b). By increasing its share in the economy, the state sought to invest in the development of country's mineral resource industry (Charman 2007), which has become a major source of state revenues (Cutler 2012: 2). During this period the government has increased the shares of the national oil companies in PSAs and oil contracts with foreign investors (Pomfret 2011: 16–17). The government's decision to re-nationalize parts of the economy was triggered by the resource nationalism policy, as discussed in subsection 2.1.7. As Libman argues (2008), this re-nationalization policy lessened the influence of foreign companies and led to the strengthening of the role of the state in the economy.

In general, privatization has proven successful for the overall economic development of Kazakhstan (Knox Thames 2007: 112).

2.2.2. Fiscal policy

Since independence the government has pursued a prudent fiscal policy (Bertelsmann Foundation 2006). This policy has aimed at increasing economic growth and facilitating reform processes, raising labour productivity, stimulating innovations and human capital (Government of the Republic of Kazakhstan 2007). Dzharkinbayev (2011: 55) notes that the state budget in the period from 2001 to 2006 was largely balanced: imbalances did not exceed 1 per cent of GDP. In the period 2007–2010, the budget deficit amounted to 2.3 per cent on average; this increase was triggered by implementation of anti-crisis measures (Dzharkinbayev 2011: 55).

There has been considerable debate on whether Kazakhstan's economic stability can be threatened by the 'resource curse', also known as the 'Dutch disease', a typical threat for resource-abundant countries (Kalyuzhnova 2011; Ustyantseva 2010; Egert and Leonard 2008; Kalyuzhnova 2006; Kutan and Wyzan 2005; Cohen, 2003; Wakeman-Linn et al. 2003; Kuralbayeva et al. 2001). By this is meant a situation when the cheap and abundant natural resources in a country may trigger a currency appreciation for a certain time, in turn leading to low levels of economic growth, price increases, stagnation and economic crisis (Polterovich et al. 2010; Humphreys et al. 2007; Sachs and Warner 1995).

Opinions vary as regards this 'resource curse' and Kazakhstan. Kutan and Wyzan (2005) identified some effects by using an econometric model in which they analysed how changes in oil prices influenced the real exchange rate in the period 1996–2003. They found a significant correlation between the changes in oil prices and changes in the real exchange rate – but without this leading to stagnation in economic development during this period. Egert and Leonard (2008) analysed the risk of 'Dutch disease' (or 'the resource curse') at a later stage of the country's development. They examined the dependency between oil price fluctuations and non-oil manufacturing industries in Kazakhstan in the period 1996–2005. They found that, even though there was an appreciation of the national currency (the Tenge) during this period, that was limited to the real exchange rate for the oil industry, and was statistically insignificant for the non-oil manufacturing industries. Indeed, avoiding the problem of the 'resource curse' has always been on the agenda of the government; in 2004, President Nazarbayev stressed that the cornerstone of fiscal policy must be to withdraw excessive petro-dollars from the economy, in order to avoid Dutch disease, decrease inflation, and avoid currency appreciation (*Gazeta.kz* 2004).

Kalyuzhnova (2006) notes that the creation of oil funds is of vital importance for resource-rich economies, as such funds can absorb excessive petroleum revenues and help to achieve overall macroeconomic and fiscal stability. She further points that the government established the National Fund of the Republic of Kazakhstan (NFRK) in 2000, with the aim of stabilizing the oil-driven economy in case of external shocks. In her later work, Kalyuzhnova (2011) notes that the NFRK accumulated sufficient assets to mitigate the negative consequences of the world economic crisis of 2008 by supporting the industries hardest hit during the crisis – banking, construction, real estate. From its establishment in 2000, the NFRK's assets grew from USD 1.2 billion to USD 33.7 billion in 2010; despite bailing-out the economy during the crisis by using the Fund's reserves, total assets increased up to 28 times (Dzharkinbayev 2011: 51). Dzharkinbayev further holds (2011: 56) that if excessive petroleum revenues were channelled not to the NFRK, but directly to the state budget, then they would totally cover the budget deficit for all the years 2000 to 2010, except for 2009.

Overall, there has been little evidence of the impact of the 'resource curse' on the economy of Kazakhstan, thanks to the government's prudent fiscal policies that have helped to generate significant fiscal surpluses (CASE 2008: 6). Moreover, government fiscal measures have been accompanied by effective institutional measures such as the creation of the NFRK and adoption of fiscal rules aimed at absorbing and managing excessive petroleum revenues (CASE 2008; Kalyuzhnova 2011).

2.2.3. Tax policy

The government has viewed simplifying the tax system and providing tax incentives as major tools to stimulate economic growth and the inflow of FDI (Morisset and Pirnia 2000). Vershinina (2007) identifies four main stages in the formation of tax policy. The first stage relates to the period 1991–1995 during which more than 40 types of taxes were introduced and the first Tax Code was adopted. The second stage covers the period from 1995 to 2000, during which the number of different types of taxes decreased to 11, indicating that the focus in this period was on improving the tax system. The third period (2000–2002) included a comprehensive improvement of the Tax Code. The fourth period started in 2002. During this period, the reform of the system has been implemented, aimed at eliminating ambiguity in the Tax Code clauses. Moreover, the tax system has been improved, to facilitate the tax regime for small and medium-sized companies (SMEs) (Vershinina 2007).

From 2007 tax calculation procedures for SMEs were simplified, with tax rates set as follows: 3–5 per cent for individual entrepreneurs and 3–7 per cent for legal persons depending on a profit amount (Tax Code 2008). In addition, preferential taxation in the form of 'special tax regimes' for SMEs has been introduced (Vershinina 2007). Today, the corporate income tax rate is 20 per cent, which equally applies to domestic and foreign companies (Tax Code 2008). The individual VAT rate has been changed twice. Until 2007 it was calculated according to a progressive scale from 5 to 20 per cent: the higher the income, the higher was the tax rate applied. After 2007 the individual VAT rate was set at 10 per cent (Tax Code 2008).

Even though tax legislation has been always directed towards reducing the tax rates for different types of businesses, still it was subject to constant change; in all, three tax codes have been adopted during this period (*Kursiv* 2012). Moreover, even though tax rates are relatively low, the complex tax administration procedures are felt as an additional burden for various companies (ibid). However, according to the report of the Bertelsmann Foundation (2012), the tax system in Kazakhstan remains among the most advanced in the post-Soviet space.

2.2.4. Monetary policy

The Law of the Republic of Kazakhstan on Currency Regulation, adopted in 1993, regulates currency transactions and operations according to the principles of market economy (Law on Currency Regulation 1993). The national currency – the Tenge – was also introduced in 1993 (Eicher 2004b) and immediately became 'a freely convertible currency' according to the IMF definition (Rakurs 2011). Before the Tenge was adopted in 1993, the National Bank of Kazakhstan (NBK) had not been involved in the implementation of monetary policy (Burke and Okulova 2009: 12). Since 1994 the NBK has controlled and implemented monetary policy by regulating credit operations, interest rates, and the exchange rate (*Zakon.kz* 2008; Burke and Okulova 2009; see also subsection 3.3.1.1).

Unofficially, in 1993 the country had introduced a 'soft' fixed exchange rate attaching the Tenge to the US dollar; having a fixed exchange rate was intended to help keep inflation low (Burke and Okulova 2009). The NBK purchases or sells the Tenge to keep the fixed exchange rate in balance (ibid).

There have been three main challenges for monetary policy. The first challenge was the financial crisis of 1998 in Russia, which caused depreciation of Kazakhstan's Tenge and led to negative implications for the economy (Burke and Okulova 2009: 11; *Zakon.kz* 2008). To mitigate the consequences, the government tightened fiscal policy and cut social payments (Burke and Okulova 2009).

Second, after the country started intensive involvement in the oil industry after 2000, monetary policy faced numerous problems (*Zakon.kz* 2008; Burke and Okulova 2009), especially the issue of an excessive inflow of oil revenues. This related to the fact that the economy is resource-dependent. To better control the inflow of petro-dollars into the economy and to keep inflation low, the NBK tightened monetary policy during this period (*Zakon.kz* 2008).

Third, the global economic crisis of 2008 has led to currency devaluation in countries which had been Kazakhstan's main trade partners (*Mir Finansov* 2010). In addition, global prices for oil and gas fell, forcing the government to target inflation and adopt currency corridors (ibid; see also Table 2.2 on inflation rate). In addition, the government implemented devaluation measures with respect to the Tenge; in 2009, a new currency corridor was introduced by the NBK (*Mir Finansov* 2010). As a result of these measures and the global increase in raw material prices, by the end of 2009 the national currency was in much better shape (ibid).

In the period from 2010 to 2012, the main goal of the NBK was to maintain price stability and keep inflation within the range of 6–8 per cent; in 2010 and 2011, the Tenge was further strengthened (National Bank of Kazakhstan 2011). Exchange-rate fluctuation of the Tenge was much less than in 2009 and did not exceed the currency corridor set in 2009; as a result, the NBK abolished the currency corridor in 2011 and shifted to a floating exchange rate for the Tenge.

Overall, the history of monetary policy in Kazakhstan demonstrates the vulnerabilities of the country's economy and its dependence on export of raw materials. However, it also demonstrates the ability and prudence shown by the government and the NBK in introducing effective measures to maintain a stable economy.

2.2.5. Social policy

Kazakhstan lost many years trying to step up social reforms, often patterned on western models, by painful trial and error.
Marat Yermukanov (2003)

The shift from a planned to a market-oriented economy imposed constraints on state capacity to effectively manage social policy (Müller 2003). Since independence the social policy system has experienced serious challenges (for more details see subsection 3.3.4). The economic collapse of the 1990s had a negative impact on state capacities to deliver on generous social policies (Alshanov 2011). The problems of poverty and low living standards in the rural areas and monotowns[6] have been serious, both during the first decade of independence and also in the new millennium (Sinicina 2006). Falkingham (2005) notes that one third of the population was living below the critical poverty level (USD 4.30 per day) in 2005. The problems of poverty complicated the effective delivery of social policies, as state funds had to be channelled towards the most vulnerable groups in the population.

Article 1 of the Constitution (1995) proclaims the Republic of Kazakhstan as a 'democratic, secular, legal and social state whose highest values are: the individual, his life, rights and freedoms.' After independence President Nazarbayev declared that Kazakhstan's development model was aimed at the creation of a socially-oriented market economy; this type of economy implies a balance between market progress and social equality in which the social realm should be considered as an important source of economic development (Dzhumambaev 2001). The government has been the main actor responsible for providing social security schemes to the population (UNDP 2005: 35). The government has reformed the pension, education, health-care systems. The pension system was built according to the Chilean system (Müller 2003); the education system has been modernized and the country has become part of the Bologna system of education (Ministry of Education 2012a). Social insurance policies, however, are in the initial phase of development and a major breakthrough is yet to be achieved (Gassmann 2011). As regards organizations which promote social policies, such as labour unions, in the 1990s they were path-dependent on weak labour unions of the Soviet period (Dzhumambaev 2001); their role hardly changed after 2000 (Kurmanov 2010). The health-care system has been reformed according to the strategic goals set in the Kazakhstan 2030 Development Strategy (see subsection 2.1.1); a major aim is to achieve

6 'Monotowns are urban settlements with economic bases dominated by a single industry or core enterprise' which were widespread in the USSR (World Bank 2010: 21). Today there are 27 monotowns in Kazakhstan, home to 16% of the urban population (*KAZINFORM* 2012).

significant improvement in the living standards of the population (Amagoh 2011). The health system has been reformed according to the New Public Management principles of public service delivery such as efficiency, quality, and civil societies and partnerships (ibid). Many problems in the health sector remain, and further reform is needed. However, in contrast to the period 1991–2000, the government has made the goal of fully implementing the health reform a strategic priority during the second decade of independence.

2.2.6. Summary of economic reform measures

The government of Kazakhstan has been confronted with many challenges in implementing economic reform measures since independence. It has pursued liberal policies as regards privatization, fiscal, tax and monetary policies; it has also been responsive to social demands, adopting various measures to promote a socially-oriented development model. Table 2.5 summarizes the main milestones of economic reform measures in the country since independence.

Privatization policy of the 1990s was aimed at attracting FDI. The government set favourable conditions for foreign investors, and key enterprises in the energy sector were sold to foreign companies via tenders and auctions. Since 2000 the government has promoted several re-nationalization processes and gained stronger control over the country's key economic sectors.

Fiscal policy has been aimed at maintaining budget balance and reducing government debt in relation to GDP; indeed, the government has succeeded in keeping the budget deficit low and reducing its debt-to-GDP ratio. Moreover, prudent state policies have helped to prevent a 'resource curse' in the economy; the government has been able to produce high fiscal surpluses and has established the NFRK to absorb and manage excessive petroleum revenues.

The *tax system* of Kazakhstan is deemed the most advanced in the post-Soviet area. Tax legislation itself has been subject to constant amendments and revision, with three tax codes having been adopted since independence. The government has established a 'business-friendly' taxation regime intended to attract FDI, and has set low tax rates for SMEs. However, despite low tax rates, Kazakhstan's complex tax administration procedures are somewhat of a drawback.

Monetary policy has been largely exercised by the National Bank of Kazakhstan, the main body responsible for regulating credit operations, the exchange rate and interest rate. Since 1991 currency regulation mechanisms have been adopted and implemented according to international standards. In 1993, the Tenge was adopted as the national currency. Russia's economic crisis of 1998 and the global financial crisis of 2008 have been major challenges to the monetary policy of Kazakhstan.

As to social policy, the government has adopted a social model in line with the criteria for a socially-oriented market economy. The pension, education, and health-care systems have been reformed, with varying degrees of success.

Table 2.5. Summary of economic reform measures in Kazakhstan

Privatization policy	– Aimed at attracting FDI in the 1990s – Key economic industries privatized – After 2000, re-nationalization processes – Stronger governmental control over key economic sectors after 2000.
Fiscal policy	– Aimed at maintaining budget balance – Success in keeping budget deficit low and reducing government debt-to-GDP ratio over time – High fiscal surpluses generated by the government – Avoiding the 'resource curse' in the economy – The NFRK established in 2000 to accumulate excessive petroleum revenues.
Tax policy	– Three tax codes adopted since 1991 – Kazakhstan's tax system among the most advanced in the post-Soviet space – Business-friendly tax legislation promoted by the government to attract FDI and help SMEs to develop – Complex tax administration procedures 'counteract' low tax rates.
Monetary policy	– Since 1991, currency regulation elaborated and implemented according to market principles – The national currency 'Tenge' adopted in 1993 – The National Bank of Kazakhstan is the main body responsible for implementing monetary policy – Russia's economic crisis of 1998 and the global financial crisis of 2008 are viewed as the main challenges for monetary policy.

Social policy	– Kazakhstan's development model aimed at the creation of socially-oriented market economy – With varying degrees of success, the government has reformed the country's pension, education and health-care systems.

Chapter 3. Institutional framework of the economy

3.1. Assessing institutional reform since 1991

After assessing the overall economic development since 1991 (see Chapter 2) it is also necessary to evaluate the emerging economic and political institutions in the country. Although there is a sizeable literature on Kazakhstan's economic performance, and its economic development since independence as well as future prospects, the scholarly literature on institutional development along the political, economic and market dimensions is by no means as comprehensive.

Limited research has been conducted on the development of political institutions in Kazakhstan, including the study of political parties (Isaacs 2011: 2). Multi-party legislation has been adopted in Kazakhstan (Omarov 2008), with one party, Nur Otan (formed in 2006), currently dominating the party system (Isaacs 2013: 1064; Armingeon and Careja 2008: 450). Other authors have analysed the way political institutions have been formed (Warkotsch 2008; Cummings and Nørgaard 2004; Cummings 2005). The main conclusion which can be drawn is that political institutions in Kazakhstan have been shaped by the complex interaction of various elites, the local, Soviet and Western ideological elements and governance approaches.

Concerning economic institutions and reform processes, Ahrens and Platje (2010), Jeffries (2003), Spechler (2004), Peck (2004), Troschke and Zeitler (2006), Ginsburg and Troschke (2005), and Leschenko and Troschke (2006) have analysed Kazakhstan's development by studying processes and characteristics similar to those set within the VoC framework, including privatization, corporate governance and FDI. Since independence, the government has sought to implement market-oriented reforms (Spechler 2004; Pomfret 2009). However, the envisaged reforms have not been complete. In their study of transition economies, Beck and Laeven (2006, in Iradian 2009) found that countries endowed with natural resources, like Russia, Azerbaijan, Tajikistan, Uzbekistan and Kazakhstan, have introduced market reforms only partially.

Scholars who have analysed market institutions in Kazakhstan include Koshanov (1995), Eicher (2004a), Pomfret (2006b), Charman (2007), Spechler (2008), Simon (2009), Rybina et al. (2010), Teal et al. (2011) and Luly (2012). According to Charman (2007: 180, 181), the economy can be characterized as a 'state-led liberal market economy', aimed at fostering the development of market economy institutions and able to serve as a model for other resource-rich and former centrally planned economies in Azerbaijan and Turkmenistan. Rybina et al. (2010: 93) suggest a similar definition of Kazakhstan's emergent market economy, which they label 'a government-dominated transition economy'. Simon (2009: 1) holds that the transition path was followed 'under conditions of a limited democracy' and that the economy has remained vulnerable to external shocks due to its dependence on mineral resources; however, there has been considerable success in liberalization and market reforms.

Eicher (2004a: 3–4) sees Kazakhstan as a 'model transition economy' in its pension and banking systems. He analyses various indicators in order to judge whether the country has a market economy, using criteria set by the USA and the EU (see Table 3.1). Eicher argues that the EU criteria are stricter than those set by the US Department of Commerce, which can explain why the USA recognized Kazakhstan as a market economy, whereas the EU granted it only 'a special market economy status' in 2000, because it did not adhere to principles concerning state interference and law enforcement according to EU standards.

Table 3.1. Market economy criteria

Criteria	**European Union**	**US Department of Commerce**
Market-determined prices	State interference must be minor	Wage rates are established by the labour market
Control of resources	Disappearance of undue state control over resources and production decisions	State ownership of resources is minimal
Accounting standards	International standards are followed	–
Property rights	Law is transparent and effective; Insolvent firms are forced into bankruptcy	–
Exchange rates	Exchange rates are not fixed	Currency is convertible
Foreign investments	–	There is potential for foreign investment

Source: Eicher (2004a: 5).

The European Bank for Reconstruction and Development (EBRD) studies the emerging market institutions in its annual transition reports. First of all, when assessing the transition path in Kazakhstan by EBRD standards, it is necessary to indicate the rise of 'the private sector in relation to GDP over time. As Table 3.2 shows, the share of the private sector amounted to 55 per cent in 1998. Within a decade, this figure rose, reaching 70 per cent in 2008. However, by 2010 this indicator had fallen to 65 per cent, which can be explained by the increased involvement of the state in the economy and the role of Samruk-Kazyna during and after the economic crisis (see subsection 3.3.2.2).

Table 3.2. Progress of economic transition[7]

Kazakhstan	Enterprises			Markets and trade			Financial institutions	
Year/Private sector share of GDP in per cent	Large-scale privatiza tion	Small-scale privatiza tion	Governance and Enterprise restructuring	Price liberaliza tion	Trade and foreign exchange system	Competi tion policy	Banking reform and interest rate liberaliza tion	Securities market and non-bank financial institutions
1998/55	3	4	2	3	4	2	2+	2
1999/55	3	4	2	3	3	2	2+	2
2000/60	3	4	2	3	3+	2	2+	2+
2001/60	3	4	2	3	3+	2	3-	2+
2002/65	3	4	2	3	3+	2	3-	2+
2003/65	3	4	2	4	3+	2	3 ↑	2+
2004/65	3	4	2	4	3+	2	3	2+
2005/65	3	4	2	4	3+	2	3	2+
2006/65	3	4	2	4	4-	2	3	3- ↑
2007/70 ↑	3	4	2	4	4-	2	3	3-
2008/70	3	4	2	4	4-	2	3	3-
2009/65↓	3	4	2	4	4-	2	3- ↓	3-
2010/65	3	4	2	4	4-	2	3-	3-
2011/n/a	3	4	2	4-↓	4-	2	n/a	n/a
2012/n/a	3	4	2	4-	4-	2	n/a	n/a

Source: Author's presentation based on EBRD Transition Reports (1998–2012).

The EBRD (2006) classification criteria for calculating the 'private sector share of GDP' indicator use official (government) and unofficial statistics. This share indicates the officially-registered revenues of private companies;[8] it may also include unofficial revenues if reliable information is available (ibid). The

7 According to the EBRD (2006: 4) classification, 'the transition indicators range from 1 to 4+, with 1 representing little or no change from a rigid centrally planned economy and 4+ representing the standards of an industrialised market economy (...) Arrows indicate change from the previous year. One arrow indicates a movement of one point (from 4 to 4+, for example), two arrows a movement of two points. Up arrows indicate upgrades, down arrows downgrades.'

8 'The term "private company" refers to all enterprises in which private individuals or entities own the majority of shares' (EBRD 2006: 4).

EBRD acknowledges the numerous data limitations, especially as regards the informal activities of the private sector. Moreover, official data frequently differ from the estimates calculated by the EBRD, due to differing definitions of 'private sector' and 'non-state sector' adopted by the EBRD and public agencies in countries in transition (ibid). Pomfret (2003) is critical to the EBRD approach, which he sees as too mechanical to capture the economic and development processes in the transition context, and argues that it is difficult to apply the standards of advanced market economies to countries in transition. Thus, the scores of the EBRD indicators should be treated with some caution.

Other indicators are grouped into three categories: *enterprises, markets and trade,* and *financial institutions* (Table 3.2). The 'enterprises' category includes large-scale and small-scale privatization as well as governance and enterprise restructuring. The scores for both types of privatization remained stable in the period from 1998 to 2012. While large-scale privatization scored '3' for the entire period, small-scale privatization scored '4', and so can be considered an area in which the country achieved the main success in transition from a command to a market economy. By contrast, progress in governance and enterprise restructuring has been somewhat limited, always scoring '2'. On the whole, the most progressive transition has been in the 'enterprises' category.

The 'markets and trade' category includes price liberalization, trade and foreign exchange system and competition policy. Kazakhstan has achieved remarkable progress also in this area. Since 2003 price liberalization has been stable, scoring '4', with slight downgrades in 2011 and 2012. Scores on the trade and foreign exchange system have fluctuated between '3' and '4' for the whole period. Finally, competition policy received the lowest score in this category: constantly '2', indicating the need for further reform.

The 'financial institutions' category comprises two elements: banking reform and interest rate liberalization and securities market and non-bank financial institutions. The score of the first element (banking reform and interest rate liberalization) shows that over time the state has managed to pursue progressive reforms in the banking sector; and since 2002 the score has not fallen below '3–'. The same tendency can be traced for the securities market and non-bank financial institutions. Since 2006 Kazakhstan has always scored '3–' on the EBRD indicators, and this shows progress compared to the period 1998–2005 when this indicator scored '2' and '2+'.

The EBRD also assesses the progress of institutional reforms in various economic sectors of a country in transition. In its country strategy, the EBRD (2010b) highlighted those key sectors in the country in which institutional reforms are deemed necessary. Significant institutional reforms are still required in the financial, enterprise and energy sectors in order for the economy of Kazakhstan to become more competitive (ibid). Moreover, according to the EBRD (2010a), the system of public procurement is weakly developed (see

Appendix 1[9]), 'accountability' and 'flexibility' scoring only 40 per cent; by contrast, 'integrity', 'transparency' and 'competition' of the public procurement system score 80 per cent, 80 per cent and 90 per cent, respectively.[10]

According to EBRD reports (2010a: 12; 2010b: 13), the economic transition in Central Asia, including Kazakhstan, is not complete. Moreover, state involvement in the economy has increased in recent years, indicating the importance of the state's role in shaping the country's economic relations. This increase in state interference is partly caused by the recent economic crisis and its negative influence on the economy. Most of Kazakhstan's major sectors – like the financial system, real estate, agriculture and construction industry – have been seriously affected by the crisis of 2008 (Mikheev 2010: 12; OECD 2011b). Since the financial system was the most integrated of all Central Asian economies in the global financial system, it was hit hardest by the crisis (Pomfret 2009). To mitigate the consequences, the state boosted its recovery by investing USD 11 bln (Laruelle 2008). As a result, a Stabilization Fund worth USD 4 billion was established, with the aim of maintaining liquidity. Esanov and Kuralbayeva (2010) have assessed state measures to mitigate the consequences of the economic crisis as effective and prudent, but international organizations have judged these measures differently (see Foster 2010; also subsection 3.3.1 on the financial system).

Overall, the impact of the crisis in Central Asia has attracted the attention of many scholars in recent years, with many of them outlining the consequences of the crisis for Kazakhstan. Spechler (2010: 1) holds that the country suffered from 'bank failures' during the crisis, whereas Pomfret (2009: 5) claims that Kazakhstan, as an active participant in globalization, is the most vulnerable of all the former Soviet Central Asian states to external shocks, as demonstrated by the crisis; conversely, it is also better prepared than any other country in the region for dealing with an economic crisis. The anti-crisis measures of the government have proved this (Scharff 2010). In order to stabilize the situation further, the state is likely to retain its increased control over the economy, through Samruk-Kazyna, as the fiscal stimulus programme is part of the industrialization plan for the period 2010–2015 (EBRD 2010a). Thus, the economic crisis of 2008 set the stage for an increasingly interventionist role of the state role in the economy (Luly 2012).

---

9 The appendix of this study is available at http://www.centralasiaproject.de or upon request from the author (roman.vakulchuk@googlemail.com).

10 'The chart shows the score for extensiveness and comprehensiveness of national public procurement laws (…) The scores are calculated on the basis of a legislation questionnaire, based on the EBRD Core Principles on an Efficient Public Procurement Framework (…) Total scores are presented as a percentage, with 100 per cent representing the optimal score for these benchmark indicators' (EBRD 2010a: 18).

3.2. Varieties of Capitalism (VoC) approach

The Varieties of Capitalism approach (VoC), advanced by Hall and Soskice (2001), serves as a starting point of the analysis of the type of market economy emerging in Kazakhstan. This analytical framework has been utilized for classifying various parts of the economy, facilitating the descriptive analysis of institutional development. The VoC approach has been successfully applied to classify the market economies in the post-Communist transition states in Eastern Europe and to a lesser degree in the CIS (Martin 2002; Cernat 2002; Knell and Srholec 2007; Buchen 2007; Mykhnenko 2007; Crowley and Stanojevic 2011; Luly 2012). Applying the VoC approach to the relationships between institutional subsystems should help identify existing institutions in the following key domains: the financial system, corporate governance, industrial relations, the social security system, vocational education and training and inter-firms relations (Hall and Soskice 2001), thereby shedding light on the type of market economy currently emerging in Kazakhstan.

However, little research has been done on institutional development or the interaction between different institutions[11] in Kazakhstan. According to the Varieties of Capitalism (VoC) approach, which is a company-centred concept, two types of market economies have been historically formed in the West: the Liberal Market Economy (LME) and the Coordinated Market Economy (CME) (Hall and Soskice 2001). This has become widely-used concept, embedded in the literature on comparative capitalism (Jackson and Deeg 2006: 21).

In this concept, capitalism is seen as based on the idea of coordination (Hall and Soskice 2001; Deeg and Jackson 2006: 22; Mendelski 2008: 4). Each system has its distinct set of features. In an LME, resource allocation among firms is coordinated by the market, whereas in a CME, market processes are complemented by intense coordination among market players (Herrigel and Zeitlin 2010: 668). These are classified as market-oriented (LME) and strategic coordination (CME) systems (Hall and Gingerich 2009: 481). Each system is organized around the concept of institutional complementarities, where complementarity is defined as '...the presence (or efficiency) of one [institution] increases the returns (or efficiency of) the other' (Hall and Soskice 2001: 17). Complementarity is seen as the result of the interconnection and a distinct type

11 The definition of an 'institution' here builds on that given by North: institutions are 'the humanly devised constraints that structure human interaction. They are made up of formal constraints (e.g., rules, laws, constitutions), informal constraints (e.g., norms of behaviour, conventions, self-imposed codes of conduct), and their enforcement characteristics' (North 1994: 360). North distinguishes between institutions (rules) and organizations (economic and political players).

of coordination mechanism in the following institutional domains: financial system, corporate governance, industrial relations, social security system, vocational education and training and inter-firm relations (see Table 3.3). These domains are central to LMEs and CMEs alike.

The type of a *financial system* is important as it determines firms' access to finance and the adaptability to the changing market conditions (Hall and Soskice 2001). The financial system in an LME differs from that in a CME. In LMEs financing through the capital market is widespread, while in CMEs credit financing of companies prevails. In an LME, the potential loss of market shares and external impact on current profitability of a firm can be mitigated if a firm is able, quickly and easily, to reduce the number of employees due to flexible labour markets (ibid: 16). Further, according to Hall and Soskice, firms in a CME have access to funding which is not linked to their current profitability. In a CME, long-term employment contracts are common. Thus, in a CME the labour market is less flexible than in an LME, and it is difficult for firms to dismiss employees. This is how the labour market in LMEs and CMEs are linked to the financial system.

Table 3.3. Key features of the VoC approach

VoC approach	Liberal market economy (LME)	Coordinated market economy (CME)
Corporate governance and financial system	Shareholder valube centred (short-term financial markets)	Stakeholder value-centred (patient long-term capital)
Industrial relations	Decentralized wage-bargaining	Coordinated wage-bargaining
Unionization level	Rather low	Rather high
Social security system	Low benefits	Generous benefits
Vocational training	General skills/high R&D expenditures	Company- and industry-specific skills
Inter-firm relations	Competitive/limited business coordination/little sharing of information	Cooperative/high degree of business coordination/high degree of sharing information

Source: Author's presentation based on Hall and Soskice (2001), Ebbinghaus and Manow (2001: 5) and Nölke and Vliegenthart (2009: 650).

Corporate governance is also an integral part of the VoC framework and is closely tied with the financial system. As Hall and Soskice (2001: 7) explain, this domain provides firms with a structure within which security of investments is made possible and returns for the investments are guaranteed. The existence of funding opportunities and the security of investment returns are crucial for operations of a firm (ibid). In a CME, private firms rely on long-term capital returns on investments, whereas in an LME short-term financial markets prevail (Hall and Soskice 2001; Ebbinghaus and Manow 2001). Firms in CMEs actively use various employer networks to facilitate market information exchange and secure access to finance; they may impose sanctions against firms that behave badly (Hall and Soskice 2001). If a firm provides false information it can be deprived of access to the industrial network; this in turn would have a negative impact on that firm's reputation and profitability (ibid: 23). In LMEs, firms do not have CME-type employer networks, and little or no information is shared among the firms. Securing access to finance depends largely on company's 'valuation in equity markets, where dispersed investors depend on publicly available information to value the company. This applies to both bonds, share issues, and bank lending' (ibid: 28).

Further, according to Hall and Soskice (2001: 7), *industrial relations* are relations between employers and employees, in which the key component is the coordination of the wage-setting process among employers, employees and labour unions. In an LME, the wage-bargaining process is usually decentralized and is driven by market forces, whereas in a CME wage-setting is exercised through industry-level bargains between trade unions and employer associations (Hall and Soskice 2001). Thus, the *level of unionization* tends to be high in a CME and low in an LME. In CMEs, labour unions and employer associations exert substantial influence on the decision-making agendas of private firms; in contrast, in LMEs labour unions and employer associations exert little influence on the decision-making policies of private firms (ibid).

The *social security system* is an important domain within the VoC approach. Social investments in employees in the form of various unemployment benefits help firms to create various pools of labour, which they may access in case certain labour skills are required (Hall and Soskice 2001: 50). In an LME, firms provide low-level benefits, whereas firms provide high-levels of benefits to their employees in a CME (Hall and Soskice 2001). The fluid and flexible labour markets in an LME require employees to invest in general, and not specific, skills. Developing general skills helps workers to remain competitive and flexible on the labour markets within an LME. In a CME, firms provide generous social benefits to their employees in order to secure their loyalty and develop skills which are company-specific (ibid). Therefore, in contrast to an LME, employees in a CME will tend to develop specific skills. The risk of being dismissed and the risk of not being able to make use of their specific skills are compensated by generous unemployment and retirement conditions that firms provide in CMEs (ibid). Hall and Soskice (2001: 51) further note that, aside from the state interests in introducing and promoting social policies, businesses in a CME are also interested in improving social benefits for the labour force. An important role is assigned to labour unions: negotiating the wage-setting process and social benefits for workers (ibid).

Vocational education and training (VET) is defined by Hall and Soskice (2001: 7) as relations between firms and a workforce, whereby firms seek to provide employees with necessary skills and employees decide which skills they want to develop. In an LME, training the workforce is based on a short general education, whereas in a CME it involves longer-term vocational training (Hall and Soskice 2001; see also Ebbinghaus and Manow 2001). The difference is explained by the nature of labour markets in LMEs and CMEs. Firms in an LME suffering from an economic downturn may lay off employees in an attempt to restructure their activities, and/or invest in R&D in order to create comparative advantages and remain competitive (Hall and Soskice 2001; Nölke and Vliegenthar 2009). Thus, dismissed employees with few or no unemployment benefits may start investing in short-term re-education courses to obtain new skills in hopes of remaining competitive in the labour market (Hall and Soskice 2001). Further, in CMEs, the labour market is less fluid and employees will generally have long tenure and companies will invest in company- or industry-specific skills; moreover, there is little risk involved in losing one's job, given the availability of unemployment benefits that firms provide in a CME (ibid). Short-term VET in an LME is explained by the necessity of being able to obtain skills quickly for a new specialization in case the previous skills are no longer in demand (ibid). In contrast, in a CME long tenure is envisaged for training employees in specific skills. Thus, as noted by Hall and Soskice (2001), the labour force is more mobile in LMEs than in CMEs.

Finally, *inter-firm relations* are defined as a firm's relations with other companies, suppliers and clients, aimed at providing a demand for its goods and services as well as establishing access to technology (Hall and Soskice 2001: 7). How do LMEs and CMEs differ in inter-firm relations? In LMEs, private firms tend not to collaborate or share market information with each other (Hall and Soskice 2001). Product competition is high and competition among firms may be fierce, driving them to compete constantly with each other for new products and customers (ibid). In CMEs, by contrast, firms tend to cooperate and build networks through which they interact and share market information (ibid: 8). In each case, firms use comparative advantages of market structure formed in CMEs and LMEs; by choosing to cooperate (CME) or not to cooperate (LME) firms ensure their access to finance and profitability (Hall and Soskice 2001). Regulations in LMEs allow friendly and hostile takeover transactions, while M&A regulations and cross-shareholding in CMEs protect firms from hostile takeovers (ibid). As a result, takeover transactions are frequent in LMEs, but are rare in CMEs (Hall and Soskice 2001; see also Jackson and Miyajima 2007: 3).

These VoC domains are interconnected by institutional complementarities; taken together they provide various advantages and benefits for firms (Hall and Soskice 2001). According to the core assumption of the VoC approach, the institutional framework in these two market systems is path-dependent: change in one particular domain will be constrained by the institutional complementarities among institutions in other domains (Jackson and Deeg 2006). Therefore, the entire system – whether LME or CME – is resistant to institutional change in one of the domains (Hall and Soskice 2001).

Hall and Gingerich (2009) provide an example of institutional complementarity. Their empirical study showed that potential deregulation of the labour market (greater market coordination) generates significant economic benefits for firms only in economies that have an LME-type of financial system; further, that greater market coordination for corporate governance provides positive effects only in countries that have fluid labour markets.

Despite the differences, each capitalist system provides firms and their employees with advantages. Examples of countries with LMEs include Australia, Canada, Ireland, New Zealand, the UK and the USA; and for CMEs, Austria, Belgium, Denmark, Germany, Japan, the Netherlands, Norway, Sweden and Switzerland, while other capitalist economies – like those of France, Spain, Italy, Greece, Portugal, Singapore and Turkey – represent a mixed type of market economy, to varying degrees combining elements of the two systems (Hall and Soskice 2001; Terjesen and Hessels 2009).

The main point of criticism of the VoC approach is that it is static and cannot account for institutional change (Herrigel and Zeitlin 2010: 670). Moreover, institutional complementarity can hardly be achieved in times of constant socio-economic change and competing interests of various actors (Mendelski 2008: 23) (see also subsection 3.3.7).

In the present work, the VoC approach is applied to classify institutional subsystems in the emerging market-oriented economy of Kazakhstan. The literature review in section 3.3 has been conducted according to VoC assumptions. Also the interview guides were composed in line with the key assumptions of the VoC framework (see section 4.5.2). Finally, key assumptions of the VoC approach were formulated as subcategories in the coding frame for content analysis (see subsection 4.8.5 and Chapter 5).

3.3. Varieties of Capitalism in Kazakhstan

3.3.1. The financial system

3.3.1.1. Evolution of the financial system

Although Kazakhstan may have been regarded as one of the more backward republics of the Union in Soviet times, a few years after independence its monetary authorities embarked on a substantial drive to reform its banking system that seems to have borne fruit...

Stephan Barisitz (2008: 67)

A 'financial system', according to the International Monetary Fund (IMF) (2006: 11), 'consists of institutional units and markets that interact, typically in a complex manner, for the purpose of mobilizing funds for investment and providing facilities, including payment systems, for the financing of commercial activity'. The major function of financial institutions is 'intermediation' in commercial and financial activities among various actors, who may be the state and non-state actors, domestic and foreign. Furthermore, in every financial system the crucial role in intermediation is assigned to 'deposit takers', which 'engage in financial intermediation as a principal activity' – banks, credit unions, financial companies, microfinance institutions and other non-banking financial institutions (International Monetary Fund 2006: 12; see also Business Dictionary 2012a). Within a traditional financial system, financial market coordination is exercised mainly by the central bank (International Monetary Fund 2006: 13), whose role is usually seen as strategic in terms of maintaining macroeconomic stability (ADB 2000; Bank for International Settlements 2009). It is the key institution in 'issuing currency, managing international reserves, and providing credit to deposit takers' (International Monetary Fund 2006: 13). Importantly, Fry et al. (1996: 2–3) argue that the central bank in an emerging economy may differ in many aspects from the central banks in developed economies. Central banks in developing countries dominate their financial system to a greater extent than do central banks in the developed world. For that reason, central banks in the emerging economies also carry greater responsibility for implementing structural reforms in their financial systems in a period of crisis or transition (ibid).

Financial systems may be variously classified. The major debate between economists and policymakers has been around two types of financial systems: bank-based (German and Japanese models), and market-based (US and UK models) (Levine 2000; Carlin and Mayer 2000). This classification also underlies the concept of a financial system within the framework of the VoC approach as outlined by Hall and Soskice (2001) (see section 3.2).

Another important type of a financial system is the Islamic financial system (Imam and Kpodar 2010; Solé 2007). Banks and other financial institutions within this system are also considered 'profit-maximizing entities' because 'they act as intermediaries between savers and investors and offer custodial and other services found in traditional banking systems', but the conditions under which Islamic financial institutions operate differ from those of Western-type financial systems (Imam and Kpodar 2010: 3). Islamic law shapes how the Islamic banking system works. Four elements in particular make the Islamic financial system different: prohibition of interest *(riba)*; prohibition of *maysir* (games of chance) and *gharar* (chance); and payments from bank profits to social benefit (*zakat*)' (Imam and Kpodar 2010: 3). Importantly, the Islamic financial system prohibits speculation, defined as 'increasing one's wealth by chance rather than productive effort' (ibid: 3; see also Maggs 2011).

There is a general assumption that the more developed the financial sector is in a given country, the higher degree of economic growth one can expect (Akimov and Dollery 2007). The case of Kazakhstan (see below) provides an example of active governmental support for the financial system – and this support has helped to build the foundations for the rapid economic growth achieved in the past decade, as well as the emergence of competitive financial institutions in the country. This in turn points to the important role of the state in the formation of a market-oriented economy in the country.

Some authors see the under-development of the financial sector as a burden for economic development in all Central Asian countries (Pavlova and Rohozynsky 2005, and Golodniuk 2005, in Ahrens and Platje 2010: 157). However, after gaining independence Kazakhstan started to build a financial system according to the principles of a market economy (Burke and Okulova 2009). Today its banking system is considered to be one of the most advanced in the CIS (Tumenbayeva 2012; Pomfret 2009; Seitkasimov 2009; Akimov and Dollery 2007; AmCham 2004; Merrill and Whiteley 2003) and is the only one in Central Asia to have become fully integrated into the global economy (OECD 2011a: 15). Luly (2012) notes that the Kazakhstan's financial system exhibits features of an 'almost-LME' type of economy.

As to the overall performance of the banking system in Kazakhstan, it performs relatively well in comparison to other CIS countries (Waikar et at. 2011; Hartwell 2013: 414). However, as noted by the former head of ATF Bank in Kazakhstan, Alexander Picker (2010), the financial system is still in an initial phase, at least in terms of the proportion of its financial stock to GDP. He points that Kazakhstan finds itself grouped along with Hungary, Russia and the Czech Republic in terms of the ratio of the country's financial stock to GDP (lower compared to the ratio of e.g. Germany, Switzerland and the USA).

Akimov and Dollery (2007: 3) hold that Kazakhstan, as opposed to other resource-rich countries, has conducted advanced and 'carefully designed reforms' in the financial sector. This, in turn, has provided the platform for substantial economic growth. During the first years of independence, the major problem in the financial sector was the significant share of 'non-performing loans', which the state solved with the help of these prudent reforms (Akimov and Dollery 2007: 5). Since 1991, the banking sector has developed significantly; with the overall number of domestic banks increasing due to the fact that the local population has trusted and used local banks more than foreign banks (Baimakhanov 2009). Moreover, as pointed by the former chairman of the National Bank of the Republic of Kazakhstan (NBK), Grigory Marchenko (2000), Kazakhstan was one of the first countries in the CIS to adopt international banking standards.

Since the 1990s, local banks have gradually adopted international norms and standards (Barsukov 2004). In 1997, in an attempt to develop the financial system, the NBK introduced 'The Programme for Transitions to International Standards by Second-Tier Banks', which helped to create a two-tier banking system in the country (Jandosov 1998: 7). Established in 1991, the NBK represents the first tier (Law on the National Bank 1995; National Bank of Kazakhstan 2012),[12] with all other banks comprising the second tier (Law of Banks 1995). The first-tier bank introduced international standards in 1998; the second-tier banks in 2000 (Jandosov 1998). The 1995 law governing the NBK stipulates that 'The National Bank of Kazakhstan shall be accountable to the President of the Republic of Kazakhstan', giving the President broad authority to approve 'the structure, overall staff size, and wage system of the National Bank of Kazakhstan', as well as its annual report (see also subsection 2.2.4 on monetary policy). By law, the President is entitled to 'appoint the Chairman of the National Bank of Kazakhstan and release the latter from his office.' Thus, even though the National Bank is considered to have a relatively high degree of autonomy, its operations can still be largely influenced by the state (Uzagalieva 2006: 413).

The major functions of the NBK are presented in Table 3.4. Fry et al. (1996) argue that the national banks heavily dominate the financial system in developing countries. This also holds for Kazakhstan, where the NBK coordinates the financial system. It shapes the legal financial regime, formulating procedures and rules for all market players by controlling 'monetary, credit and exchange rate policy and licensing, regulation and supervision of commercial banks' (Kalyuzhnova and Trimidas 1998: 684). The NBK and the government set the official interest rates (National Bank 2012),

12 In addition, 'the National Bank of Kazakhstan represents the interests of the country in its relations with the central banks of other countries, international banks and other financial institutions' (Law on the National Bank 1995).

thus limiting the influence of the market forces in this regard. However, as Schäfer et al. (2010: 704) note, the NBK is an effective supervisor of the financial system, and the supervision system itself corresponds to widely adopted international standards (Arner and Park 2011: 129). The NBK is prohibited by law from crediting the government (Uzagalieva 2006: 413). Importantly, the government does not intervene in the bank's credit operations; however, the NBK provides financial advisory services to state agencies (Law on the National Bank 1995).

Table 3.4. Major functions performed by the National Bank of Kazakhstan

– Maintaining price stability
– Issuing currency and implementing monetary policy
– Servicing the state debt
– Granting credits to banks and setting the official interest rate
– Formulating procedures for carrying out banking transactions
– Setting market rates for remuneration on the financial market
– Setting the official rate of the national currency
– Formulating procedures for exercising payments and money transfers
– Controlling and regulating foreign exchange operations
– Publishing legal regulatory documentation
– Developing financial reporting standards
– Setting the rules for operations with the currency
– Publishing external sector data (balance of payments, investment position and gross foreign debt)
– Servicing the unified treasury account for budget execution
– Setting the legal regime and structure of bank accounts

Source: Author's presentation based on Law on the National Bank (1995).

The banking sector shows a degree of high concentration, according to the Herfindahl-Hirschman index [13] (Baimakhanov 2009). The sector is further distinguished by the special conditions emplaced on the operations of foreign capital (Baimakhanov 2009; Akimov and Dollery 2007). A ban on foreign financial organizations opening representative offices in the country was lifted in 2005; as the International Finance Corporation (IFC) (2009: 21) observed, 'the country lifted the ban gradually during a transitional period, when it

13 'The Herfindahl Hirschman Index (HHI) is a measurement used to understand the level of competition that exists within a market or industry, as well as give an indication of how the distribution of market share occurs across the companies included in the index' (Modern Analyst 2012).

mapped out certain restrictive rules to ensure that domestic banks could compete fairly with foreign newcomers.' Since then, foreign banks have typically established their own representative offices, instead of acquiring shares in domestic banks (ibid). Further, foreign banks are restricted to holding a 25 per cent ownership share in local banks; in 2008, the share of foreign capital in the domestic banking sector amounted to 4.5 per cent (ibid).

In 2007, Kazakhstan's financial system included 35 second-tier banks (Table 3.5) with a loan portfolio of USD 60.4 million. Importantly, some 70 per cent of the loans concerned the real estate sector, directly or indirectly (International Finance Corporation 2009: xi).

Table 3.5. Market size of banking organizations

Type of organization	No. of organizations	Assets (USD mln)	Per cent of financial sector assets
Second-tier banks	35	76.6	81.9
Pension funds	14	7.4	7.9
Nonbanking organizations	22	4.6	4.9
Securities dealers	99	2.4	2.6
Insurance firms	41	1.2	1.3
Mortgage companies	10	1.2	1.3
Total	221	93.4	100

Source: Author's presentation based on Financial Markets Supervision Agency (2007, in International Finance Corporation 2009: 30).

Table 3.6 shows the distribution of two-tier banks as of 2011. Note that the overall number increased from 35 banks in 2007 to 39 by 2011.

Table 3.6. Structure of the banking sector (June 2011)

Number of two-tier banks, including:	39
Banks with 100 per cent state participation	1
Subsidiaries of two-tier banks	371
Number of additional offices of two-tier banks	1,889
Number of offshore offices of two-tier banks	16
Number of foreign banks on the territory of the Republic	29
Number of two-tier banks participating in mandatory deposit insurance	35
Number of two-tier banks with licenses for custodian activities	10

Source: Author's presentation based on Financial Supervision Committee of the NBK (in Rakurs 2011).

The government of Kazakhstan retains control over all leading financial market players in the country (Barsukov 2004). The NBK plays a key role in that regard: it largely defines how other financial organizations develop, and also sets the official interest rate (Law on the National Bank 1995). In 2012, it reduced the official interest rate from 6.5 per cent to 6 per cent (*Zakon.kz* 2012b). Moreover, most of the assets of the financial sector are currently within the scope of the Samruk-Kazyna's control (US Department of State 2011). That has important implications, as it indicates the important role of the state in coordinating economic processes and relations between private economic actors, as we will see.

3.3.1.2. Development of the credit market

Kazakhstan's credit market developed gradually during the first decade of independence. Soon after the turn of the millennium, the country experienced a tremendous rise in domestic credit provision to the private sector by the banking system, equalling 26.8 per cent of GDP in 2004 (Charman 2007: 170). In the period 2000–2007, GDP grew by an average of 10 per cent every year (Conrad 2008: 1). Bank lending was channelled mainly into trade, construction, real estate and banking industries (Charman 2007: 170; EBRD 2010b); and economic development was largely the result of capital investment in the last three sectors (EBRD 2010b: 20).

Between 2000 and 2008, the banking industry saw a significant development, with two-digit annual growth rates for assets (Baimakhanov 2009). 'Private credit bureau coverage'[14] grew from 5.5 per cent in 2006 to 13.7 per cent in 2007 (International Finance Corporation 2009: 39). Kalyuzhnova and Nygaard (2009) explain the increase in credit levels by rising global oil prices, coupled with the development of new oil fields and energy exports after 2000. They also note the important role of Samruk-Kazyna in boosting credit growth (see subsection 3.3.2.2).

In 2008, the financial sector felt the effects of the global economic crisis, which led to a significant decrease in foreign funding (EBRD 2010b: 121) and called into question the strength of Kazakhstan's entire financial system (Barisitz and Lahnsteiner 2010). The system was on the verge of collapse, mainly because between 2001 and 2008, local banks had become dependent on loans from abroad (Muzalevsky 2009): 60 per cent of financing for the corporate sector came from foreign loans in this period (Spechler 2010: 3). With no effective risk management system in place (Sahin 2011: 315), the financial

14 According to the World Bank, it is 'the number of individuals and firms covered by a private credit bureau as a percentage of the adult population' (see International Finance Corporation 2009: 39).

sector was particularly vulnerable to external shocks. As a result, the share of non-performing loans increased rapidly – from 7 per cent in 2008 to 38 per cent in 2009 (Barisitz and Lahnsteiner 2010: 62).

The government's anti-crisis measures helped the financial system to make a recovery from the crisis. Main measures included the nationalization of two big banks, BTA and the Alliance Bank, and the re-capitalization of other banks (Barisitz and Lahnsteiner 2010). The World Bank supported the government in implementing these measures, whereas the foreign crediting organizations criticized it, as the government's banking restructuring policy brought significant losses for creditors (Foster 2010). Government policy measures included provisioning of non-performing loans and strictly controlling the flow of external funding by toughening lending conditions from abroad (EBRD 2010a: 121). The NBK proved crucial in the post-crisis recovery of the banking system, mitigating the consequences by 'providing short-term liquidity support to commercial banks totalling over USD 10 bln' (Conrad 2008: 6).

3.3.1.3. The capital market

Kazakhstan's major stock exchange was established in 1993 (KASE 2012). Between 1991 and 1993, some 50 stock exchange platforms had mushroomed in the country (Rakurs 2011). However, the establishment of the National Commission on Securities proved effective in regulating the capital market (KASE 2012; Rakurs 2011). It reduced the number of players by introducing strict regulations for market participation, and in 1997, the Central Securities Depository was organized in an attempt to adopt international standards in capital market regulations (Rakurs 2011). Gradually, the stock market became an integral part of the financial system (Shalgimbayeva 2001); and today, it is slowly gaining even more importance (Rakurs 2011).

However, according to the Index of Economic Freedom (Heritage Foundation 2012), the capital market in the country is still 'underdeveloped'. The supervising body of the stock market is the National Bank of Kazakhstan (Barsukov 2004; National Bank of Kazakhstan 2011). Kazakhstan's stock market, along with its Russian equivalent, is considered to be relatively advanced within the CIS (Golodniuk 2005) and had 62 shareholders in 2011 (Rakurs 2011). During the first decade of independence, government securities were the major item in the capital market, although by the second decade, the composition of the market had changed: by 2011, foreign exchange transactions accounted for 56 per cent, REPO on government securities 37.5 per cent, government securities 3.8 per cent, and other transactions 2.7 per cent of the market (Rakurs 2011).

The size of the stock exchange is relatively small. KASE's market capitalization is only USD 60 bln, while it accounts for USD 16,000 bln at the New York Stock Exchange (Rakurs 2011). As of 2012, a total of 79 companies are listed in the KASE (KASE 2012). The market capitalization of listed companies (percentage of GDP) was 42.48 per cent in 2010 – the highest value being 53.93 per cent in 2006 and the lowest value being 5.44 per cent in 2001 (Index Mundi 2012a). However, legislation aimed at regulating securities still has considerable shortcomings. Market entry for many companies remains problematic, and government intervention in the stock market remains too high: as a result, 'equity capitalization' and 'local issuance of equity' are still largely underdeveloped (EBRD 2010b: 23).

The economic crisis of 2008 has also affected the capital market (Rakurs 2011; *FXTrade.kz* 2011), with foreign investors experiencing losses on the securities market (Rakurs 2011). In response to the crisis, the government introduced the New Concept of Financial Sector Development in the Post-Crisis period (President's Decree 2010; Rakurs 2011). The concept stresses the important role of the capital market and is aimed at reducing 'the volume of transfers from the National Fund, hence increasing its assets and investments revenues'; moreover, state support of the capital market is to 'provide savings for funding the non-oil budget deficit' (Rakurs 2011).

Given the relatively small size of the capital market prevailing in LMEs, and the dominance of the credit market as the main financing channel for companies, Kazakhstan's financial system can be clearly categorized as being of the CME type.

3.3.1.4. Microfinance organizations

Formally, microfinance organizations (MCOs) 'can be established as microloan organizations (either as for-profit or non-profit organizations), or credit partnerships (which are similar to credit unions)' (International Finance Corporation 2009: xii). In terms of the role of MCOs in Kazakhstan, the development of the sector can be divided into two periods: from 1991 to 2008, and from 2008 to 2012.

During the first period, microfinance was poorly developed and microfinance companies were generally 'weak and unsustainable' (International Finance Corporation 2009: xii). According to the Agency of Statistics of the Republic of Kazakhstan, 1,086 microcredit companies were officially registered in 2008 (DAMU 2012). However, there were only 100 active actors in 2008, with the 10 largest companies possessing 80 per cent of market assets. Most of the microcredit organizations are based in the south of the country, mainly in Almaty (DAMU 2012). This geographical trend is explained by the 'population density, level of entrepreneurship activity and demand for microcredits' in various regions of the country (DAMU 2012). According to DAMU (2012), during the first period, 57 microcredit organizations established the Association of Microfinance Organizations of Kazakhstan (AMFOK). According to AMFOK, in 2006, 98 per cent of the sector's investments were of international origin and only 2 per cent were of domestic origin (DAMU 2012). Various studies on MCOs in Central Asia, conducted by international organizations (e.g. MIX and CGAP 2011), have shown the low efficiency of MCOs in Kazakhstan compared to those in other Central Asian republics (DAMU 2012). Moreover, operating costs are the highest among microfinance organizations in the region; they are also ineffective, as one average MCO serves only 47 customers in Kazakhstan (compared to 251 in Kyrgyzstan, 771 in Tajikistan and 2,428 in Uzbekistan) (ibid). Other barriers in the first period included 'the lack and high cost of borrowing for MCOs; the insufficiency of MCOs' own resources; the lack of qualified staff; the lack of methodologies and training programmes for microcredit system actors; poor technical facilities; and poor community awareness of microcredit opportunities and conditions' (ibid).

During the second period, 2008–2012, the state started to invest more resources and devote more attention to MCOs. The state is currently overseeing a large-scale reform of the sector within the 'Action Programme of Small Entrepreneurship Development Fund JSC to Develop Microcredit Organizations in the Republic of Kazakhstan for 2008–2012' (DAMU 2012). The Programme targets the 'institutional development of the microcredit system in the Republic of Kazakhstan, 2008–2012, and aims to identify the priority activities of the Small Entrepreneurship Development Fund JSC to support and develop the country's microfinance sector as a third tier of the financial system' (ibid). This Fund, which has been established within the Programme, aims to provide quick assistance to MCOs and SMEs, which lacked the opportunity to attract resources before and during the economic crisis. The scope and major functions of the Fund are presented in Table 3.7.

Table 3.7. Goals of the Small Entrepreneurship Development Fund 'DAMU'

– 'The main goal of the Programme is to facilitate the qualitative development of the microfinance sector as a third tier of the country's credit system through financial and non-financial support to MCOs'
– Enhancing the access of ongoing MCOs to affordable loans on a competitive basis
– Providing incentives for MCOs to improve the quality and transparency of operations
– Improving microcredit market data collection and analysis
– Developing microcredit standards
– Developing MCO performance assessment technologies
– Training and enhancing the skills of microcredit market stakeholders

Source: Author's presentation based on DAMU (2012).

The total amount of microcredits provided by MCOs increased sharply from 55.4 bln Tenge in 2010 to 104.8 bln in 2011, then declined and reached 75.5 bln Tenge in 2013 (Table 3.8). The overall number of microcredits declined from 378,589 in 2010 to 231,137 in 2013.

Table 3.8. Credits provided by microfinance organizations

	2010	2011	2012	2013
Number of microcredits	378,589	486,082	228,453	231,137
Total amount, bln Tenge	55.4	104.8	77.8	75.5

Source: Author's presentation based on AMFOK (2014).

Another ambitious goal set within the programme was to increase the market share of the fund to 10 per cent by 2012 (DAMU 2012), which in 2008 accounted for 5.1 bln Tenge. However, no comprehensive analysis of the set goal and the effectiveness of the fund has been conducted; thus, its effectiveness and the progress of its implementation are yet to be analysed.

Therefore, as regards the microfinance sector, it can be argued that the state began seriously supporting MCOs in the period 2008 to 2013, with DAMU playing a key role in this regard.

3.3.1.5. Islamic banking

In 2009, the government made amendments to its financial legislation in an attempt to prepare the ground for the introduction of Islamic banking principles, aimed at attracting more foreign investment (Maggs 2011: 369; Rakurs 2011). The government was influenced by 'multinational businesses seeking a profitable market position' (Maggs 2011: 370) and was driven by the idea of diversifying its financial system (*The Business Year* 2011). As of 2011, one Islamic bank (the 'Al Hilal' Bank, from the United Arab Emirates) had established a representation office in Kazakhstan (Rakurs 2011), and more banks plan to follow suit (ibid: 370). Since 2003, several local banks have adopted the basic principles of Islamic banking within their operations (BankTuran Alem, CenterCredit, Alliance Bank, KazCommerzBank), including introducing 'an interest-free deposit' (Rakurs 2011). In 2010, Kazakhstan signed the 2010–2012 Islamic Finance Development Roadmap, intended to attract FDI from other members of the Organization of Islamic Conference (*The Business Year* 2011), which Kazakhstan chaired in 2011/2012 (Akorda 2013). The government has shown interest in using 'Islamic bonds *(sukuk)* as an alternative source of foreign investment', in order to facilitate financing 'projects aimed at diversifying its economy in the areas of petrochemicals, renewable energy, tourism, agriculture' (Rakurs 2011). With the growing interest of local banks in Islamic banking, the use of Islamic bonds may expand. As yet, however, the real market share of Islamic banks' transactions has remained low (*The Business Year* 2011). Considering the success of Islamic banking in Muslim countries in Southeast Asia – Malaysia in particular and in emerging markets in general (*Halal Journal* 2011) – the popularity of Islamic banking seems likely to rise among the population of Kazakhstan, 65 per cent of whom are nominally Muslim (Maggs 2011: 370). If so, and if Kazakhstan continues to adopt Islamic banking standards, the constellation of financial players and the financial sector itself may well change.

3.3.1.6. Summary of the financial system

The financial system of Kazakhstan has developed in line with international standards since independence and currently has two tiers of banks. The NBK plays a key role in coordinating and controlling the entire financial system in the country. The capital market is still in its infancy and is controlled by the NBK. Domestic financial organizations have limited autonomy, but also they receive state support. Foreign financial organizations are active, and foreign banks receive preferential treatment from the state.

The market for microfinance organizations has remained relatively underdeveloped, and many organizations find it easier to receive funds from foreign sources than from domestic ones. Kazakhstan is also gradually adopting certain elements of Islamic banking. Coordination and control of the financial system is exercised largely by the state.

Differing access to finance (through credit market in CMEs and capital market in LMEs) for firms is the most important difference between CMEs and LMEs (Hall and Soskice 2001). On the whole, the financial system of Kazakhstan resembles a CME type of system more than an LME one: companies are mainly financed through credit market, with the capital market playing a minor role (Table 3.9).

Table 3.9. Summary of the financial system

Type of system	Two-tier banking system; key international banking standards have been formally adopted; the financial system combines more elements of CME and fewer from LME; the structure of the system is largely predetermined by the state
The National Bank of Kazakhstan	The Central Bank in Kazakhstan is crucial for understanding the nature of reform in the financial sector and the establishment of the financial regime; it officially sets the interest rate

Credit market	The credit market largely dominates as a financing channel for domestic companies; the major credit growth took place from 2000 to 2008
Capital market	The market is slowly emerging; largely controlled by the NBK and the government; international organizations view it as underdeveloped; foreign exchange operations prevail over other transactions
Domestic financial organizations	Banks have limited autonomy; long-term planning and risk management strategies are poorly developed
Foreign financial organizations	The state actively cooperates with foreign banks; foreign capital is welcomed; 29 out of 39 second-tier banks are foreign-owned
Microfinance organizations	There are huge institutional gaps with respect to the status and financial performance of MCOs; MCOs are funded mainly from foreign sources; the government established the Small Entrepreneurship Development Fund 'DAMU' to increase funding and communication between MCOs and public institutions
Islamic banking	The sector is gradually adopting elements of the Islamic financial system, although its market share remains low
VoC in the financial sector	Credit financing of companies is widespread; the share of the capital market is negligible. Thus, the financial system is more similar to a CME type of system than an LME one. In assessing the institutions in the financial sector, it is necessary to account for the role of the state, as the banking sector is heavily coordinated by the state. The VoC approach should be complemented by explicit acknowledgement of existing mechanisms for state coordination of financial institutions.

3.3.2. Corporate governance

3.3.2.1. Development of corporate governance

The OECD (2005b) defines 'corporate governance' as 'procedures and processes according to which an organization is directed and controlled. The corporate governance structure specifies the distribution of rights and responsibilities among the different participants in the organization such as the board, managers, shareholders and other stakeholders and lays down the rules and procedures for decision-making.' According to the Cadbury Committee (1992: 13), corporate governance implies the way in which companies are managed and control over them is exercised. In international practice, the widely-recognized OECD principles of corporate governance assist both 'OECD and non-OECD governments in their efforts to evaluate and improve the legal, institutional and regulatory framework for corporate governance in their countries, and to provide guidance and suggestions for stock exchanges, investors, corporations, and other parties that have a role in the process of developing good corporate governance' (OECD 2004: 11). Importantly, the corporate governance framework is closely related to the legal and institutional regime of a country; however, there exists no one 'best-practice' model for corporate governance (ibid: 11–13).

As defined by Hall and Soskice (2001: 7), corporate governance is the sphere 'to which firms turn for access to finance and in which investors seek assurances of returns on their investments. The solutions devised for these problems affect both the availability of finance for particular types of projects and the terms on which firms can secure funds.' In coordinated market economies, private firms rely on long-term capital returns on investments, whereas in liberal market economies short-term financial markets prevail (Hall and Soskice 2001; Ebbinghaus and Manow 2001). Luly (2012) argues that Kazakhstan's corporate structure resembles the LME type of corporate structure in which the hierarchy of corporate power plays an important role.

Troschke and Zeitler (2006: 1) note that the evolution of corporate governance related to the 'separation of ownership and control' has been investigated in detail for Russia, but very little for Central Asia after the former Soviet republics gained independence.

As for the types of legal entities existing in Kazakhstan, national legislation includes the standard group of legal entities: general partnerships, limited partnerships, limited liability partnerships, additional liability partnerships and joint stock companies (Baker&McKenzie 2009: 12). The most common legal entities are limited liability partnerships, joint stock companies and branches of foreign firms (ibid).

Foreign companies may set 'a Kazakhstani legal entity that is either entirely foreign owned, or co-owned as a joint venture with a Kazakhstani partner; and/or establish a branch or a representative office' (Baker&McKenzie 2009: 10). Limited liability partnerships can be established by any number of legal persons and there are no restrictions in this regard; in turn, joint stock companies also have no limit on the number of shareholders; according to law, shares of joint stock companies can be freely transferred (ibid: 11, 17). Troschke and Zeitler's study (2006: 22) of the food industry found that the 'board of managers' (directors) is the most common type of company management in local firms, while 'biggest shareholder' and 'group of shareholders' are less common types. The board of managers is also responsible for areas such as investment and finance policy, and their role has expanded since independence (ibid).

Companies in the food industry are occasionally subject to state intervention with respect to their decision-making processes in such areas as 'investment, sales and distribution, social institutions', but they face no constraints from the state with respect to their 'wage setting, mergers and acquisitions' processes (Troschke and Zeitler 2006: 26 and 37). In Kazakhstan, the degree of state intervention in a company increases with the proportion of shares the state possesses (ibid: 53). Troschke and Zeitler compare Kazakhstan and Uzbekistan, and find that corporate governance in private companies is better developed in Kazakhstan, measured by 'performance indicators' (ibid).

Lee et al. (2008: 80) argue that local SMEs are not Soviet path-dependent, because most of them were formed 'in a market driven environment' in the 1990s. This is an important observation, as it indicates that Kazakhstan's economy includes a range of actors, from big state-led corporations and monopolies (many of them Soviet path-dependent), to small and medium-sized enterprises – which are more market-oriented.

3.3.2.2. Samruk-Kazyna

As regards the organization and governance of state-owned companies, the key role in terms of shaping corporate governance structure in the state sector is played by Samruk-Kazyna. This is a state-owned corporation, with the government exercising control over its activities (Satpaev and Umbetalieva 2011). The Sovereign Wealth Fund 'Samruk-Kazyna' was established in 2008 in an attempt to make the economy more competitive and sustainable, as well as to protect it from external shocks (Samruk-Kazyna 2012a). According to one IMF report (International Monetary Fund 2011b: 18), public enterprises largely control the economy today, and the assets of major domestic companies belong to Samruk-Kazyna, which accounted for almost 55 per cent of GDP in 2010. Its holdings include shares in key industries of the economy. Table 3.10 shows the industries controlled and organizations owned by Samruk-Kazyna (Samruk-Kazyna 2012b).

The corporation fully controls the shares of the Development Bank of Kazakhstan, Kazyna Capital Management, the National Innovation Fund, KazMunayGas, and several airports (Samruk-Kazyna 2012). Importantly, the main task of the Development Bank of Kazakhstan is 'to financially support infrastructure initiatives in the private sector and the state by extending long- and short-term, low-interest loans, including export credits, as well as by issuing guarantees on loans and credits granted by other credit institutions' (International Finance Corporation 2009: 20).

Table 3.10. Major companies owned or part-owned by Samruk-Kazyna

Aktobe Airport	air industry: 100 per cent of shares belong to Samruk-Kazyna
Kazakhstan Development Bank	development: 100 per cent
Kazakhstan Electricity Grid Operating Company	energy: 100 per cent
Kazakhstan Temir Zholy	railways: 100 per cent
Kazatomprom	nuclear energy: 100 per cent
KazMunayGas	energy: 100 per cent
Kazpost	postal services: 100 per cent
Kazyna Capital Management	capital market: 100 per cent
Maikainzoloto	gold industry: 100 per cent
National Innovation Fund	innovation development: 100 per cent
Pavlodar Airport	air industry: 100 per cent
SK-Pharmaceuticals	pharmaceuticals: 100 per cent
Samruk-Energo	energy: 93.42 per cent
Kazakhstan Mortgage Company	real estate: 91 per cent
Air Astana	air industry: 51 per cent
AES-Ekibastuz	coal industry: 50 per cent
Kazmortransflot	sea industry: 50 per cent
KazakhTelecom	telecommunications: 45.9 per cent
Astana Finance	finance: 26 per cent

Source: Author's presentation based on Samruk-Kazyna (2012b).

Officially, the basic goal of Samruk-Kazyna 'is to manage shares (interests) of national development institutions, national companies, and other legal entities it owns to maximize their long-term value and competitiveness in the world markets' (Samruk-Kazyna 2012a). Within the framework of its responsibilities, it officially exercises the functions shown in Table 3.11.

Samruk-Kazyna serves as the major source of finance for most of the largest companies in Kazakhstan (International Monetary Fund 2011b: 18). It is used by the government as a tool to promote and foster economic diversification. According to the International Monetary Fund (2011b: 18), working together with companies from key partner countries like China, Russia, South Korea and the EU states, Samruk-Kazyna seeks to invest almost USD 40 billion in strategic industries in the coming years.

Table 3.11. Major goals of the Samruk-Kazyna Fund

– Developing and financing regional, national and international investment projects jointly with domestic and international companies through equity and loans
– Managing the '30 Corporate Leaders of Kazakhstan' Programme and other strategic projects defined by the government
– Contributing to the diversification of the economy and purchasing assets within and outside Kazakhstan
– Developing innovative investment policies in the country, along with the active support of local companies
– Financing projects implemented by SMEs
– Coordinating financial and investment activities within the group of companies, which are part of Samruk-Kazyna
– Developing economic relations with other Central Asian states
– Contributing to regional development in Kazakhstan, via social–business partnerships

Source: Author's presentation based on Samruk-Kazyna (2012a).

The Investment Fund of Kazakhstan (IFK) is another important channel of finance for domestic business. Its main aim is to 'lend financial support to private sector initiatives in the economy's non-mineral sectors by participating in the authorized capital (i.e. acquiring shares or non-controlling packages) of enterprises in Kazakhstan.' The Fund was formed as a joint stock company with 100 per cent government ownership in July 2003 (International Finance Corporation 2009: 20). The IFK seeks to contribute to economic diversification, in particular diversifying away from the dependence on oil and gas resources (IFK 2012; Simon 2009: 73).

Samruk-Kazyna plays an important role in the economy, as it unites and manages the capital of several state-owned companies under one umbrella. This indicates a specific type of capitalism which has emerged in Kazakhstan since 1991. Organizations similar to Samruk-Kazyna can hardly be found in CMEs or LMEs, in which the state exercises less coordination and control over the major capital flows in the economy. Thus, applying the VoC approach to Kazakhstan, it is essential to account for the coordinating role of the state in the economy.

3.3.2.3. Problems in the corporate sector

Over the past few years, the role of Samruk-Kazyna in the corporate sector has grown (EBRD 2010a). However, many international organizations view state intervention in the corporate sector as disputable. For instance, when it comes to the security of property rights for private companies, Kazakhstan scored 35 points on the Index of Economic Freedom in 2010 (Heritage Foundation 2011). Kazakhstan's position is only slightly above the critical level on this index.

In addition, Kazakhstan ranks 88th of 125 countries on the 2010 International Property Rights Index, and foreign investors are concerned about the security of their property rights (Heritage Foundation 2011). In the EBRD 2010's transition report (2010a: 12), Central Asia in general, and Kazakhstan in particular, are identified as having low standards of corporate governance. The functioning and operation of SMEs have previously been thoroughly investigated within the framework of the EBRD-World Bank 'Business Environment and Enterprise Performance Survey' (BEEPS), which identifies obstacles preventing the growth of small and medium-sized companies. In this survey, firms usually rank their most pressing problems in doing business and cooperating with the state. In the 2005 BEEPS survey, the following two problems were identified by SMEs as being the most acute: 'the cost and difficulty of accessing finance; and cumbersome tax administration and high tax rates' (International Finance Corporation 2009: 12).

Table 3.12. Obstacles to doing business in Kazakhstan

Firm	Main obstacles to doing business
Small firms (1–49 employees)	Cost of financing (about 21 per cent of surveyed companies) Tax rates (about 18 per cent) Tax administration (about 14 per cent)
Medium-sized firms (50–249 employees)	Cost of financing (about 15 per cent) Corruption (about 14 per cent) Tax administration (about 12 per cent)
Large firms (250 employees or more)	Anti-competitive or informal practices (about 15 per cent) Tax administration (about 13 per cent) Economic and regulatory policy uncertainty (about 13 per cent)

Source: Author's presentation based on World Bank (2005, in International Finance Corporation 2009: 13).

BEEPS indicators show that the cost of financing has been a key obstacle for SMEs in Kazakhstan, along with tax rates and tax administration (International Finance Corporation 2009: 13), despite attempts by various financial organizations to improve their services to SMEs. Similarly, according to the ADB report of 2005, the lack of capital has been the main obstacle for SMEs. The banks do not usually finance start-up projects and representatives of SMEs stress that banks set too high and complex requirements for obtaining business development loans (Ostrowski 2010: 120). Until 2005, the main source of financing had been own sources, support from families and friends and borrowing from individuals in the informal economy (ADB 2005: 2).

However, the situation changed after 2005. There has been a substantial increase in lending capital to SMEs (ADB 2005). Small business lending soared from USD 2.2 billion in 2004 to 12.5 billion by the end of 2007 – (an increase of 78 per cent) (ibid). Troschke and Zeitler (2006: 53) found that private companies faced constraints in the form of excessively high interest rates, set by the National Bank of Kazakhstan in the period 2000–2006. Moreover, private companies in the food industry view the existing laws and their enforcement as 'inconsistent' and 'unpredictable' and see it as the main barrier to their activities (Troschke und Zeitler 2006: 32).

The BEEPS survey from 2009 (Figure 3.1) showed a changed situation from the 2005 survey. 'Tax rates' and 'corruption' were reported as the most important impediments in the private sector, with 'access to finance' ranking third (World Bank 2009). On average, the financing situation changed for the better for private companies. However, although this holds for SMEs, large firms stressed 'access to finance' as the main problem that hindered their operations (ibid), which had been much less a problem in 2005. This is explained by toughening conditions for external borrowing imposed by the government in connection with the 2008 financial crisis (EBRD 2010a: 121). In addition, the state promoted SMEs by launching the special microcredit 'Action Programme of Small Entrepreneurship Development Fund JSC to Develop Microcredit Organizations in the Republic of Kazakhstan for 2008–2012' (DAMU 2012). Thus, for them access to finance was no longer a serious obstacle. However, tax rates and corruption became major barriers for firms of all sizes.

Overall, the 2008 crisis directly contributed to worsening financial conditions in many industries. In some sectors, access to finance is critical – not least in agriculture. An OECD report (2011b: 65) found that 40 per cent of the private companies in the agricultural sector saw access to finance as 'a challenge' for them, and almost 60 per cent felt 'the cost of financing' was excessive.

The 2008 economic crisis severely hit Kazakhstan's public and private corporate sector alike, which prior to the crisis could easily borrow from various banking organizations, domestic and foreign (EBRD 2010b: 16). After the crisis 'access to cheap borrowing' from international organizations and banks was limited, and local banking organizations could not service their debts, leading to 'a painful process of de-leveraging'; in reaction to the post-crisis situation, the government launched 'an ambitious programme of quasi-sovereign bilateral borrowing', aimed at diversifying the economy in the long run (EBRD 2010b: 27).

Figure 3.1. BEEPS data. Enterprise surveys in Kazakhstan (2009)

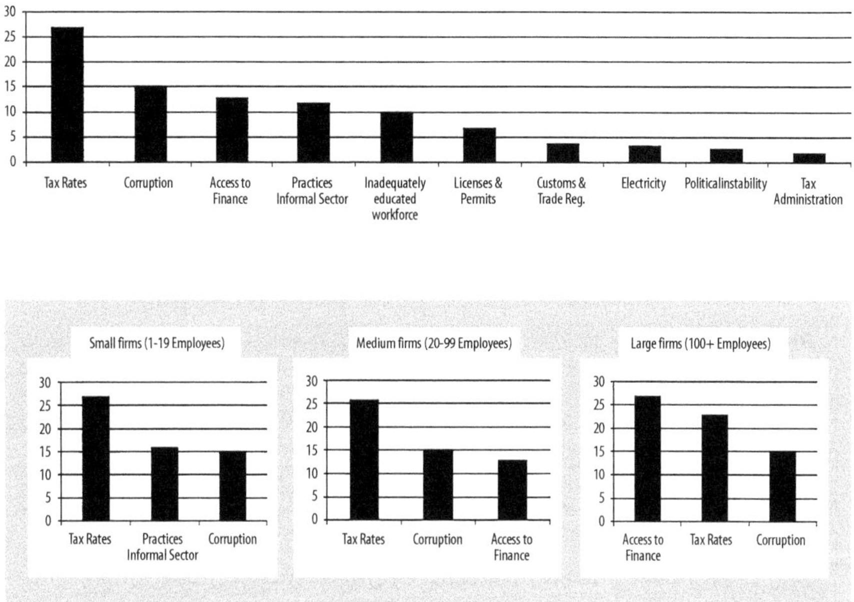

Source: Author's illustration based on World Bank (2009a). Note: Percentage of firms identifying the problems as the main obstacle.

3.3.2.4. Summary of the corporate system

Table 3.13 summarizes the corporate system in Kazakhstan. The most widespread types of firms are Limited Liability Partnerships, Joint Stock Companies and representation offices or branches of foreign firms. When it comes to corporate decision-making, the board of managers (directors) is the most common decision-making body. The key actor in the corporate sector is Samruk-Kazyna, the state corporation which unites a range of big national corporations. Major issues in the corporate sectors include limited access to finance; state involvement in economic processes; property rights are not always protected; and a complicated tax regime.

We may conclude that state-owned companies largely follow a CME type of economy, whereas private companies belong to the LME type. The corporate sector is heterogeneous; the large corporate sector is coordinated and controlled by the state, whereas SMEs operate in a more market-oriented environment. Importantly, access to finance is complicated for SMEs and big business alike.

Table 3.13. Summary of the corporate system

Type of system	Heavily coordinated by the state; SMEs perform largely according to market economy principles; big business is under the umbrella of the state
Types of companies	Limited Liability Partnerships, Joint Stock Companies and branches of foreign firms are the common types
Corporate structure of foreign companies	Foreign companies usually establish legal entities which are entirely foreign owned, or co-owned as a joint venture with domestic partners; they may also establish a branch or a representative office
Decision-making	The board of managers (directors) is the most widely used decision-making body in corporate decision-making
Role of Samruk-Kazyna	The state holding 'Samruk-Kazyna' owns most of the assets of the biggest state companies in the economy; it has shares in key industries and is a shareholder of the major domestic companies; the corporate structure of state-owned companies is largely shaped by Samruk-Kazyna
Major sources of finance for the private sector	Small domestic companies use bank loans; large domestic business is financed through Samruk-Kazyna and big domestic and foreign banks
Major obstacles for the corporate sector	Access to finance; state involvement in many sectors of the economy remains significant and the degree of state intervention in private companies increases with the proportion of state shares; the tax regime is complicated
VoC in the corporate sector	The corporate sector is heterogeneous; the large corporate sector is coordinated and controlled by the state, whereas SMEs operate in a more market-oriented environment. State-owned companies largely follow a CME type of economy; private companies belong in the LME model. Access to finance is complicated for both SMEs and big business. In applying the VoC approach to the corporate sector, consideration must be given to existing mechanisms of public control and coordination within the sector.

3.3.3. Industrial relations

3.3.3.1 Milestones in industrial relations development

In the definition of the European Commission (2003: 23–24), industrial relations are viewed as 'structuring and regulating the employment relationship by means of interaction, dialogue, bargaining, argument and dispute between the employers' and employees' sides'; they are 'participatory' relations between employers and employees. These relations are shaped at the company level and at the level above the company, with the former concerning relations within the company (between employers and employees), and the latter 'external regulations' (government, trade unions, employer associations) (Huiskamp 1995: 29, in European Commission 2003: 25). Hall and Soskice (2001: 7) see industrial relations as relations between employers and employees, where 'the major problem facing companies is how to coordinate bargaining over wages and working conditions with their labour force, the organizations that represent labour and other employers.' Within an LME, the wage-bargaining process is usually decentralized and market-oriented, whereas in a CME it is exercised through industry-level bargains between trade unions and employer associations which seek to take each other's interests into consideration (ibid).

The Constitution of Kazakhstan declares 'a number of rights of people in the field of labour and industrial relations, including the right to freedom of forming associations', as well as 'freedom of labour and the free choice of occupation and profession, the right to safe and hygienic working conditions, to just remuneration without discrimination, as well as to social protection against unemployment', as well as providing for 'the right to individual and collective labour disputes' (Kryvoi 2006). Thus, the legal conditions for coordinating industrial relations are generally in line with Western standards.

As of 1999, the labour market was among the least developed segments in the economy; moreover, there was no comprehensive analysis of labour supply and demand, which left many potential employees unaware 'that their labour was in demand and that there were vacancies' (Zhatkanbaev and Mukhtarova 1999). *The Economist* (2008a) and the European Training Foundation (ETF 2002) identify the key indicators of labour market development in the period 1991–2008 as shown in Table 3.14.

Major problems faced by domestic companies have included the weak linkage between the available labour force and the types of jobs available. In addition, during the first decade of independence, a significant proportion of the population were involved in the shadow economy (ETF 2002; 2003). This problem of illegal employment had serious implications for the labour market, as it involved some 38 per cent of the economically active population in the early 2000s (ETF 2003: 10). Illegal employees do not pay taxes or contributions to their pension funds (ibid).

Table 3.14. Key features of the labour market (1991–2008)

Key features for domestic companies
– Employers impose their conditions on employees, especially in the private sector
– A significant proportion of people was employed in the shadow economy
– Contradictions between actual labour potential and the types of jobs available
– No real link between work and wages
Key features for foreign companies
– Introduction of a quota on foreign labour, set annually by the government as a percentage of the domestic labour force
– Foreign firms are required to hire more local workers
– Introduction of a work permit system, making it difficult for foreign companies to bring in a highly skilled workforce, as work permits must be renewed annually
– The government places increasing emphasis on foreign investors to train and employ local workers and ensure that they receive the same remuneration as foreign workers.

Source: Author's presentation based on ETF (2002) and *The Economist* (2008a).

Government pressure on foreign companies concerning the hiring of local workers increased in 2000, with the introduction of work permits and quotas for foreign employees. Kazakhstan's 2001 Foreign Labour Regulations Law contains a provision that work permits may be issued to foreign workers only if no suitable local candidates are found. In general, foreign companies are considered to have more favourable labour relations compared to domestic companies, as the former usually have more competitive salary packages (ibid). Foreign specialists tend to be paid more than local specialists in most foreign companies (Syroezhkin 2009). UNESCO (2005) found that the average foreign specialist has a salary 10 times higher than what local counterparts receive. Yermukanov (2005) notes the case of a labour conflict between local and Turkish workers at the Turkish Senimdi Kurylys company based in Kazakhstan, where local employees earned only USD 207 per month, while their Turkish counterparts earned USD 1,769.

Today, the labour market is rather uncompetitive (Mashuri 2010: 34), inflexible and 'shallow, lacking a sufficient pool of skilled labour' *(The Economist* 2008a), and highly skilled professionals are difficult to find locally (Mashuri 2010). This applies to the state and private sectors alike (*The Economist* 2008a). In agriculture, which is a priority sector in the country (Government of the Republic of Kazakhstan 2012a), the lack of highly qualified specialists at the top management level is an obstacle for agri-business, so firms in this sector seek various investment opportunities for professional education and training of local personnel (OECD 2011b: 260). However, the Heritage Foundation (2011) regards Kazakhstan's labour regulations as 'flexible' and 'the non-salary cost of employing people quite moderate.' Nevertheless, in their 2012 report they note that even though the labour market remains flexible, implementation of the Labour Code remains weak (Heritage Foundation 2012).

A major issue in the labour market has been the disproportionate distribution of highly skilled labour force due to the high incomes in the natural resources sector (Kozhumov 2011). Much of the highly skilled labour force has shifted from the manufacturing and process industries to the energy sector. This 'shift' has led to an ineffective distribution of human capital in the economy (ibid), and can partly explain why labour costs in Kazakhstan have been estimated to be the highest in the CIS (*The Economist* 2008a).

3.3.3.2. The wage-setting process

The minimum wage in Kazakhstan is the guaranteed minimum cost of labour, which totalled 13,717 Tenge or USD 90 per month in 2009 (*Neweurasia.net* 2010; Baker and McKenzie 2009: 43), 17,439 Tenge (USD 117) in 2012 and 18,660 Tenge (USD 123) in 2013 (Agency of Statistics 2013: 421; Agency of Statistics 2014b). There has been a tendency for the minimum wage to increase annually since independence, and the Ministry of Labour and Social Protection is seeking to raise the minimum wage further by 2015 (*Neweurasia.net* 2010). According to the Federation of Trade Unions of the Republic of Kazakhstan (UNESCO 2005), the legally set minimum wage does not correspond to the real 'basket of goods' and cost of living; it would need to increase by an average of 30 per cent to reach this level. In practice, however, the minimum wage is not paid, as it is far too low (*The Economist* 2008a).

There are no wage restrictions in Kazakhstan (Baker&McKenzie 2009). According to Article 77 of the labour code, the working week is limited to 40 hours per week (Labour Code 2007). Article 36 stipulates that the initial probation period can last no longer than three months (Labour Code 2007). In case of cancellation of the employment contract an employer is to provide 'one month's prior written notice (…) unless the employment contract or collective bargaining agreement envisages a longer notice period'; the same applies to an employee's decision to cancel the contract (ibid). Formally, assessments of employee performance and the wage-setting process are 'determined by the collective bargaining agreement and in its absence, by the employer' (ibid).

3.3.3.3. Labour unions and employer associations

The literature on *labour unions* is scarce, and assessments of their role and importance for the economy differ. Luly (2012) points out that industrial relations can hardly be subsumed under any of the two VoC categories, given the ambiguous role of labour unions in coordinating industrial relations.

During the first decade of independence, the development of industrial relations was not a priority; trade union membership fell drastically throughout the country (Borisov and Clarke 2006: 609). Under the 1993 Law on Trade Unions, trade unions are provided 'with legal protection under Kazakhstani law, and their right to exist and act is also protected by the Constitution' (Kryvoi 2006). Three major documents regulate the activities of trade unions: the 1993 Law on Trade Unions, the 2007 Labour Code, and the 1996 Law on Collective Labour Disputes and Strikes. The legal norms reflected in the Law on Trade Unions shape 'the process of collective bargaining, in which trade unions may represent employees that are members of those trade unions' (ibid). Any employee has a right to establish a labour union, although a minimum of 10 members is required (Law on Trade Unions 1993). According to Article 10 of the Law on Trade Unions, a legally established labour union has the right to 'collectively bargain with the management of the enterprise, negotiate collective labour agreements, oversee the work conditions and safety of its members, and perform other activities aimed at protecting rights of its members' (Kryvoi 2006). Trade unions are 'to oversee observance by the enterprise, of all aspects of the collective labour agreement, as well as the enforcement of statutory labour norms' (ibid).

As regards the official institutional platforms used by trade unions to communicate with the government, the sole viable platform is currently the Federation of Trade Unions of the Republic of Kazakhstan, established in 1994 (Federation of Trade Unions 2012). Today, the Federation is the most representative organization of employees, with almost 2 million members throughout Kazakhstan (Federation of Trade Unions 2012). It includes 26 republic-level labour unions, four regional labour unions and the Labour Union Council of Astana (ibid). Its aims are to protect employees' rights and promote Kazakhstan's market economy.

The work of the Federation is organized according to the tripartite agreement among the government, employers and employees (Federation of Trade Unions 2012), which formally resembles the institutional structure adopted in South Korea between 1960 and 1980 (Root 1996). Participation in this trilateral social partnership is considered to be the major function of the Federation (Federation of Trade Unions 2012). Once a year, representatives of the Federation, the government and employer associations meet in order to sign a general agreement which serves as the basis for signing collective sectoral treaties between members of the Federation and members of employer associations at the republic, regional and local levels (ibid). As Kurmanov (2010) notes, one important function of trilateral commissions is to agree upon the minimum wage before it becomes part of the state budget.

In the Soviet era, labour unions were meant to promote the state's social policy, although they mainly had responsibility for sending employees to various resorts and providing them with additional wages (Panova 2008). Their current role does not go beyond the Soviet framework: *defacto*, labour unions exert little influence on industrial relations in the private sector (Dzhumambaev 2001). They are industry-based, with relatively effective trade unions mainly in the mining and energy industries – another legacy of the Soviet past (Kurmanov 2010).

In the 1990s, labour unions regularly organized strikes in the public sector, due in particular to delays in the payment of wages (Kurmanov 2010). However, the privatization of heavy industry in the period 1995–1997 led to the collapse of many trade unions which had been formed in the Soviet period mainly within the mining industries (ibid). During the second decade of independence, the number of strikes fell considerably (*The Economist* 2008a).

As for *employer associations*, the existing literature sees them as relatively weak in terms of institutional and organizational influence. An institutionalized mechanism for exchanging information between business and the state does exist, but it is not effective. According to Duvanova (2007: 190), associations are integrated in vertical and horizontal networks. She notes the case of the Kazakh Business Forum, established in 1992; it is a business association that serves as a platform of vertical and horizontal integration for business associations. The presence of regional offices within the Forum implies vertical integration, whereas horizontal integration means that it also includes independent associations which, although part of the Forum, retain their autonomy (ibid).

Apart from the Kazakh Business Forum, private domestic business and the state also interact through the Ata-Meken Association and through smaller business associations (*Kazahstanskaya Pravda* 2007). Ata-Meken unites small and medium-sized businesses and represents the interests of the entire domestic business sector at the state level, provides consultancy services to SMEs, as well as actively engaging in the legislative processes in Kazakhstan (*Kazahstanskaya Pravda* 2007; Ostrowski 2010: 136).

The formation of these associations may herald the emergence of lobby groups, and it should be noted that a draft law on lobbying was under consideration in 2010 (USAID 2010), but was not adopted and fully withdrawn from the Parliament in 2012 (*Mir Finansov* 2011; Government of the Republic of Kazakhstan 2012b). The draft law stated that its major objective was to facilitate communication between the private sector, the government and the Parliament.

Big business associations lobby the state by other means. Duvanova (2007: 192) holds that a better term for their interaction with the state is 'representation', implying a less powerful role played by business associations. Through 'representation', associations seek to express their interests through such formal communication channels as meetings with the President within various working groups, contacting the ministries, public bodies, participation in regular sessions of various public bodies and local governments (ibid). Large foreign and domestic businesses have often met directly with the President to raise their concerns (Duvanova 2007; Libman 2008), whereas SMEs lack this possibility.

Foreign companies play a significant role in shaping industrial relations. Since independence, Kazakhstan embarked upon a strategy of active cooperation with other states and private foreign business (Ostrowski 2010). This serves as an important and distinctive characteristic of the emerging economy in Kazakhstan. An example of effective interaction between the government and foreign players can be seen in the public–private initiative of the American Chamber of Commerce in Kazakhstan. It has various working groups that look into various issues that affect the business environment and the flow of FDI into Kazakhstan, and acts together with the representatives of the Prime Minister's Office and other ministries (AmCham 2011). Another platform which the government uses in order to attract FDI and cooperate with foreign business is the Foreign Investors' Council, where communication between big investors, mainly from the extraction industries, and the government is conducted on a regular basis (Foreign Investors' Council 2012). As 'the priority group' (Libman 2008), big foreign companies have become members of today's successfully functioning Council. Meetings are regularly held between government officials and company representatives within the Council, and President Nazarbayev serves as the chair of the Council (Foreign Investors' Council 2012). There are also several smaller foreign employer associations which promote the rights of various segments of foreign business. Thus, an effective institutional platform for encouraging active cooperation with foreign private business and for attracting FDI has been established.

3.3.3.4. Summary of industrial relations

Table 3.15 summarizes the main results regarding the development of industrial relations in Kazakhstan. Formal international standards in labour regulation have been adopted in Kazakhstan, based on Western standards. The labour market remains uncompetitive; the lack of a skilled workforce is a serious problem. Due to this deficit of a skilled workforce, labour costs in Kazakhstan are among the highest in the CIS. Foreign companies usually offer better employment conditions.

The state sets the minimum wage, and collective bargaining is commonest form of wage-setting. Labour unions are relatively weak; overall, industry-based trade unions prevail. Employer associations are somewhat more powerful than labour unions. Making lobbying activity official had been under consideration several times, but the draft law was not adopted and withdrawn from the Parliament in 2012. Big businesses meet with key public officials through various formal communication channels in order to promote their interests. With certain reservations, this system of industrial relations can be formally classified as belonging within the LME model. The reason is that even though many labour unions exist, in practice they exert little influence on the industrial relations decision-making agenda in private firms, as in LMEs.

Table 3.15. Summary of industrial relations

Type of system	International standards in labour regulation are adopted; the system is based on Western standards
Labour market	Non-competitive, inflexible; lack of highly skilled labour; foreign companies more advanced in terms of labour relations as they provide competitive salary packages; labour costs among the highest in the CIS
Differences within the economy	Labour market suffers from a disproportionate distribution of the workforce due to the high incomes in the natural resource sectors; a big proportion of the high skilled labour force from the process industries has shifted to the energy sector, leading to ineffective distribution of human capital in the economy
Wage-setting process	Minimum wage is set by the state; formally, collective bargaining is widely accepted; no wage restrictions exist in the private sector
Labour unions	Labour unions are weakly organized; little influence on industrial relations in the private sector; the Federation of Trade Unions acts according to the tripartite agreement between the government, employers and employees
Types of unions	Industry-based trade unions prevail
Strike record	1991–2000: frequent strikes; 2000–2010: fewer strikes
Employer associations	Employer associations relatively weak in institutional and organizational influence; main employer associations are the Kazakh Business Forum and Ata-Meken for domestic companies, and the Foreign Investors' Council and AmCham for foreign businesses

Lobbying activity	The draft law on lobbying had been under consideration several times, but was not adopted and finally withdrawn from the Parliament in 2012; big businesses use various formal state–business communication channels to promote their interests
VoC in industrial relations	*Dejure:* the labour code, trade union and employer association regulation based on international standards adopted; *defacto:* labour law is relatively poorly enforced. With certain reservations, the system of industrial relations formally belongs in the LME model.

3.3.4. The social security system

3.3.4.1. Evolution of the social security system

According to the Business Dictionary (2012b), a social security system is 'a government program aimed at providing basic needs to citizens who are retired, unemployed, or unemployable due to a disability or disadvantage. It is funded usually by mandatory payroll contributions from both the employees and the employers, and from the government's tax revenue.'

According to Hall and Soskice (2001), in an LME, firms usually provide low-level benefits, whereas in a CME they tend to provide high benefits to their employees. An important role is assigned to labour unions, which are intended to protect the rights of retired, employed and unemployed workers and guarantee certain benefits to them (ibid). A key aspect of the social security system is pension provisions for retired employees. Pension accumulation starts from the beginning of an employee's career and ends at retirement age, which may differ from country to country.

In Kazakhstan, the social security system has changed from 'a completely unitary system of social protection to a mixed one' (UNDP 2005: 55). The legal concept, adopted in 2001, 'offers a model system of social protection, including elements of both solidarity and targeted systems of mandatory and voluntary insurance' (ibid). By 2007, Kazakhstan had formulated a social protection model relevant for a market economy, as new legislation incorporated provisions for effective regulation of labour relations, and a pension system (ETF 2007: 2). The government has remained the main actor, responsible for providing social security schemes and most social benefits to the population (UNDP 2005: 35). This also applies to setting the 'rules of the game' as regards job security, the pension system and the regulation of trade unions. However, government spending on social assistance as a percentage of GDP has remained low. In 2009, government spending on social assistance was slightly above 1 per cent of GDP; this was lower than in Kyrgyzstan and Russia and much lower than Ukraine, which spent 2.5 per cent (see World Bank 2009b, in Gassmann 2011: 16).

According to the ADB classification, labour market protection in Kazakhstan accounted for only 0.1 per cent of GDP, social assistance 0.7 per cent and child protection 0.2 per cent, while the overall level of social insurance amounted to 3.4 per cent (see Table 3.16). In comparison, Uzbekistan spent 7.9 per cent of its GDP on social insurance and Kyrgyzstan 5.3 per cent.

Table 3.16. Social protection expenditure, percentage of GDP (2008)

	Social insurance	Social assistance	Labour market	Child protection
Armenia	2.5	1.9	0.0	0.0
Azerbaijan	3.2	1.8	0.0	0.2
Kazakhstan	3.4	0.7	0.1	0.2
Kyrgyzstan	5.3	2.9	0.1	0.3
Tajikistan	0.3	0.4	0.1	0.1
Uzbekistan	7.9	0.5	0.0	2.4

Source: ADB (2008), International Labour Organization (2010) and Gassmann (2011: 16).

3.3.4.2. The pension system

As Eicher argues (2004a: 3), in areas like the pension system, as well as the banking industry, Kazakhstan is a 'model transition economy'. The pension system was put on a market track very quickly, with the pension reform of 1998 allowing companies working with pension assets to operate with them on the organized stock market (Alibaev 1998). Already in 1996, the Law on Non-State Pension Funds on a Voluntary Basis had been elaborated, but this law proved ineffective as the poorest segments of the population were pessimistic to contribute to these funds (Yermukanov 2003). As a reaction to the failure of the first law, in 1998 a second law was adopted, which mirrored the Chilean pension system (Yermukanov 2003; James 1998; Becker et al. 2009). The mastermind of the reform, Grigory Marchenko, who headed the special working group for pension reform at that time, was inspired by the World Bank's reports on advantages of the Chilean-type pension system. In the end the reform was promoted with assistance from USAID and the World Bank (Lim 2005). The government changed the system from a pay-as-you-go (PAYG) 'defined-benefit scheme to one based on a fully funded, defined-contribution principle' (Rakurs 2011).

According to the new pension reform, 10 per cent of an employee's monthly salary is forwarded to a pension fund chosen by the employee, where the pension is accumulated (Marchenko 2003). Kazakhstan's pension reform was conducted more quickly than any other reform in the CIS (ADB 2003: iv; Simon 2009: 71). It proved successful, stimulating an improvement in the services provided by the managers of pension funds (Yermukanov 2003) and also boosting the development of pension funds (Rakurs 2011). Within the new system, employees may now easily shift from one pension fund to another, which sharpens the competition among funds (Yermukanov 2003). Retirement age is set to 63 years for men and 58 years for women (ibid).

In 2012, twelve pension funds officially operated in Kazakhstan (*Invest-Market.kz* 2012), with pension assets mainly concentrated in government securities (Rakurs 2011). However, because of the low interest on government securities, the funds have become 'increasingly attracted to blue-chip bonds' (ibid). In 2001, the total assets of the pension funds totalled USD 2.5 bln; by 2010 this figure had grown to USD 12 bln. Such a rapid increase occurred because, by law, all contributions are mandatory; however, a major problem is that most pension assets are concentrated in only a few major pension funds (ibid). Moreover, the economic crisis of 2008 has had a negative impact on the social security system (ISSA 2010), including companies operating in the pension sector.

In 2011, the minimum monthly pension amounted to 16,047 Tenge equivalent to USD 109.4 and 19,066 Tenge (USD 125.3) in 2013 (Agency of Statistics 2014b).

3.3.4.3. The insurance sector

The insurance industry of Kazakhstan was poorly developed in the period 1991–2002. The major breakthrough occurred between 2002 and 2007, due not least to the huge volumes of foreign funding which poured in from abroad, with local banks with excess capital hurriedly investing in insurance companies (Rakurs 2011). Major profits were earned by companies in certain periods – the profits of insurance companies in 2004 increased by up to 39 per cent compared to the 2002 level, by 68 per cent in 2005, and 79 per cent in 2006 (ibid). Subsequently, as companies in other segments of the financial sector, insurance companies were severely hit by the crisis and incurred huge losses (Rakurs 2011; *Fingramota.kz* 2011). The situation improved in 2010, when companies were back on a profit track, as the overall economy recovered and measures taken by the government proved effective (National Bank 2011). In 2012, there were 38 insurance companies in Kazakhstan (AFN 2012).

We should distinguish between individual insurance and corporate insurance. The latter is much more popular and developed compared to individual insurance (Rakurs 2011). The general population tends to avoid individual insurance due to the low-quality services typically provided by insurance companies (Bekbaeva 2009). The Financial Supervision Agency (FSA)[15] and its plan for 2011–2015 set the goal of educating the population about the benefits of individual insurance; nevertheless, due to low average income levels, insurance is far from being actively used (Rakurs 2011). Insurance companies suffer from having a poorly developed statistical database, which obstructs them from assessing insurance risks properly (ibid). Moreover, the marketing strategies employed by insurance companies are underdeveloped, and companies often fail to guarantee insurance payments to their customers, in turn resulting in negative attitudes towards individual insurance (Bekbaeva 2009). In general, it is only big foreign and domestic firms that provide a wide range of insurance benefits to their employees, with SMEs lagging behind in this regard (*Insur.kz* 2012). In 2009, the share of the insurance market in the economy was less than 1 per cent of GDP (Bekbaeva 2009; Rakurs 2011) – whereas in Russia it was 3.5 per cent, and in the EU and the USA 13 per cent (Bekbaeva 2009). The market remains underdeveloped and only large private firms provide a generous package of benefits (like health and unemployment insurance) to their employees. In the public sector, the state also provides social benefits to its employees.

3.3.4.4. Summary of the social security system

Table 3.17 summarizes the main findings with respect to the social security system of Kazakhstan. The pension system reflects the Chilean pension model. Most pension assets are concentrated in 'government securities'. Employees pay 10 per cent of their salary to the pension fund.

The government remains the main actor responsible for providing social security schemes; it sets the 'rules of the game' concerning job security issues, the pension system and regulating trade union activity. Only some big private firms and state-owned companies guarantee job security and provide a wide range of insurance benefits (health and unemployment insurance) to their employees; the share of the insurance market in the economy is less than 1 per cent of GDP. Corporate insurance remains more popular than individual insurance. In general, the insurance market is in the initial stage of development.

15 'In 2004, a separate agency was established for regulating and supervising the financial market and financial organizations (or the Financial Supervision Agency). The primary intention was to develop an independent and effective system of consolidated supervision over financial entities. The FSA took over some of the functions of the NBK in supervising the financial sector, mainly the banking sector; after 2004, the regulation and supervision of the country's financial sector was conducted by both the NBK and FSA. This split of the authorities mainly related to the rapid development of the country's banking sector in the early 2000s' (Rakurs 2011).

The system can be classified as partly belonging to the LME type of economy, as private firms generally provide only limited social security benefits to their employees.

Table 3.17. Summary of the social security system

Type of system	The legal concept of the system was adopted in 2001; *dejure*, it includes social protection, with elements of solidarity and targeted systems of mandatory and voluntary insurance; it is considered appropriate for a market economy; the government is the main body responsible for coordinating the system; public spending on social assistance remains low
Pension system	A pension system has been developed; it was put on a market track after the pension reform of 1998 and operates according to the Chilean pension model; 12 pension funds officially operate in Kazakhstan; pension assets are mainly concentrated in 'government securities'; however, most pension assets are concentrated in a few pension funds; 10 per cent of employees' salaries are paid into the pension fund
Insurance market	The insurance sector accounts for a tiny share of the financial sector, and is viewed by domestic and foreign participants as underdeveloped; a breakthrough came in 2002–2007, mainly due to huge volumes of foreign funding; corporate insurance is more popular than individual insurance; the share of the insurance market in the economy is less than 1 per cent of GDP; only some large private firms and state-owned companies provide insurance benefits, like health and unemployment insurance, to their employees
VoC in the social security system	The government remains the main actor responsible for providing social security schemes; the government sets the 'rules of the game' regarding job security, the pension system and regulating trade unions. Generally, only some big foreign and domestic private firms provide a wide range of social security benefits to their employees; SMEs rarely provide these services. In the public sector, social benefits are provided to public employees by the state. The system can be classified as partly belonging in the LME type of economy.

3.3.5. Vocational education and training

3.3.5.1. Development of vocational education and training

Hall and Soskice (2001: 7) define vocational education and training (VET) as relations between firms and the workforce where 'firms face the problem of securing a workforce with suitable skills, while workers face the problem of deciding how much to invest in what skills.' The outcome of this coordination may trigger an increase in the competitiveness of companies and workers as well as the economy as a whole (ibid). In an LME, training the workforce is based on a short general measures, whereas it involves longer-term vocational training in a CME (Hall and Soskice 2001; Ebbinghaus and Manow 2001). Public and private spending on VET can help to improve worker skills and enhance labour productivity (OECD 2011b: 260).

According to Charman (2007), Kazakhstan's education system is similar to an LME-type of economy. It is based on obtaining general education and skills (by contrast, the education system in a CME targets specific skills for employees). However, Luly (2012) notes that 40.9 per cent of firms provide training to permanent employees (7 per cent above the regional average and very close to the average OECD level, 41.1 per cent). This particular aspect places Kazakhstan's VET system in the CME type of economy. Thus, the VET system can be classified as a mixed model, with elements of both LME and CME.

One of the underestimated challenges after 1991 was educational reform. The system had to be transformed from the Soviet type to one which could meet the requirements of a market-oriented economy (Anderson and Heyneman 2005). As a USAID report (2005: 8) noted: 'Kazakhstan's educational system is patterned after the Soviet Union model and is practicing a knowledge-based approach built around an obligatory school curriculum.' Education is valued in local society, and this has its origins in the Soviet education system (ibid). Moreover, in the course of the past 20 years the country has made progress in improving the overall level of education (Ngozi Okonjo-Iweala 2011), but as of 2000, the education system was not market-oriented (Pleskovic et al. 2000). Kalyuzhnova and Kambhampati (2007: 620) hold that the educational system has gradually shifted from 'a system suited to a centrally planned economy to a system suited to a market economy.' Today, education in Kazakhstan consists of four levels: primary schools, middle schools, secondary/high schools and professional schools – the latter considered 'colleges' (USAID 2005: 8). In 2010, Kazakhstan became part of the Bologna higher education process (Ministry of Education 2012a), with the introduction of a three-level degree system: Bachelor – Master – Doctor of Philosophy; a shift towards a 12-year secondary education is also gradually taking shape (Decree of the President 2010; Zakirova et al. 2009: 25). The education system is clearly oriented towards European standards (Sagitova 2012) and in 2010 Kazakhstan ranked first according to the UNESCO Education for All (EFA) Development Index with primary education amounting to 99 per cent, adult literacy 99.6 per cent, and gender parity 99.3 per cent (UNESCO 2012; World Bank 2014: 6). Public expenditures on education increased in the period 2012–13, although they were lower than the OECD average of 6–7 per cent (World Bank 2014: 6).

As regards VET, the lack of highly skilled human resources is a serious problem (OECD 2011b; Mashuri 2010). Terjesen and Hessels (2009: 556) found that Kazakhstan, along with Thailand and the Philippines, had the lowest ratio of export-driven entrepreneurial activity in the world – perhaps partly due to the low quality of its VET system. However, this situation has forced the government to pay increasing attention to professional education in recent years. With the launch of the Innovative Industrial Development Strategy, set for 2003–2015, and the State Programme on Accelerated Industrial-Innovative Development, set for 2010–2014, the VET sector has become a priority sector (Ministry of Education 2012b; Smirnova 2014: 639–640). The problems of the underdeveloped VET system and its negative influence on the labour market were officially recognized in 2006, when, in a meeting with foreign investors, the President announced that Kazakhstan 'faces an acute shortage of skilled technical specialists' (OECD, IBRD and World Bank 2007: 37). Hawley (2006) notes that in 2006 the government explored possibilities of investing in the VET sector and sought to involve employers; in order to develop the VET sector, it was necessary to engage employers in the teaching and learning process, cost sharing and development of VET educational standards. Recognizing these needs, the state VET Programme (NPVET) for 2008–2012 was adopted in 2008, aimed at modernizing the system of professional education and training, and integrating it into the international educational space (NPVET 2008; Decree of the President 2010).

Officially, the VET system is intended to contribute to better implementation of the objectives of the State Programme of Accelerated Industrial-Innovative Development (*Obrazovanie.kz* 2011). Before the adoption of the NPVET, all state efforts to modernize the VET system had failed (NPVET 2008). In 2006, the level of financing in the VET sector accounted for a mere 0.2 per cent of the country's GDP, as against almost 1 per cent in the Czech Republic, 0.58 per cent in Slovakia and 0.56 per cent in Poland (ibid). For the first decade of independence, VET in Kazakhstan relied heavily on teaching specialists who had obtained their qualifications during the Soviet period. No succession of cadres was possible because most professional and technical schools had ceased to exist during the *perestroika* period (OECD, IBRD and World Bank 2007; NPVET 2008). Promising teaching specialists usually shifted to the private sector, because of low remuneration in the VET sector (OECD, IBRD and World Bank 2007). Table 3.18 summarizes the major problems in the VET sector, 1991–2008.

Experts from IBF International Consulting (2010) have pinpointed the lack of a VET standards database, supporting the NPVET analysis that consultancy services are not systematically provided. A further important impediment: VET has been the least-financed educational sector in Kazakhstan (NPVET 2008; OECD, IBRD and World Bank 2007). Indeed, there is usually 'no regular provision for equipment, books and teaching materials' at VET schools (OECD, IBRD, World Bank 2007: 36). The deficit of highly-skilled specialists stimulates companies to sponsor professional training programmes for local highly-skilled and low-skilled employees (OECD 2011b: 260).

Table 3.18. Problems with VET

– Uncompetitive salaries and benefit packages for teaching staff
– No system of in-depth training for students in state and private firms; lack of a dual education approach
– No refresher training for instructors in technical disciplines
– Lack of a systematic institutional approach to coordinating the work between VET institutes and schools
– Poor connection between firms and VET schools, leading to asymmetries in supply and demand for specialists
– VET school programmes not market-oriented, cannot satisfy private-sector demand for specialists
– VET schools do not have a PR policy or adequate consulting services to promote their services and educational standards
– Lack of institutional platforms for cooperation between VET schools and public and private firms
– No clear responsibility between republic-level and local authorities in decision-making, attracting resources and budgetary allocation in the VET sector
– Big companies do not coordinate their human resources policies with VET organizations
– Lack of private/public monitoring mechanisms to assess the demand among firms for specialists and the supply potential of VET schools
– Ineffective state planning mechanisms with respect to VET
– No normative legal basis with respect to business commitment to provide VET for employees
– Lack of continuity among the various levels – state, republican and regional – in VET programmes
– Insufficient employer sponsorship
– Institutions of higher education enjoy far higher prestige than VET schools

Source: Author's presentation based on National Observatory (2005), OECD, IBRD and World Bank (2007), NPVET (2008) and ETF (2009).

The NPVET 2008–2012 provided for adequate financing for the development of international educational standards and curricula. There have also been attempts to create a National Human Development Plan, which would promote the NPVET (OECD, IBRD and World Bank 2007: 38). The NPVET includes the organization of new VET programmes with the involvement of employers, who are to cover around 50 per cent of programme expenses (ibid).

The inclusion of employers is a new dynamic in the VET system, largely missing prior to 2008. In addition, new VET levels are planned to be added within the National Programme: 'from the basic or initial level, which will prepare students for specific occupations, through to a second level, which aims at achieving more complex and higher skills, to a third level, which will train students for junior technician jobs after four years of training' (NPVET 2008; see also OECD, IBRD and World Bank 2007).

As regards responsibility for VET development, the Sectoral Council and the Ministry of Education are the main government actors in charge (IBF International Consulting 2010), with the overall quality of new VET programmes to be tested at the National Qualification Centre, including input from employers in the process (OECD, IBRD and World Bank 2007: 38). The total budget for the project is USD 33.2 mln, with 4 mln to come from the republic-level budgets and 29.23 mln in the form of a World Bank loan (*Newskaz* 2011).

The first fruits of the NPVET are already evident. By 2012, the number of VET schools had increased to 804 (Agency of Statistics 2012c), a doubling from the mid-1995 level. Moreover, within its framework, the business community (the Corporate University Samruk-Kazyna, for example) has been contributing to the development of teaching materials aimed at improving vocational education (IBF International Consulting 2010). Business associations and large companies also contribute to VET development. Ata-Meken, KazMunayGas, Kazenergy, Kazakhstan Temir Joly and ENRC Management KZ laid the ground for a bottom–up approach in helping to elaborate and adopt professional standards (Edu.gov.kz 2010). In an attempt to improve vocational education, the government has also established the basis for a trilateral social partnership involving business, the state and the education sector; moreover, international actors such as the EU, GIZ and USAID have contributed additional initiatives to VET curricula development (ibid). However, as experts from IBF International Consulting (2010) have argued, donor organizations promote their own approaches, leading to 'inconsistency and incoherence' in VET curricula development in Kazakhstan. Moreover, the 'best experience, even from international organizations, is not disseminated. Local knowledge is not incorporated' (ibid). At present, the most effective instrument of VET development is available within the framework of the Foreign Investors' Council, which holds regular consultations with the government and representatives of foreign oil companies, working together to elaborate VET programmes for the petroleum industry (Foreign Investors' Council 2012). Although both parties seek to improve the qualifications of local labour, their efforts have focused mainly on the oil and gas industry.

3.3.5.2. Summary of the VET system

Unlike the Soviet period, VET in Kazakhstan today is weakly promoted by private actors. It suffers from the lack of financing: it is the least financed part of the education sector. Connections are poorly established between labour market needs and the availability of locally trained specialists. The lack of a systematic dialogue between educational institutes and business adds to the problem.

The state is the only actor to pay attention to VET development, whereas private firms do little to invest in the education and training of their employees, due largely to lack of infrastructure and experience. Thus, the 'vocational education' indicator, as part of the VoC framework, should be approached mainly through the lens of state involvement and participation in VET development (see Table 3.19). Kazakhstan's education system is similar to an LME-type of economy, based on obtaining general education and skills (whereas, as noted, the education system in a CME targets specific skills of employees). However, private firms do provide training to employees, as under the CME type of economy. Thus, the VET system in Kazakhstan can be classified as a mixed model, with elements of both LME and CME.

Table 3.19. Summary of VET

Type of system	System suffers from lack of financing and of training capacity, in relation to labour market needs; the concept of 'general education' follows the LME type of the economy, based on obtaining general education and skills
Education	In 2000, the education system was not market-oriented. During the second decade of independence, the system became more attuned to market economy; from 2010, the education system is part of the Bologna process
Problems in VET	During the Soviet period, VET was highly developed; today, it is underdeveloped and uncompetitive in Kazakhstan; financing in the VET sector was only 0.2 per cent of GDP in 2006; teaching specialists move to the private sector because of the low pay in the VET sector; VET is the least financed part of the education sector; activities of international organizations in developing VET have been fragmented; there is no systematic dialogue between education and business at the national level. To improve VET, the government has established a three-way social partnership involving business, the state and education
VoC in VET	Generally, there is only limited literature on VET development among private firms, especially concerning the first decade of independence. Private firms invest some efforts in training/educating their employees, but suffer from lack of infrastructure and experience. VET as part of the VoC framework

	should be approached mainly through the lens of state involvement in VET development. Kazakhstan's system is a mixed one, following LME standards in education and CME standards in re-educating and training of employees.

3.3.6. Inter-firm relations

3.3.6.1. Evolution of inter-firm relations

Within the framework of the VoC approach, inter-firm relations are defined as 'relationships a company forms with other enterprises, and notably its suppliers or clients, with a view to securing a stable demand for its products, appropriate supplies of inputs, and access to technology' (Hall and Soskice 2001: 7). In an LME, private firms do not normally collaborate with each other; competition is high, driving firms to compete constantly with each other for new products and customers. In a CME, by contrast, firms tend to cooperate and build networks through which they interact and share market information (Hall and Soskice 2001: 7). As Hall and Soskice (2011: 27) note, inter-firm cooperation does not pay off in LMEs where competition between private firms is intense, but it is beneficial for firms in CMEs.

Overall, there has been a scarce academic literature on inter-firm relations in Kazakhstan, with limited information on relations between companies and other enterprises, suppliers, clients, access to technology, etc. Aspects of inter-firm relations such as standard-setting, technology transfer, and collaborative research and development (Hall and Soskice 2001) require further study. As Luly (2012) notes, 'little information is available regarding inter-firm relations in (...) Kazakhstan and thus classifying (...) remains difficult in this sphere.' However, with certain reservations, inter-firm relations can be viewed as combining the elements of both an LME and a CME.

The economy of Kazakhstan suffers from the problem of limited competition between local firms in the domestic market (Simon 2009: 90). An OECD (2011b) study of sector competitiveness in Kazakhstan evaluated market competition between firms in the agricultural sector, including wheat export, the meat industry, dairy production, the chemical sector and logistics for agribusiness. The major finding was that the sector itself is fragmented: as a result, access to finance for firms is limited; the lack of new technology and know-how adds to the problem. A related negative outcome is that companies are restricted in their 'ability to invest in farm inputs and equipment' (ibid: 75) which creates impediments to higher productivity. Moreover, firms in the agricultural industry must purchase technical equipment from abroad (ibid), which means that local firms do not cooperate with each other within the framework of 'supplier–customer' horizontal relations. The major solution proposed in this OECD study is to facilitate access to finance by means of 'supply chain financing' and by developing retail chains.

Another study related to 'inter-firm' relations was conducted by Griffith et al. (2001, referred to in Wu et al. 2004: 449) who examined joint ventures formed between foreign and domestic companies in Kazakhstan. They found that local–foreign ventures with higher levels of knowledge transfer usually have higher levels of commitment and satisfaction within their mutual relationships. This means that local companies which integrate or form cooperation partnerships with foreign companies seek more cooperative relations with their foreign peers than those companies which do not collaborate with foreign companies. This also implies that the level of knowledge transfer is significantly lower in companies that choose not to become involved in collaborative ventures (ibid).

The government has sought to control and coordinate the development of inter-firm relations. It tries to promote knowledge transfer between private firms, technological education and R&D activities, whereas the private sector has remained passive. For instance, there are student exchange programmes and cooperation programmes at the state level with universities in the EU and the USA, including the Bolashak Programme (ISTOK-SOUYZ 2009; Government of the Republic of Kazakhstan 2012a), which promotes the engineering profession in particular (ISTOK-SOUYZ 2009). The Bolashak (the word means *'future'*) Programme was launched by President Nazarbayev in 1993 to support talented young people for studies abroad. According to the Presidential Decree:

> In Kazakhstan's transition toward a market economy and the expansion of international contacts, there is an acute need for cadres with advanced western education, and so, it is now necessary to send the most qualified youth to study in leading educational institutions in foreign countries (Bolashak 2012).

Programme graduates are expected to return to Kazakhstan and work for three to five years (Bolashak 2012). Until recently, it was possible to work only in the public sector; however, Bolashak graduates may now work in the private sector as well. After graduation, newly-qualified specialists return, and the state tries to accommodate them in national and private firms, thereby seeking to facilitate R&D activities in the private sector. This fits well with the overall goal of diversifying the economy through R&D and high-tech production (Government of the Republic of Kazakhstan 2012a).

However, real R&D projects have been few, and the sector remains 'underdeveloped' (OECD, IBRD and World Bank 2007: 174). R&D in the field of communications, for instance, does not receive state support and there are no government programmes, policies or regulations to assist it: main priority sectors have remained agriculture, construction, defence, energy, heavy industry and medicine (ISTOK-SOUYZ 2009: 12).

Nevertheless, the government has been attempting to diversify the economy (Government of the Republic of Kazakhstan 2012a) and to develop R&D and general know-how across the economy. The National Innovation Fund (NIF) is the major public body responsible for promoting R&D in Kazakhstan, established in 2003 as a development institute to support innovation, with the objective of creating venture funds and boosting innovation (National Innovation Fund 2011). However, its activity has been heavily criticized and the NIF is currently undergoing restructuring and optimization, as not all the goals set within the State Programme of Accelerated Industrial-Innovative Development have been met so far (*Invest-Market.kz* 2011).

Also other agencies have been established by the government in order to develop and facilitate R&D exchanges between domestic firms. These include the Science Fund, the Centre for Marketing and Analytical Research, the Centre for Engineering and Technology Transfer, and the Development Bank of Kazakhstan (OECD, IBRD and World Bank 2007: 174). But these organizations are inexperienced and have yet to make a significant impact on R&D (ibid). Today, innovative R&D is funded mainly by the state (Sitenko 2011), with 43 per cent of spending in this area coming from regional budgets (Toxanova et al. 2008: referred to in Sitenko 2011: 110). The private sector has little involvement in R&D and relies heavily on the supply of technologies from abroad (Sitenko 2011: 110). As Mendelski (2008: 9) argues, a private firm can be considered a key player in the transition context if it fulfils the criterion of being the key driver of R&D, innovation and technologies. In the context of Kazakhstan's economy, private firms have remained passive in that regard so far. It is hard to assign them a key role in R&D, and the state continues to be the main player.

In order to boost the growth of innovation, the government has initiated several development programmes for small and medium-sized state-owned and private firms. Recent programmes are the 'Business Road Map–2020' launched in 2010, and 'Productivity–2020' started in 2011, which aim to create new enterprises and help existing SMEs upgrade their R&D strategies and productivity, and optimize their business processes (*Kazakhstan Democracy* 2012; *Caspionet.kz* 2012). Within the framework of these two programmes, it is planned to lay the ground for employing more than 20,000 people; in January 2011, a total of 1,175 SMEs were provided with new projects to render various types of services in a range of industries (ibid). But their effectiveness is yet to be seen. The most important point is that there is a commitment from the state to help SMEs develop further. According to former Prime Minister Serik Ahmetov, the state is interested in further active involvement of domestic business in implementing programmes on economic modernization and development, as well as in making domestic business a more active player as regards innovation policy (*Kazahstanskaya Pravda* 2012).

3.3.6.2. Summary of inter-firm relations

On the whole, there has been little research on how relations among firms in various industries are shaped (see Table 3.20). There appears to be limited competition among private firms, and many segments of the same industry can be fragmented. In agriculture, for instance, cooperation or competition among firms is limited due to the weak integration of various parts of the industry. Companies in a range of industries also face other problems, like limited access to finance, lack of resources to purchase and apply new technologies and know-how, and the poor state of R&D development. The state is the main actor in promoting knowledge transfer and R&D activities among private firms. Private firms have remained relatively inactive here. After 2000 the government initiated several large-scale programmes to develop innovative growth of SMEs.

In general, there is little literature describing other aspects of inter-firms relations, which makes it difficult to classify inter-firm relations in Kazakhstan according to the VoC approach.

Table 3.20. Summary of inter-firm relations

Type of system	On the basis of available research, it is not possible to define the type of system
Competition among private companies	Limited competition among firms in various sectors/the problem of fragmentation of various industries
Problems with inter-firm relations	Market competition in agriculture is weak, and access to finance for firms is limited. Lack of new technologies and know-how add to the problem; firms in the agricultural sector purchase all technical equipment from abroad
R&D development	The state attempts to coordinate the development of inter-firm relations; the government tries to promote knowledge transfer and R&D activities among private firms; however, the real state of the art in R&D projects is weak and the sector is underdeveloped; the private sector remains passive in promoting R&D
VoC in inter-firm relations	Given the scant literature, it is difficult to generalize on the development of inter-firms relations from the VoC perspective, although might be said to combine elements of the two systems.

3.3.7. Summary of the VoC approach

Based on the literature review, it is necessary to assess whether the VoC approach can serve as an effective analytical framework for explaining the type of an emerging economy in Kazakhstan. Table 3.21 presents the main findings from the literature review.

Table 3.21. The VoC approach in Kazakhstan

VoC approach	Liberal market economy	Coordinated market economy	The economy of Kazakhstan
Corporate governance and financial system	Shareholder value centred (short-term financial markets)	Stakeholder value-centred (patient long-term capital)	Short-term markets (LME); state corporations belong in the CME; private firms in the LME
Industrial relations	Decentralized wage-bargaining	Coordinated wage-bargaining	Collective wage agreements in the state sector and individual bargaining in the private sector (similar to the LME type)
Unionization level	Rather low	Rather high	Formally high, but remains ineffective (formally the CME type, informally LME)
Social security system	Low benefits	Generous benefits	Low benefits (partly the LME type)
Vocational training	General education (short tenure)/Rare trainings	Vocational training (long tenure)/ Frequent trainings	The LME type as regards education; the CME model as regards vocational training
Inter-firm relations	Competitive/limited business coordination/little sharing of information	Cooperative/high degree of business coordination/high degree of sharing information	Limited coordination among firms/the state is the main coordinator (difficult to classify)

Source: Hall and Soskice (2001), Ebbinghaus and Manow (2001: 5) and author's own elaboration.

As regards corporate governance and the financial system, short-term markets prevail – as is typical with an LME. One striking difference is that state corporations operate according to the CME principles, whereas private firms operate mainly within an LME type of market environment. State corporations are united by Samruk-Kazyna, which coordinates the relations and interaction among them, thus making it similar to a CME. However, the nature of this coordination is different from a typical CME: employer associations play a coordinating role for firms in CMEs, whereas the state performs this function in Kazakhstan. Thus, state-owned companies can be characterized as belonging to a state-led CME. In turn, private firms operate in a more competitive environment. That implies little coordination among firms and little exchange of market information through business associations, as is typical in an LME.

For ease of classification, industrial relations should be divided into two sectors: public and private. In the public sector, collective bargaining is widespread; in the private sector, individual bargaining over wages prevails. We may conclude that, with respect to wage-setting, Kazakhstan's economy is similar to an LME. The level of unionization is formally high (as in a CME), but the real impact of labour unions on industrial relations is insignificant. Thus, informally it should be rather characterized as LME.

The social security system is characterized as partly LME, because most private firms do not provide social benefits to their employees. Only big private firms and state companies provide some social benefits, and the overall level of benefits provision remains low.

The VET system represents a mixed model. The education system is similar to the LME type, as it is based on obtaining general skills and not specific skills (as would be the case in CMEs). The VET itself is based on CME principles, as 40 per cent of private firms tend to provide frequent trainings and improve qualifications of their employees.

Finally, it is difficult to identify the type of inter-firm relations. The review of the scarce literature on inter-firm relations indicates limited coordination between firms. Overall, the state remains the main actor which coordinates R&D activities and promotes innovative policies at SMEs and big companies. However, further research is required to enable inter-firm relations to be classified more comprehensively.

As can be seen from Table 3.21, the VoC approach helps to shed light on the emerging economy and the type of institutional subsystems, but with limitations. The state in Kazakhstan exerts influence within the main dimensions of the VoC approach. Since this approach does not account for the major role of the state and state involvement in economic processes, it renders the necessary explicit account of the key role of the state beyond the scope of the VoC approach.

Second, given the transitional nature of the economy, it is hard to grasp the dynamics of economic development and changing relations involving the state, state-owned companies and private firms. Within this transition context, institutions cannot be viewed as static elements of the economic system in transition, but should rather be seen as dynamic ones (Mendelski 2008: 6). The main problem with the VoC approach is that it is a static approach (Lane 2007), and fails to account for or explain economies undergoing institutional change (Deeg 2005; Herrigel and Zeitlin 2010; Luly 2012). As Luly (2012) notes, the VoC approach falls short when it comes to explaining the sources of frequent institutional changes that have taken place in Kazakhstan since 1991. Similarly, Mendelski (2008) considers that institutional complementarity is difficult to attain when economic changes are frequent. According to Hall and Soskice (2001), institutions can change or be modified under the conditions of strong competitive pressure, but only gradually; institutional change, however, is unlikely to occur when institutions are complementary to each other. In advanced market economies, complementary institutions generate efficiency gains; thus economic actors will try to keep these efficiency gains (ibid: 18). It can be assumed that the more institutions complement each other, the more resistant will these institutions be to change.

Thus, the VoC approach fails to account for sudden institutional change in a transition economy like that of Kazakhstan. However, it has served an important starting point for classifying and categorizing the institutional subsystems in the economy, and has facilitated the descriptive analysis of its main institutional elements.

In order to account for the role of the state and institutional dynamics I conducted 159 semi-standardized interviews (see Chapter 4). The major concern was to identify respondents' subjective perceptions of how the economy and economic institutions function in Kazakhstan, as well as how the 'rules of the game' are shaped and determined by the state and the private sector. The interviews helped to identify and shed light on institutional dynamics and change over time, in light of the key role and influence of the state on the formation of the economy. Moreover, the interviews helped to reveal the complexity of interaction between private business and the state, covering formal as well as informal practices between various players. The analysis of the existing literature did not fully cover the peculiarities of informal practices in state–business and inter-firm relations. On the other hand, the literature review helped identify certain research gaps – such as the fact that little research has been done on analysing inter-firm relations in Kazakhstan. The use of semi-structured interviews helped to fill these gaps.

To account for shortcomings of the VoC approach and in order to account for institutional change over time in a context of transition, I later apply a core–periphery framework. Use of this framework became possible after the preliminary analysis of the interviews, coupled with advice from my colleagues and my own experience and knowledge obtained in the field (see subsection 4.8.2 on preliminary analysis of interviews). This analytical framework became the main approach in the analysis, with the VoC approach playing a supplementary role. Interview results are presented in Chapter 5.

Chapter 4. Research design: qualitative cross-sectional interview study

4.1. Cross-sectional research

This study employs a qualitative research design, including qualitative cross-sectional interviews. Qualitative methods for data collection and data analysis were used throughout, with semi-structured interviews as the main method of data collection and qualitative content analysis as the main method of data analysis. The underlying strategy is investigator triangulation strategy. Prior to and during data collection, various researchers were involved in preparing for the field trip, jointly elaborating interview guides, and conducting pilot and main interviews. Several researchers were also involved in the data analysis.

Qualitative research has been criticized for being overly descriptive, lacking in analytical rigor and generating data that cannot provide generalizable conclusions (George et al. 2005). However, qualitative research also has its clear strengths. The qualitative type of research design is transparent (Bryman 2004, referred to in George et al. 2005). Moreover, as opposed to quantitative methods, 'qualitative methods are typically more flexible – that is, they allow greater spontaneity and adaptation of the interaction between the researcher and the study participant (…) the strength of qualitative research methods is that participants may provide an answer in their own words, whereas in quantitative research they are usually forced to select one of the fixed responses' (Mack et al. 2005: 4).

This study includes the elements of both cross-sectional and cross-cultural qualitative research design. Cross-sectional design represents data collection on subsets of a population in a given time-period (Bryman 2004: 41). In this study, the 'more than one case' type (Bryman's typology) of cross-sectional design has been applied, as I seek to identify and describe variation within the economy. In cross-sectional and cross-cultural research, qualitative methods usually have greater methodological strength than quantitative methods (Rajshekhar et al. 2011). Despite the common use of quantitative methods in cross-cultural research, they often fail to provide 'an in-depth understanding of underlying end-user actions or phenomena under investigation' (ibid: 157). I did not investigate the causality mechanisms of how various parts of the economy interact with each other. Rather, I have sought to provide an in-depth descriptive analysis of the type of a market-oriented economy in Kazakhstan and its institutional structure – the main purpose of the research in this study.

As regards the elements of a qualitative research design, it was important to consider 'respectful listening, difficult and challenging engagements (…) and a critical, long-term consideration of the implications of methods in the construction of meaning' (Howitt and Stevens 2005: 30, in Wesche et al. 2010:

60). Attention to these points was important because this type of field research is generally complex (Twyman et al. 1999, in Wesche et al. 2010: 60) – as indeed was the research conducted for this project.

This complexity is embedded within the 'cultural differences between Western and non-Western contexts', as 'such contexts are internally diverse, making it difficult to generalize fieldwork within them' (Wesche et al. 2010: 60). During fieldwork in Kazakhstan, special attention was paid to cross-cultural considerations, and certain elements of my research design were adjusted to the specific local cultural traditions. It is important to consider the cultural context when doing fieldwork in Central Asia (Mollinga 2008: 12). The qualitative research conducted for this study consisted of elements of cross-cultural research, where the cultural background of the region, as well as that of study participants, mattered greatly. Citizens of Kazakhstan and respondents of other nationalities working in Kazakhstan were approached, enabling observation of how different business cultures interact with local ways of doing business. Subsection 5.1.1 on the role of the state in the economy discusses how different cultural backgrounds influence respondents' perceptions of economic development in Kazakhstan.

4.2. Doing fieldwork in Central Asia

Conducting research in the field is rarely a straight-forward business. The most careful planning can mean little once the researcher moves into the field and encounters the real world.
Matthew Willis (2005: in Mollinga 2008: 1)

Doing field research has never been easy. First of all, observing or studying the social world involves an enormous complexity, so any method utilized to analyse and understand this complexity will have its limitations (Perecman and Curran 2006: xviii). Field research in a foreign country becomes even more complex: in addition to preparing a standard set of tools for conducting a study, researchers must also account for 'differences in customs, tacit cultural assumptions, and institutions that (…) may manifest some greater or lesser similarity from place to place' (ibid).

Central Asia is a particularly difficult place for fieldwork (Wall and Mollinga 2008; Kuzmits 2008, Wilkinson 2008; Wall 2008; Veldwisch 2008), not least because research may be seen as politically sensitive (Mollinga 2008: 11). On the other hand, as Mollinga (2008: 15) also notes, such sensitivity is common within development research in general – Central Asia is not necessarily exceptional in that regard.

There were significant barriers which prompted me to collect primary data. One of the major issues is the lack of reliable data concerning the economic sphere (European Community 2007; World Bank 2008; Wilkinson 2008; International Crisis Group 2010; Petrick 2011; Smith 2012; UNECE 2012b). According to the OECD, existing data sets are usually unreliable in the region (as reported in World Bank; 2008: 8). Among Central Asian states, data availability is particularly serious in Turkmenistan, which complicates in-depth analysis of the country's economy (European Community 2007: 53), but also in other Central Asian countries, data reliability is a key problem. For instance, Smith (2012) holds that the lack of reliable data in the transport sector in Central Asia complicates economic analysis of the sector. Another example is the lack of accurate data on migrant flows and their economic effects in the region and the CIS (International Crisis Group 2010: 1).

Moreover, collecting primary data helped to fill research gaps (e.g. on inter-firm relations in Kazakhstan) as described in detail in subsection 3.3.7. Therefore, for this study, the collection of primary data in the form of semi-standardized interviews was seen as a necessary tool for obtaining reliable data and enabling valid research results. The primary data collected for this research include direct communication with 159 respondents directly involved in economic processes and policy-making. However, I realize that respondents may not always speak openly or truthfully in interviews. To mitigate this concern and enhance the validity of the data obtained, observation and investigator triangulation were employed, as explained in section 4.4 and subsection 4.5.4.

Collecting primary data in Central Asia has long been a challenge in the region (European Community 2007: 39; Petrick 2011). One underlying problem is that often there is a gap between the use of a method in theory and in practice (Mollinga 2008: 1). As Kuzmits notes (2008: 40), standard methods and tools may fail 'to stand the test of cultural adaptability' in the region. After coming to the field, foreign researchers may need considerable time to adapt to the environment and adjust their methods and techniques of data collection (Wilkinson 2008).

Problems of fieldwork in the difficult political environment of Central Asia have been highlighted by Kuzmits (2008), Wilkinson (2008), Wall (2008) and Veldwisch (2008). Kuzmits (2008: 27) explains that studying microeconomic issues in Tajikistan and Uzbekistan is difficult due to the significant share of the 'shadow economy', meaning informal cross-border trade in various commodities. Thus, he argues, in order to avoid potential problems, it is best to focus the research on less sensitive economic issues in these countries. He also underscores the point that it is hard to involve the local population in Central Asian republics in social science research, given the lack of social science traditions. For many people in Central Asia, field study activity is a completely new phenomenon, and is often viewed with mistrust (ibid). Kuzmits further notes that one should be prepared to deal with bureaucratic barriers and unexpected events; and 'intercultural adaptability in timing interviews' is indispensable (ibid). Holidays, election campaigns or local political tensions should be always considered in terms of time management. On a different note, the researcher should also be prepared for the extreme hospitality of the local people (Wilkinson 2008: 58). Kuzmits (2008: 35) supports this point, noting that while doing research on borderland management in provinces of Tajikistan he 'nearly suffocated in hospitality.'

Wall (2008) agrees that doing field study in Central Asia poses many difficulties for foreign researchers. For instance, in Uzbekistan the government largely controls and sets restrictions on the research activities of international research institutes. Veldwisch (2008) adds that the problem of censorship leads to 'protective attitudes' during data collection, as well as to a lack of trust in foreign researchers. In his study of water distribution problems in Uzbekistan, Veldwisch had difficulties conducting interviews with selected respondents, who often avoided answering certain questions or provided ambivalent responses (ibid: 171). In order to obtain valid data, the researcher must be flexible and should exert all efforts to win respondents' trust and confidence (ibid).

Mollinga (2008: 4–5) offers a list of key 'boundaries that need to crossed, negotiated and managed' in a difficult research environment. He stresses the importance of cultural differences: the ability of a researcher to speak the local language, to be familiar with local norms, habits, customs and ways of self-expression. That is why persons from Central Asia who met these specific criteria were selected as researchers for the present research project.

Another important issue is to ensure the ethical legitimacy of a research project. This requires adapting to local norms and behaviour, as well as the ability to understand hidden hints of respondents which sometimes cannot be directly expressed (Mollinga 2008: 11). Kuzmits (2008: 40) argues that support through a strong local partner is vital for the successful implementation of a field study in the region. When I raised this point during informal conversations with local experts prior to my fieldwork, I was assured that it would be necessary to find a local research partner in Kazakhstan, as purely international research projects are usually received with scepticism by elite respondents. Within our project I concluded a cooperation agreement with a prominent academic institution in Kazakhstan, which facilitated establishing contacts with various respondents. This proved important, as many respondents felt enthusiastic on hearing that this was a joint research project supported by a well-known local institute.

Finally, given the complex political environment in Central Asia, the method of observation appears to be highly relevant (Mollinga 2008: 12). Its use proved well justified in this project, as it helped enhance the validity of the data obtained. This method is introduced in detail in subsection 4.5.4.

4.3. Interviewing elites in Kazakhstan

Few studies focused on key aspects of interviewing elites in Kazakhstan. White et al. (1996) hold that public employees in Central Asia are largely Soviet path-dependent, which means that power distance plays a significant role and makes such persons highly inaccessible. On the other hand, many scholars have studied the specific aspects of interviewing elites in Russia, including Rivera et al. (2002) and Ledeneva (2006; 2008). However, as Rivera et al. point out (2002: 683) interviewing elites in post-Soviet republics remains largely under-researched, as most academic work on interviewing elites has been biased towards Western countries, disregarding the theoretical and practical aspects of interviewing post-Soviet elites. Therefore, it remains questionable whether the application of purely Western-based methodological tools for interviewing elites in Central Asia can be successful. Rivera et al. (2002) note that the Central Asian countries exhibit several specific features which make them different from other states; moreover, there are differences from one country in transition to another, because of the unique reform paths each chooses to pursue.

In view of the lack of literature on interviewing elites in Kazakhstan, I had to move in a trial-and-error way in my field study, gradually learning and adjusting the practical tools for successful interviewing. On the other hand, many parts of my approach to conducting interviews in Kazakhstan were based on a more universally applied set of criteria for interviewing elite respondents. For instance, I tried to prepare myself for dealing with elite respondents, who may exaggerate their roles (Berry 2002: 680) and engage in self-promotion during an interview (Ball 1994: 97–98, in Walford 1994). I also considered it important to avoid establishing contact with elite respondents through mediators, like secretaries or other 'gatekeepers' (Becker and Meyers 1975: 607), as such administrators usually aim at fending off interviewers. Direct communication with the potential respondent was the best way to get an interview arranged.

4.4. Sampling

4.4.1. Sampling procedures: snowball sampling and direct contact

A major concern prior to my field research was to select an appropriate sampling procedure, and here the choice fall on the snowball sampling method. Although this sampling procedure implies using informal channels in reaching respondents and the lack of a systematic approach (Hendricks et al. 1992), this strategy proved highly appropriate. This type of sampling procedure involves reaching respondents who have been recommended by other respondents (Boehnke et al. 2011; Noy 2007). It is often employed in qualitative research, especially when other avenues have been exhausted (Noy 2007). Snowball sampling is particularly suitable for otherwise highly inaccessible groups of respondents such as top-management employees in private companies, public officials (Boehnke et al. 2011: 111) and elites in general (Forsythe 1977). Moreover, this procedure was particularly suitable for my study, given the important role that personal ties and networking play in Kazakhstan (Schatz 2004; 2005; Cummings 2005; Fast 2004). That meant that in order to succeed in reaching respondents in Kazakhstan it is crucial to know someone who can personally recommend selected respondents, and here snowballing can be effective. In order to minimize the bias associated with this method, I utilized it only with respondents who corresponded to the criteria set in my stratified sample (see subsection 4.4.2). If a recommended person did not meet these criteria, I did not interview him or her.

However, it was not possible to reach all respondents by snowball sampling. In some cases, the chain of recommended persons came abruptly to an end and I did not have access to further respondents in a particular group. Then I employed another procedure: 'direct contact' of selected respondents. I had initially assumed that attempts to reach respondents directly would be less successful. Surprisingly, I found that 'direct contact' may be used successfully in Kazakhstan, though few important issues arose in that regard (see subsection 4.6.3). Within the entire sample, 65 per cent of respondents were reached by the snowball procedure, and the remaining 35 per cent by direct contact, usually by contacting the respondent's administration, without knowing an interviewee in person or having personal references. In general, I sought to employ a balanced approach in reaching respondents, in order to minimize any potential bias in the research results. The results would probably have been more biased if I had relied solely on the snowball procedure.[16]

16 It was not possible to employ the snowball sampling method with representatives of a category like 'state-owned companies'.

In practice, I utilized the two sampling procedures as follows:

Snow-ball approach. I generally gave a call to a person who had been recommended by another person – a colleague or partner. During the talk I first mentioned who had recommended him or her for the interview, introduced myself, the project, goals and then requested an interview. Occasionally, I would be asked to send more detailed information about the project; however, in most cases people agreed almost at once to be interviewed. The 'snowball' strategy proved successful when it came to approaching respondents and arranging the interviews. Still, I did not interview everyone who was recommended, but only those who fit my categories in the sample. For instance, if a respondent recommended someone from an industry that was not among those selected for study, I explained politely that interviewing this person would not suit the specific objectives of this project. Using the 'snowball' approach, it did not matter how I contacted the recommended respondents, by email or by phone.

Direct contact. First contact was made by phone call or an e-mail to set up an interview. I introduced the topic of the interview, project as well as project partners, provided the reason for wishing to interview this particular person, and mentioned that confidentiality would be ensured. If the person agreed to be interviewed I provided my contact details and asked him or her to suggest a date and place. As mentioned, I tried to always avoid going through administrators or secretaries because this could minimize my chances of getting an interview. Figure 4.1 below shows the successful strategy of organizing the interviews through direct contact.

Figure 4.1. Arranging interviews via direct contact

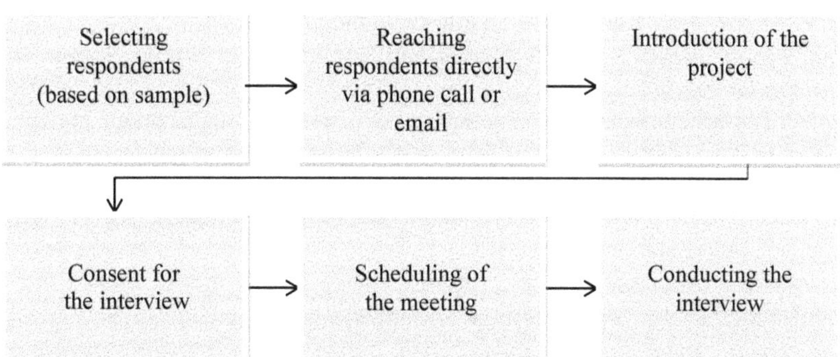

The best way to establish first contact with respondents was generally over the phone. Unlike in the snowball approach, emails were less successful with the direct approach, as respondents found it much easier to refuse in writing than when talking on the phone. After several futile attempts to contact respondents via email, I decided to always establish first contact by a telephone call.

It was important to remain flexible and always prepared for sudden changes in the schedule and respondent's availability. For these purposes, I created an emergency interview guide (for situations when I was running out of time, etc.), a strategy for unexpected scenarios (e.g. discussing illegal practices) and always kept the various interview guides together, as a respondent might qualify for several categories. Case in Point 4.1 below show the importance of being flexible in arranging interviews.

Case in Point 4.1. Snowball sampling in practice

While interviewing a representative of one big foreign company, I asked him whether he could recommend someone else for our interviews. I indicated that I would be interested in other foreign companies. Fortunately, I had no other interview planned afterwards, as he was very enthusiastic and offered to talk to some friends (representatives of other foreign companies) who worked in the offices nearby. The building in which his company was located proved to house several other foreign companies, working together and sharing the same floor. He suggested that after I finished I should go and interview the top management of those companies. He took us to the directors of three foreign companies, one after another. He introduced us and our research goals nicely and in a clear way, so that they agreed to be interviewed. Thanks to the first respondent, without any prior planning I managed to interview four persons in a row on the same day. Moreover, these companies all met the criteria set in my sample. The first interview started at 10 am and the last one finished at 4.30 pm.

4.4.2. Composing the sample

This research was aimed at identifying the type of economy that has been emerging in Kazakhstan and explaining how the entire economy functions, in terms of the VoC framework. While designing this research project, my main goal was to achieve a high representativeness of the sample. However, the research design did not imply having a representative sample as in quantitative research. Rather, it meant to present the variety of perceptions of the key economic and political stakeholders. With the sample I sought to achieve equal representation of various actors' perceptions on a market-oriented path for Kazakhstan, so I prepared a set of target categories in advance, according to the specific criteria elaborated below.

The key economic players representing the largest industries and the most important countries (in economic terms) operating in the country were identified.

Moreover, the sample included the most important, and thus most representative, players in economic policy-making. It was important to be able to draw general conclusions from my sample to the population, so that the interviews with actors from the biggest industries in the economy could provide insights into the overall formation of the economy. The *population* in my study is the economy of Kazakhstan as represented by key economic industries, whereas the *sample* is key economic players and political decision-makers. The *units of research (elements)* are industries, which are the constituent parts of the economy (population). The *data sources* are key economic players, political decision-makers and experts. As I wanted to explore how constituent parts of the economy function and interact with each other in order to identify what type of economy is emerging, I interviewed key decision-makers and economic players. Thus, data sources and units of research are not identical here. And finally, the *units of analysis* in this study are semi-structured interviews conducted with the selected categories of respondents.

In the sample I was interested in variation within the population. However, what I used was not a random stratified sample, but a *qualitative sampling guide,* as that served the research purpose better. The guide also included an element of a stratified sample in which the population is grouped into various strata, each of which corresponds to a certain criterion (Boehnke et al. 2011: 104).

As regards sample composition, a heterogeneous sampling procedure was utilized, because various players (respondents) in the economy were contacted, on the basis of criteria such as the position of the employee, industry, home country and size of firm. Representatives of companies were selected from the biggest industries in the economy, and foreign companies were chosen from the most active foreign countries operating in Kazakhstan. Experts and academics researching economic policy-making in the country were also contacted in order to enable a more objective and neutral assessment of economic development. Finally, public officials were interviewed, as well as key representatives of international organizations dealing with various aspects of the economic reform processes and familiar with the situation from within. Thus, the sample was able to span the entire spectrum of opinions and views as to the kind of market economy that is emerging in Kazakhstan.

I composed my sample during the project workshops organized prior to the field study. At these workshops, major issues related to the composition of the sample were discussed. First, workshop participants identified the major decision-makers in economic policy-making in Kazakhstan, mainly by analysing secondary sources and applying prior knowledge of the country. Seven major categories of respondents were identified; the same procedure was applied with respect to key industries and countries within the economy. For this purpose, trade statistics were analysed, and the countries selected have been major economic partners of Kazakhstan (see subsection 2.1.7 on FDI).[17] Initially, I had planned to conduct 25–30 interviews in each category of respondents, in hopes of obtaining a representative picture of economic decision-makers, economic actors and respective industry.

There are six levels in the sample: target categories; target employees; target industries; target countries; target companies by size; and target interview locations (see Table 4.1).

The first level, *target categories*, consists of public employees, representatives of employer associations and labour unions, experts, representatives of international organizations, representatives of state-owned companies, private domestic companies and private foreign companies.

The second level, *target employees*, includes high-ranking public officials; directors and heads of employer associations and labour unions; prominent domestic and foreign experts; and representatives of the top managerial level, mainly chief executive officers, heads, directors, and owners of state-owned, private domestic and foreign companies and international organizations.

The third level, *target industries,* includes agriculture, construction, finance, information technologies, manufacturing, natural resources, services and trade. With these categories I wished to explore perceptions of the overall economic development and reform processes, rather than focusing on the development of a specific industry. These particular industries were selected as they represent the major economic sectors in Kazakhstan (see subsection 2.1.1 on the structure of the economy). To achieve a sample with high representativeness, it was essential to include the industries that contribute most to GDP.

The fourth level of sampling, *key countries,* is nested within the target categories 'international organizations' and 'foreign companies'; it consists of China, France, Germany, Japan, Russia, the UK, the US and a group of seven smaller states. The target category 'experts' includes prominent domestic and foreign experts and academics. The remaining target categories 'public employees', 'employer associations and labour unions', 'state-owned companies' and 'private domestic companies' consist solely of domestic actors.

As for the fifth level, *target companies by size,* the aim was to achieve equal representation of small, medium-sized and big companies.

In the sixth level of sampling, *target interview locations*, I aimed for even coverage of the main regional economic centres in Kazakhstan. The geographical distribution of respondents by Almaty, Astana and Karaganda adequately matches the economic importance of each city. Subsections 4.4.3–4.4.8 provide descriptions of the actual sample as well as the justification for the choice of each level.

---

17 The same procedure was conducted by the research team responsible for Uzbekistan.

Table 4.1. Sample

Population	Constituent parts of the economy of Kazakhstan (see target industries)
1) Target Categories	1) Public employees 2) Employer associations and labour unions 3) Experts 4) International organizations 5) State-owned companies 6) Private domestic companies 7) Foreign companies
2) Target Employees	1) High-ranking public officials such as members of Parliament; heads of ministries, state agencies and governmental departments; regional public officials 2) Directors and heads of associations and unions 3) Prominent domestic and foreign experts 4) to 7) Representatives of top-managerial level, preferably CEOs, heads of international organizations, companies and owners of companies
3) Target Industries within categories 4–7	1) Agriculture 2) Construction 3) Finance 4) Information technologies 5) Manufacturing 6) Natural resources 7) Service industry 8) Trade
4) Target Countries for categories 4 and 7*	1) China 2) France 3) Germany 4) Japan 5) Russia 6) the UK 7) the USA 8) 7 small countries * Other categories (1–3) represent domestic players
5) Target Companies by Size for categories 5–7	1) Small-sized companies (1–20 employees) 2) Medium-sized companies (20–100 employees) 3) Big companies (more than 100 employees)
6) Target Interview Locations	1) Almaty 2) Astana 3) Karaganda

4.4.3. Categories of respondents

Here and in the following subsections the composition of the sample is presented in greater detail. I decided to approach stakeholders and key economic players who represent both the private and public domains: private domestic companies, foreign companies, state-owned companies, international organizations, experts, public officials, labour unions and employer associations. For each category of respondents I elaborated a specific interview guide covering specific areas of expertise of target respondents (see Appendix 2). The major economic industries of the economy – agriculture, construction, finance, information technologies, manufacturing, natural resources, services and trade – are nested within such categories of respondents as representatives of private domestic companies, foreign companies and state-owned companies. A detailed distribution of respondents by industry in the actual sample is presented in subsection 4.4.4.

As seen in Figure 4.2, the most representative category in the actual sample is 'international organizations'. I conducted a total of 46 interviews with respondents representing international organizations. As there were no refusals in this category, it contains the greatest number of respondents in the entire sample. The second largest category is the category of 'experts'; here I approached 39 experts and academics. The categories 'private domestic companies' (23 respondents), 'public officials' (21) and 'private foreign companies' (19) were less represented, with 'employer associations and labour unions' (6), 'state-owned companies' (3) and 'education' (2) being under-represented. However, the category 'employer associations and labour unions' should not be considered under-represented, because there are not many functioning associations and unions in Kazakhstan. Thus, the number of respondents (6) in this category may be regarded as adequate in terms of proportion of the entire group of employer associations and labour unions.

Initially, there was no plan to interview experts from the 'education' category, so they cannot be considered as part of the initial sample. This idea arose during the field study, as I felt such persons could provide valuable information on the educational system and its implications for the development of the labour market and overall economic performance.

A major issue in the sample relates to under-representation in the category 'state-owned companies', which made it impossible to generalize from the sample to the broader population. Still I managed to conduct three semi-structured interviews with representatives of the largest state-owned companies, and these have been utilized in the analysis of the data obtained. Respondents in this category proved highly inaccessible – which might be explained by unwillingness to share critical information, as well as the busy schedules and excessive workloads of public-sector employees. Finally, their relative inaccessibility may also be explained by the fact that it was not possible to employ the snowball approach with this category, as I did not have connections and access to top managers of national companies[18] in the first place.

Figure 4.2. Categories of respondents

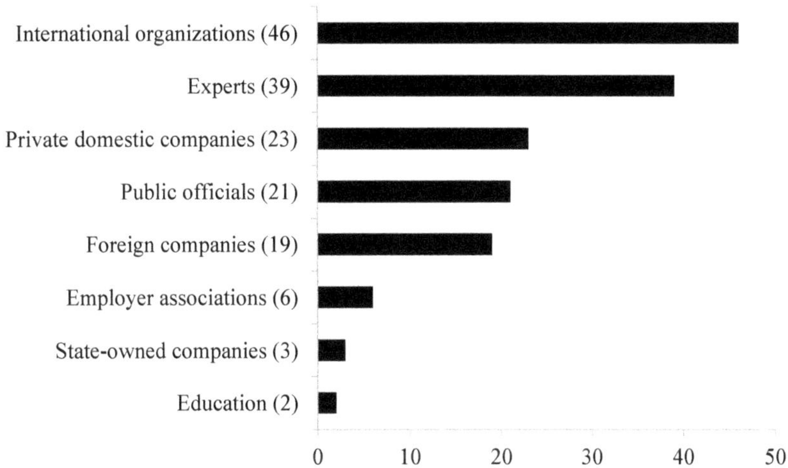

4.4.4. Selected industries

Figure 4.3 shows the composition of selected industries in the sample. As they were considered to be the most important and largest in the economy, I approached representatives of these industries.

Altogether, 33 interviews were conducted with representatives of the service industry, nine in construction, five in the oil and gas, five in manufacturing, four in trade, two in finance and one in agriculture.

Agriculture, manufacturing and trade proved under-represented mainly because not so many foreign actors are active in these sectors in Kazakhstan. By contrast, the oil and gas industry has many foreign corporations; however, only five interviews could be conducted, as representatives of oil and gas companies were generally unwilling to be interviewed. After all, this is a sector of strategic importance which may involve sensitive issues.

18 National companies which are state-led (the state owns a controlling share) under the umbrella of Samruk-Kazyna (see subsection 3.3.2.2).

Figure 4.3. Sampled industries

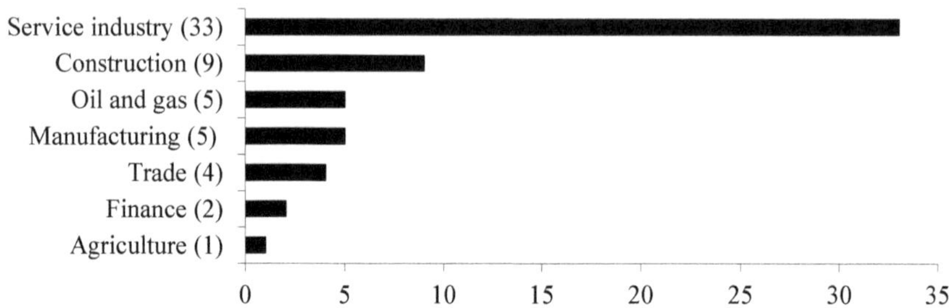

Most representatives of companies in the finance sector and legal services agreed to be interviewed, but the respondents refused to talk specifically about their own company, preferring to be interviewed as 'experts'. If I considered that the person could be regarded as an 'expert', taken into consideration his or her working experience and academic background, we agreed that I would conduct an expert interview. In case he or she did not qualify for an expert interview, I thanked the person, expressing regret that it was not possible to talk about the activities of the company. As the interview guides for 'experts' and 'international organizations' were almost the same, except for three questions, I decided to use the 'international organizations' interview guide if the person represented a foreign company, and used the 'expert' interview guide if the respondent was from a local company. In that case, I tried also to identify that person's perceptions concerning not only general points about the economy of Kazakhstan, but also subjective opinions on how his or her company (in finance and legal services) functioned, and the major obstacles and opportunities for doing business. Thus, the opinions of representatives of the financial industry and legal services were widely reflected in the sample as well.

Initially, I had intended to use 'information technologies' as a separate category, but merged it later with 'services' because of the many similarities. The scope of activities in this industry is very diverse. For instance, the state-owned company Kazakhtelekom provides telecommunication services, but also offers a great variety of other services, such as logistics, which can only be indirectly classified as belonging to telecommunications. Therefore, in order to facilitate categorization of industries, companies providing information technologies of various kinds were subsumed under the 'service' category. In the end, the *service sector* came to include the following subcategories: retail, education, legal services, consulting, franchising, research and academic services, logistics, medical services, environmental services, and hotel business. For the purpose of analysis of the entire service industry, these subcategories were placed into one category. The importance and dominance of the service industry in the economy is evident: in 2009, the share of services in relation to GDP amounted to 55.5 per cent in Kazakhstan (Index Mundi 2010) and to 51.8 per cent in 2010 (Index Mundi 2012b).

4.4.5. Selected countries

I sought to select interviewees from the largest industries and the countries most economically active in Kazakhstan. The target countries are *Russia, Japan, China, Germany, France, UK,* and *the USA,* which all have a considerable trade turnover with Kazakhstan, with many active companies. Some of these countries also exert significant political and economic, direct and indirect, influence on the states of Central Asia, including Kazakhstan. In addition, I also interviewed representatives of companies from countries that are economically less active in Kazakhstan, to see whether the conditions for doing business are similar for any foreign company, or whether the volume of economic and trade relations with Kazakhstan matters in terms of receiving favourable or less favourable treatment from the state. For instance, there are many private companies from the USA, with various channels through which to exert influence, from the American Chamber of Commerce to the US Embassy. I hypothesized that private companies from smaller countries like, say, South Korea or Finland would enjoy less favourable treatment from the state than ones from big and powerful states.

Figure 4.4 shows the overall distribution between the interviewed representatives of local (113) and foreign (46) companies and organizations. Local respondents accounted for 70 per cent of those interviewed. Actually, I had sought to achieve exactly this proportion, 70/30, in the sample, as it reflects the relative participation of domestic and foreign capital in the economy as a whole (Alshanov 2011).

I received a total of 33 refusals from local representatives and 15 refusals from representatives of foreign companies and experts. In total, there were 159 persons who agreed to be interviewed and 48 whom I approached, but who for various reasons decided not to give an interview. This introduced a bias into the sample. I sought to deal with this problem by always trying to approach potential respondents representing the same category, similar organizations by industry, size and ownership structure so that they would be equivalent to organizations whose representatives would not grant interviews.

Figure 4.4. Distribution between local and foreign respondents

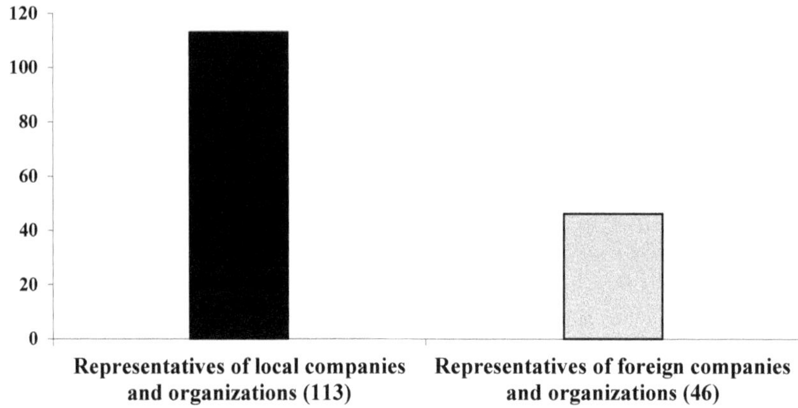

The country that is most prominent in the sample is the USA, with many private companies operating in Kazakhstan. Almost all US respondents were easy to access and expressed interest in my study. The second and third largest foreign countries were Germany (seven respondents) and the UK (six). Four respondents in my sample represent organizations founded or based in more than one European country: they are subsumed under the category 'EU' (see Figure 4.5).

Even though China is one of the leading economic partners for Kazakhstan, I was able to conduct only one interview with a representative of a Chinese company. Six heads of Chinese companies declined to be interviewed – which did not really come as a surprise, as I anticipated that Chinese companies would be unwilling to share information with us, in line with the well-known closedness of Chinese companies. Therefore, private companies from China are generally under-represented in this sample. The same holds for Russia (only one interview). I received three rejections from representatives of Russian companies and organizations.

A flexible strategy was applied in approaching potential respondents from foreign companies. When, for instance, no candidate from France agreed to be interviewed, I simply omitted France from the sample, and chose instead a country with a similar level of economic relations with Kazakhstan – Denmark in this case.

Figure 4.5. Distribution of respondents by country

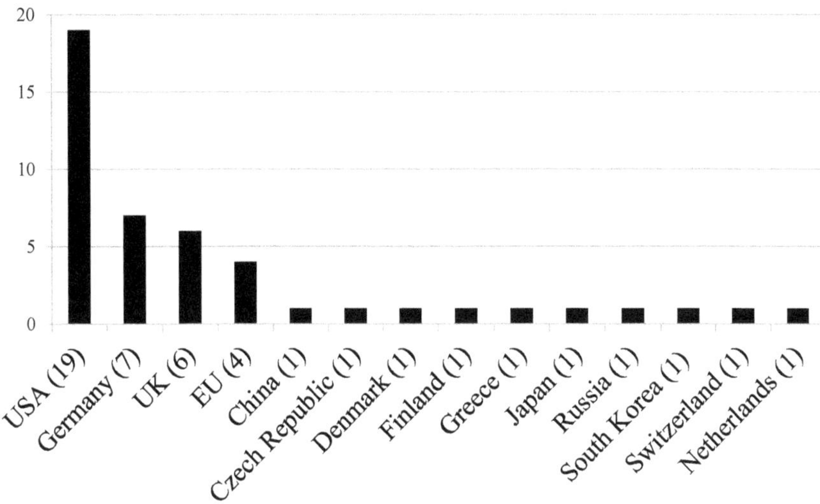

4.4.6. Company size

Small, medium-sized and big companies are evenly represented in the sample. I approached 15 small-sized companies, 23 medium-sized and 24 big domestic and foreign companies. There were some difficulties in arranging interviews with heads of small companies, who tended to be reluctant to share information; in many cases they referred to their busy schedule. This distribution of companies captures the actual distribution of companies in the economy (Figure 2.3).

As explained, in total there were 159 persons who agreed to be interviewed and 48 persons who declined. Of the latter group, 28 persons came from private domestic and foreign companies (the remainder: ten representatives of state-owned companies, five public officials, three experts, two representatives of employer associations and labour unions).

4.4.7. Gender distribution

Altogether 51 female respondents and 108 male respondents were interviewed. In view of the persisting patriarchal elements in local society, this serves as a positive indication of a changing situation with respect to a more equal gender distribution in top managerial and political positions.

Here it should be noted that women often prefer to work within public administration. According to the majority of the public employees interviewed, there are no great gender imbalances within the public administration. No restrictions, formal or informal, preclude women from public employment. Women interviewees proved to be equally satisfied with employment benefits and conditions in public administration as their male colleagues. Most respondents pointed out that women had been less active in seeking positions in the government as well as public agencies during the first decade of independence. The public sector had been more traditional and heavily dominated by men. However, the situation has changed slightly since 2000. This change in women's attitudes towards employment in public administration was stimulated by more competitive salaries and social packages that were introduced and offered to public officials. According to the majority of respondents, this is also explained by the modernization of the system of public administration after 2000. However, this change occurred mainly within the high ministerial apparatus of the government: employment benefits for women in rural areas have remained basically unaltered. Thus, the number of women seeking positions within local municipalities is generally lower than for positions at higher policy-making levels.

4.4.8. Interview location

I sought even coverage of Kazakhstan's regional economic centres. The geographical distribution of respondents adequately corresponds to the volume of economic activities in each particular region. Most interviews were conducted with companies based in Almaty and Astana, which are the political and economic centres of the country (*Expert Kazakhstan* 2012). A smaller part of the interviews were conducted with companies based in Karaganda, an important industrial centre. 106 interviews were conducted with representatives of companies and organizations based in Almaty, 49 in Astana and 4 in Karaganda.

In fact, regional representation was better than shown by these statistics. There were also respondents from other regions and cities. Many entrepreneurs in Kazakhstan have branches in several regions or cities, so in interviews I was also able to ask and identify how economic relations had been shaped in all the regions where they worked. Such persons were approached while they were on business trips in Almaty or Astana. This proved a good strategy, as I faced some logistical constraints and it was not possible to travel across the whole vast territory of Kazakhstan to cover other regions. Such interviews were conducted in Almaty or Astana, but in terms of content they covered the economy of other regions as well. Twenty respondents formally placed in the 'Almaty' and 'Astana' categories actually represented two or more regions or cities. Respondents were categorized under 'Almaty' and 'Astana' because they were generally affiliated with company headquarters in one of those two cities. In addition, it was not always possible to identify clearly in which regions such persons spent most time, and which less.

4.5. Methods of data collection

4.5.1. Semi-standardized interviews

Semi-standardized interviews were used as the major method of primary data collection. Primary data have more importance and relevance to my research, given the problem of unreliable secondary data as discussed before. Moreover, the literature review showed that many aspects within the Varieties of Capitalism framework, such as corporate governance or inter-firm relations, are largely under-researched topics. There is little literature on interaction involving institutions in these areas in Kazakhstan. Therefore, by collecting primary data I sought to fill in these and other gaps (see also subsection 3.3.7). In general, semi-structured interviews serve as a primary data source for qualitative research (DiCicco-Bloom and Crabtree 2006). There were two reasons for my choice of semi-structured interviews as a method for primary data collection.

First, during my field study I interviewed experts, representatives of domestic and foreign private business, public officials, and representatives of international organizations, labour unions and employer associations. The key issue of interest was respondents' subjective views on how the economy, economic and political institutions function and interact with each other. A major advantage of semi-standardized interviews is that they primarily aim at elucidating and understanding respondents' perceptions (Rabionet 2011; Grodeland et al. 1998). That was precisely my goal: to collect, assess and understand shared information and respondents' perceptions. It is impossible to collect individual perceptions and views through business-surveys, for instance. Semi-structured interviews require active interaction with interviewees, and that makes them different from business surveys (Bavdaz 2009: 2).

Second, in the context of Central Asia, semi-structured interviews coupled with researcher flexibility better suit the specific cultural environment (Kuzmits 2008: 36). Usually, talking directly or using check-off questionnaires are not viewed positively: in interacting with Central Asia respondents it is better to proceed with open-ended questions and be ready for lengthy conversations (ibid). In my view, semi-structured interviews should be a preferred tool for primary data collection in the region: respondents tend to trust such interviews, so the chances of obtaining authentic information and reliable data are higher.

What characterizes semi-structured interviews? First of all, as with other types of interviews, semi-structured interviews 'are usually scheduled in advance at a designated time and location outside of everyday events' (DiCicco-Bloom and Crabtree 2006: 315). They are based on fixed questions, but also allow asking questions that arise during the interview (DiCicco-Bloom and Crabtree 2006; Patton 2002). For this study, the use of semi-structured interviews proved particularly relevant as it allowed me to focus on my particular topics of interest while remaining flexible and open to accommodating other relevant topics not covered by the interview guides. As argued by Rabionet (2011: 564) 'a completely un-structured interview has the risk of not eliciting (…) the topics or themes more closely related to the research questions under consideration.' Questions within the conversational interview are almost always different from each other; there are no predetermined questions, and therefore these interviews may be different from each other in terms of content (Patton 2002: 342, 343). This also requires flexibility on the part of the researcher (ibid: 342), but there is no structure to allow for a quick and convenient systematization of the data obtained. In this particular study, it was important to elaborate some questions in advance according to the theoretical structure of the VoC approach, in order to achieve the research objective. I applied this theoretical framework in my study and incorporated theoretical considerations into the interview guides (see subsections 4.5.2.1–4.5.2.5).

I needed to conduct interviews that could be easily systematized and analysed. Purely conversational interviews are hard to systematize and analyse along a unified set of criteria, unlike the case with semi-structured interviews. Standardized interviews involve a predetermined set of questions, put to all respondents, using the same wording, in order to reduce variation in the questions as such (Patton 2002: 342). That also rules out asking any additional questions during the interview. Such lack of flexibility was unsuited for the purposes of this research, so semi-structured interviews were judged most appropriate.

In the interviews my major concern was to identify respondents' subjective views on how the economy and economic institutions function, as well as how the rules of the game are shaped and determined by the state and the private sector. It was important to conduct semi-standardized interviews, as institutions cannot be viewed as static elements of the economic system in transition: they must be seen as dynamic ones (Mendelski 2008: 6). Using semi-standardized interviews facilitated identifying and understanding the formal and informal role of the state in the market economy as well as institutional dynamics and change in the country over time. Interviews help reveal *defacto* interaction between private business and the state sector. Identifying informal practices through analysis of the literature was difficult, and interviews helped fill that gap. That is not to underestimate the importance of the literature review, as it enabled the comparison between the official position and the subjective views of respondents as to the type of market economy now emerging in Kazakhstan.

4.5.2. Construction of interview guides

4.5.2.1. General approach

An interview guide contains the list of issues to be identified during an interview and serves as a framework for structuring and developing questions (Patton 2002: 343, 344). The chief aim of the guide is 'to ensure that the same basic lines of inquiry are pursued with each person interviewed' (ibid: 343). My interview guides were based on key assumptions of the VoC approach (see interview guides in Appendix 2). The major focus while constructing interview guides was placed on the analysis of the economy within its six institutional domains: financial relations, corporate governance, industrial relations, inter-firm relations, social security system and vocational education and training. The interview guides for all categories included sections that covered aspects of these domains. The general thematic structure for all guides followed the logic of these six institutional domains of the VoC and their interaction with each other. In addition, I examined institutions within the public administration, as they may trigger the development of economic institutions in transition countries (Ahrens 2008: 25). Some of my questions incorporated these considerations in the interview guides for public officials, experts and international organizations. For instance, questions concerning political institutions such as the independence of regional politicians, the effectiveness of the court, the transparency of public officials, the predictability of policy-making as well as the persistence of Soviet economic and political institutions were formulated and included in the interview guides.

Seven interview guides were elaborated for the field study, as respondents were grouped into the following categories:

- private domestic companies;
- foreign companies;
- state-owned companies;
- international organizations;
- experts;
- public officials;
- employer associations/labour unions.

All seven interview guides were elaborated in advance, in varying degrees of detail. This helped to make the entire process of interviewing more structured by identifying the aspects of research in advance, as recommended by Patton (2002). Other important and relevant issues that arose during the interviews were taken into account and transformed into new questions, and new respondents provided answers to newly formulated questions as well. Thus, the interview guides allowed for flexibility in terms of structuring the interviews and changing the questions. I agree with the views expressed by Mack et al. (2005): the strength of qualitative methods as opposed to quantitative research methods is that they allow for identification of new and potentially highly relevant issue-areas during interviews.

Subsections 4.5.2.2–4.5.2.5 provide detailed descriptions of the interview guides, with examples and explanations of some central questions. The interview guides described below are the final versions, as adjusted during the pilot phase. All unsuitable and overly sensitive questions were eliminated during that phase. Additionally, a few questions were reformulated during the field study, as I constantly asked respondents for feedback. I was particularly interested to learn whether some questions were phrased in an uncomfortable way. Having received feedback, I reconsidered these questions and adjusted them accordingly, for use with subsequent respondents. On the whole, however, there were few such instances. Thus, the pilot phase proved successful, as the interview guides underwent only minor changes in the course of the main phase of data collection.

4.5.2.2. Interview guides for private domestic, foreign and state-owned companies

The company interview guides covered such points as basic facts, relationships with other companies, relationships with investors, education and employment, relationships with workforce, which are part of the VoC approach. Each of these sections contained several key and follow-up questions. I always kept in mind that new issues could arise which were not covered by the interview guides; I might also ask new questions if I saw that the respondent possessed appropriate expertise in a particular area.

The interview guides for private domestic, foreign and state-owned companies all contain a similar 'basic facts' section, with questions on the respondent's background, the projects and industry in which the company is involved. Under 'basic facts' I also asked about the approximate number of employees in the company, date when the business was established, and form of first registration. As explained, all interview guides are based on key assumptions of the VoC approach. In the first section, on relationship with other companies, I would ask: *Do any kinds of contacts exist between you and your competitors?* With this question I sought to identify whether private companies tended to cooperate with each other or to compete. This was a central question, because, as noted earlier, according to the VoC approach, in a CME private firms prefer to cooperate with competitors, whereas in an LME private firms tend to compete with each other (Hall and Soskice 2001). After this question I also asked the follow-up question: *Are there any activities (e.g., research and development, collaborative vocational training, marketing) in which your company cooperates with the competitors?* Here I sought to identify in which particular area cooperation may take place.

Throughout the interviews, I kept utilizing a flexible strategy. If I understood that a respondent had expertise in a particular area and was eager to talk I asked more follow-up questions, to elicit as much detailed information about the topic as possible. A few questions were standardized. I asked respondents such questions at the end of several sections in order to identify the overall attitude of the respondent to a particular process or phenomenon. For instance, at the end of the section on relationship with other companies I asked: *Taking the questions above into consideration, how would you describe your relationship with other companies in your industry: very competitive – competitive – neutral – cooperative – very cooperative?* In answering this question, the respondent characterized the relationship between private firms in a particular industry in general.

In the interview guide for firms I also placed a special emphasis on networking activities between and among employers: *Does any network exist between employers?* I was interested to learn whether top management sought to coordinate the firm's relations with other companies through employer associations. In an LME, inter-firm coordination is usually limited, whereas in a CME private firms rely heavily on deep inter-firm relations (Hall and Soskice 2001). Thus, knowing the type of coordination between firms would help in identifying the type of market economy in which private firms operate.

Throughout, I placed special emphasis on such central elements of inter-firm relations as tools for conflict solution. What instruments do private businesses use in case of conflict with competitors, suppliers, investors, and public authorities? Here I wanted to see whether informal tools are employed along with formal ones in conflict resolution, and so in each subsection I asked the following question: *In case of a conflict, how do you deal with your suppliers? (Competitors, investors, public authorities).*

Another important aspect of state–business interrelations, one which largely defines how corporate governance is shaped in Kazakhstan, is the interest shown by private firms in making short-term or long-term investments. In an LME short-term capital investments prevail, as the invested capital may be returned within a short period of time, whereas in a CME private firms will employ a different strategy, as return on investment takes longer (Hall and Soskice 2001). Unlike the case in a CME, private firms in an LME tend to maintain short-term relations with competitors, suppliers, and customers. In order to explore the situation, I included the following questions: *Do you have long-term relations with your investors? (competitors, suppliers)* and *Does your company worry about making long-term investments?*

In order to account for the role of the state and identify whether private companies face obstacles within the investment regime, I asked: *Does your company worry about making long-term investments?* If the response was 'yes', I continued with two follow-up questions, to elicit to what extent the government policies complicate/facilitate company investment policies: *Have there been some unexpected laws introduced, which influenced your strategic decisions?* and *Have there been any laws introduced recently but then reconsidered?*

Regarding education and recruitment policy I was interested in how recruitment policy is organized, and whether training is provided for employees to upgrade their skills. This is an important distinction between LME and CME types of economy. As explained in section 3.2, companies in an LME invest in short-term training and general skills of employees, whereas companies in a CME generally provide long tenure and invest in company- or industry-specific skills (Hall and Soskice 2001). So I asked: *Does your company provide any training for the employees?*

The final section of the guide concluded with general remarks. I would always ask whether the respondent had any questions, or wished to comment on the interview guide. Here it should be noted that there are only few differences across three interview guides. The guide for state-owned companies is shorter, without questions about the relationship of a company with the government. I also skipped the questions about conflict solution tools a state-company uses in dealing with public agencies. After all, state-owned companies are often part of public agencies and implement the projects of certain governmental agencies and departments.

4.5.2.3. Interview guide for public officials

Constructing an interview guide for public officials was a challenge. I had to consider a wide range of specific political and cultural aspects in preparing every question. Kazakhstan, like any other Central Asian state, is a difficult place for interviewing elites. I had to avoid questions that could negatively affect the flow of the interviews with public officials. I made good use of the assistance of local experts, who helped me in omitting, re-phrasing and changing several questions during the pilot phase of the research project.

The interview guide for public officials consists of the following sections: basic facts, role of the state in the economy, and functioning of the agency. In the first section on basic facts I asked general questions on the respondent's career path, motivation for becoming a public official as well as main duties and responsibilities. Then I asked: *How often does the rotation of public officials in your agency take place?*

Responses to this question could help me better understand how rotation processes influence the efficiency and effectiveness of public administration, thus shedding light on the role of the state in promoting economic reforms in Kazakhstan. I wanted to see whether frequent/infrequent rotation causes problems for economic policy-making and has any implications for state–business interrelation. Thus, it was crucial to include this question in the interview guide. Then, I added the following question: *According to your perception, is there a country or a group of countries that could serve as a suitable reference model for Kazakhstan?*

If a respondent had difficulties in naming a particular country, the interviewers suggested possible options from the list below: *Continental Europe, USA, China, Russia, East Asian economies (Japan, South Korea etc.), or other (please specify).*

The choice of selected countries was based upon the analysis of official government's declarations, announced development programmes and official speeches of high-ranking government officials. Those countries are often mentioned as models for development in Kazakhstan. The task was to identify whether officially announced reference models are implemented in practice. I did not immediately mention the examples of countries, waiting until respondents provided an answer. Only when the respondent failed to come up with a specific country would I suggest the above options.

During the interviews I tried not to influence the flow. I also tried not to anticipate possible answers from respondents. I wanted the public officials to feel comfortable, answering freely without being forced or prodded.

Then, as a follow-up question, I asked: *Is there anything that differentiates Kazakhstan from its reference models according to your perception? Please describe.* With this question I sought to find which elements were incorporated into the economy from foreign development models and which were specific to Kazakhstan's development path.

In the final section on the functioning of the agency (department or ministry) I asked questions aimed at elucidating the detailed structure of the agency, its decision-making structure, duties and responsibilities across various departments of the agency as well as the effectiveness of communication channels among various public agencies. I also included a question about the influence of the official Development Strategy of Kazakhstan 2030 on the daily routines of public officials: *In which ways does the announcement of the Strategy 2030 influence your daily work?* This aimed at revealing whether there was a link between the tasks performed by a particular agency, and the overall principles of the Development Strategy. In general, no questions for public officials were negatively perceived by those interviewed, nor did any respondent voice serious concern with respect to the sensitivity of the questions asked.

4.5.2.4. Interview guides for experts and international organizations

The interview guides for experts and representatives of international organizations were rather similar, as I expected that representatives of both categories possessed more or less the same expertise. The guides varied only in some aspects, as when questions concerned the specific activities of international organizations. In general, the questions addressed key macroeconomic issues as well as the overall economic development of Kazakhstan. Both interview guides included the same sections: basic facts, functioning of the economy, rule of law, reform need, and future outlook and planning.

At the very beginning of the interview guide, I included a question for representatives of international organizations, on the role of an international organization in Kazakhstan: *Does/did your organization shape or somehow contribute to the economic policy making and emergence of new institutions in the country? If yes, could you please describe how?* Moreover, I assumed that powerful international organizations had contributed to the entire reform process since independence. Hence, the follow-up question was: *How did your decisions/projects influence economic policy making of the country over time?* This question helped to clarify to what extent international organizations had participated in the reform process over time, as well as how they contributed to the emergence of new institutions.

The remaining questions were the same for the two interview guides. In the first section on the functioning of the economy, I started with a general question intended to shape the further flow of the interview: *According to your perception, what is the role of the state in the market economy?*

Then, a question on the wage-setting process was asked: *How are wages in Kazakhstan usually set?* I was interested to learn which actors are involved in the wage-setting process, especially whether the state influences the process in the private sector by setting wage limits for firms. So I added a follow-up question: *Does the state influence the wage-setting process?*

When preparing this interview guide I had included a question on sources of finance for local companies. Given the problems in the cost and difficulty in gaining access to financial resources (see subsection 3.3.2.3), the following question was asked: *What is the usual source of finance for local companies?* I expected experts and representatives of international organizations to have expertise in this area. It may well be that official data on sources of finance differ from actual practice. Based on my local knowledge I expected that 'on paper' private firms might report that they used bank loans or capital markets, but would in practice use other channels as well, such as own sources and informal borrowing from private persons. The latter are usually not officially indicated as sources of finance. Since it is hard to identify the existence of informal sources while analysing official documents and statistics, I wanted experts to shed light on informal practices in this area.

As in the interview guide for companies, there was also a question on the financial motives of investors: *According to your perception, are big corporate investors mainly driven by long-term (strategic) or short-term (financial) motives?* This was supplemented with a follow-up question on the role of the state in establishing a favourable investment regime for investors: *Does the state try to promote the long-term commitment of investors and companies to certain projects/industries?* Subsequently, I asked a question focused on the respondent's general views on business opportunities and obstacles: *What do you consider the major opportunities and major obstacles that private entrepreneurs and investors face in Kazakhstan?* Respondents were asked to briefly list the major opportunities and major obstacles. In order to summarize their answers the following closed question was asked: *According to your perception, how easy is it to do business in Kazakhstan?* with possible answers on a scale from 1 to 5:

easy 1 2 3 4 5 difficult

In order to understand the nature of the current investment climate and account for the important role of foreign investors in shaping Kazakhstan's economy, I asked several questions concerning interrelations between the state and foreign investors. For example: *Are foreign investors welcome to invest in all sectors of the economy, or are there some industries where they have only limited access?*

Another important question dealt with the security of property rights of companies. Seeking to find out whether the law is applied equally to both domestic and foreign companies, I asked: *Does partial foreign ownership of a company have a* de facto *effect on the security of property rights?*

After conducting 40 interviews, I decided to include a new and important question in the interview guide for experts, relating to the logic of path-dependence. Previously I had no questions that could help to show what, if any, elements of the Soviet institutional system have persisted in Kazakhstan. In my first field-study experience, some of the experts interviewed had argued that the current administration builds and maintains several institutions identical to the

Soviet governance model. I discussed this point with all team members, and we decided unanimously to ask two questions that could help us to identify institutions originating from the Soviet era: *Do elements of the Soviet practices still remain in policy making practices of the country? If yes, what are they?* and *Do these elements/institutions have just another form, but the same gist?* I decided that asking these questions might help us better understand why some market economy reforms have succeeded or failed in Kazakhstan.

The final section on the need for reform, future outlook and planning contained key questions to experts and representatives of international organizations. First of all, it was important to identify whom respondents consider to be the key actors in the economy: *Who, according to your perception, are the key players in the economy?* A similar question followed on key political decision-makers in the country: *Who, according to your perception, are the key political decision-makers in the economy? Could you please name three most important decision-makers?* Here the aim was to compare official opinions about key players and decision-makers with the respondents' own views. This could help us identify any 'grey eminences' in the economy, with influence on decision-making process in the economic sphere.

It was also important to explore respondents' views on the effectiveness of public administration. Since my study was part of a larger research project the interview guides also included theoretical assumptions from the New Institutional Economics, the New Political Economy and modern governance research. Here a special set of questions on accountability, participation, predictability and transparency of public officials was prepared. These were based on the model of effective governance proposed by Ahrens (2002), who stresses that these four dimensions are the constituent pillars of the credibility of the public administration. In its turn, credibility is an all-encompassing element necessary for effective governance (ibid: 132). I built the questions around these principles. For instance, as regards transparency of policy-making, I asked: *How transparent are the actions and policies of public officials, according to your perception?*

I was also interested to see the extent of communication between private business and the state: do both parties interact with each other regularly? I asked representatives of two categories the following question: *What are the ways to exchange information between business and the government?*

Finally, two concluding questions intended to gradually wrap up the entire interview. The first one concerned the impact of the economic crisis of 2008 on Kazakhstan: *Could you mention two things which have changed because of the recent economic crisis?* The second question was on the future of economic development and economic reforms: *What is your general perception concerning the intermediate future of Kazakhstan?*

4.5.2.5. Interview guide for employer associations and labour unions

The interview guide for employer associations had a section on the activity of an employer association and its relations with other employer associations. As the other interview guides I began by asking about the professional and academic background of the respondent. Then I continued with a specific set of questions for representatives of trade unions and employer associations. One of the questions I was particularly interested in was the following: *What is the main reason for companies to join your organization?* I sought to understand the motivation that drives private firms to establish labour unions and employer associations, and what goals various stakeholders pursue in that regard.

The relationship with the government was an important element, so I asked: *Does your association (union) interact with the government in any way?* If the labour union or employer association interacted with the government, I continued with a follow-up question: *What are the forms of such interaction? Do you have any joint projects with the government?*

Apart from the relationship with the government, the decision-making process within associations and unions should be clarified. This could help explore the distribution of decision-making power in an association/trade union as well measure its influence on individual companies. A low impact of labour unions/employer associations on decision-making processes in private firms is usually inherent in an LME-type of economy; and high impact of labour unions/employer associations is usually observed in a CME. Thus I asked: *How does your association influence the decisions in the companies which belong to your association?*

Finally, there was a question on the general importance and influence of labour unions/employer associations on economic processes: *How would you evaluate the importance of employer associations/trade unions for the economy of your country?*

4.5.3. Workshop on interview technique and pilot interviews

'Good qualitative study based on semi-structured interviews relies on the knowledge, skills, vision and integrity of the researcher doing that analysis. Training and experience are crucial for this endeavour' (Dingwall et al. 1998, in Rabionet 2011: 565). Various measures were undertaken to ensure that the research team met these criteria. In order to learn necessary skills for conducting semi-structured interviews, a workshop on interview technique was organized in Göttingen in April 2009. During the workshop all project researchers gained a better understanding of the nuances involved in conducting interviews, as well as obtained skills necessary for organizing and conducting interviews.

Interactive sessions with an expert on interview technique allowed strategies of conduct to be elaborated before, during and after the actual interview. Moreover, in the course of the workshop the expert advised us to test the interview guides by conducting several pilot interviews with similar groups of respondents. Between May and August 2009, pilot interviews were conducted in Almaty, as well as in Tashkent, Uzbekistan, and in Celle, Germany. The group of researchers responsible for interviews in Kazakhstan conducted pilot interviews with Russian entrepreneurs in Celle in July 2009. These interviews were done jointly by two researchers. After each interview both researchers exchanged ideas and observations.

These pilot interviews were helpful and useful for two main reasons. First, they provided feedback on the interview guides, and some questions were rephrased, changed or omitted. Moreover, new questions and those questions that were changed as a result of a pilot study were introduced in the final version of interview guides. Second, conducting pilot interviews helped to improve the interviewers' communication skills in interacting with respondents.

4.5.4. Observation and investigator triangulation

As noted earlier, the use of the observation method was important for this research. This method serves as a supplementary tool for applied semi-structured interviews and can be used at any stage of the research process (Mack et al. 2005: 14, 16). Often the accurate and joint application of several qualitative methods can increase the validity of the results obtained (Lambert and Loiselle 2008: 234–235; DeWalt et al. 1998). The method is widely used in research on culture, anthropology and ethnography (Spradley 1980). Participant observation is a method in which the researcher participates in 'the daily activities, rituals, interactions, and events of a group of people as one of the means of learning of the explicit and tacit aspects of their life routines and their culture' (DeWalt and DeWalt 2011: 1). The method helps reveal various practical and theoretical aspects of human life embedded in everyday activities (Jorgensen 1989: 14). Importantly, as Mack et al. note, 'data obtained through participant observation serve as a check against participants' subjective reporting of what they believe and do' (2005: 14). Moreover, the method 'is also useful for gaining an understanding of the physical, social, cultural, and economic contexts in which study participants live; the relationships among and between people, contexts, ideas, norms, and events; and people's behaviours and activities – what they do, how frequently, and with whom' and allows exploration of factors about which the researcher was not aware while designing the research, but which are important for finding an answer to the research question (ibid: 14). In practice, the researcher keeps notes on his or her own observations, informal interactions with participants, and by documenting relevant observations from newspapers, radio and television (ibid: 13).

The method is time-consuming – that is one of its major disadvantages (Mack et al. 2005: 14). However, in my case this was not a problem, as I spent more than one year doing the field study, with ample time to observe economic processes as well as participants, i.e. the respondents. Sometimes I had follow-up informal meetings with respondents. For instance, after conducting an interview, I might invite the respondent to dinner, or be invited myself. In such cases, we could discuss more informally how the economy is developing and could explore the issues that might not have been identified during the formal interview. As a result of these conversations, I sometimes adjusted certain questions or added new ones to the interview guides, as appropriate. Based on my observations and notes I also altered some aspects of my behaviour during the interviews, and made changes to the interview guides.

In this study it was the observation method that was used. Participant observation implies that the researcher takes part in the field as a regular actor, which could not apply in my case. I was only observing economic processes, events and respondents' behaviour during the fieldwork. In the end, it emerged as a helpful strategy for cross-checking and ensuring the quality of the interviews. The observation method proved useful for distinguishing between truthful and false, authentic and non-authentic information. By thoroughly analysing patterns of respondent behaviour, I tried to become aware of whether a respondent was giving authentic information or not. To that end, I made notes during the interview and discussed them in our research group afterwards.

Furthermore, I utilized the strategy of investigator triangulation for both the data collection and the data analysis phases. This strategy 'involves using several different investigators in the analysis process' (Guion et al. 2002: 1–2). The necessary condition should be the participation of several colleagues of one research project in the data collection process using 'the same qualitative method', done so as to evaluate the consistency of employed methods, increase validity of obtained data and gain 'a broader and deeper understanding of how the different investigators view the issue' (ibid). Members of our research team conducted semi-structured interviews, using the same interview guides, with representatives of the same group of respondents. Afterwards we were able to compare our experiences and observations. Moreover, since the same research project was being conducted in two countries at the same time, I could share experiences and compare methods of data collection with the research team working in Uzbekistan. If our observations and conclusions largely coincided, that indicated that the data collected were valid and that the methods we employed were used in a consistent way.

Guion et al. (2002: 1–2) hold that even though this method is a good tool for validating the results, it cannot always be implemented in practice. It requires bringing all researchers together – and, due to the time constraints and busy schedule of each researcher, that may not always be possible. However, I had enough flexibility in terms of time and adjusting individual schedules of all researchers, because I could spend more than one year in the field.

4.5.5. Team collaboration

It was essential to work as part of a united team in this project. Collaboration took place at every stage of my study, also as part of the investigator triangulation process. Working as a team provided synergy effects that benefited all project researchers. I could engage in constant exchange of field research experiences and ideas from Kazakhstan and Uzbekistan, and compare the data obtained. This also enhanced the overall validity of my own data. This point may well support the argument that teamwork in the social sciences may prove highly useful and mutually beneficial for all research participants, as is already widely recognized within the natural sciences.

4.6. Field research: data collection

4.6.1. Before the interview

Field research methodologies have to be done, philosophically, technically and socially, and doing them is (hard) work that involves the negotiating of a complex set of issues and circumstances.
Caleb Wall and Peter Mollinga (2008: 13–14)

For the field study I elaborated three strategies – *before the interview, during the interview* and *after the interview*. The strategies are based on the results of the workshop on doing interviews and on the pilot interviews. In addition, I took account of cultural elements specific to the region's economic and political environment. All interviews were conducted by two interviewers: normally myself as leading interviewer, and a research assistant as second. Sometimes we exchanged roles, in which case I also actively participated in the interview and asked follow-up questions. Below is the step-by-step guide for the interviews conducted by the research team in Kazakhstan.

Before the interview:

1. I printed out an interview guide with topics and tables for systematic information. I also highlighted some important questions adjusted to the specific knowledge and experience of a respondent, and elaborated universal signs.

2. I created an emergency interview guide (for situations when I was running out of time, etc.), prepared a strategy for unexpected scenarios (e.g. discussing informal practices) and always kept the seven interviews guides together, as a respondent could qualify for several categories. It also happened a few times that the respondent unexpectedly called other employees so that I could speak with them right away, without planning in advance.

3. Most interviews were scheduled to last between 70 and 90 minutes. It was important to have at least one hour free after the planned interview in case the respondent arrived late or the interview itself lasted longer than expected. In the beginning I was sometimes unable to arrive in time for a subsequent interview because the previous interview had exceeded the expected time limit: therefore I tried to schedule as much time as possible between two interviews each day.

4. In general, I planned to conduct only one or two interviews a day. If more than two interviews were arranged, the schedule could be disrupted if a respondent failed to arrive on time or wished to postpone the interview for later that day. On the other hand, there were also exceptions when three or even four interviews had to be conducted on the same day. In that case, our research team split and conducted the overlapping interviews separately.

5. In advance, I tried to collect as much information as possible about the interviewee and the company/organization, to be better prepared for the interview as well as have an understanding of why that person's views and perceptions might be like this or that.

6. In arranging the interview I followed two approaches: *snowball approach* and *direct contact,* as explained in subsection 4.4.1 on sampling procedures. With both approaches, I always sent respondents the cover letter either in Russian or English presented in the box below.

Cover Letter

Dear Mr/MS…,

Hereby we would like to give you a brief description of our research project 'Emerging Market Economies in Central Asia.' Currently, an international group of researchers from Central Asia and Europe work on the project. The project is coordinated by the Private University of Applied Sciences in Göttingen, Germany and the University of Groningen, the Netherlands. In Kazakhstan, we cooperate with the Public Policy Research Centre as well as the KIMEP University in Almaty.
The main objective of the project is to analyse the emerging market economies in Central Asia, in particular the economies of Kazakhstan and Uzbekistan. Particularly, we are interested in exploring under which conditions local and foreign enterprises operate in Central Asia. In this context, we focus not only on institutional and legislative conditions, but also on peculiarities which are embedded within the culture of the country. As for the interview guide, we have the following sections: functioning of the economy, rule of law, reform need and future economic outlook.
Your experience and knowledge are of great interest for us. Please note that no preparation for the interview is required from your side. We assure that the information you provide us will be used only with your permission. Moreover, the results of the interviews will be used anonymously.

If you have any further questions regarding our project or the interview, please contact us any time.

Kind regards,
Research team

7. I usually suggested that we meet at the respondent's workplace, but some respondents preferred to be interviewed in less formal places like cafes or restaurants. If an informal setting had been suggested as the place for an interview I tried to avoid disturbing elements (no music, minimum background noise), though this was not always possible.

8. I created an ID of the interviewee. Each respondent was assigned his or her own unique number which could be recognized only by the interviewers.

9. I thought carefully about the dress-code, prepared our business cards, and sought to ensure that all the necessary items and technical equipment – pens (at least two), pencils (at least two), dictaphones (two), batteries for dictaphones, paper, seven interview guides – were in place. This was usually the responsibility of the research assistants.

10. I always had to be prepared for an interview to be postponed several times.

4.6.2. During the interview

11. Before going to the interview, I double-checked that the respondent would be available, by contacting him or her directly or through a secretary, usually one hour in advance.

12. If the interviewee was not available or had limited time, I always asked for another appointment, trying to stay flexible, and letting the interviewee select a better time.

13. On meeting a respondent, I tried to create a relaxed atmosphere by asking a few non-relevant questions (about the weather, etc.), and telling 'easy' jokes and other social small-talk.

14. Initially, I had considered giving small presents to the respondents; however, I decided not to, in order to remain strictly impartial and not exert any kind of influence on respondents' answers.

15. Prior to the interview, I briefly introduced the research project and explained the purpose of the interview. Case in Point 4.2 below demonstrates nuances related to arranging interviews.

Case in Point 4.2. Importance of 'symbolic power'

A high-ranking public official was approached by us directly. I phoned his secretary, who immediately put me through to him. I briefly introduced myself and the purpose of my call. This public official was very busy and he asked whether I could be even briefer and tell him why I was calling. I explained again why I was calling precisely him. During my short presentation he heard that our project partner was one of the leading international organizations. On hearing about this partner, he agreed immediately to be interviewed. Next day I was interviewing him in his office. However, in the middle of the interview he asked me whether I represent the organization that I had mentioned during the introduction yesterday. I replied that it was just our cooperation partner. It turned out that he had expected the organization to be conducting the research. I had to disappoint him, and then he said: 'I was confused yesterday when you mentioned that organization. I thought you were from there. If I had realized it was just your partner, I would probably have said "no" to the interview.' However, the rest of the interview went fine and he responded to the remaining questions with interest and respect. In that case it was just a matter of luck for us to reach him as he had misunderstood when I had been introducing the entire

project and our partners. This situation also showed how 'symbolic power' may matter for arranging interviews.

16. I explained how the respondent had been selected, mainly referring to his or her working experience and expertise in the field. I started as follows: *'I decided to talk to you, since you possess a lot of knowledge in the area and are an expert on this subject...'*

17. Then I explained the structure and format of the interview, introducing major topics within the interview guide as well as the time frame for the interview. It was critical for us to always ask a respondent right before the interview whether he or she had enough time to talk. Sometimes it emerged that the person could devote just 30 minutes, with no any chance to talk again on a later occasion. In such cases I selected the most important questions and asked them quickly. I had also to be prepared for sudden interruptions by colleagues of the respondent; in such cases I agreed to come back later, or simply wait if I had no other interviews scheduled afterwards.

18. I always explained what would I do with data, how the information would be treated. I also assured respondents of confidentiality.

19. If the respondent was interested, we agreed that I would send him or her the research results as soon as they become available.

20. Before recording I always asked for permission to do it.[19] In some cases, people were reluctant to be taped. This could be for various reasons, such as lack of experience with interviewing, fear that despite guarantees in confidentiality provision I might use the information publicly. In case a respondent refused to be taped, the interview was written down verbatim, usually by a research assistant.

21. I began by asking an easy 'bridging' question (about his or her career, success, sometimes encouraging the interviewee to answer demographic questions).

22. I remained friendly and respectful throughout the interview.

19 As argued by Kuzmits (2008: 36), there is no golden rule with respect to the use/non-use of tape recorders in Central Asia. Flexibility and sensitivity are required and the researcher's good intentions must in any case be clear to respondents (ibid).

23. In many cases I tried to make the interview more relaxed, more like a conversation, not a formal question-and-answer session.

24. I stayed focused and showed interest through on-verbal language, always, however, remaining neutral to what the respondent was saying.

25. I tried to ask the questions exactly as they were written, avoiding yes/no questions as much as possible.

26. If the respondent did not provide answers to a question or seemed confused, I repeated the question in a slightly different form. I also encouraged him or her to continue talking by using non-verbal language as well as trying to help in case of confusion.

27. I used plain language, and avoided jargon or special terminology. However, if the respondent preferred to use such language, I encouraged him or her to do so, as it was in our interest that respondents expressed their opinions and perceptions in the way they wished, with no constraints from the interviewer. This helped to ensure that the information we received was authenthic.

28. Throughout the interview I took care not to impose my opinions on the respondent.

29. In particular, it was important not to finish a respondent's sentences and answers for him or her.

30. I used various kinds of probes to get further information – silent probe, overt encouragement, etc.

31. Very often in order to dig deeper into the issue or problem I asked respondents for clarification. For instance, 'a minute ago you were talking about the experience you had in (...) Could you tell me more about that?' or 'you mentioned this problem before, could you please elaborate more on that?'

32. I would always take notes, even if interview was being recorded. Having notes helped me in case the background noise was loud, or the respondent spoke too softly.

33. I used a kind of special shorthand while making notes. This saved our time and helped in case a respondent tried to read what I was writing –

he or she quickly lost interest in what I was writing when my shorthand proved impossible to decipher. Otherwise, the course of interview could be disturbed and an interviewee could get confused.

34. I always asked if the respondent had any questions or suggestions. In particular, I drew the respondent's attention to any changes that he or she might wish to suggest with respect to the interview guide.

35. I finished the interview by asking the following question: 'Now you've received a general picture of the questions we are interested in! Is there anything else in particular you think might be interesting for us and you would like to tell us?'...

36. I always asked for interviewee's business card, if it had not already been provided.

37. I asked about any suitable new contacts that I might perhaps interview.

38. In the end, I warmly thanked the interviewee for his or her time and effort.

4.6.3. After the interview

39. I evaluated and graded the quality of the interview (detailed description of the grading system is provided in the following subsections).

40. Right after the interview, I filled in the Interview Form (IF) (see sample in Appendix 3). If I had no time to finalize this immediately, I went through the notes once again, while everything was fresh, to make sure that they were legible and understandable.

41. I sent the interviewee an e-mail, expressing our thanks, assuring once again of confidentiality, and giving our contact details.

42. Taking into consideration any comments and feedback on the interview guide, I tried to rework it accordingly.

As mentioned, based on my observations and notes I decided to change some aspects of my conduct during the interviews as well as my interview guides. All interviews were conducted by two interviewers. In general, the main interviewer asked questions and follow-up questions based on the interview guide and led the whole interview; the second interviewer asked follow-up questions and both interviewers probed further if the respondent proved to know much more about the subject than covered in the interview guide. Moreover, in case a respondent declined to be recorded, the second interviewer would write down the responses, verbatim. The second interviewer also took intensive notes for the IF, highlighting the main points of the interview. This IF, which was completed immediately after the interview, contained the following key points:

- Interview number;
- Name of organization;
- Name of interviewee;
- Duration of the interview;
- First impression;
- Changes concerning the interview guide (if any);
- Remarks;
- Points to be clarified (mentioned during the interview, but not so much clear to interviewers);
- New contacts (recommended potential respondents);
- Organization of the interview (how many phone calls, e-mails, etc. were necessary to arrange the interview);
- Overall grading.

The idea of using such a form was based on considerations of refreshing our impressions on the interview, thinking it over and better digesting the information received. In addition, the IF served as a vital source for improving the work quality of interviewers and the interview guides: I could spot my mistakes, discuss them and make an effort to eliminate them. Also, I received frequent feedback on Interview Forms from the project director, my supervisors and our colleagues in Uzbekistan. This form was introduced exclusively for internal purposes.

Most interviews were in Russian; there were a few in English and German, mainly with representatives of foreign companies and international organizations. My native language is Russian and I speak English and German. Thus, respondents were always offered a choice of languages: Russian, English, and German (for representatives of German and Swiss companies). Most of our interviews were conducted at the respondents' workplaces, with a few conducted in the office of our project partner in Almaty or in cafes and restaurants.

Throughout the fieldwork I sought to follow the common set of agreed rules. While doing interviews I took care never to start with provocative statements or ask leading questions. It was also critical for the interviewers not to talk as big experts on a topic or to demonstrate too much in-depth knowledge of a subject, as that might unnerve the respondent.

One noteworthy observation from our field study relates to the strategy for approaching potential respondents, whether the ‘snowball’ strategy and ‘direct contact’ (as explained above). In the case of Kazakhstan, 65 per cent of the respondents were approached by the snowball method, and the remaining 35 per cent by direct communication. The striking difference between the two strategies was that ‘snowball’ respondents appeared eager to talk, and would share important and relevant information. They showed a high degree of trust in us, were respectful and interested in our academic research. By contrast, when respondents – except for public officials – were approached directly, many of them agreed to be interviewed, but they often proved rather reluctant to talk much or provide full, rich answers. They tried to look interested, and asked a few questions; however, they provided mainly short answers and sometimes tried to rush through the entire process. This experience underscored the importance of personal relations and trust in the context of Central Asia. If someone had recommended a person, that basically entailed an ‘obligation’ to meet with us and fully satisfy our research needs by giving almost a perfect interview. Trust proved to be central in that regard.

Why, then, did the respondents whom I contacted directly agree to be interviewed in the first place? I think that there are three major reasons. First of all, agreeing was a sign of transparency: all respondents wanted to show that their company was transparent, could be easily accessed by a third party, and that an interview could be easily arranged as long as this did not contradict official policy. Public relations increasingly matter in Kazakhstan, and so many persons agreed to be interviewed – but most these interviews proved to be of low quality, as the respondents’ main goal was simply to express consent and accessibility, not really to share relevant information. Second, since the research team represented a foreign project, many respondents were interested in establishing contact with us. It is currently ‘trendy’ and may offer various economic opportunities for local companies to develop relations with foreign partners. Third, the country has a deeply rooted culture of hospitality, so sometimes people agreed to talk to us merely out of politeness. The issue of hospitality in Central Asia has been mentioned already. My field study confirmed the point that researchers should recognize ‘hospitality concerns’ as an important element in conducting fieldwork in Kazakhstan.

Even though most of the interviews with directly contacted respondents were not particularly rich in information or comprehensive, I did not eliminate them from the overall sample. The selection of interviews for my analysis is based not on the sampling strategy. It is based on a system of grades (see subsection 4.6.5). That said, more than half of the interviews with directly contacted respondents scored relatively poorly (less than eight) on this scale.

4.6.4. Recording statistics

Most respondents agreed for the interview to be recorded; 148 interviews out of 159 were recorded. The 11 interviewees were reluctant to be taped for various reasons, generally not explained to us.

In most cases I came to understand the underlying reasons for not wanting to be taped in the course of the interview. For many respondents, it was the issue of sensitivity as well as lack of trust in us, the interviewers, possibly because of previous negative experiences. In line with the ethical framework I did not insist on recording; as explained, the second interviewer would then try to write down the responses word by word. Nevertheless, the fact that 148 interviewees out of 159 agreed to be taped demonstrates a very positive trend in terms of general openness of elite respondents in Kazakhstan and transparency in sharing important information.

4.6.5. Measuring the quality of interviews: grading scale

The grading scale was introduced at the very beginning of the fieldwork in order to measure the quality of the interviews according to the key quality criteria elaborated by the research team (see list below). The grading scale was intended to help to cut budget expenses, since interviews which did not score 5 on the scale would not be translated or transcribed. To make the assessment of interviews transparent, the grades and their definitions were elaborated in advance, as follows:[20]

1 – The interviewee agreed to be interviewed and arrived for the interview; however, this person provided nothing (whether intentionally or unintentionally) that could be of interest to the project. All in all, the interview was of no use to the project.

2 – The interview guide proved largely inappropriate, due to the current business activity status of the company and/or the fact that the interviewee refused to answer most of the questions or became extremely defensive. All in all, the interview was of no use to the project.

3 – The interviewee appeared to be providing falsehoods for some reason. In addition, the interviewee was defensive and refused to answer some of the questions. All in all, the interview was of no use to the project.

4 – The interviewee gave answers which were not explicit, mentioned no cases and wanted to finish the interview as soon as possible. No internal or

20 This grading scale has been elaborated jointly with Farrukh Irnazarov.

external motivations to provide an interview with better content could be observed. No data, or data of very limited value, were provided.

5 – The interview guide was covered, but some questions were either irrelevant and/or the interviewee was very reticent and the answers had to be dragged out. No explicit examples were provided, and the interview had to be firmly guided.

6 – The interview guide was covered, a minimum amount of examples and cases was provided; many fairly simple questions appeared suspicious to the respondent and thus affected the answers. However, some of the answers were full of information.

7 – Cases and examples were provided on request, answers were rather short but seemed pertinent. The respondent was not particularly willing to contribute, and skipped some questions; however, he/she provided valuable and informative answers to the questions to which he/she did respond.

8 – The interview guide was covered; however, some questions were avoided. The respondent expected many issues to be known by the interviewers and urged us to read between the lines rather than expressing everything explicitly. Most of the answers were full of information. The respondent may have not been totally frank, but did give many interesting examples and cases, and contributed to the project with the information provided.

9 – Excellent interview! The respondent covered the interview guide fully, provided many good and interesting examples, was highly willing to contribute and shared as best he or she could. Answers were frank, full of information and straight to the point, with no prevarications noticed. The interview was a great asset to the project.

10 – The respondent covered far more than the interview guide initially required, and provided with good, vivid, relevant and interesting examples and cases. Was willing to contribute, and answers were structured in a frank, logical and analytical manner. The interview was conducted in a friendly atmosphere. The interviewee exceeded expectations and the information provided was a great asset to the project.

Upon completion of each interview, the two researchers involved assigned a grade to the interview based on the above scale. In order to avoid or reduce the bias, each assigned the grade independently and discussed the grade whenever assessments did not match. In those cases, we managed to reach consensus through discussion. However, our grades generally did match, presumably due to the transparent grading criteria set at the very outset. The same grading was used by the research team in Kazakhstan and in Uzbekistan.

Out of the 159 interviews conducted in Kazakhstan, 13 scored '9' and 13 scored '10', whereas the most common grades were '6' and '7' and somewhat less common '8' (Figure 4.6). Interviews marked grey (from '5' to '1') were not used for subsequent analysis. It was inevitable that some interviews would be of low quality. It was also obvious that some respondents were deliberately telling falsehoods or were not willing to share much information. Still, of the entire sample only 15 interviews were deemed not suitable for further analysis.

Figure 4.6. Distribution of interview grades

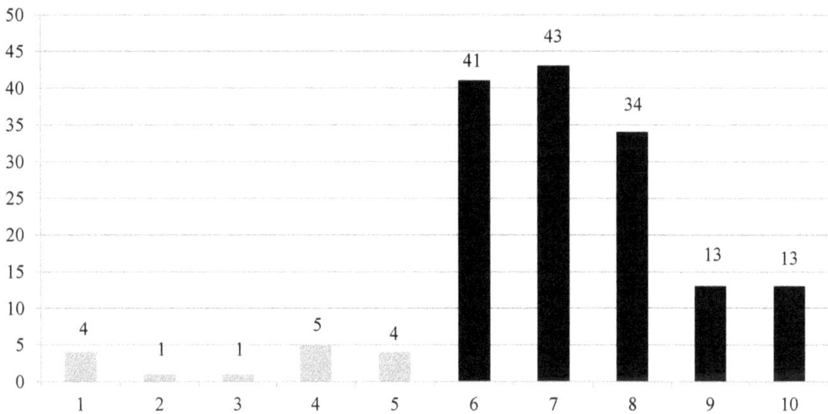

4.6.6. Dealing with various categories of respondents

The interviews involved the top management of companies, high-ranking public officials as well as prominent experts, directors (heads of departments) of international organizations. I tried to avoid interviewing middle management and administrators, as that proved useless from the very beginning. I tried first also to approach middle-range employees; but such interviews were of poor quality. The major reason is probably that middle-range employees are not accustomed to being interviewed; as a result they prefer not to be involved in such activity.[21] If it proved impossible to arrange interviews with the heads of big companies, I tried to interview their deputies.

One important classification of interviewed respondents based on fieldwork experience should be mentioned: 'easy' and 'difficult' respondents. 'Easy' respondents were readily accessible, and willing to share information. 'Difficult' respondents were far less accessible, unwilling to be interviewed, reluctant to share any information, cautious in their answers. It was time-consuming to arrange an interview with such persons. I found 'easy and 'difficult' respondents

21 Project team members faced the same problem in Uzbekistan.

across all categories, although this was always a matter of degree. In Uzbekistan, the division between 'easy' and 'difficult' respondents was much as the research team had expected: the 'easy' respondents came from private domestic companies, foreign companies, international organizations and experts, whereas 'difficult' respondents came from the categories of public officials and state-owned companies.

In Kazakhstan, however, I found a different situation: 'easy' respondents came from the categories public officials, international organizations, experts, employer associations and labour unions and foreign companies – whereas the 'difficult' respondents came from private domestic companies and state-owned companies. In fact, representatives of private domestic companies proved to be poorly accessible, whereas public employees were accessible and eager to talk. It was necessary to spend considerable amounts of time arranging interviews with local entrepreneurs. Their schedules were usually busy, hectic and unpredictable. I also faced the same schedule conditions with other categories, but nowhere was the situation as extreme as with representatives of private domestic companies. Many of the interviews were postponed and finally not conducted at all. Some interviews were repeatedly postponed – in two cases, seven and ten times.

I tried to elaborate a strategy which could minimize risks and save time: I always tried to contact representatives of private domestic companies in advance. I contacted their secretaries sometimes one day before the meeting, sometimes one hour prior to the meeting, and would receive positive confirmation. But then, on arriving to the interview location I was told that the respondent was far too busy to be able to talk to us or had just left to attend a business meeting. In some cases, I could neither wait nor re-schedule the interview again if I was offered such a possibility by the administrators, or I was politely told that it would not be possible to do an interview due to that person's busy schedule. In my view, such reactions on the part of representatives of private companies go deeper than their busy schedule. Two other factors were also involved: the intercultural aspect, and the potential benefits for the respondent. The intercultural aspect matters to the extent that some respondents were unwilling to say directly 'no' and thereby risk offending us. In fact, this factor may be of minor importance, whereas the question of potential benefits may be more important. Representatives of private domestic companies are businessmen with a rational way of thinking. When I contacted them by phone and introduced my research project, they would ask often: 'How can I benefit from it?' or 'What do you offer us in return?' They wanted their time and efforts be somehow compensated in material terms. I always responded that I would provide them with the research results; yet, this often proved insufficient for getting an interview. After receiving such responses I needed to reconsider my strategy for local entrepreneurs. I tried to present the project to them by linking it directly to probable benefits to their enterprise. I also spoke with various stakeholder groups on this issue and realized that such businessmen tend to think in material terms, so the benefits have to be tangible. Simply offering them the results of the study was useless in many cases. However, I could not do more than that, as I had decided from the very beginning not to provide any material compensation to respondents. In that way I hoped to avoid any bias, as compensated respondents could feel obligated to give some kind of answer to each question, even if they had nothing to say or did not possess relevant expertise. I wanted respondents to share with me only their real expertise.

Finally, I also faced considerable difficulties in arranging interviews with representatives of state-owned companies. The heads of state-owned companies tended to be inaccessible. In general, it was difficult to organize interviews with heads of state-owned companies due to various corporate policy restrictions. In theory it is possible, but in practice it might take several weeks until a request for an interview is considered by the administration. When I was not able to contact anyone except employees holding deputy or even middle-range positions in state-owned companies, I decided to use this opportunity and to interview them. Otherwise, I risked getting no interviews with representatives of state-owned companies at all.

Respondents in all other categories were much easier to work with. In particular, I was surprised how accessible high-ranking public employees were – I could contact them directly. Problems of power distance to public officials are gradually disappearing. Although I took care to appear as subordinate in the process of interviewing, they still treated me as an equal. For arranging interviews with public officials, both the snowball and the direct contact strategies proved successful – in fact, the latter was even more effective (see Case in Point 4.3).

Case in Point 4.3. 'Recipe' for arranging interviews with public officials

When interviewing public officials, at the end of the interview I asked politely if they could recommend other public employees for an interview. However, when I asked one respondent to recommend someone else among those whom she knew, she replied that 'personal recommendation would hardly help you approach other state employees, as they are all very busy throughout the week. Even if they agree, they would not simply find time for an interview.' Thus, after few futile attempts I realized that the snowball strategy would not always work. But I also learnt that by law in Kazakhstan, all state employees are required to respond to individual and collective requests from the public and private business, whether by telephone or via email, in a timely manner. From other public employees I learnt that the law is well enforced and everyone who sends a request almost always receives a reply. Thus, the alternative to the snowball approach became direct contact which turned out to be effective in arranging interviews with public employees.

According to my observations, public employees are becoming more and more public figures who are eager to be interviewed. Public relations increasingly matter within domestic politics. Therefore, I was able to contact high-ranking officials without serious problems. For instance, all interviewed Members of the Parliament of the Republic of Kazakhstan were contacted directly by the research team and agreed to be interviewed without delay. Some 90 per cent of the public officials I interviewed were approached directly without being personally recommended by someone else. As opposed to the interviews of directly contacted respondents, our interviews with public officials were generally of high quality. Moreover, I expected that public officials would be unwilling to deal with the few sensitive topics that were included in the interview guides. In fact, I rarely noticed any hesitance when they responded to potentially sensitive questions.

As regards overall openness and expression of interest to the project and interviews, four categories stand out: experts, foreign companies, international organizations and public officials. The reason was presumably that giving interviews and being interviewed are part of their daily activities, and they are well accustomed to this practice. This was noticeable in their behaviour. Often respondents from these categories were 'professional' interviewees, well-prepared for a long interview and aware of how to provide concise and relevant answers. By contrast, representatives of state-owned companies and private domestic companies often asked us before the interview what kind of answers they should provide – long or short. In the beginning of the interview they were often nervous and tended to behave rather artificially. By the middle of the interview they could relax because they had learnt what was expected of them. This probably reflects the fact that representatives of these four categories are more frequently interviewed than representatives of the two other categories (private domestic companies and state-owned companies). This may also help to explain why representatives of private domestic companies were generally so inaccessible for interviews.

4.7. Caveats and limitations in data collection

4.7.1. Methodological problems

Most of the problems in data collection process and how I dealt with them have already been mentioned. Still, three methodological problems should be noted here. First, one of the major limitations of the field study was the financial crisis of 2008, which had severely affected the economy. Most of the economic sectors suffered from the world economic crisis (Kairlenov 2009). During the interviews many respondents became emotional when talking about the crisis and its consequences. Those entrepreneurs who suffered from the crisis held negative views on development of the economic system; their perceptions were greatly influenced by the negative impacts of the crisis on their businesses. Their answers could become biased and misleading, as these respondents focused only on the short-term impact of the crisis, whereas prior to the crisis their firms had experienced 15 years of successful economic growth. They often drew parallels between the overall economic development and their current entrepreneurial downturn. In order to better elicit the interrelation between the economic crisis and respondents' answers, I elaborated special questions. In particular, when interviewing representatives of private companies I posed two crisis-related questions at the end of the interview: *Could you mention two things which changed in the economic or political environment since the crisis? And how did the crisis impact your company?*

It became clear during the interviews that some respondents directly or indirectly attached special importance to the economic crisis and how it influenced their business. However, by asking these questions at the end of the interview I sought to make sure whether the crisis was important for them. It allowed for double-checking because many respondents mentioned only the crisis-related problems of other businessmen. Asking them directly about the impact of the crisis on their own activities helped clarify whether their views were based on personal experience or on what they had heard from other businessmen. In fact, more than half of entrepreneurs interviewed shared the view that the consequences of the crisis were significant and negative; there were only few who held that the crisis presented an opportunity for them and had a positive impact on the economy.

Second, I sought to always maintain a balance between flexibility and structure while conducting interviews. It could be difficult to adjust the interview guides according to the specific area of expertise of a respondent. Instead, I conducted the interviews in a way that allowed me to ask representatives of each category the same set of questions. If in the course of an interview it became evident that the respondent had in-depth knowledge and expertise in a certain area of my interest, I proceeded to ask more detailed questions about that particular area.

Third, a minor problem with which I eventually coped but which should be acknowledged was that different respondents may attach different meanings to the same terms, and this might confuse the further process of data analysis (Patton 2002). Thus, at a later stage while using content-analysis one may end up with some codes that are technically similar, but have different meanings, sometimes even opposing ones (ibid). In conducting the interviews I always kept this concern in mind and asked questions to check exactly what an interviewee meant by a specific term.

4.7.2. Interview ethics

According to Kuzmits (2008: 40), 'cultural sensibility, transparency on intentions and honesty about competencies are essential of ethical dimension of field research' in Central Asia. I always tried to adhere to those principles while doing the field study. An important consideration was to follow the ethical rules, because it was crucial not to do anything that could prove harmful to my respondents. Before each interview I guaranteed absolute confidentiality unless a person agreed to be quoted personally (which was only occasionally the case in Kazakhstan). I promised to send respondents the recorded piece of the interview if they asked for it. It was critical for us not to pose a threat to any respondent by misusing the information obtained. Adhering to the principles of interview ethics also relates to the analysis of information. For instance, in analysing the data I tried to avoid saying something like 'the manager of the Agricultural Union claims...' If this were the only union that existed and worked for the rights of farmers, it would be easy to trace the identity of the respondent. Information should be presented neutrally, like 'a representative of the agricultural industry argues...', so it would not be possible to identify the person's identity.

4.7.3. Quality criteria: validity and reliability

To ensure validity and reliability of the obtained results, I employed various strategies. Validity in qualitative research means that the methods employed helped to obtain necessary information (Kvale 2007: 122–126). Reliability is one of the evaluation criteria of the quality of a study, and is closely interrelated with the validity criterion (Golafshani 2003: 601). In my qualitative study I employed a quantitative approach to measure reliability.

Assessing the degree of validity requires the researcher to provide a detailed step-by-step description of what was done in the field during data collection (Nuttall et al. 2011: 162; Teddlie and Tashakkori 2009). In the previous subsections, the entire process of data collection was presented in detail. I largely achieved the goal of collecting the data according to my sample, covering all stratification criteria.

As to the degree of *external validity*, it is difficult to assess it as my sampling criteria were not designed so as to yield a representative sample in quantitative terms. Rather, its structure aimed at presenting the views and perceptions of the main groups of economic actors and decision-makers, industries and countries so as to be able to speak about equal representation of various actors' perceptions on Kazakhstan's market-oriented economic development. Moreover, it should be acknowledged that samples not obtained by random sampling cannot be considered representative.

I was able to achieve the research objectives that had been set, although I must acknowledge that not all categories were fully covered, as some industries and countries were slightly under-represented. Still, except for the generally under-represented category of 'state-owned companies', I was able to achieve high representation of all levels in the sample. When using the snowball approach, I selected only those recommended respondents who met the criteria of the sample – in target categories, target employees, target industries, target countries and target companies by size. Likewise with my use of direct contact with respondents: I selected only those who met the criteria of the sample. Using both approaches enabled me to enhance the validity of the data obtained.

Moreover, I was able to gain access to the most important respondents and conducted a large number of high-quality interviews according to the grading criteria outlined above. As noted most interviews scored six or higher, with only 15 scoring five or lower (Figure 4.6). Thus, 144 interviews qualified for an analysis. The process of data collection went largely according to plan. This enabled the presentation of perceptions of a large number of economic actors regarding the type of market economy in Kazakhstan. As a result, some general conclusions regarding the type of the economy can be drawn – with certain caveats, as mentioned and discussed earlier and will be touched on later in section 5.5.

Employing the various interviewing strategies described above, I tried to provide all necessary conditions under which each respondent would be authentic in his or her responses. However, it should be acknowledged that no data should be viewed as being more or less authentic than other. And even if a person is authentic in his or her perceptions and tells what he or she believes, the information provided may still differ from the actual facts and events. Thus, to find out whether the information provided in the interviews matches or contradicts the actual facts, I employed the methods of *observation* and *investigator triangulation*. The second interviewer and I made notes on respondents' psychological behaviour during the interview. These notes, and the media analysis of actual information, helped to establish whether the information provided was authentic. I would make notes not only about a respondent's behaviour, but also about interesting facts or events mentioned in the course of the interview. In order to learn more about specific issues or facts I used the media or internet sources, or spoke with relevant experts. As far as I can judge, in most interviews the information provided was authentic.

Various triangulation methods employed in this research were designed to complement each other and achieve a high degree of validity and authenticity. The method of *investigator triangulation* was utilized. Since the study was conducted simultaneously in Kazakhstan and in Uzbekistan, and the researchers used identical methods for data collection, I was able to double-check the flow of the entire process of data collection and compare my own observations with those of my colleagues. The project phases during which investigator triangulation was employed were as follows:

1) *In September 2009*, the whole research team gathered at Issyk-Kul, Kyrgyzstan, in order to discuss the first conducted interviews in Kazakhstan and Uzbekistan. By then, nine interviews had been conducted in Kazakhstan and we could share our first field-study experiences. Some questions were removed because they were sensitive, or were inapplicable to local elite respondents. New questions were formulated and added to the interview guides. The same revision procedure relates to interviewing as a process. Importantly, on the basis of our first experience I adjusted the criteria for conduct in interviewing and in implementing the observation method.

2) *In April 2010*, I spent two weeks in Tashkent, Uzbekistan, in order to ensure comparability of methods for data collection and compare our observations. During that period I conducted several interviews with Uzbek respondents, jointly with Uzbek colleagues. This helped to identify gaps in the strategies of data collection used by the two teams as well as facilitate the use of methods at a later stage. This exchange of experiences, ideas and observations proved extremely helpful in improving our interviewing techniques.

3) *In May 2010,* an Uzbek researcher came to Astana to support the Kazakhstan team in conducting interviews with public officials. The feedback given by this Uzbek colleague on the use of data collection methods in Kazakhstan allowed us to compare observations and identify points for further improvement. Eight interviews with public officials and experts were conducted interchangeably (I switched the role of the leading interviewer) with the Uzbek colleague in Astana.

4) *In June 2010*, part of our research team from Germany went first to Uzbekistan and then to Kazakhstan in order to check and further ensure consistency of the interview methods employed. They also conducted several interviews and their contribution further enhanced the consistency and reliability of the methods employed.

5) *In June 2010*, seeking to improve interview quality, I organized a workshop jointly with our local partner in Almaty. I invited prominent

experts in order to present and discuss the preliminary analysis of data collection. Through this active interaction with invited experts and their feedback, we enhanced the consistency of the methods used for data collection and improved the validity of the data obtained. Consulting with experts at various stages of the research process on methods and analysis of data obtained has been an appropriate tool for improving the quality of interviews (Rabionet 2011: 564), thereby obtaining more valid data. Based on these experts' feedback, I incorporated important remarks and comments into the interview guides and strategies of communication with respondents.

6) *In June 2011*, an expert workshop was organized in Göttingen, Germany. Prominent experts on Central Asia and project researchers were invited. The main intention was to conduct a preliminary analysis of the interviews and discuss them. The workshop helped identify new theoretical approaches in our research (see subsection 4.8.2) and the strategy for subsequent interview analysis.

The use of the investigator triangulation method also helped to enhance the *reliability* of data collection methods and data. According to Patton (2002, in Golafshani 2003: 602), reliability is 'a consequence of the validity in a study.' Importantly, trustworthiness is essential for ensuring the validity and reliability of the data obtained (Seale 1999: 266, in Golafshani 2003: 601). At every stage of the research process I tried to make sure that this condition is met.

I employed the inter-rater reliability approach as one of the approximations of reliability in a qualitative study. For that aim, investigator triangulation was applied as described above. Inter-rater reliability means 'evaluating the degree of agreement of two observers observing the same phenomenon in the same setting' (Teddlie and Tashakkori 2009: 212). Two, or sometimes more, researchers conducted interviews in a similar manner, using identical methods and technique with respondents of the same category (possessing similar expertise). After that I was able to compare our methods and the data obtained, and if necessary to adjust our data collection methods accordingly.

In this cross-sectional study, in order to ensure reliability of the methods employed at all stages of the project, we constantly exchanged ideas on concepts, notions and terms used in conducting semi-standardized interviews. However, I also recognize that in qualitative research it is impossible to achieve complete reliability (Carcary 2009: 14). Even if respondents provide similar answers or researchers' observations are similar to each other, they will never be totally identical (ibid). All I could do was to seek to minimize the differences in our methods and interpretation of observations.

4.8. Qualitative data analysis

4.8.1. Preparing the data for analysis

After 159 interviews had been conducted, the next step was to transcribe the 148 audio-files from the recorded interviews. However, as described in subsection 4.6.5, only those interviews that scored six or higher were transcribed (144 interviews in total).[22] When transcribing these interviews we followed the same guidelines: interviews were transcribed verbatim in their entirety, and any para-verbal information was also added.

The next step was to translate the Russian-language interviews into English, as it was planned that the entire team should be able to use them and there were some project researchers who did not speak Russian. This was done by a group of translators, selected on a competitive basis. The quality of translated interviews was randomly checked at each stage of the translation process. Importantly, these translators also participated in conducting semi-structured interviews in Kazakhstan and in Uzbekistan. This was a distinct advantage, as they were highly familiar with the nuances of the respondents in Kazakhstan and could translate the interviews as closely as possible to the original text. Nevertheless, it was not always possible to find full equivalents to the original words and phrases, and in many instances it was a challenge to provide correct translations in English. Indeed, issues relating to language equivalence are recognized as an important concern in cross-cultural studies (Matsumoto and van de Vijver 2011: 9; International Test Commission 2010; van de Vijver and Tanzer 2004). He and van de Vijver (2012: 8) note that there is a problem that certain words in one language lack equivalents in other languages, which complicates the translation and data analysis processes. Therefore, it is necessary to acknowledge that the translation process may add a layer of interpretation to the original data.

To minimize this risk, the translators took care to place the original Russian terms in brackets for those words and sentences that were difficult to translate into English. If there were problems with understanding certain translated words or there were doubts regarding equivalent translation, I always referred to the original material in Russian. This helped to ensure that original words were understood correctly. It turned out that in several instances the translation was not fully equivalent to the original text. In these cases I always stuck to the original data and tried to find an equivalent translation for a particular word.

Thus, this strategy proved effective and minimized the risk of incorrect understanding of the material and avoided potential data distortions.

22 The grading scale was introduced at the very beginning of the fieldwork in order to measure the quality of the interviews according to the key criteria elaborated by the research team (see subsection 4.6.5).

Furthermore, para-verbal information was also used to ensure translation accuracy. It was also helpful for better understanding the context of respondents' answers. This strategy facilitated the analysis of the interviews. Therefore, I was aware of methodological caveats and challenges at every stage of the data analysis process. Often referring to the material in original language makes it possible to argue that concept equivalence was achieved to a significant extent.

4.8.2. Preliminary analysis of interviews

After the interviews were transcribed and translated, an expert workshop was organized in Germany in June 2011. Prior to this workshop, project researchers and experts conducted a preliminary analysis of the interviews. Based on the results of the workshop, it was concluded that the VoC framework could not fully comprehend the type of economic system which has evolved over the past 20 years. Since the VoC approach is based on company-centred assumptions, it fails to explain the massive role of the state in coordinating economic processes (see also subsection 3.3.7). The VoC approach had served as a central starting point of my research, as its theoretical framework helped identify key areas of this study – but it could not fully bring out what type of a market economy has been emerging in Kazakhstan.

Given the preliminary analysis of the workshop, the VoC framework was complemented by a second analytical approach, a 'core–periphery' framework, which could cover other important aspects and account for an active role of the state in the economy, allowing the research questions in this study to be more fully answered. The inclusion of this analytical framework resulted from the preliminary technical analysis of the interviews. This preliminary analysis as well as the inclusion of new aspects to the research became the data-driven part of the entire analysis of the data which I obtained during the study.

A preliminary examination of the interviews revealed aspects pointing to two types of economies co-existing within the economic system. The first type is a 'core' part of the economy, dominated by the state; the second type is a 'periphery' part, which is a more market-oriented type in which private actors enjoy considerable economic freedom. Preliminary analysis of the interviews done by experts and workshop participants showed that most state-owned companies and large foreign and domestic private companies belong to the 'core' and are influenced, directly and indirectly, by state regulatory mechanisms. Most private small and medium-sized enterprises (SMEs) belong to the 'periphery' part of the economy which exhibits features of a market economy, with little state involvement. Before applying content analysis, it is important to acknowledge that this framework has been used at the general level; it is assumed that there are 'state-led' and 'market-oriented' parts of the economy.

In order to better understand the nature of the emerging market economy it is necessary to account for the role of the state in the economic realm and state–business interaction in the country. The VoC approach does not explicitly account for the role of the state and state–business interaction (data-driven aspects). However, as the preliminary analysis revealed, accounting for these aspects is central for understanding how the economy is shaped. Therefore, based on the results of this workshop, my analysis of the data obtained was structured around theory-driven and data-driven categories. I used content analysis for data analysis, as this method helped identify distinct characteristics of these two types of the economy. At that stage, it was not possible to define the 'core' and 'periphery' in further detail, as further detailed characteristics were unknown, but the subsequent content analysis helped identify the distinct characteristics of these two types of the economy. The results of content analysis provided in Chapter 5 help characterize in detail the 'core' and 'periphery' parts of the economy. After defining the key features of the two parts of the economy, it was possible to identify what type of market economy is emerging in Kazakhstan – which has been the major aim of this work.

My coding frame for content analysis was mainly based upon seven key questions (Table 4.2), which were elaborated during the workshop by experts and project participants and based upon the preliminary analysis of the interviews. The coding frame also included the key aspects of the VoC approach, which, however, played a supplementary role in my analysis.

These seven questions target the two countries studied during the research project: Kazakhstan and Uzbekistan. For the purposes of my research I focused the analysis and composed the coding frame for content analysis around questions 3, 4, 5 and 7. There are two reasons which explain and justify the selection of these four questions for data analysis. First, as follows from the preliminary analysis of the interviews, the aspects embedded within these questions were identified as most important and crucial ones by respondents. These aspects are both theory-based (based on the VoC approach) and data-driven (see also subsection 4.8.5 below). Second, according to the experts at the workshop, these four questions were more suitable in the context of Kazakhstan than the other three. The questions point to key aspects of state–business interaction, and shedding light on them would help identify in detail the key 'core' and 'periphery' characteristics of the economy. Thus, I hold that answering these particular questions should help in identifying the type of market-oriented economy emerging in Kazakhstan.

Table 4.2. Seven questions

1. With whom do 'core' and 'periphery' buy their supplies and equipment? – public procurement system and price control – do actors outside the company/organization influence these decisions? – is it market-driven or non-market-driven?
2. How do 'core' and 'periphery' hire and fire people? – what are the key requirements for hiring and firing people? – are there differences between the public and the private sector? – which incentives make public officials stay in the public sector considering that salaries and social package are usually much more competitive in the private sector?
3. How do objectives of state and business actors interact? – level of interaction – state attitude towards business (foreign and domestic) and business (foreign and domestic) attitude towards the state
4. What are the major problems facing business (foreign and domestic)? – what are the most common problems facing private business? – which instruments are used by business to solve them? – are problems and solutions different across industries? – formal and informal ways of achieving goals – are businesses failing or expanding in specific industries? Which ones and why?
5. Has the scope of state involvement increased or decreased over time period? – how and why did the shift in various degree of involvement occur? – what are the main mechanisms that the state uses to intervene in the economy? – what are/were the particular stages of state involvement?
6. Constellation of coordinating actors and pattern of their changing duties – what are the key ministries and public agencies responsible for economic coordination? – what are their tasks? Have their duties undergone any changes over time period? – why did these changes occur? – how and why does rotation take place in the public sector?
7. Interaction within the private sector – how do companies within the private sector interact with each other (degree of cooperation, competition, regulation of competition, mergers and acquisitions)? – do size of business, activity, industry, state regulation requirements matter for cooperation or the lack thereof between private companies with each other? – what is the influence of other market players (labour unions and employer associations) on inter-firm and state–business relations?

Questions 3, 4, 6, 7, which are relevant for the present study, were refined as follows (see also Chapter 1):

1. What is the role of the state in steering economic processes in Kazakhstan and how does the interaction between the state and private business take place? (Based on Questions 3, 4 and 6)
2. How do relations between private economic actors shape the emerging economy in Kazakhstan? (Question 7)
3. What is the role of other market players, such as labour unions and employer associations, in influencing state–business interaction and in shaping economic relations in the country? (Question 7)

4.8.3. Methods for data analysis: qualitative content analysis and frequency analysis

It would have been possible to use two methods for data analysis in this research – conceptual coding and content-analysis. However, for the purpose of this research, I used qualitative content analysis as the main method of data analysis, because the data analysis must be systematic (Schreier 2012). I have large masses of data, equal to 2400 pages of A4 format (on average, each interview is 15 pages long). With such masses of data and trying to keep track of everything, ‘it is easy to get lost’ in the data, as Schreier (2012: 4) notes. The major advantage of content analysis is that it avoids the confusion associated with processing huge amount of data and forces the researcher to focus only on the selected and relevant aspects of the material (Schreier 2012: 8–9). Answering my research question required systematizing the results obtained, then selecting only those parts of the data which are relevant to the research question. It is also necessary to have a systematic overview of respondents’ perceptions and answers to questions, in identifying the kind of a market economy now emerging. From the classified and systematized data, it will be possible to show how respondents answered particular questions. The use of content analysis is perfectly suited to these purposes.

In addition to content analysis, I also used frequency analysis, a method that helped me to present the results of content analysis. Using content analysis helped compose frequency tables of respondents’ answers and present them, along with direct quotations, as my research results. The use of frequency tables facilitated the presentation of the results. In my analysis, I also identified patterns in respondents’ perceptions and how their various characteristics – academic and professional background, place of work, personal affiliation, type of company’s activity, country of origin, status, position – influence their views. To demonstrate patterns in respondents’ perceptions I used cross-tables, a specific type of frequency table that helps to illustrate certain patterns between and within different categories of respondents.

An important concern relates to the analysis of the data obtained and the use of frequency tables. From the results shown in frequency tables, I will be able to make general conclusions to the whole economy in case respondents' opinions largely coincide. In fact, if respondents from different categories hold the same views and perceptions, this would mean that my conclusions gain more validity.

If perceptions diverge, the reasons why they may differ, within each category and among them, should be identified. There might be systematic variation in respondents' official position and status. That will make it necessary to identify patterns in particular perceptions of respondents on the basis of their academic and professional background or place of work, personal affiliation, type of company's activity, country of origin, status or position. For instance, theoretically, it may well be that when it comes to the assessment of the state's role in the economy, most public officials will deem the level of state involvement in economic processes to be low, whereas most private entrepreneurs may well view the level of state involvement as excessive. In that case the perceptions of public officials may be explained by the fact that they, as representatives of the state, cannot express themselves differently as to the level of involvement. By contrast, private entrepreneurs deal with state and public agencies in their daily activities; if they encounter problems, they may regard the level of state involvement as excessive. Thus, the perceptions of public officials might be influenced by their affiliation with the state, whereas the perceptions of entrepreneurs might relate to the type of their activity and the type of interaction with public agencies.

If the perceptions of respondents differ and are largely category-specific, that means that I say that these respondents argued in this or that way because they possess a certain status, or that there are other reasons that could influence their opinions and perceptions. In that case, it becomes more difficult to generalize about the findings. They can only be generalized separately for each category or group of categories of respondents, whereas generalizing for the entire economy is far more difficult and requires further research. So, in this context the interpretations should be treated with caution.

4.8.4. Selected interviews for analysis

The total number of interviews selected for analysis was 48 out of 159 and there were two main criteria for their selection. The first criterion is that of equal representation of all seven categories of respondents. According to the second criterion, the best interviews from highly represented categories of respondents, scoring from seven to ten, were selected and analysed (see the grading scale in subsection 4.6.5). Therefore, for the purposes of data analysis, the eight best interviews from categories public officials, representatives of international organizations, representatives of private domestic and foreign companies were selected. Furthermore, three interviews with representatives of employer associations and labour unions and three interviews with representatives of state-owned companies were also content analysed to ensure the inclusion of all the categories of respondents, both highly represented and under-represented. The overall number of selected interviews for content analysis was 38 in these six categories.

Regarding the category of experts, the ten best interviews from this category were not analysed via content analysis, but used in their entirety without reducing the data. The expert interviews were the most information-rich interviews. At the same time, they appeared to be less structured. Often, an expert would focus on his or her area of expertise, disregarding other sections of the interview guide in which he or she had little or no expertise. Sometimes experts gave an answer to one particular question or told a story some three to four pages long. Thus it would be difficult to analyse expert interviews according to the structure of my coding frame, as many issues were not covered by the interviewees. And yet, the major value of these expert interviews was that experts could provide in-depth analysis of many areas as well as important aspects of state–business interaction and economic development. They introduced a more detailed and more profound layer of analysis of certain events, providing important context information helpful for interpreting the findings of the content analysis. Therefore, considering these points and not wishing to reduce this rich data, I used the expert interviews for background and context information, with the stories and direct quotations given by experts complementing and accompanying the absolute frequency tables and cross-tables composed via the content analysis. The information provided in the expert interviews helped to supplement and better contextualize the results of the content analysis.

The criteria used in selecting interviews for analysis became clear only after all interviews were finished. It was impossible to say *a priori* exactly how many interviews would be in each category. Based on the grading scheme used to rank the interviews, only those interviews which scored seven or higher were selected for analysis. Interviews scoring six or lower were disregarded, as they would be of little or no use to the analysis. The rate of excellent interviews (scoring nine or ten) was rather high in comparison to the low-quality interviews (scoring from one to six). Thus, 48 units of analysis (interviews) were employed, and 38 units of analysis were analysed via content analysis.

Furthermore, based on the assumption that the economy exhibits features of two distinct subsystems, the *core* and *periphery* systems, the company interviews were selected for content analysis according to the 'core', 'mixed' and 'periphery' types. From the preliminary analysis of interviews, it was possible to select interviewed companies according to this analytical framework.

The 'mixed' category was used for companies which do not belong to either the core or the periphery but which clearly exhibit some elements of both subsystems. Moreover, if there were difficulties in assigning a certain company to one of these categories, it was also placed in the 'mixed' category. This division represented an important step for analysing the selected interviews in-depth. The categorization of interviews helped to better identify various patterns in respondents' perceptions. In total, eight interviews with representatives of private domestic companies, eight with foreign companies, and three with state-owned companies (19 interviews) were classified according to the core–periphery framework: seven companies in the 'core' (three companies representing the petroleum sector, two telecommunications, one the logistics sector, and one the finance industry), eight in the 'periphery' (three companies in construction, two in digital technologies, one in trade, one in consultancy, and one in manufacturing) and four in the 'mixed' category (one company in construction, one in service industry, one in trade, and one in finance). Public officials, experts and representatives of labour unions and employer associations are not part of this classification because, unlike companies, they are not economic actors in the strict sense of the term.

In order to ensure data confidentiality and protect the anonymity of the respondents, all interviews were assigned special codes:

EAR – Representative of an Employer Association
Ex – Experts
FCR – Representative of a Foreign Company
IOR – Representative of an International Organization
LUR – Representative of a Labour Union
PDCR – Representative of a Private Domestic Company
PO – Public Official
SOCR – Representative of a State-Owned Company

As a next step, a number was assigned to each selected interview. Thus, quotations of respondents' opinions and perceptions could be used without threatening their anonymity. For example, one representative of an international organization said the following:

> There has been relatively strong government control of food-stuff, which was introduced in 2008, after the first wave of the crisis in Kazakhstan, to prevent high inflation and a negative social impact. It worked reasonably well.

This respondent will be presented as follows: 'IOR8' – IOR meaning 'representative of an international organization' and 8 referring to the number of this respondent on the list of selected interviewees, available only to the author.

Removing the respondent's name does not always suffice to ensure confidentiality because the content of a quote may reveal the identity of the respondent or the company. If a respondent talks about his or her own company and describes its size, number of projects, country of origin, activities undertaken or gives a concrete example of a problem the company dealt with, then its business partners can easily identify the speaker and the company. I have given consideration to this important concern in presenting the results of my study, and have sought to ensure that it is not possible to ascertain the respondent's identity from the direct quotes provided. I have provided only quotes that would not reveal that person's identity, or I have omitted specific phrases. Respondents' views are not always presented in the form of direct quotes: in several cases I have re-phrased statements and then provided the coded reference to the respondent.

4.8.5. Constructing the coding frame

This section describes how the main categories and subcategories (see Appendix 4 for the coding frame) were derived. The structure of the coding frame is presented in detail, including the number of levels and how all categories and subcategories relate to each other. It should be noted that the categories and subcategories described below were used in the main coding; they do not include the subcategories used for pilot coding.

First, I introduced the main overarching data-driven category *core–periphery* (A)[23] into my content analysis, which includes the following subcategories: 'core', 'periphery' and 'mixed'. This main category relates to the overall analytical concept adopted in the study for the data analysis phase and is embedded within research questions 3, 4, 5 and 7 presented in Table 4.2. The first value 'core' implies the part of Kazakhstan's market-oriented economy which is led by the state, characterized by high degree of state involvement in regulating and coordinating economic processes and providing investment conditions for economic actors. The second value 'periphery' implies the part of the economy which is driven by the market, characterized by a low to medium degree of state involvement in regulating and coordinating economic processes and providing investment conditions for economic actors. Finally, the third value 'mixed' relates to the situation when the respondent explains the features of both the 'core' and 'periphery' parts or when it is hard to recognize about which particular part of the economy the respondents speaks. This main category underlies all subsequent main categories and subcategories below and it was applied to all units of coding in the coding scheme. All 423 units of coding were analysed and classified according to this main category.

23 Coding letter in the coding frame.

When presenting direct quotes of respondents in Chapter 5, I introduce another coding level based on the overarching data-driven 'core–periphery' category of my coding frame. According to this coding scheme I indicate whether a respondent representing the company category belongs to the 'core' or the 'periphery'. Moreover, I indicate whether a respondent talks about the 'core' or the 'periphery'. In the example below this is indicated as follows:

> 'Red tape' is greater in banking sector than in any other industry (FCR 1/Core: Core).

FCR 1/Core: Core means 'representative of a foreign company' (FCR 1) belongs to the 'core' and talks about the 'core'. The second example:

> Q: *Would you agree with the argument that in order to be successful one needs to be in constant cooperation with the government?*
> R: Yes, I would say so. To have things done, it is necessary to have friendly relationship with the government… (IOR23/Core)

IOR23/Core – the respondent represents an international organization and not a company. Thus she does not belong to any of three categories ('core', 'periphery', 'mixed'), and 'core' means that she talks about the 'core' part of the economy. Furthermore, if a respondent represents a company in the unrecognizable 'mixed' category and talks about the 'periphery', then it is indicated as 'FCR1'/Mixed: Periphery'. If a respondents talks both about the 'core' and the 'periphery', it is indicated as: 'Core–Periphery'.

This categorization helped to better identify patterns in respondents' views and perceptions, shedding light on the essence of the hybrid economy evolving in Kazakhstan.

Aside from the overarching 'core–periphery' category, I chose three main categories to describe the type of market-oriented economy in Kazakhstan: *state–business interaction, inter-firm relations* and *the role of other market players.* Only the interview material relating to these key categories was analysed, with *state–business interaction* as the main focus of analysis. The category *state–business interaction* is partly data-driven and partly theory-driven, whereas *inter-firm relations* and *the role of other market players* are largely theory-driven. Therefore, as explained, a mixed inductive-deductive strategy was used to elaborate subcategories in the coding frame.

State–business interaction: From the preliminary analysis, the dimension state–business interaction emerged as highly important, as it concerns interrelations between the state and private business. It covers the role of the state in the economy; the level of state involvement over time; success criteria for private business; reasons for differing treatment of small and large businesses; firm's preferred type of investment policy; and instruments for solving problems facing private business. The rationale behind composing these categories is based on the preliminary analysis of the interviews during the expert workshop (see subsection 4.8.2) which showed them to be the key aspects of state–business interaction. This main category corresponds to research questions 3, 4, 5 presented in Table 4.2.

The role of the state in the economy (1.1)[24] is a theory-driven category. It refers to how respondents perceive the role of the state in the economy, in terms of regulation (monetary policy, design, implementation and enforcement of laws), of discretionary (industrial policy, subsidies, etc.) and of inter-firm coordination policies. It has the following values: 'dominant', 'moderate', 'non-intervention'. It is important to find out how respondents perceive the level of state involvement and coordination in the economy, as it can help identify the key characteristics of the 'core' and the 'periphery'.

The next data-driven category, the level of state involvement over time (1.2) extends the first subcategory by helping to identify how the role of the state and the level of involvement in the private sector changed over time. I divided the 19 years of Kazakhstan's independence into two periods (two subcategories): 1991–2000 (1.2.1) and 2000–2010 (1.2.2), each with the following values: 'the involvement of the state is excessive'; 'the involvement is moderate'; and 'little involvement' of the state.

The third data-driven subcategory, success criteria for private business (1.3), helps to show whether constant communication with the state is an important factor for the success of private business. It has three values: 'communication with the state is crucial'; 'communication with the state is necessary only in some situations and is not always a key factor for success'; 'no communication with the state is required' for private business to achieve its goals and solve problems. This subcategory helps to indicate whether private business can operate independently and successfully within the economic realm, or if state support is really necessary.

The fourth data-driven subcategory, reasons for the differing treatment of small/large businesses (1.4), helps reveal why the state treats various types of companies in a different way. The reasons may be as follows: size of the business, meaning that if a business is small, it is of little or no interest in terms of potential economic benefits for the state and vice versa; company ownership, meaning that if a company is foreign/private vs. state-owned, it has more benefits because the state involves less in its activities and vice versa; strategic considerations, meaning that the government is interested in cooperation with companies working in strategic industries; lack of state capacity, meaning that the state lacks sufficient capacity to coordinate different types of private business equally, and focuses on companies from industries highly profitable to the entire economy; the merging of state interests with business interests,

24 Coding number of the category here and in the subsequent categories and subcategories as used in the coding frame.

meaning that when the state has certain stakes in big businesses, they are more likely to receive necessary support.

The fifth theory-driven category, the firm's preferred type of investment policy (1.5) was introduced to help identify the type of strategy private companies choose, based on the conditions provided by the state. There are three values: 'long-term investment policy', 'short-term investment policy' and 'other'. 'Long-term policy' (three or more years) indicates a private company is confident in its future prospects because the security of their investments is guaranteed and appropriate conditions are provided by the state. 'Short-term investment policy' means that a private company is not confident in the security of its investments, as the appropriate conditions for long-term investment are not provided, meaning they plan only for the short term (one or two years). Moreover, the investment regime set by the government is somewhat unpredictable and the rules are constantly changing. In an LME, private firms will prefer short-term investments due to the structure of the financial markets, whereas in a CME private firms will invest on a long-term basis. Knowing the preferred type of investment strategy helps to determine whether Kazakhstan's economy exhibits the features of an LME or a CME.

The sixth data-driven subcategory, instruments for solving problems facing private business with the state (1.6), helps identify the tools that private companies use in case of problems or conflicts while dealing with the state. There are four major sets of tools. First, 'the use of state mechanisms' means that private companies interact directly with the state/and or resort to the economic courts in order to find a solution to their problems. Second, private companies may use 'domestic business mechanisms', meaning that they use negotiation mechanisms and/or communication platforms such as various entrepreneur forums or business associations. Third, private companies may turn to 'international platforms' such as international economic courts or various international associations in Kazakhstan or abroad. And fourth, depending on the problem, private companies may use 'a combination of tools'.

Inter-firm relations: This second dimension includes the following subcategories: type of interaction between private firms; key criteria for interaction; regulation of competition; merger and acquisitions; instruments for solving problems between private companies. This dimension covers relations between an enterprise, and notably its suppliers or clients, aimed at securing stable demand for its products, and access to technology. This is important in view of the implications of the state's indirect influence over private firms. With the example of the interaction between private firms, we can identify the nature of inter-firm relations, the role of the state in coordinating relations between private firms, and better understand the key characteristics of the 'core' and 'periphery' parts of the economy. This main category corresponds to research question 7 (see Table 4.2).

The first theory-driven subcategory within this dimension is the type of interaction (2.1), which points to the type of interrelations between various types of firms with each other (private, foreign, state firms). This subcategory has the following values: 'mainly cooperative approach between firms', meaning that firms tend to cooperate with each other; 'mainly competitive approach between firms', meaning that private companies tend to compete with each other; 'mixed approach', which means that it may well be that private or state companies use both approaches (cooperative and competitive), depending on the particular business project. According to the theoretical assumptions of VoC, a high level of competition between competitors is inherent in an LME, as opposed to the high degree of cooperation found in a CME.

The second data-driven subcategory (2.2) is aimed at revealing the factors which drive competitors to cooperate with each other. Knowing this is important for understanding the type of market environment in which private companies operate. This subcategory has the following values: 'market conditions matter', meaning that relations between competitors are market-driven and companies are free to choose whether to cooperate with each other or not; 'business size matters', meaning that private companies interact with each other depending on the size (turnover) of their business activities or joint projects; 'the type of industry matters', meaning that competitors cooperate with each other as the type of industry they represent requires private companies to collaborate closely; 'state regulation matters', meaning that the state requires and/or prepares the ground for cooperation/non-cooperation between private companies.

The third theory-driven subcategory within the second dimension, regulation of competition (2.3), indicates the degree to which the state regulates competition between private firms. It has four values: 'strong regulation', 'moderate regulation', 'little regulation' and 'no regulation at all'. This subcategory should help identify whether the state heavily regulates various industries, or whether some industries are heavily regulated while private firms in other industries may face little or almost no regulation from the state. In CMEs, the degree of regulation of competition between private firms is high, whereas it is low in LMEs (Hall and Soskice 2001).

The fourth theory-driven subcategory, merger and acquisitions (M&A) (2.4), is intended to indicate the frequency of merger and acquisition transactions between private companies and between private and state companies. Having determined the frequency, I should be able to assess the degree of competition between firms in various industries and identify the type of inter-firm relations. There are three values here: 'frequent M&A', 'rare M&A', and, 'no M&A in the industry'. M&A are frequent in LMEs, whereas takeover transactions are rare in CMEs (Hall and Soskice 2001; Jackson and Miyajima 2007: 3).

The fifth data-driven subcategory concerns instruments for solving problems between private firms (2.5): the tools to which private companies usually resort in case of a problem or conflict with other private companies. There are four major sets of tools, parallel to those described for 1.5 above: the use of state mechanisms; domestic business mechanisms; international platforms; and a combination of these tools. This subcategory is aimed at comparing the tools private companies use in dealing with other private companies, vis-à-vis the tools they use in dealing with the state. Differences may shed light on state–business interaction and help to identify key 'core' and 'periphery' characteristics.

Role of other market players: This third dimension focuses on actors like labour unions and employer associations, and their impact on state–business interaction. It includes the following subcategories: the influence of labour unions; the influence of employer associations; reasons for the weak influence of other market players. This main category corresponds to the last aspect of research question 7 on the influence of other market players (see Table 4.2).

The first theory-driven subcategory, the influence of labour unions (3.1), describes the extent of labour union influence on state–business interaction, showing whether labour unions assist private business in solving problems and in promoting the interests of employees with employers and the state. This influence is categorized as follows: 'rather strong influence', 'rather moderate influence', 'rather low influence' or 'no influence at all'. The role of labour unions will be less significant in an LME than that in a CME; the level of unionization and influence on industrial relations will be lower in an LME than that in a CME (Hall and Soskice 2001).

The second theory-driven subcategory, the influence of employer associations (3.2), describes the extent of influence of employer associations on state–business interaction, showing whether employer associations assist private business in solving problems and promoting business interests before the state. Also here, the values are 'rather strong influence', 'rather moderate influence', 'rather low influence' or 'no influence at all'; and also here, the role of employer associations will be less significant in an LME than that in a CME (Hall and Soskice 2001).

The third data-driven subcategory and the final subcategory of the coding frame, reasons for the weak influence of other market players (3.3), builds on my personal observations as well as the preliminary analysis of the interviews. It indicates the reasons which may lead to the insignificant influence of labour unions and employer associations on state–business interaction. First, there is the possibility of 'Soviet path-dependence' as a limiting factor on the influence of labour unions and employer associations; second, 'private firms may view them as ineffective', and third, 'other' – any other reasons indicated by respondents.

In the final analysis, these three dimensions and their subcategories will be part of the coding frame used for the content analysis. As noted by Schreier

(2012: 58), a coding frame as part of content analysis is 'at the heart of the method', and is aimed at systematizing and structuring the data obtained. The frame usually includes main categories, which are the core elements in the analysis, and subcategories, which specify what in the material relates to main categories (ibid). The structure of a coding frame is a tool to reduce obtained data. Schreier (ibid: 60) explains that using a coding frame 'you reduce the many different things that are said in your material about a particular topic to these subcategories.' Each coding frame must have at least two levels: one main category and its subcategories (ibid: 63). The more levels a frame has, the more complex is the frame (ibid: 67–71). The coding frame in my analysis (see Appendix 4) can be considered as a frame of high complexity, as it consists of three categories and four hierarchical levels, with all categories based on a three-level structure, except for one, which is based on a four-level structure.

In constructing this coding frame, I followed the requirements of unidimensionality, mutual exclusiveness, exhaustiveness and saturation (Schreier 2012), ensuring that my dimensions were not intermixed.

Unidimensionality is important as it allows describing more clearly and concisely the collected material and helps achieve *mutual exclusiveness* of the subcategories (Schreier 2012: 74). The subcategories should exclude each other so that only one part of segmented material can be coded with one subcategory *'within a given dimension'*, whereas it is possible to assign the same unit of coding to other subcategories in the coding frame (ibid: 75). I followed Schreier's strategy (2012: 72–73) to ensure that my coding frame meets these criteria. First, to ensure I do not mix the dimensions with each other I checked whether subcategories in my coding frame can be considered as examples of the main categories. If some of the subcategories were not instances of the main categories, then I revised them accordingly and ensured they are the instances of the main categories. Second, two categories in my coding had the same subcategory names. This can be an example of 'mixed' dimensions if these categories have the identical function (Schreier 2012: 73–74). However, this was not a problem in my coding frame as category names in two dimensions served functions (see the categories 1.6 and 2.5 in the Coding Frame in Appendix 5). Third, to ensure the subcategories in my coding frame exclude each other, I selected the units of coding so that each of them corresponded only to one subcategory.

Exhaustiveness of a coding frame (Schreier 2012: 76) implies that within a coding frame each unit of coding should be assigned to at least one subcategory. Introducing a residual category can help in achieving this target – but if the residual category is used more frequently than the substantive subcategories, then the coding frame should be considered insufficiently valid and will need revision (ibid). To ensure the exhaustiveness criterion, I included residual subcategories for data-driven categories. This requirement is related to the validity requirement of the coding frame (ibid), to be assessed and discussed below.

Saturation means that each subcategory should be coded at least once. Since my coding frame is a mixture of data-driven and theory-driven subcategories, different saturation criteria have to be applied (Schreier 2012: 77). As regards data-driven subcategories and their values, they all stem from the collected material and so the saturation criterion is met by definition. The theory-driven subcategories build on the VoC concept and represent the main aspects of the concept. In the case of theory-driven subcategories it is not necessary for each subcategory to be coded at least once (ibid).

Regarding the process of constructing the coding frame, it should be noted that the second coder was involved from the very beginning. He was thoroughly familiar with the research project, having participated in all stages of the research process from the very start. To begin with, I discussed each selected category with him and asked his opinion about the applicability of categories and subcategories. Before the actual discussion of the coding frame, he went through the material and the coding frame. Sometimes, during our discussion we could not immediately arrive at a common understanding of particular aspects in the coding frame, he occasionally had a different understanding of some categories. In the end, we discussed each and every category and subcategory in detail and agreed on how to understand and utilize the coding frame. His feedback was helpful as it allowed redefining some of the categories, adjusting the coding frame, and discovering overlaps in categories.

While examining the coding frame and before proceeding with actual coding, the second coder recommended including the subcategory 'instruments for solution of problems between private companies'. This subcategory is indeed relevant, as it enables comparison between private companies and the state on this point. I may mention a further contribution of the second coder: initially the values of the subcategory 'key criteria of success' read as follows: 'cooperation with the state is crucial', '*ad hoc* cooperation with the state', and 'no cooperation with the state is required'. Here, the second coder proposed replacing the term 'cooperation' with 'communication'. He held that 'cooperation' is a broad term, with various forms and interpretations that may lead to confusion. The questions in my interview guides did not deal with cooperation of private companies with the state as such, but focused on a narrower aspect – *communication* with the state. There was a specific question on this issue in the interview guide for public officials, experts and representatives of international organizations: *What are the ways to exchange information between business and government? Prompt: Are there regular meetings?*

The responses showed that being able to communicate regularly with the state is an important factor in success for private companies. Using the word 'communication' instead of 'cooperation' (see definition of subcategory 1.2 in Appendix 6) helps a better understanding of this important aspect of state–business interaction.

Also helpful was the feedback from several experts on the coding frame before trial coding, as it helped to show that one dimension in the first version of the coding frame was mixed with another one. The subcategory 'justification of state involvement in private business' looked as follows:

Justification of state involvement in private business
- Excessive involvement
  - Justified
  - Partly justified
  - Non-justified
- Moderate involvement
  - Justified
  - Partly justified
  - Non-justified
- Little involvement
  - Justified
  - Partly justified
  - Non-justified

Here, respondents' perceptions as to the level of state involvement (excessive, moderate, little) were mixed with their opinions on whether such state involvement was acceptable (in terms of being justified, partly justified, non-justified). After receiving the feedback from colleagues, I split the subcategory in two to ensure unidimensionality. The first subcategory became as follows:

Level of state involvement in coordinating private sector
- Excessive involvement
- Moderate involvement
- Little involvement

And second subcategory:

Justification of state involvement
- Justified
- Partly justified
- Non-justified

After several revisions while building the coding frame I made sure that the coding frame met all the necessary requirements for a coding frame, as outlined by Schreier (2012): unidimensionality, mutual exclusiveness of the subcategories, exhaustiveness, and saturation. Thus, the coding frame for the pilot coding was composed according to these criteria (see Appendix 4).

4.8.6. Pilot coding

4.8.6.1. Preparatory phase

The pilot coding was conducted by two researchers. This was a necessary step before proceeding with the main analysis phase. The pilot coding involves three main stages: trial coding procedure, consistency check of the coding frame, and revision of the coding frame (Schreier 2012: 146). The pilot coding was applied to part of the material selected for data analysis (details on the selection criteria are provided below). The major goal in this phase is to optimize the coding frame so that in the main analysis phase all important aspects of the material will be covered. Moreover, it helps to reveal whether some categories and subcategories are not applicable, and whether some categories may be re-named or merged with other categories (ibid: 146–147). Conducting the main research phase without doing pilot coding may lead the researcher in the wrong direction, as some parts of the coding frame may prove inapplicable to the material (ibid: 147). Therefore, trial coding is a necessary step for identifying possible problems in the coding frame and making the necessary adjustments.

The material for the pilot coding should be part of the main data selected for qualitative analysis: since qualitative research implies the in-depth description of a certain phenomenon and not testing of a hypothesis (as in quantitative research), it is better to use part of the material for the main coding phase (Schreier 2012: 148). In my study I sought to provide an in-depth description of Kazakhstan's market economy. Thus, in the main coding I used the material which I analysed also in the pilot coding phase. In deciding how much material to use in the trial coding, I was concerned about *variability* and *practicability*, which serve as two criteria necessary for selecting material for the pilot coding in content analysis (ibid: 151).

First, in selecting part of the material for trial coding I was driven by *variability* concerns, which mean that both coders should try all categories and subcategories of the coding frame, and all categories and subcategories should be applied to various types of the material (Schreier 2012: 149). Two interviews from each of the categories were selected for the pilot coding. Given the differences across the applied interview guides for these categories, it was reasonable to expect considerable variation among interviews. By selecting two interviews from each category of respondents I tried to ensure that all possible differences in the material could be covered. This approach follows the logic that the more the variable material is used in the pilot phase, the more likely it is that all categories and subcategories will be covered (ibid: 150).

Second, it was necessary to account for the *practicability* criterion; usually, a researcher should choose only part of the material for pilot coding in order to reduce the amount of time spent on the procedure (Schreier 2012). In order to strike a balance between variability and practicability, 10–20 per cent from the total material may be used (ibid). I used 35 per cent of the material (12 interviews out of 38) for pilot coding.

I applied a *thematic criterion* for segmenting the data into units of coding. One code may represent several answers that arise within different parts of the same interview (Schreier 2012). For analysing the interview material, a thematic criterion has a definite advantage over the formal criterion such as a full answer of a respondent (ibid: 136). As respondents may occasionally return to the questions asked earlier in the interview, such an interview usually lacks a firm, exact structure (ibid). In my work, units of coding are based on various themes. In some cases units of coding correspond to the structure of the interview questions. However, this is not always the case, as various themes may emerge in various parts of the interview as well. Applying a thematic criterion was more appropriate for the analysis of my research material as it could bring together the pieces of the same topic scattered throughout the entire interview. On the one hand, the use of the thematic criterion may give rise to the problem of ambiguity, as it is not always evident where one topic ends and another starts (ibid: 138). In order to reduce ambiguity I chose my units of coding so that they would fit only one subcategory within the coding frame, as suggested by Schreier.

I employed the segmentation strategy proposed by Schreier (2012: 142):

1) two coders agreed what constitutes a unit of coding;
2) first, each researcher independently from each other, and then together, chose the code, which was later used for the selected unit of coding ('blind coding');
3) both coders discussed the way the coding of this particular unit was done.

I was interested to see whether some aspects emerge in interview responses at all. However, if these aspects are repeated throughout the interview, they do not provide any additional information to my research question. Therefore, both coders coded the material according to a *synthetic* procedure based on such a criterion as presence/absence of subcategories (Schreier 2012: 156).

4.8.6.2. Running the trial coding

The coding scheme for the pilot coding consisted of three main dimensions and 18 subcategories (see Appendix 4), or 21 in all. While running the pilot coding, the strategy was to do simultaneous coding of all dimensions and subcategories. As Schreier (2012: 153) notes, mental abilities allow most people to keep in mind not more than about 40 (sub)categories at the same time. Thus, with two coders it was possible to code the selected material simultaneously, one interview at a time. They coded according to the units of coding and dimensions, an approach deemed appropriate for working with interview data (ibid: 154). Coding of the interview material was done simultaneously according to the following categories:

- role of the state in the economy;
- level of state involvement in coordinating private sector *(removed after trial coding)*;
- level of state involvement over time;
- criteria of success of private business;
- reasons for differing treatment of small and large business;
- justification of state involvement *(removed after trial coding)*;
- firm's preferred investment policy;
- instruments for solving problems of private businesses;
- type of interaction between private firms;
- key criteria for interaction;
- regulation of competition;
- merger and acquisitions;
- influence of labour unions;
- influence of employer associations;
- reasons for weak influence of other market players.

Both coders used blind coding, working independently of each other.[25] This procedure helped comparison of results, as well as identifying weaknesses in the coding frame. Both coders agreed to make a note of any difficulties encountered, in order to discuss them after completing the coding procedure and making the necessary adjustments. To facilitate comparison between two coders (Schreier 2012: 157), each coder used the coding sheet, as summarized in Table 4.3.

After the trial coding, the two coders discussed all units of coding, which were coded differently. Out of 117 units of coding, only seven had been coded differently. Both coders discussed the reasons for their differing interpretations in these seven cases. Few examples of the differences were as follows:

---

25 MAXQDA software was used in the pilot coding and the main coding.

1) Interviews 5 and 11 revealed a serious problem with one of the categories in the coding scheme. First of all, the subcategory 'justification of state involvement' proved less applicable for trial coding, appearing in only two interviews out of 12. Moreover, each times it was coded differently by both coders. As the coders realized after the discussion: first, none of the respondents had been asked a direct question about justification of state involvement; secondly, two times two respondents mentioned this issue indirectly but in contradictory ways, so that it was not possible to agree on the same code. Respondents' answers were subject to ambiguous interpretation. If there was such a question in the interview guide and if it was asked explicitly by the interviewers, then it is more likely that two coders would find it easier to agree on the same code. However, since that was not the case, I decided to remove this category from the coding frame for the main coding phase (see Appendix 5 for the final version of the coding frame).

2) With Interview 6, the first coder assigned the unit of coding 2.2 ('key criteria for interaction with competitors') the code number 1 ('market conditions matter'), whereas the second coder assigned the code number 6 ('other'). Following discussion, the conclusion was that both interpretations were equally valid. The first coder had decided that market conditions determine whether or not private companies cooperate, with no other factors motivating companies to cooperate with each other: thus, competitors are free to choose whether or not to cooperate, depending on their market strategies. In the view of the second coder, the respondent was pointing to the fact that participation in industrial associations is ineffective, and therefore companies do not cooperate with each other. In other words, if participation in associations were fruitful and effective, then this particular company would cooperate with other competitors. Since there is no criterion 'effective associations', the second coder felt it should be coded as 'other'.

Given that both coders provided equally reasonable arguments for different coding, it was decided to follow the technically more convenient approach and use the reasoning of the second coder. That second approach was more 'convenient' as it permitted collecting other criteria that lead competitors to interact with each other, whereas the first one would require additional interpretation and justification each time.

3) In Interview 8, discussions between two coders led to the conclusion that only instruments that in practice were employed for solving problems should be taken into account, and not instruments that might hypothetically be used as was mentioned by the respondent. In this research I focus on practices for problem-solving between companies as part of their interaction with each other. Therefore, the decision rule was added; purely hypothetical speculations should be discarded.

Table 4.3. Pilot coding sheet

Interview 1 (6)[26]	1.1	1.2	1.3	1.4	1.5.1	1.5.2	1.6	1.7	1.8	2.1	2.2	2.3	2.4	2.5	3.1	3.2	3.3
Coder 1							1[27]			2[28]	5	1	1		4	1	
Coder 2							1			3	5	1	1		4	1	
Int. 2 (7)	1.1	1.2	1.3	1.4	1.5.1	1.5.2	1.6	1.7	1.8	2.1	2.2	2.3	2.4	2.5	3.1	3.2	3.3
Coder 1										2	3	1		1			
Coder 2										2	3	1		1			
Int. 3 (7)	1.1	1.2	1.3	1.4	1.5.1	1.5.2	1.6	1.7	1.8	2.1	2.2	2.3	2.4	2.5	3.1	3.2	3.3
Coder 1												3		1		2	4
Coder 2												3		1		2	4
Int. 4 (8)	1.1	1.2	1.3	1.4	1.5.1	1.5.2	1.6	1.7	1.8	2.1	2.2	2.3	2.4	2.5	3.1	3.2	3.3
Coder 1			1							1		4				1	2,1
Coder 2			1							1		4				1	2,1
Int. 5 (9)	1.1	1.2	1.3	1.4	1.5.1	1.5.2	1.6	1.7	1.8	2.1	2.2	2.3	2.4	2.5	3.1	3.2	3.3
Coder 1	2	2		3	3	2	1	4	3	1	3	4	1		4		
Coder 2	2	2		3	3	2	1	4	1	1	3	4	1		4		
Int. 6 (8)	1.1	1.2	1.3	1.4	1.5.1	1.5.2	1.6	1.7	1.8	2.1	2.2	2.3	2.4	2.5	3.1	3.2	3.3
Coder 1	3				2	2	2	2		2	1	3		2		1	
Coder 2	3				2	2	2	2		2	6	3		2		2	
Int. 7 (8)	1.1	1.2	1.3	1.4	1.5.1	1.5.2	1.6	1.7	1.8	2.1	2.2	2.3	2.4	2.5	3.1	3.2	3.3
Coder 1	1	2					1	1		2	6	4	3	2	3	3	1
Coder 2	1	2					1	1		2	6	4	3	2	3	3	1
Int. 8 (9)	1.1	1.2	1.3	1.4	1.5.1	1.5.2	1.6	1.7	1.8	2.1	2.2	2.3	2.4	2.5	3.1	3.2	3.3
Coder 1		2	1				3	2		1	4,6	3	3	2	4	3	
Coder 2		2	1				3	2		1	4,6	3	3	4	4	3	
Int. 9 (10)	1.1	1.2	1.3	1.4	1.5.1	1.5.2	1.6	1.7	1.8	2.1	2.2	2.3	2.4	2.5	3.1	3.2	3.3
Coder 1	2	1	2	1	1	2	2	1		3		3	1	2	3	2	2
Coder 2	2	2	2	1	1	2	2	2		3		3	1	2	3	2	2
Int. 10 (10)	1.1	1.2	1.3	1.4	1.5.1	1.5.2	1.6	1.7	1.8	2.1	2.2	2.3	2.4	2.5	3.1	3.2	3.3
Coder 1	1	1	1,2,3				1					3	1	1	4	2	4
Coder 2	1	1	1,2,3				1					3	1	1	4	2	4
Int. 11 (10)	1.1	1.2	1.3	1.4	1.5.1	1.5.2	1.6	1.7	1.8	2.1	2.2	2.3	2.4	2.5	3.1	3.2	3.3
Coder 1	3	2	1	3	1	3	1		1						1	2	
Coder 2	3	2	1	3	1	3	1		2						1	2	
Int. 12 (9)	1.1	1.2	1.3	1.4	1.5.1	1.5.2	1.6	1.7	1.8	2.1	2.2	2.3	2.4	2.5	3.1	3.2	3.3
Coder 1		1	1		2	2	1	2				2			4	3	
Coder 2		1	1		2	2	1	2				2			4	3	

26 Grade of the interview.
27 Assigned value.
28 Marked grey are the instances when units of coding were coded differently by two coders.

4) In Interview 9, the subcategory 'instruments for solution of problems of private business' (1.7) was coded 1 ('use of state mechanisms') by the first coder and 2 ('use of business mechanisms') by the second coder. Here the second coder made a mistake in assigning the code number 2, as the respondent had said that private companies use courts in order to solve their problems. In this case the code number 1 ('use of state mechanisms') should be applied.

> It's not an exception anymore when an entrepreneur goes to court against public agencies and wins the case.

After finding the differences in coding seven units of coding, both coders revised the coding frame. The major change was the removal of two subcategories: 'justification of state involvement' and 'level of state involvement'. The former was removed because there were no direct questions on the justification of state involvement, so respondents rarely mentioned the issue. The latter was discarded due to significant overlaps with the subcategory 'role of the state'.

4.8.6.3. Evaluation of the coding frame

First of all, the *reliability* of the coding frame has to be assessed. It is necessary to apply the reliability criterion as that helps to evaluate the quality of a coding frame (Schreier 2012: 166–167). The strategy applied was 'comparison across persons', whereby two persons code the material independently and then compare their results with each other (ibid). After this comparison one coefficient for all subcategories in three main categories was calculated. As a full 94 per cent of the material was coded the same way and only 6 per cent of the material was coded differently, it can be argued that the coding was sufficiently consistent. Consistency is a synonym of reliability if applied in a qualitative content analysis; and since, as Schreier (2012: 167) notes, 'reliability is always a matter of degree', the degree of consistency of the coding scheme can be said to be rather high. As explained above, the two coders also discussed in detail the differences in coding that occurred during the pilot phase and in the end they both agreed on future use of decision rules. This procedure is recognized as relevant and important for assessing reliability of the coding frame in a qualitative content analysis (ibid: 175). Thus, it can be argued that the coefficient of agreement with respect to the entire coding frame between the two coders was high.

The reliability of the coding frame was assessed from another perspective as well. When there are large amounts of data for analysis, it is necessary to test whether the categories have been used consistently across the entire data (Schreier 2012: 168). In my coding frame, the meaning of the categories was in fact generally present in the analysed material. Moreover, if both coders come to significant agreement with respect to the meaning of the material – as was the case in this research – then it is highly likely that also other members of the academic community will understand the material in basically the same way and thus accept it (ibid: 169).

Concerning the results of the pilot coding, it is necessary to point out one tendency. In the coding sheet (see Table 4.3) low-scoring interviews have few subcategories, whereas high-scoring interviews cover almost all subcategories; thus, the higher an interview is graded, the more material it contains. This is in line with the definition of the grading scale that was employed during the data collection period. As explained, the grading scale was introduced at the very beginning of the fieldwork in order to measure the quality of the interviews according to the key quality criteria elaborated by the research team. For instance, in interview number one, which received a grade of 6, the respondent covered only seven subcategories out of a total of 17. By contrast, the respondent in interview number 9, which was given the top grade of 10, covered 15 subcategories out of the 17.

The use of the coding sheet also helped to double-check the quality of the grading scale employed. As the results of pilot coding show, most of the 12 interviews were graded correctly according to the criterion 'presence of subcategories'. That indicates that, in general, the higher the interview was graded, the more subcategories it contained, and the converse for low-graded interviews.

As explained by Schreier (2012: 175), another important step is to assess the *validity* of a coding frame. Validity means the degree to which a coding frame 'captures what it sets out to capture' (ibid). Like reliability, validity is measured in terms of degrees. Face validity and content validity are usually applied to assess the validity of the coding frame (ibid: 185). *Face validity* is applied to evaluate a data-driven coding frame and *content validity* is applied to a theory-driven coding frame (ibid: 186, 189). This coding frame is a mixture of data-driven and theory-driven subcategories. Both criteria must be applied in assessing the overall validity of the coding frame.

First, face validity must be assessed. Out of 15 subcategories, eight had residual categories 'other'. In two subcategories out of eight, residual categories were coded. The first such subcategory was coded three times out of eight (the remaining five were applied to substantive categories). The second subcategory was coded two times out of six as 'other' (the remaining four were applied to substantive categories). Face validity can thus be considered as relatively high, as only in two subcategories was material assigned to residual categories. In the next step, both coders revised these two subcategories, to ensure that all substantive categories covered all important aspects of a phenomenon. To that end, one additional substantive category was added.

In judging whether the coding frame corresponds to the efforts invested in the research, it is necessary to assess whether the frame captures all important aspects of the material, or only part (Schreier 2012: 187). After the pilot coding phase, both coders concluded that those aspects which had been missing were now included in the coding frame. The results of the pilot coding did not reveal any significant gaps in terms of differentiation of the material, as the coding frame covered all important aspects necessary for answering my research question. The subcategories in the coding frame contain various levels of abstraction, both low and high levels, and are combined with each other. For instance, the abstract subcategory 'role of the state in the economy' is logically combined with the less abstract subcategory such as 'level of state involvement over time' (see the final version of the coding frame in Appendix 5).

Moreover, the differentiation criterion plays an important role in measuring face validity (Schreier 2012). As regards coding frequency, my coding frame was well differentiated as there were no subcategories which would be coded many times more than other subcategories. From this perspective, the level of face validity was also quite high. However, there was another problem: certain subcategories were not coded at all in some interviews. There were two main reasons. First, in low-quality interviews (graded 6 or lower) respondents skipped some of the questions or did not possess enough expertise to answer them. Thus, some parts of the material in high-quality interviews (graded from 8 to 10) was simply not present in low-quality interviews. Second, some of the questions in the interview guides for public officials, experts and representatives of international organizations differed from the questions used in the interview guides for representatives of private domestic and foreign companies, state-owned companies and employer associations and labour unions. Such partial differences in the interview guides resulted in some subcategories being coded in one group of the interviews but not coded in the other group.

However, this will have no negative impact on the main coding: unlike the pilot coding phase, only interviews scoring from 7 to 10 will be analysed in the main coding, with the exception of two interviews in the under-represented 'state-owned companies' category and one interview with a public official (all three scored 6). The reason behind analysing these three interviews in the main coding is that it was important to analyse all the interviews with representatives of state-owned companies, precisely because this category of respondents was under-represented. Excluding from this category interviews that scored 6 would lead to further under-representation, and there would be only one interview (score 7) in the data analysis phase. Including one score-6 interview with a public official was also due to representation concerns with respect to the category 'public officials'. As a result, I assumed that most subcategories would be covered in each interview during the main coding.

As regards the seven theory-driven subcategories, they must be evaluated by content validity (Schreier 2012: 189). First, before doing pilot coding, both coders concluded that the coding frame was sufficiently valid, as the categories and subcategories adequately represented the aspects of VoC approach utilized in this research project. Second, a third expert involved in the research project was consulted and he agreed that these seven categories adequately represented the 'core–periphery' framework and the VoC concept. Finally, the distribution of coding frequencies cannot be applied as a criterion for assessing the validity of a theory-driven subcategory, as such subcategories are based on a certain concept; thus, the researcher cannot change subcategories in case of high frequency, because that would entail a change in the concept itself (ibid: 190).

In the end, assessing the validity of the coding frame, we may conclude that the coding frame was sufficiently valid, as face validity was relatively high. The overall coding frequency for residual data-driven subcategories was low; the level of differentiation was high; and finally, even though some of the categories were abstract, the overall level of abstraction was not too high, as the abstract categories were supplemented by less abstract ones, which helped to achieve a balance between them. Content validity was also sufficiently high, as categories and subcategories represented the underlying theoretical concepts (the 'core–periphery' framework and the VoC approach) in a comprehensive way and the expert was invited to assess content validity.

4.8.7. Main coding

4.8.7.1. Preparatory phase

As during the pilot coding, the material was segmented in the form of 38 semi-structured interviews into units, with each unit corresponding to one dimension of the coding frame. I segmented my material according to the thematic criterion. Each interview contained on average 8,000 to 10,000 words, so it generally took three or four hours to indicate the relevant parts of the material in one interview and mark the units of coding within them. Often respondents spoke about the same issue in different parts of the interview, so to indicate relevant parts I had to read each interview carefully and connect different parts of the material together in case they related to the same unit of coding. I considered parts of the material as 'relevant' if they related to the units of coding within the coding frame, which is based upon my research question. In segmenting the material I had to keep in mind a total of 17 categories (three main categories and 14 subcategories). As coders can usually follow not more than 40 categories at a time (Schreier 2012: 195), I was able to follow 17 categories while separating relevant parts of the material; and, as suggested by Schreier, I assigned numbers to the units of coding after marking relevant parts of the material.

4.8.7.2. Running the main coding

No changes must be introduced into the coding frame during the main coding (Schreier 2012: 198). I utilized the coding frame that had been revised after the pilot coding, without making any changes during the main coding (see the coding frame for the final coding in Appendix 5). I ran the main coding on my own, and conducted coding and recoding procedures after a period of 18 days. During this second procedure I recoded all the material again. Although the pilot coding frame was not substantially revised or changed for the main coding, I still recoded the material from the 12 interviews used for the pilot coding.

During the main coding I experienced only minor shortcomings with the coding frame. As Schreier notes (2012), no coding frame is perfect, and this should be taken into account while running the main coding. In particular, I faced two problems: First, in the midst of the process I realized that it would make sense to include a subcategory on the importance of introducing best practices from abroad, as many respondents mentioned that the economic model of Kazakhstan exhibits many features adopted from foreign models. In the part where the results are presented I partly solved this problem by presenting respondents' perceptions in a qualitative way and summarizing their opinions in one table, without conducting content analysis (see Table 5.2).

Second, there were also few other instances where subcategories could be composed. I wrote down these subcategories separately and again introduced them in the results part, either as a *case in point* or by directly quoting the respondent. This helped to underscore those points which were not covered by the coding frame, but which seemed important for my research question.

As a next step, I compared codes which were coded differently during the first coding and subsequent recoding: this applied to 16 out of 423 codes. With different codes, it is necessary to decide on the meaning of these units (Schreier 2012: 203). I presented the results of the main coding in one coding sheet, with three columns: one for the two points in time, and one for the final code (see Appendix 7 for the final coding sheet). In the coding sheet I indicated all units which had been coded differently. Overall, 96.8 per cent of the material had been coded the same and only 3.2 per cent had been coded differently at two different times. During the trial coding I had coded 94 per cent of the material the same way and 6 per cent differently, so this indicates a slight improvement of the coding frame used in the main coding. However, it should be recalled that two coders were involved in the pilot coding, whereas I ran the main coding on my own, at two different time-points. In the final coding sheet I put the same codes from the first two columns into the third column. For the 16 differing categories I checked why I had assigned them different codes. I found that there were five typographical errors; moreover, the meaning of seven codes was ambiguous and so I had interpreted them differently two times (indicated in red on the coding sheet). Then I decided not to use them and did not enter them in the coding sheet. The remaining four codes were less ambiguous; here I asked my colleague for help in deciding the final meaning (indicated in green on the coding sheet).

Given the fact that my units of analysis (interviews) were larger than units of coding, I had to attach my results to the units of analysis (Schreier 2012: 207). In presenting the results I use absolute frequencies accompanied by continuous text and illustrated by both direct quotes and cross-tables, which is a specific type of frequency table (see Chapter 5). They help to demonstrate various patterns in respondents' perceptions.

4.8.7.3. Final round of evaluation

Assessing the overall quality of the content analysis method in this work, I can conclude that content analysis was consistently conducted according to the guidelines outlined by Schreier (2012). In the pilot coding phase, two researchers had been involved. I built my coding frame according to the following criteria: unidimensionality, mutual exclusiveness of the subcategories, exhaustiveness, and saturation. The inter-rater agreement in the pilot coding phase was 94 per cent. This shows the high degree of coding consistency, and thus indicates the high degree of reliability of my coding frame. The coding frame was also sufficiently valid, as face validity and content validity were relatively high. The coding frame reflected the underlying theoretical concepts (the 'core–periphery' framework and the VoC approach) in a comprehensive way, and the expert was also involved to assess content validity. The coding frame was revised after trial coding and then applied in the main coding phase.

In the main coding, 96.8 per cent of the material was coded the same and only 3.2 per cent was coded differently. Compared to the degree of coding consistency in the pilot phase (94 per cent vs. 6 per cent), this shows the slight improvement of the quality of the coding frame used in the main coding. Also here, it should be borne in mind that two coders were involved in the pilot coding, while in the main coding phase I coded the material on my own. This may indicate a minor limitation of content analysis. Involving a second researcher for the main coding would certainly have added another value while using the method. However, since the main coding was expected to be time-consuming, and given the time constraints and practical considerations of other researchers, it was not possible to involve a second rater for the final phase.

Thus, I coded the material at two different time-points, which is standard procedure in case a second coder is not available (Schreier 2012).

In general the method largely helped me to achieve my research objectives in the data analysis phase. The coding frame fully represented the theoretical concepts which are applied in this work and the results from content analysis helped to answer the research question. Chapter 5 offers a detailed discussion of the results of data analysis.

Chapter 5. The emerging hybrid market economy: the 'core–periphery' model

5.1. Studying state–business interaction

5.1.1. The role of the state in the economy

Before presenting the results of the content analysis, it is necessary to highlight several caveats and limitations in connection with the data analysis and interpretation of results (recall also subsections 4.7.1 and 4.7.3, on caveats and limitations in data collection). First, for data analysis, only 48 interviews out of 159 were used: that was a smaller sub-set of the entire sample. Using a smaller sample reduces the degree to which the sample can be considered representative and increases the probability of error, which may negatively affect the results obtained. Second, the results of the interview analysis are based on people's perceptions and thus cannot be viewed as the 'ultimate truth' as regards comprehending the essence of market economy in Kazakhstan. Perceptions are based on respondents' subjective judgments and personal observations, so the element of subjectivity and possible biases should be taken into account in interpreting the interview results. That said, systematization and content analysis of respondents' views helped to reduce these biases and made it possible to draw some general conclusions regarding the type of market economy in Kazakhstan (see also section 5.5).

The first main category of the coding frame is 'state–business interaction' and the first subcategory is 'the role of the state in the economy'. The question was: what has been the role of the state in shaping a market economy in Kazakhstan? I begin with a general overview of respondents' perceptions of the role of the state in the economy, which covers most areas of interrelation between the state and private business. This category includes an assessment of the level of state involvement in coordinating economic processes and in regulating the activities of private actors. Shedding light on the role of the state will help clarify the nature of state–business interaction in Kazakhstan. Analysis of each of these aspects is provided in detail in subsections 5.2.2–5.4.3 below.

As explained, the VoC approach holds that the level of inter-firm coordination is low in a Liberal Market Economy (LME), whereas in a Coordinated Market Economy (CME) the level of inter-firm coordination in the private sector is high (Hall and Soskice 2001). Unlike LMEs and CMEs, the state largely coordinates economic processes and inter-firm relations in Kazakhstan. Thus, it is necessary to assess this role of the state. According to thirteen of my respondents,[29] the state dominates how the economy develops (see Frequency Table 5.1). Twelve respondents hold that the role of the state is moderate with respect to regulating and coordinating the economy, whereas only six respondents saw the state's role as non-interventionist, i.e. that the state does not seek to control and regulate economic development, but seeks to provide as much freedom to private entrepreneurs as possible.

Frequency Table 5.1. Assessment of the role of the state

Role of the state in the economy			
Dominant	Moderate	Non-interventionist	Other
13	12	6	0
5 IORs[30] 3 PORs 3 PDCRs 2 FCRs	4 PORs 3 FCRs 2 IORs 2 PDCRs 1 EAR	3 FCRs 1 POR 1 PDCR 1 IOR	–

Importantly, some respondents – but not all – see this role as justified. For instance, IOR5 (Core–Periphery),[31] views the state's role as 'dominant', and also thinks that it is justified:

> It (*the role of the state*) is rather significant, I think. In relation to the entire market economy structure, the bulk of industries are heavily regulated by the state. The energy sector, for example, is heavily controlled due to its social component. All the reforms in this sector have already been made and these reforms were made quite quickly. If we compare our situation to Russia's, they have been undertaking pension, social and utility reforms for decades and they have always run up against strong resistance from the population, which is rather active in protecting its position. While in Kazakhstan, it (*reform*) was made unilaterally right after the collapse of the Soviet Union and was simply taken for granted. From one perspective, this was an acute pain that should have been overcome. Banking and other sectors were quite quickly

29 Coding abbreviations: EAR – Representative of an Employer Association; Ex – Experts; FCR – Representative of a Foreign Company; IOR – Representative of an International Organization; LUR – Representative of a Labour Union; PDCR – Representative of a Private Domestic Company; PO – Public Official; SOCR – Representative of a State-Owned Company.

30 The frequency table summarizes the responses of 31 respondents out of 38, as not all 38 interviewees responded to the question on the role of the state in the economy. The same holds for subsequent frequency tables, in which the total number of responses does not always match the total number of interviews analysed.

31 See subsection 4.8.5 for detailed description of the 'Core–Periphery' coding level and indications of respondents' belonging to the 'core' or the 'periphery' and mentioning the 'core' or the 'periphery' or both in their answers.

> reformed during that period. At the moment we are receiving dividends from the reforms undertaken during that period. We have experienced difficult times, just like every other country in the former USSR, but unlike us, they did not dare go for these reforms. We have a combination of elements, of a market economy with state interference; certain sectors are under strict state control. There are also sectors that continue to be subsidized.

This excerpt sheds some light on the nature of economic reform in Kazakhstan since independence. The first years of independence were especially painful for the economy, as the state implemented various radical market reforms using a 'shock therapy' approach – but these reforms proved successful and today the economy is enjoying the results. As regards state coordination of the economy, some industries are under state control ('core').

However, IOR2 (Core–Periphery) has a completely different opinion, arguing that this 'dominant' role is hardly justified:

> I think the role is excessive. I think if you start talking about the American or German model, none of them are appropriate for describing in this case. Because in Germany, for example, the state has strong regulation which is not bad, actually, because relying purely on the market to self-regulate is fraught with dangers. At the same time, the countries such as Canada that had quite specific productive requirements to financial institutes turned out to be more stable, right? Norms and regulations are rather clear and strict there (...) The very first difference from the German model is that with the state interference there is little freedom for entrepreneurship. There are too many controlling authorities. The government itself realizes that and speaks about that but not many things are done in this respect. Unfortunately, the efforts to change the system and ensure good functioning of business without additional bureaucratic requirements are not very productive.

This respondent sees the state's efforts at coordinating the economy as rather ineffective. The role of the state is here considered significant: but it is ineffective and therefore not justified. IOR2 (Core–Periphery) gives an example of bureaucratic burden involved in doing business:

> What is the cost of doing business in Canada with turnover up to USD 5 million? It will cost you an annual report only. For a small business, that means one accounting officer who will cost you USD 400 to make a report. In Kazakhstan even on annual basis it is hard to find an accountant who would agree to serve the company for USD 400. The requirements of making reports on a quarterly basis and paying taxes on a frequent basis lead to high cost of administering a business. There are too many different factors where the government requires too much from small businesses including the time that a business wastes to implement the requirements set by the government which in the end, give nothing to the government. The regulation is excessive.

Varying opinions exist – but these opinions can be explained. The reason why IOR5 views state coordination as justified may be explained by the fact that he has mainly worked for international organizations throughout his career. Perhaps he has a more neutral view of the role of the state, never having been directly involved in state–business relations. On the other hand, IOR2 had significant experience in working as an entrepreneur in Kazakhstan before joining an international organization. Both respondents agree that the role is excessive, but differ in their understanding of that role.

The main conclusion to be drawn is that the state is heavily involved in regulating and coordinating the economy in Kazakhstan, and sets the rules for the development of private business. This is an important observation in light of the company-centred approach within the VoC framework, which cannot fully account for the fact that the state may play a leading role in shaping and coordinating economic relations. In view of that observation, accounting for the more prominent role of the state in regulating the economy and in shaping the rules of the game became imperative for my research.

The 'dominant' role of the state is also expressed by IOR17 (Core):

> The state's position in the economy is significant, given the direct ownership and the way they regulate everything. So, it is a significantly state influenced economy (…) The economic crisis of 2008 has increased that role, especially as regards controlling access to finance.

However, this respondent, like most of the others, did not provide a personal opinion on whether such role is justified. Public officials, by contrast, shared the perception that high involvement of the state is justified. According to one public official (PO2/Core):

> Kazakhstan is the leader among the Central Asian countries. Among the CIS countries, I think we are on the same level as Russia: in some things Russia leaves us behind; in terms of certain state regulations we leave them behind. Until recently, in matters of budgetary financing and building transparency we have been ahead of Russia. They have only just arrived at implementing the stages we had passed through some time ago. However, in some matters of economic development they are better because they had a very strong base from the start and the programmes that have been financed so far were orientated towards maintaining that level. I think we have good prospects among developing countries in terms of our future; there are defined courses in economic policy made by the government which ensures our leadership in some of the areas. We are not talking about leadership in all areas; but in terms of some indicators we can surely be so.

From the perceptions and views of various respondents, an important pattern can be identified. IOR2 has work experience in developed Western countries and his cultural, academic and professional background has its origins from Canada. His view and perception of the state's role in the economy are partly influenced by his background. In turn, IOR5 is less critical to the role of the state; also this can be partly explained by his background. IOR5 grew up in Kazakhstan and has worked mainly there; his perceptions have been shaped by his background and he applies other standards from those of IOR2 in assessing the role of the state in the economy. Thus we see that the cultural background and origin of a respondent seem to play an important role in shaping that person's views and perceptions. The country of origin of a respondent is equally important as other factors (academic and professional background, age, institutional affiliation) which influence respondents' views. This cross-cultural aspect adds a new layer to the analysis, but is also a further limitation of my study that must be taken into account (see also section 5.5). Therefore, one can expect that for instance respondents from Russia will be influenced by their cultural background and country experience, and would probably apply their own set of criteria (based on Russian experience) to assess the economy in Kazakhstan. Similarly, respondents from Germany could be expected to apply their own criteria based on their experience of the German market economy.

Given this cross-cultural element, it is also important to note the presence of a large number of foreign actors in the country. Since independence, Kazakhstan has been open to foreign direct investment. Moreover, the government has also wanted to learn from the development models of other states. Thus, the subject of models of economic development should be taken into account, and the elements which Kazakhstan has adopted in the course of its development. In terms of openness to international experience in economic development, Kazakhstan can be considered a leader among the CIS countries. The government has been keen on learning from the experience of other countries. From the interviews conducted for this research, it was possible to identify the systemic elements that have been adopted. The literature review in Chapter 3 showed that the *pension system* is based on the Chilean pension model, and the *banking system* contains some elements of Islamic banking, based on the experience of Arab countries. The interviews helped reveal that the banking system has also drawn on the German financial system, at least to some extent.

Interviewees also mentioned many other foreign models which the government has referred to in connection with economic development. Table 5.2 summarizes areas of reforms made by the government which are based on models from other countries. The *presidential system* and the *Parliament* are based on elements of the French model; the *public administration* is based on models from EU countries, Singapore and South Korea; the *tax system* contains certain elements of the US and South Korean tax systems; the *National Welfare Fund 'Samruk-Kazyna'* was established based on the Norwegian model of oil revenue accumulation and management, as well as Singapore's 'Temasek' Wealth Fund, and the Japanese experience; *construction and infrastructure* development has drawn on the experience of the United Arab Emirates,

Malaysia and Finland; *innovation policy* has developed according to some elements of the Finnish model; *education policy* is partly based on German, South Korean, Finnish and US models;[32] and the development of *agriculture* has drawn on the experiences of the USA and of Russia.

As all respondents noted, Kazakhstan follows a multi-vector approach in terms of learning from foreign economic models. Respondents stress that Kazakhstan has learnt from economic development of the four Asian Tigers – Singapore, Hong Kong, South Korea and Taiwan. Moreover, it seeks to learn lessons from economic development in China, Turkey, the United Arab Emirates and Russia. Overall, the state has been keen to learn from the diversity of successful experiences in other countries, with two main strategies used to adopt this knowledge and experience. First, as one of the interviewed experts (Ex7/Core–Periphery) notes, consultants from various countries are invited to come to Kazakhstan and share their experience. They may even participate in the elaboration of various development programmes under 'Strategy 2030'. For instance, as Ex5 (Core) notes, Professor Michael Porter from the Institute for Strategy and Competitiveness at Harvard Business School was invited in 2004 to Kazakhstan to do research and identify priority sectors in the economy within the 'Diversification of Kazakhstan's Economy through Cluster Development in Non-Extracting Sectors of Economy' development programme, adopted that same year. Professor Porter suggested developing a cluster within machine building, metallurgy, tourism, food industry and agriculture, transport and construction industries, drawing on the successful experiences of the USA in cluster development. However, this cluster programme failed, as no adequate infrastructure was put in place to implement it (Ex5/Core; IOR15/Core).

Importantly, models from foreign countries are not copied directly: attempts are made to first adjust them to local conditions and existing infrastructure, and only then are they implemented in practice (Ex20/Core).

Second, public officials themselves travel to South-East Asian countries, as well as to the EU area, to learn from the development models offered by these countries through various government programmes. After they return, they also participate in elaborating development projects (IOR15/Core).

32 As PO6 (Core) explains, 'I was in the working group in the Ministry of Education and was responsible for switching to a credits-based system of education. The American system was taken as the model for transition. It was a totally new thing for us.'

Table 5.2. Kazakhstan's development model[33]

Presidential system/Parliament	– French model
State and economic development models	– China, Hong Kong, Singapore, South Korea, Taiwan – Russia – Turkey – United Arab Emirates
Public administration	– EU model – Singaporean model (National School of Public Policy draws on the Lee Kuan Yew School of Public Policy in Singapore)
Tax system	– South Korea – the USA
Pension system	– Chilean model
Sovereign Wealth Fund	– Japanese model – Norwegian model (Government Pension Fund) – Singapore's 'Temasek' Wealth Fund
Construction and infrastructure development	– Finland – Malaysia – United Arab Emirates
Innovation policy	– Finnish experience in innovation policy
Banking and finance industry	– German financial system – Islamic banking from Arab countries
Education	– Finland – Germany – South Korea – the USA
Agriculture	– Russia – the USA

A vivid example of this approach is the creation of Samruk-Kazyna (see subsection 3.3.2.2), the largest national corporation in Kazakhstan, which was founded along the lines of Singapore's 'Temasek'.[34] IOR1 (Core) justifies the creation of Samruk-Kazyna:

33 This table is based upon respondents' views.

34 Temasek is a big investment company in Singapore. 'Its portfolio covers a broad spectrum of industries: financial services; telecommunications, media and technology; transportation and industrials; consumer and real estate; energy and resources; and life sciences' (Temasek 2012). Similarly, Samruk-Kazyna unites the largest companies from the largest industries in Kazakhstan (see Table 3.10).

> The most positive shift (in government policy in the last few years) is the creation of 'Samruk-Kazyna'; it was created, united under one roof and received huge financing from the government; I think it is a very positive aspect. Also, it was used to rescue the 'BTA Bank' (…) there are different opinions, but I view the rescue of the 'BTA Bank' as state interference in the market economy. Sometimes some changes are taking place in the oil sector. But it is a fully state-controlled sector, so we should not be surprised at that.

Thus, Kazakhstan has been eager to learn from the diversity of experiences in other countries and adopt elements of a range of models within its institutional setup. In turn, however, the adoption of various institutions complicates the analysis of the structure of the economy. It may be seen as a 'patchwork', with several subsystems within the economy sometimes functioning according to different rules, standards, incentives and structures. If Kazakhstan had followed the institutions of *one* other country, that would have made its economic system easier to analyse. What is irrefutable is that the country has managed to achieve high indicators in terms of economic performance in the years since independence. The adoption of different institutional models may complicate the analysis of the economy, but might also help to explain why Kazakhstan has been able to achieve high economic growth.

An important observation, from all respondents, is that the economy has not only elements of strong state regulation ('core'), but market elements as well ('periphery'). Table 5.3 shows this tendency. In this table only representatives of private companies are categorized on the basis of their perceptions of the role of the state. Analysing industries and the size of companies represented by the respondents helps to identify noteworthy differences. In particular, big companies tend to perceive the role of the state in the economy and the level of involvement as massive, in contrast to small and medium-sized businesses (SMEs). Thus, these big companies can be assigned to the 'core' part of the economy. According to the representative of a large foreign company in the banking industry (FCR11/Core: Core), 'red tape' is greater in the banking sector than in any other industry. Finance was always a target for the state (…) as it involves huge capital.' This view is supported by the head of a big HR company in the oil and gas industry (PDCR9/Core: Core), who said, 'a lot of the agencies conduct frequent inspections of companies. They come without notification and business gets disrupted.' This perception is also shared by representatives of international organizations. However, as IOR1 (Core) argues, high-levels of state involvement in big business is not what makes Kazakhstan distinct from other countries:

> Among the shareholders, the state can interfere in large companies as much as it wants; it is a right, I think, and justified approach. The closer the company or the business is to the extractive sector – oil and gas – and services around it, then, of course, government decisions influence them because it is all related to government

> purchases and government enterprises. I am sure this phenomenon can be observed in every country. It is not something that is peculiar to Kazakhstan.

By contrast, most representatives of small companies saw the role of the state as rather liberal. According to the head of a small consultancy company (PDCR8/Periphery: Periphery), 'the state does not intervene. Private entrepreneurs do everything on their own. All we have to do is pay taxes on time. And we have to do our accounting on time, exactly what we do all the time.'

Table 5.3. Perception of the role of state, by company representatives

	The role of the state is dominant	
Company	**Industry**	**Company size**
1. PDCR (core[35])	Oil and gas	Large
2. PDCR (core)	Oil and gas	Large
3. FCR (core)	Finance	Large
4. FCR (mixed)	Trade	Medium
5. PDCR (periphery)	Manufacturing	Medium
	The role of the state is moderate	
1. FCR (core)	Oil and gas	Large
2. FCR (mixed)	Service	Large
3. PDCR (periphery)	IT services	Medium
4. PDCR (mixed)	Finance	Small
5. FCR (periphery)	Construction	Small
	The role of the state is minimal	
1. PDCR (periphery)	Consulting services	Small
2. FCR (periphery)	Trade	Small
3. FCR (periphery)	IT services	Small
4. FCR (core)	Logistics services	Small

35 According to the 'core-periphery' classification of company interviews (see subsection 4.8.4).

The head of a small foreign company (FCR2/Periphery: Periphery) which distributes digital software supported that view, saying, 'since there is no production in our industry, as such, and only services are sold, the state does not acquire shares in private companies in our industry.'

SMEs view their development largely through a liberal lens, with little involvement from the state. These companies represent the 'periphery' part of the economy. According to representatives of SMEs (PDCR8, FCR1, FCR2, FCR4, FCR5), the state deliberately provides 'freedom of manoeuvre' for small companies. But there is also a perception on the part of SMEs that the state should be more involved in effective coordination of the market, as the conditions for small business are currently unstable (PDCR8, FCR2, FCR4, FCR5). A sometimes 'chaotic' evolution is characteristic of SMEs, and this leads to lower predictability and short-term investment strategies among private firms. Representatives of SMEs hold that state intervention is necessary for effective law enforcement, as small companies often face market distortions and need the support of the state in tackling them (PDCR8, FCR2, FCR4). Moreover, public financial support of SMEs and big businesses is significant. As PO3 (Periphery) argues, the state regularly allocates funding to SMEs in the form of subsidy programmes and crediting, but, unlike big businesses, there are no proper mechanisms to provide effective control over its flows in the SME sector.

Thus, the question arises: are small and medium-sized private companies deliberately provided with a high degree of economic freedom by the state? Again, opinion differs. Public officials generally share the perception that it is a deliberate state policy to provide as much freedom to private business as possible. But there is also an alternative view. As Ex19 (Periphery) notes, many new industries in the economy emerged after Kazakhstan had gained its independence. As a result, the state had to start regulating these industries 'from scratch', having no experience in dealing with these new type of industries. The state rarely intervenes in these new areas, as it needs to acquire more understanding of the appropriate mechanisms to elaborate for dealing with these industries. The question remains open, though, and requires further research.

The fact that representatives of big companies within the large and capital-intensive industries tend to view the state as dominant, whereas small companies from less capital-intensive industries see it as liberal, serves as an important indicator of the existence of two different parts of the economy – the 'core' and 'periphery', demonstrating differing degrees of state involvement based on the size of business, understood in terms of its number of employees and operating capital. This categorization of respondents into two camps, one perceiving the state role as substantial in scope and the other as non-interventionist, indicates that one part of the economy is heavily regulated and coordinated (the 'core'), whereas the other part is much less coordinated (the 'periphery'). However, PO5 (Core–Periphery) notes that the differences between the two economies are often blurred, as is the degree of regulation; as a result, the degree of economic freedom may vary from sector to sector.

The key challenge is to characterize the two parts of the economy and to show how they both function. In order to better identify and understand the main differences, the essential aspects of state–business interrelations and their dynamics are analysed in the next subsections.

5.1.2. State involvement over time

What has been the role of the state in the economy since independence? In order to address this question, the extent of the state's involvement in coordinating private business, as perceived by interview respondents, must be considered. The values employed in content analysis are as follows: 'the involvement of the state is excessive'; 'the involvement is moderate'; 'there is little involvement' on the part of the state. Two periods are examined: 1991–2000 and 2001–2010. Frequency Table 5.4 shows how respondents assess the degree of state involvement in coordinating the activities of private business over time.

Frequency Table 5.4. State involvement in the economy over time

Level of state involvement					
1991–2000			**2001–2010**		
Excessive	Moderate	Little	Excessive	Moderate	Little
7	3	6	3	10	4
4 IORs 1 PO 1 FCR 1 PDCR	2 FCRs 1 PO	5 POs 1 FCR	1 PDCR 1 IOR 1 PO	5 POs 3 FCRs 1 IOR 1 EAR	1 PO 1 FCR 1 PDCR 1 IOR

Seven respondents perceive the level of state involvement in the activities of private business, 1991–2000, as excessively high; three respondents view it as moderate, and six respondents see little involvement. The second period, 2000–2010, is assessed as follows: three respondents view state involvement as extremely high; ten respondents view it as moderate; and four respondents consider that there was little state involvement.

This frequency of perceptions reveals several interesting patterns. In general, the distribution of answers indicates that state involvement in the first period (1991–2000) is seen as moderately high, whereas during the second period (2001–2010) it is perceived as moderate. As regards the six respondents who said that there was little state involvement in the first period, five of them are public officials, who are likely to support the view that the state did not intervene too much in the affairs of private business. First, they are themselves state representatives, and since excessive state involvement is usually perceived negatively, they may be reluctant to acknowledge that it was excessive. Second, the first period of independence is officially viewed in a positive light, given the radical reforms the government had to implement in shifting from the command to market economy, so market reforms as such are usually associated with economic freedom. These five public officials, however, acknowledged that during the second period, the state strengthened its role in coordinating private business activities – which they see as justified, given the debilitating impact of external shocks (like the economic crisis of 2008) on the economic situation. The state had to intervene in order to mitigate the consequences of these external shocks; and indeed, it succeeded in overcoming the negative impact of the crisis on the economy. The first period is generally viewed by public employees as a 'learning period' during which the state provided much economic freedom to economic actors. It also accumulated knowledge and gained capacity to become a more active regulator of economic processes. The economic crisis of 2008 became the culminating point in the changing role of the state, with a shift towards more active coordination of economic processes.

As regards the four respondents who said that there was little state involvement during the second period, the first respondent represents a small foreign company in the construction industry (FCR5/Periphery), the second a small domestic firm operating in the finance industry (PDCR1/Mixed). The third respondent is a high-ranking public official (PO2) directly involved in economic policy-making. It seems likely that she said there was 'little involvement' because of her own direct participation in the official decision-making processes. This was her response:

> We have already reached the stage of attracting capital and investment. We think this level of development is sufficient to sustain certain rates of economic growth. The reforms in the social sector have been passed successfully. In some areas we introduced abrupt market mechanisms that many developed countries in the West tried to avoid. We escaped subsidies in the housing and communal sector. Here, we have target support which implies the involvement of market mechanisms and work on compensation mechanisms. In 2005, a serious reform process in the housing and communal sector was started; since 2002 we discontinued controlling tariffs which are currently not subsidized at all. They are based on market principles or the break-even point (PO2/Core–Periphery).

Moreover, this respondent concludes that Kazakhstan has been able to take an enormous step forward in terms of implementing market reforms: 'I would say we have had fundamental reforms in almost in every sector. The "market economy coefficient"[36] in this entire system of reforming the economy from the

36 A term coined by the respondent during the interview.

command administrative to the market system makes it around 90 per cent.'

Finally, the fourth respondent (IOR23/Core–Periphery) is the head of an international organization which has operated in Kazakhstan for many years. As regards the second period, this respondent explained:

> The government is trying to be very active in the economy in terms of encouraging business development, encouraging foreign investment, encouraging whatever priorities they may have set for the development of the economy. And their current priorities are SME development, technology development – certain things they identified as being very important for Kazakhstan to really push it ahead apart from oil and gas, which develops by itself.

IOR23 considers that there was little state involvement during the second period, because this respondent had been advising the state on various projects devoted to introducing market reforms for many years. Given the enormous efforts the state invests in order to develop its market economy, the state's interference might, by definition, be viewed by IOR23 as 'little'.

In general, and as all respondents noted, learning from other development models and implementing market reforms has not been a smooth or easy process. The role of the state and the level of state intervention have depended heavily on Kazakhstan's economic performance since independence. During times of crisis, the state intervened in the economy to the extent needed to save the country from collapse (PO3/Core–Periphery), and this is how the state justifies its involvement.

Thus, since independence the state has played an ambivalent role, shifting from one approach to another. The role of the state in the economy is actively and widely debated in Kazakhstan. Respondents noted that the economic crisis of 2008 forced the state to intervene and bailout the hard-hit banking and construction industries (IOR15/Core–Periphery). During the second period, the government introduced so-called 'manual control' over economic processes (PO2/Core–Periphery).

In general, the first period was characterized by a high level of state involvement in economic processes, but during the second period private actors faced only 'moderate' involvement from the state. Respondent IOR1 (Core–Periphery) said that state involvement in the first period of independence was high; however, the state lessened its involvement over time:

> I started my work experience here in the 1990s. When I was in consultancy my first work in Kazakhstan was on privatization. If we compare what I experienced during my first three years of work to what was happening in 2001, they are, of course, two different things. If we compare what I have seen in Uzbekistan in the mid-90s with what is happening at the moment, I guess it is almost the same with slight changes. In Kazakhstan the situation is different today (*less state involvement*). I would not say it is 'state control' in Kazakhstan; it is more 'state supervision'.

In his opinion, even though Kazakhstan remains an active reformer in the region and its development path differs from those pursued in neighbouring countries, many processes associated with state–business interaction are still overly complicated. He explains:

> However, through my 'Western' eyes many things look absurd. For example, if I want to make payment, or at least transfer a 'laughable' amount of money, I need to get a bank contract and show that it is legitimate money and prove it has nothing to do with terrorism or drug sales. In the US you transfer as much money as you want. At the end of the year you just have to show everything to the tax office and they make selective inspections. There are totally different paradigms in terms of government interference. Here you are under constant supervision and the government for some reason always thinks that businesses are not doing things properly. But again, compared to Uzbekistan, it is a totally different story. It's total control in Uzbekistan. Compared to the situation in other Central Asian states, Kazakhstan looks much better and solid. Especially, compared to Uzbekistan and Turkmenistan in terms of business interference. Or we can see what is happening now in Kyrgyzstan as regards raid actions, etc. I guess this kind of things happened here in the 1990s. I think it is a bad luck that Kazakhstan is located in this region and perhaps a lot should be merited to the government that they do not tend to compare themselves much to Uzbekistan (IOR1/Core–Periphery).

The interviews revealed another pattern pertaining to big foreign oil companies. The state's attitude and level of involvement concerning big foreign business has changed in line with different patterns. Note that this pattern was also revealed in the literature review (see subsection 2.1.7). During the first decade of independence, the government provided especially favourable conditions to large foreign oil businesses, with little intervention from the state. However, as PO1 (Core) observes, 'they (*foreign investors*) thought that our favourable treatment was in fact our weakness.'

After 2000 the situation changed. The government tightened the conditions governing big foreign investors, and the introduction of the Law on Subsoil and Subsoil Use of 24 June 2010 became the key indicator of this changing attitude. IOR15 (Core) highlights the fact that Kazakhstan experienced significant economic growth after 2000, and thus gained political levers for influencing investors – levers that the state had not possessed during the first decade. Kazakhstan is now in a position to dictate its 'rules of the game' to big investors, unlike in the 1990s. For instance, as another respondent noted, the state may now require large foreign oil investors to invest significant sums in social responsibility projects, and this is exactly the area that the state is currently promoting (IOR3/Core).

Therefore, we can conclude that the level of state involvement during the first period is generally perceived as rather 'excessive' by private players, except for most big foreign oil businesses. During the second period, state involvement is perceived as rather 'moderate' by most private economic players and 'excessive' by big foreign oil companies (see Frequency Table 5.5).

Frequency Table 5.5. Summary of state involvement over time

Level of state involvement	
1991–2000	**2001–2010**
1 pattern: Viewed as 'excessive' by every type of business	**1 pattern:** Viewed as 'moderate' by every type of business
2 pattern: Viewed as 'low' by big foreign oil businesses	**2 pattern:** Viewed as 'excessive' by big foreign oil businesses

These patterns reflect the general situation, based on the perceptions expressed by my interviewees. These patterns may not always accommodate the specific cases of various foreign and domestic companies, which may have different attitudes concerning the level of state involvement in the period 1991–2010. Nevertheless, it is important to note how the majority of respondents view the changing role of the state over time. These patterns, as central economic and policy background, can help to explain the nature of state–business interrelations. Given the constant and dynamic change in the degree of state involvement in the activities of private business, it is difficult to identify clear patterns in state–business interaction and assign various businesses to either 'core' or 'periphery'. The degree of state involvement has been subject to dynamic change caused by modified government priorities in different periods since independence. Even though clear patterns are difficult to identify, this observation is an important indicator in itself, as it indicates that the background conditions for the emerging market economy in Kazakhstan have been dynamic and constantly changing since 1991. It is thus important to account for these dynamics when analysing the nature of state–business interaction in greater detail.

5.1.3. Factors for the success of private business

How can private businesses ensure that they follow a successful strategy and solve their problems? What are the factors involved in private business success? In order to shed light on successful strategies, we need to investigate the effects of communication between private businesses and the state. This section will show the importance of constant communication between private companies and the state for problem solution of private business. Here, 'communication' refers to private actors voicing their problems to the state, discussing and trying to solve them. Other aspects of communication (lobbying, advocacy, mutual informal support, etc.) are not dealt with in too much detail here, and would require further in-depth research. This work specifically focuses on 'communication channels for problem solution of private business', seeking to shed light on how the flow of interaction between the two actors occurs in Kazakhstan. Due to high transaction costs for operating of private business, private actors have to resort to the use of direct channels of interaction with the government. This is in line with findings of Vakulchuk et al. (2012: 198): in order to solve the problems and overcome barriers, local companies resort to the use of contacts with the government.

For the content analysis, three values were employed:

- 'communication with the state is crucial' for private business to achieve its goals or solve problems;
- 'communication with the state is necessary only in some situations' and is not always a key factor for success: private business can manage without assistance from the government and may employ communication channels on an *ad hoc basis*;
- 'no communication with the state is required' for private business to achieve its goals and solve problems: private business does not use communication channels with the state, as it manages to solve its problems and perform without state support and assistance.

As Frequency Table 5.6 shows, the majority of respondents (16) felt that for a private company to operate and perform successfully, it was necessary to have access to communication channels and interact regularly with the government. Eleven respondents considered the *ad hoc* use of communication channels to be important: if a private business faces a problem, it should communicate directly with the state. Of course, that requires already having access to communication channels with the state. Only four respondents felt that communication with the state was not important, and that business can solve its pressing issues without its support. Three of these respondents are from small private domestic companies and one represents a small foreign company. The pattern appears to be that SMEs, which represent the 'periphery' economy, may not require constant access to the government to the same extent that big business ('core') does.

Frequency Table 5.6. Success strategy for private business

Factors important for the success of private businesses			
Communication with the state is crucial	*Ad hoc* communication	No communication is required	Other
16	11	4	1
5 POs 5 IORs 4 FCRs 1 PDCR 1 EAR	4 IORs 3 FCRs 2 PDCRs 1 PO	3 PDCRs 1 FCR	1 PO

We find further important patterns within this subcategory. First, five public officials hold the opinion that private business should deal with a range of public agencies and maintain frequent communication. They view this as justified: they see the state as the key economic player, so private business should learn from the state. As PO2 (Core–Periphery) argues, the state provides necessary support for private business, as private business itself is not able to deal with existing market inefficiencies:

> I would describe our economic policy as based on market mechanisms. The only sector where I think the government has taken strong control is in the capital intensive sectors. This is what the Keynesian model suggests as well. Today in Kazakhstan we do not have any single financial-industrial group that would be able to manage the implementation of large capital-intensive projects or the creation of big industrial production units. Here we need state intervention and support, so the state has developed its own position and policy line and allocates resources to this participation scheme. However, the participation scheme and the system of management are built on market principles which were the reason for separating political and economic functions. The founding of Samruk-Kazyna and similar holdings is a continuation of market functions: the state is involved in this, but by indirect means. I mean, the people who occupy political positions – the ministers and prime ministers – are not involved in the development and implementation of these projects. They are involved in creating conditions; that is very important because it ensures a balance and does not let state regulation become archaic and kill off entrepreneurial activity in the country. The government is the one to define when to put the objects into operation. When certain levels and rates are reached, and the breakeven of a particular enterprise is guaranteed, the government lets the enterprise go, can offer it for sale or can decrease its share in it. This is what we have observed over the past few years. According to the legislation, we do not have nationalization in the country; it is prohibited.

In my view, the key point of this public official (PO2/Core) is that the state participates in the economy and this 'participation scheme and the system of management are built on market principles.' This respondent sees state involvement and support as vital, and cites Samruk-Kazyna as an example of state intervention in the economy by indirect means.

On the one hand, the state takes care of private business in capital-intensive industries, 'as parents take care of their children' (PO5/Core). On the other hand, private businesses in the 'core' may sometimes face excessive bureaucratic involvement on the part of the state. The same holds at the local level of politics. Regional officials want to remain key decision-makers so that private business cannot do without them. Some of them are old bureaucrats who still operate with a Soviet mind-set: they may talk about market reforms and changes, but they think within the old framework (IOR15). In other words, the Soviet path-dependence matters in that context. The five public officials mentioned constant communication with private business as a natural and inevitable thing (by contrast, in advanced Western market economies the state usually seeks to provide as much economic freedom to private business as possible, and to minimize the contact between the state and entrepreneurs). As the head of a foreign construction company (FCR5/Periphery: Periphery) argues, contact with the state requires a lot of bureaucracy, which may prove too costly and burdensome for a private company. Thus, that company will decide not to seek access to the government, and, according to this respondent, will even view communication with the government as a burden. As shown below, such attitudes may be the result of ineffective communication channels between the state and private domestic SMEs.

As PO2 (Core) noted, big local private business is not strong enough to be fully independent of the state, manage big investment projects and develop completely on its own. This may relate to the lack of market and entrepreneurship traditions in Kazakhstan due to the Soviet past and the command economy. In Case in Point 5.1, PO3 (Core–Periphery) describes the lack of market traditions and the attitude of entrepreneurs toward market reforms during the first years of independence.

Case in Point 5.1. Entrepreneurs' attitudes toward the first market reforms

'When we first obtained independence and became a sovereign state, of course, no one really understood what the *market* was. It was some chaotic movement which was understood differently by different people. I remember that in 1991 I started my business and in 1993 tax inspectors came to me. I could not understand why they came to me and why I had to pay taxes. This is how the situation looked like. Then everything started to normalize and we became actors in the market economy: you should not interfere, the market is free, the market regulates everything; we were so much taken up by the romanticism. But the two crises of 1998 and the recent one have shown what it really is; in 1998 the state did intervene much in the market processes; but since there were too many complaints and things like that and after the prices went up, after terrible inflation and social conflicts started…That's when the state decided to intervene. Actually, we were the first to start this process; maybe we received the information late, but I know that among our neighbouring countries we were the first to start working on its implementation. After that, we started to regulate these processes. Of course, there were many complaints because the people could breathe the freedom; but now the state is intervening. There have been lots of conflicts and debates and now they came up with this concept of 'manual control'. But we will see how it is going to work in the future. I think that the world is shifting towards these processes…' (PO3/Core–Periphery).

Another pattern relates to attitudes of representatives of private companies. The distribution of respondents' perceptions by industry and size of company helps to illustrate this pattern. As can be seen from Table 5.7, it is hard to draw clear-cut conclusions concerning what kinds of companies (in terms of size and industry) view communication with the state as crucial for success and problem solving. However, from the overall Frequency Table 5.6, it appears that most companies generally deem regular communication with the state as central to success.

Table 5.7. Perception of communication by companies

Communication with the state is crucial		
Company	**Industry**	**Company size**
1. FCR (core)	Oil and gas	Large
2. FCR (core)	Banking	Large
3. PDCR (periphery)	Manufacturing	Large
4. FCR (mixed)	Trade	Small
5. FCR (core)	Logistics	Small
***Ad hoc* communication with the state**		
1. FCR (mixed)	Service	Large
2. PDCR (core)	Oil and gas	Large
3. PDCR (mixed)	Construction	Medium
4. FCR (periphery)	IT services	Small
5. FCR (periphery)	Trade	Small
No communication with the state is required		
1. PDCR (periphery)	Construction	Large
2. PDCR (periphery)	IT services	Medium
3. FCR (periphery)	Construction	Small
4. PDCR (periphery)	Consulting services	Small

From Table 5.7, another clear pattern emerges. Communication with the state is crucial for various types of foreign business, although it may not necessarily be important for representatives of private domestic companies. As noted by IOR15 (Core–Periphery), the constantly changing rules of the game and dynamic business environment make it difficult for foreign companies to operate in Kazakhstan, whereas local entrepreneurs find it easier to operate in this familiar environment. Such companies may have established close relations with local bureaucracies and know how to solve problems quickly, or avoid them. Foreign companies may not have these advantages, and thus often face greater problems in dealing with regional public officials. In the end, the operating environment may be equally complicated and challenging for local and foreign entrepreneurs alike, although the former will generally be more aware of existing problems and have appropriate tools for dealing with them. Especially when entering the market, foreign companies may experience such problems and need state support, advice and consultancy assistance (IOR15/Core–Periphery). Later, once they have adapted to the local rules of the game and have been operating in the country for a while, representatives of foreign companies tend to report fewer issues and concerns, and assess the operating environment more positively. As Ex1 (Core–Periphery) notes:

> There is the official entry mode through the 'Welcome to Kazakhstan' slogan, and there is the unofficial entry mode. You see, a business cannot enter the local market on its own. It doesn't work in a classical way when investors come, invest and operate. This is true when investors work with the central government which is transparent. But when they come to the regional level, they first have to get their decisions endorsed by the local authorities.

Endorsement from regional authorities is what may make the entry point complicated for foreign firms. Then foreign investors may rely on support of the central government or appeal to their respective embassies. In any case, they need access to effective communications channels to be able to raise their concerns and get their problems solved.

Domestic and foreign entrepreneurs may seek governmental support and assistance through various channels of communication. This is where the main lobbying activities of private business take place. Channels for communication are important at all levels of entrepreneurial activity and play a central role also for the government in coordinating economic processes. Here we should distinguish between communication channels for foreign businesses and for domestic ones.

Foreign businesses

According to the majority of respondents, the most effective communication channels are as follows: the Foreign Investors' Council (FIC), the American Chamber of Commerce, and the European Business Association of Kazakhstan (EUROBAK). In addition, there are two other associations – KAZENERGY, and the Association of Mining and Metallurgical Enterprises (AMME) – that bring together domestic and foreign energy players (KAZENERGY) and mining companies (AMME), both seen to be effective.

These associations serve as platforms for representing and promoting the interests of large foreign businesses vis-à-vis the state. According to IOR23 (Core), regular communication with the state through FIC is absolutely necessary for the success of private businesses:

> To get things done, it is necessary to have a friendly relationship with the government. The Foreign Investors' Council is the biggest platform for communication. It is a well-respected organization. A lot of companies take part in it and they even fight to get into it so their voices can be heard.

During sessions of the Foreign Investors' Council, consultations are conducted between big investors and the government. In contrast to KAZENERGY, which includes domestic and foreign energy players, only big foreign companies belong to the FIC.[37] Its current membership consists of foreign companies mainly from extraction industries. Thus, the Council represents the interests of foreign oil and gas businesses. In 2012, the FIC had five working groups: Investment Image Enhancement Group, the Taxation Working Group, the Oil and Gas Working Group, the Legal Working Group and the Operations Working Group (Foreign Investors' Council 2012). In 2014, three working groups functioned at the FIC: Operations Working Group, Investment Policy Working Group and Innovative-Technologies and Economy Diversification Working Group (Foreign Investors' Council 2014). These working groups aim to support foreign business through regular communication with key local stakeholders (FCR1/Mixed: Core).

According to most respondents, meetings are held regularly between government officials and representatives of the companies within the Council. President Nazarbayev acts as FIC chair and frequently invites high-ranking businessmen, like the CEOs of Shell, Exxon, or Chevron, to discuss their activities, problems and future projects (FCR1/Mixed: Core). The same

---

37 Officially, 'the Council is an advisory body established by the "Order of the Head of State" (Order 3985 dated 30 June, 1998) to promote direct dialogue between the Kazakh government and foreign investors in order to address key issues related to the investment activities of foreign companies in the country as well as improve the investment climate in Kazakhstan' (Foreign Investors' Council 2012).

respondent also notes that the Council is widely seen as successful, as both parties actually listen to each other's concerns, and the FIC serves as a useful tool for companies to voice their interests and make the state work to solve their problems. As PO5 (Core) argues, state officials have been making enormous efforts to coordinate the country's oil and gas policy with the multinational oil and gas companies, and thereby improve the investment climate.

Another effective institutionalized communication channel is the public–private initiative of the American Chamber of Commerce (AmCham). It has various working groups which address issues that affect the business environment and private foreign business in Kazakhstan. As IOR23 (Core) notes, AmCham has more than 200 members, although not all of them are representatives of private business, as there are NGO representatives as well. Further, according to this respondent, members can be divided into four main groups: oil and gas, financial services, consumer goods, technologies. Social networking, including lobbying and advocacy, is important in AmCham activities (ibid). As IOR23 (Core) goes on to explain,

> AmCham prepares big public presentations on outstanding issues and problems in the business environment, trying to raise public awareness about what these issues are and why they are important. Importantly, it involves the government. When these events take place in Astana, there is usually a huge government contingent. The Prime Minister, ministers and deputy ministers attend AmCham events; there are also representatives of the Supreme Court and Justice among speakers. So, this is unique because it brings the government and business community together. It is very important that within AmCham the government discusses the issues that the business community raises. This makes them aware of what needs to be worked on to improve the business environment.

AmCham acts together with the representatives of the Prime Minister's Office and other ministries, and all parties participate in working groups and develop policy recommendations. In contrast to the FIC, AmCham represents the interests of various industries; according to FCR1 (Mixed/Core–Periphery), it also unites small and medium-sized companies. AmCham serves as a clear example of a state–business platform, organized in a structured way, which effectively attains its goals, this respondent adds.

A third important communication platform which promotes the interests of European business is EUROBAC. As FCR1 (Mixed: Core) explains:

> R: There are all sorts of institutions established particularly for foreign investors. At the senior level, you have the Foreign Investor's Council. Then, we have EUROBAK and AmCham, which represent a lower level.
>
> *Q: Is there real interaction between the government and private business?*
>
> R: Yes, because guest speakers turn up and field questions and there are lots of panels; lots of committees working on specific projects. I know about the judicial system and the tax system in particular – all the accounting firms, large ones, are

> involved in viewing and approving and advising on tax reforms and similar activities. If you ever ask for clarification with EUROBAK or AmCham, you do get a response.

The FIC, AmCham and EUROBAC mainly unite and represent big foreign companies. The interests of foreign SMEs are somewhat under-represented as not all of them are members of these organizations. FCR1 (Mixed–Periphery) sees this as a disadvantage for these SMEs, as they cannot effectively communicate their problems to the state. Several respondents mentioned other, smaller, associations which support small and medium-sized foreign businesses, like the German Chamber of Commerce in Kazakhstan – but such smaller associations remain less influential. Thus, big foreign business enjoys a generally privileged position in its relations with the state.

Domestic businesses

In order to assess the 'maturity' of local business in terms of its ability to protect its rights and communicate its problems with the state, it is important to see what communication channels are currently available, and how effective they are. Large domestic businesses can communicate their problems through the Forum of Entrepreneurs in Kazakhstan, the Association of Entrepreneurs and Ata-Meken (IOR2/Core), although these are not as effective as the channels for large foreign businesses. As one of the experts interviewed put it, 'at least, they meet. However, the results is a different question' (Ex5/Core). According to another respondent (IOR2/Core–Periphery):

> The Forum and Association are making great efforts to deliver their concerns to the government. And the government cannot be silent. So, in response it organizes councils of economic consultants on different aspects of economic activity. However, I have not seen these structures to be very effective. And yet, when these structures talk too loudly, the government tries to put out the fire somehow.
> *Q: Do these meetings between business and the government take place on a regular basis? Or does it depend on a particular problem?*
> R: It depends on the particular problem. If the tax authorities go wild, business complains (…) I mean, not everything works out for these associations, but at least they are showing that they are pro-active.

Ata-Meken unites small, medium-sized and large businesses, and represents the interests of the entire domestic business sector to the state. In addition, it tries to engage actively in law-making and in initiating draft laws. However, Ata-Meken has remained relatively weak (PO9/Core–Periphery), and only large domestic companies receive significant support (EAR1/Core–Periphery). The majority of SME respondents held that there was a great need for effective associations – otherwise, public agencies would not listen to the business sector. Further,

EAR1 (Periphery) notes, an institutionalized mechanism for exchanging information between SMEs and the state does exist, but this mechanism itself is currently not effective, and is generally weak in institutional and organizational influence. Domestic SMEs lack an effective mechanism for regularly voicing their concerns and solving their problems quickly (EAR1/Periphery). The most common problems mentioned by representatives of SMEs were the following: selective law enforcement and interpretation of laws, frequent tax inspections, sudden changes in legislation.

Foundation for small business support DAMU is one of few channels where small businesses can express and effectively promote their interests. DAMU's main aim is to provide state support to SMEs in various areas (see also Table 3.7) (DAMU 2014). Quite often, if a problem is of acute importance for SMEs and requires state involvement, both parties may also meet to find a solution under *ad hoc* conditions. However, small businesses have to be active and united if they want their problems to be heard and action to be taken. As PO5 (Periphery) put it, 'small business should really make a lot of noise in order to be heard.'

Table 5.8 provides a summary of communication platforms by business size, as assessed by respondents.

Table 5.8. Communication channels by business size

Type of business	Communication channel with the state
Large Foreign Business	Foreign Investors Council, American Chamber of Commerce, EUROBAK
Large Domestic Business	Ata-Meken, Forum of Entrepreneurs of Kazakhstan, KAZENERGY, the Association of Mining and Metallurgical Enterprises
Foreign SMEs	Associations of entrepreneurs, foreign embassies; German Chamber of Commerce in Kazakhstan
Domestic SMEs	Financial Institutions' Association, National Export and Investment Agency KAZNEX INVEST, Foundation for small business support DAMU

The effectiveness of the state–business interaction depends on the level of interaction: the higher the level, the more effectively can problems be solved and more accessible will public officials be. By 'effectiveness' is meant the ability of private firms access public employees officially, arrange meetings, discuss acute problems and find solutions. With a big oil company, for instance, it is highly likely that a problem will be resolved effectively, taking into account the interests of both parties, and in a timely manner, because large businesses have access to communication channels with the state ('core'). The overall situation with decision-making can be seen as a pyramid, at the top of which the effectiveness of decision-making and agenda-setting is seen as optimal by most respondents. The issue of accessibility of public officials plays a crucial role. Ex1 (Core–Periphery) expresses the view that public officials are generally accessible:

> In Kazakhstan it is easy to meet, talk and find a compromise with public officials. For instance, it is quite easy to meet *akims* (mayors; the heads of provincial government) and ministers. The country is not that closed in this regard. You can meet any public official if your projects are intelligible; you can easily find a compromise with them. It's not Russia where it is quite difficult even to meet a minister. Or try to meet the Prime Minister or any other minister in China…

Ex1 draws a relevant comparison between public employees in Russia, China and Kazakhstan. That comparison is relevant because both Russia and China are emerging economies at a somewhat similar stage of development, but on a different scale. The respondent notes that it is much more difficult to access public officials in those countries, whereas it is relatively easy to do so in Kazakhstan. Indeed, I can confirm this, as I was able to meet and interview many high-ranking public officials: they agreed to be interviewed, and proved to be open, easily accessible and helpful with respect to recommending other public officials for my study (see also subsection 4.6.6 and Case in Point 4.3).

Despite the ease of accessing public officials, communication of business with different categories of public officials can still be problematic and ineffective, but for other reasons. We should distinguish between communication with the central government and with regional authorities. Respondents saw the problem of frequent team rotation in public administration in the regions as the main barrier to effective state–business communication. Public officials also acknowledged that intra-governmental rotation is a serious issue. They argued that rotation as such is an effective tool for maintaining a healthy public administration, as it helps avoid entrenchment and corruption. Frequent rotation should help bureaucrats stay competitive and committed to constant self-development. It is also meant to ensure that they stay loyal to the central system rather than the institution and location where they work. However, rotation has also some negative implications.

Major changes in the personnel structure usually occur once a new public official is appointed. He or she will bring in own people, and the composition of the previous staff in the department may change dramatically. There are no restrictions from the state on 'dragging the team', meaning that team members can easily shift from one state department to another if their former director offers them a post. Respondents from private firms all acknowledged this as a serious problem with negative implications on efficient functioning within public administration, as it leads to a lack of continuity and stability in the work of state bodies. This also reduces responsibility of the new appointees, who may reasonably argue that employees need more time to adapt to the new tasks before they can deliver efficient results. This 'learning' period may take a long time, impeding efficiency in the meanwhile. It also leads to Weber's 'fragmentation of responsibility' in public agencies, with direct impacts on state–business interaction. As a result of frequent team rotation, representatives of private companies must constantly adjust to new staff in the ministries and public agencies, which slows down business projects in the long run.

At the top governmental level (the central government and ministries), rotation is relatively rare and the Foreign Investors' Council, AmCham or the European Business Association of Kazakhstan ensure regular and stable communication between high-ranking public officials and representatives of private business. However, state–business interrelations at the regional level (deputy *akims*, heads of local municipalities) suffer from frequent rotation of public employees. As pointed out by the head of one employer association of 'periphery' companies (EAR4/Periphery), 'the key regional public official understands your problem. You come inspired the next day and open his door, but cannot find him there. There you see a completely new team of employees. This happens often…' Because of constant rotation, SMEs find it difficult to cooperate and communicate with public agencies at the regional level. As IOR3 (Periphery) notes, 'it is difficult for private business to consider regional public agencies as stable partners, because of constant rotation in the regions.'

Another issue which affects state–business interaction is that highly-skilled public employees work mainly in the central apparatus and are poorly represented at the regional level; moreover, employment in public administration in oblasts (regions) is not as attractive as in the central apparatus. Thus employees with advanced education, primarily Bolashak graduates (see subsection 3.3.6.1), are under-represented at the regional level. Bolashak graduates work mainly in the central government and ministries, whereas there are almost no public servants with foreign education working at the regional level. Private companies face difficulties in communicating with regional bureaucrats, who tend to retain the Soviet mode of thinking and largely stick to traditional administration and informal practices. According to one expert interviewed:

> Public administration practices between public officials at the governmental level and regional public servants differ (…) There are obvious differences in administration approaches between advanced public employees with Western education in the central apparatus and regional politicians, who have never been abroad and who still have the Soviet mindset (Ex12/Core–Periphery).

So, while representatives of foreign and domestic companies noted the presence of highly-skilled, well-educated and competent public officials at the top governmental level, they found it much harder to work with many regional public employees. As a result, private companies often try to communicate and solve their problems with regional governors through the central government in Astana, which may slow down business operations and project implementation significantly.

In this regard, the communication problems of SMEs are particularly evident. As EAR1 (Periphery) explains:

> R: We are trying to engage in a dialogue with the government, with public agencies, which represent the ministries here in Almaty and other central bodies. It is not because it is modern to do so; but we are trying to make them listen to the problems at lower levels. It is evident that they cannot always see very far below and what under them; public officials do not have relations with the real sector of economy and small business. Therefore, their perception is a bit distorted and here we are trying to show that in reality the situation is different. They sometimes listen to us; sometimes not. I would not say they agree with our argumentation and opinion right away; most likely not. We always have serious debates and disputes with them on different matters.
> *Q: Are you usually the one who is the initiator of such joint projects?*
> R: As a rule – yes.

SMEs are often the drivers of change and work hard to attract the state to deal with their problems. They may organize various initiatives or working groups to interact with the state. By contrast, the state takes a more proactive stance with respect to communication with big businesses and is often the driver of change. Importantly, these communication processes indicate the emergence of new culture and traditions of state–business interaction unheard-of during the Soviet era.

Another important observation is that the higher the level of communication, the more predictable is state policy seen to be by private business. The formation of the Customs Union between Russia, Kazakhstan and Belarus came as a surprise for representatives of SMEs – but not for the representatives of big business, who had been in regular contact with the government through established communication platforms and were prepared for changes (PDCR4/Periphery: Core–Periphery). The Customs Union was created on a highly accelerated track in 2010, without SMEs being properly or fully informed about the changes for business and the potential consequences for certain industries:

> I think that the law on the Customs Union's formation between the three states is unclear and the Union came as a surprise for small business. This will negatively impact small and medium-sized business, especially producers of goods as it is very difficult for domestic companies to compete with companies from Belarus and Russia. Even though my own company does not produce anything, still I think this is a problem for small private business (PDCR4/Periphery: Core–Periphery).

Big business enjoys greater predictability as to policy-making than do private SMEs, who may find it difficult to anticipate state measures and policies. In general, and unlike large businesses ('core'), small and medium-sized companies ('periphery') do not have effective channels for communication with the government and find the operating environment less predictable. However, the financial sector is an exception: there is a well-established institutional platform in the form of the Financial Institutions' Association of Kazakhstan, which has been successful in promoting the interests of small, medium-sized and large financial organizations with the state (see Case in Point 5.2).

Case in Point 5.2. The effective association of bankers

The Financial Institutions' Association of Kazakhstan (FIAK) is considered to be a successful example when it comes to promoting local business interests in finance with the government. It has close relations with the National Bank and elaborates a common position for the whole banking sector on particular issues. All banks are constantly emailed by the State Agency for Financial Control. The number can reach ten to twenty files with respect to three to four issues a day. All issues which relate to the financial sphere, legislation, taxation are covered and discussed by the Agency. For all the innovations which the state promotes, the Agency informs the banks. The public sector considers this form of cooperation a useful bridge between the government and private banks. Cooperation between the Association and Agency is considered effective. If a new law or a draft is introduced, then it is discussed by both sides. Opinions of both parties are collected and expressed to all stakeholders. In some instances private banks must reply to requests from the Agency, even though the implementation of certain decisions is done on a voluntary basis.

Every financial organization is informed of new laws through the communication platform between the Association and the State Agency. Moreover, all second-tier banks are updated on legislation from the database '*Zakon*' (Law), which is constantly revised by the Republican Centre of Legal Information. A lively exchange of information takes place concerning concrete issues which the Agency takes up and circulates to banks. Opinions from all financial institutions are collected. The same relates to any state bank. For instance, Halyk Bank may circulate a request regarding a particular issue. The Agency then facilitates communication between the public bank and private organization. From this perspective, law-making is perceived as a lively and transparent process by participants in the financial sector, as all players have a right to express opinions and can trace every legal development that may impact their activities. Thus, it would be more difficult for a private bank to protect its interests on an individual basis. In this regard, the financial sector has structured communication mechanisms that help the state to better cooperate with the private sector (PDCR1/Mixed: Core–Periphery; FCR11/Core: Core–Periphery).

As noted, most respondents see frequent communication with the state as crucial for a private company to operate and develop successfully in the business environment of Kazakhstan. Here we can conclude that big businesses, especially foreign ones, are in a better and more privileged position ('core') than small and medium-sized companies ('periphery'), because the former enjoy direct access to effective communication channels, which helps to facilitate problem-solving. The 'periphery' companies are also disadvantaged because they deal mainly with regional authorities who represent local level of politics. Respondents see the frequent rotation of public employees at the regional level as the main barrier to effective state–business communication as regards 'periphery' companies.

Thus, different companies differ in their capacities for communication and interaction with the state. It is natural that big companies ('core') have more resources and capacities than SMEs ('periphery') for participating actively in state–business interaction and promoting their agenda. Probably this is the case in any economy and it should not be surprising. However, in the case of Kazakhstan this distinction is noteworthy as it indicates the broader structure of the economy. Further analysis of the differences between various companies and differing state attitude towards them is provided in the next subsection.

5.1.4. Reasons for differing state treatment of private business

Another important indicator of state–business interrelations are state attitudes towards small, medium-sized and large businesses. The previous subchapter showed that private businesses in the 'core' have the advantage of more effective channels of communication with the state than companies in the 'periphery'. That there are effective and less effective communication platforms also reflects the fact that the state may treat various businesses differently – providing support and attention to companies depending on their size, ownership structure, strategic considerations, compatibility of state and business interests, and other reasons. Content analysis has helped to identify why some businesses may experience varying treatment from the state.

This subcategory was used in order to capture respondents' views on why the state treats various types of business differently. An especially important factor was the *size of business*: if a business is low in capitalization, it may be a subject to little regulation and involvement from the state. In Kazakhstan, small-sized companies, measured in terms of personnel, are usually small in terms of capitalization as well. Other factors are *company ownership*: if a company is foreign/private and not state-owned, it has more benefits, as the state will regulate and involve less in its activities; *strategic considerations*: the government protects strategic industries and is interested in cooperating with companies working within these industries; *lack of state capacity*: the state lacks sufficient capacity to treat all types of private business in the same way, and thus focuses only on companies from industries deemed highly profitable for the entire economy; and *the merging of state interests with business interests*: when the state has certain stakes in big businesses, they are more likely to receive necessary support. Additionally, respondents mentioned other reasons, which are presented below.

The majority of respondents – 19 people – held that 'size of business' is one of the major reasons for differing state attitudes towards various businesses (Frequency Table 5.9). Twelve respondents mentioned that 'company ownership' matters; and six thought that, due to 'strategic considerations', the state may treat different industries and types of private businesses differently. Six respondents viewed 'strategic considerations' as the main reason for differing state attitude towards private companies. Four respondents saw 'merged interests of state and business' as important. Finally, 3 POs provided other reasons for differences in state attitudes.

Frequency Table 5.9. State attitudes to private business

Reasons for differing treatment of private business				
Size of business	Company ownership	Strategic considerations	Merging of state interests with business interests	Other
19	12	6	4	3
5 POs 5 IORs 4 PDCRs 3 FCRs 2 EARs	8 IORs 2 FCRs 1 SCORs 1 PDCR	4 IORs 2 POs	3 IORs 1 EAR	3 POs

Most respondents say that the *size of business* can be a decisive factor for differential treatment. This view is supported by all types of categories of respondents, which makes the finding even more valid. What does the size of business mean? It means that after achieving a certain level of capitalization, a private company may risk higher state regulation or a potential take-over, but it may also enjoy more state support and gain access to platforms for effective communication. Thus, private companies have a choice of expanding and becoming a subject of higher state regulation, or remaining at a lower level of economic activity. Here I should note that greater state involvement is not always perceived negatively, and opinion on this subject differs considerably. For instance, a public official (PO2/Core) holds that substantial state involvement is justified because large businesses are not capable of implementing huge capital-intensive projects.

Examples 1 and 2 (see Table 5.10) show how the expansion of a business may lead to increased attention from various interest groups or even a hostile take-over. Therefore, a company may decide not to exceed a certain range of capitalization, so as to be able to continue operating in an environment with less regulation. Moreover, from Example 3 we see that, in certain industries, companies cannot expand because the market in question is shared by many small private companies. Because of the lack of big companies and low capital-intensity in the market, the state is not particularly interested in active regulating and coordinating this sector, so companies here operate in a more market-oriented environment ('periphery').

Example 4 shows that private companies in the mining sector are exposed to state influence and regulation because of the high capital-intensity of the sector ('core'); and that small companies are more vulnerable than large ones ('periphery').

Example 5 also supports the argument of the interconnection between the capital-intensity of a sector and the rate of state involvement. Moreover, FCR4 (Periphery: Core–Periphery) holds that companies in a capital-intensive sector have a say as regards their interaction with the state, since these companies usually enjoy the support of employer associations. In contrast, companies in sectors that generate little turnover are disadvantaged, because any associations representing their interests are less powerful (see subsection 5.1.3). This respondent adds that big business usually enjoys favourable treatment from the state ('core') – transparent registration procedures, constant updates on new amendments in legislation, etc.

In Example 6, a representative of an international organization provides an example of a special programme for SME development ('periphery'): entrepreneurs supplying bottled water were offered to expand their activities, which would increase their sales volumes. However, these entrepreneurs argued that 'if we do what you are saying our sales will be increased and we will come to the "surface".' And so, they opted not to expand in order to operate in an environment with less regulation. EAR1 (Periphery) says that private entrepreneurs may sometimes split one company into two or more smaller ones in order to stay 'invisible', so that they can remain within the more market-oriented environment. Why do small companies prefer the market-oriented environment? As EAR1 (Core–Periphery) notes, small companies can use a simplified declaration in reporting on their activities, and they pay lower taxes to the state:

> In contrast to medium-sized business individual entrepreneur is a more convenient form of operation today which is characterized by simpler taxation policy. For middle-sized and big business the taxation policy is much harder: they have to pay corporate income tax; therefore, many of them split off and transformed into small businesses in order to pay less taxes.

Until 2010, one entrepreneur could establish two or more enterprises at the same time, in order to pay lower taxes and work in a business environment which implies little regulation and coordination by the state. As a result, the state introduced a change in the legislation, prohibiting entrepreneurs from founding two or more enterprises at the same time (EAR1/Periphery).

This example shows that even though the 'periphery' companies operate in a more market-oriented environment by being subject to simplified regulation and experiencing little involvement from the state, they are also more vulnerable than big companies. Many 'periphery' companies are afraid to grow and expand. However, growth is what usually drives economic development. Firms have to grow gradually; otherwise the overall economy may suffer and stagnate. For instance, German Mittelstand (SMEs) has been viewed as the main driver of the economic development in Germany; on average SMEs contribute to more than 50 per cent of total economic output in Germany (Federal Ministry of Economics and Technology 2012). Unlike Germany, SMEs in Kazakhstan contributed to only 14 per cent of GDP and to 20.2 per cent in 2011 (ADB 2005; Agency of Statistics 2011) (see also subsection 2.1.1).

In Example 7 a public official acknowledges that SMEs do face numerous problems, especially access to finance and frequent inspections. Even though small companies may operate in an environment with less direct state influence, they still have to deal with sudden and apparently uncalled-for public inspections that may disrupt their activities ('periphery'). This official goes on to explain that the state is now seeking to restrict such inspections, further simplify licensing and other procedures for SMEs. In his response, PO8 (Periphery) notes the commitment of the state to improve operating environment for SMEs. That is a central point: that the state is less involved in SME activities not only because of the low capitalization of SMEs, but also as a matter of a deliberate state policy to provide as much economic freedom to SMEs as possible (PO5/Periphery; PO8/Periphery) – while being deliberately interventionist with respect to big companies in capital-intensive sectors (PO2/Core; PO18/Core).

Table 5.10. Size of business as a reason for differential treatment

Ex. 1 'You see, when a business reaches a certain scale, it becomes an object of focus for certain groups. As long as you are in one particular turnover range, everything is quiet and regulation is insignificant. In Kazakhstan it's almost the same as in Russia' (IOR5/Core–Periphery).
Ex. 2 'A company which has got too big in size may become an attractive candidate for a hostile take-over' (IOR24/Periphery).
Ex. 3 'Depending on the volume and turnover the interest of the state toward a particular industry changes (…) If you take the entire [elevator] business in Kazakhstan, of course, the volume and turnover is huge. However, each separate business is privately owned. For instance, last

year the turnover of my business was very small. The major part of it was spent abroad to purchase equipment. About 10 million Tenge left on my account. Who would ever be interested in this amount?' (PDCR3/Periphery: Periphery).

Ex. 4

'Some small Korean companies in mining had a tough time here, because local partners decided to have the whole company and not just the part of it. It is a problem, particularly with small companies that seem more vulnerable than big companies. It is very difficult to go to the economic courts. They are not very competent at dealing with these economic cases' (IOR23/Periphery).

Ex. 5

'I think that the government is strongly influenced by the sectors that generate budget earnings: the oil and gas sector, for example. These are the main ones. It is quite obvious that the state will receive less tax from smaller scale companies and correspondingly, the associations representing them will be less influential' (FCR4 /Periphery: Core–Periphery).

Ex. 6

'I can give you an example. There were bottled water suppliers. We offered them to expand their business and instead of 200 bottles of water to supply 500 bottles per day to cut costs and increase sales volumes. The water supplier refused and said: "Why do we need it? If we do what you are saying our sales will be increased and we will come to the 'surface'. We prefer the work stay low". So they prefer to work in this mode' (IOR3/Periphery).

Ex. 7

'No one argues that SMEs do not have any problems in Kazakhstan. There is a problem with access to financial resources. We have these problems. We tackle them. For that we have a special programme called Road Map Business 2020. It is aimed at assisting private business to receive more financial resources for concrete projects, for specific industrial needs. Here we seek maximum simplification of things. Literally, the Ministry of Economic Development and Trade recently launched the project of a law to the Parliament of the Republic on simplification of a licensing system. It would not be like that, when a state body itself issues a directive and goes to inspect business. This will have to be done only through a directive of the government. It has to be a decision of the government. This makes things complicated. It is not like someone wants to go on inspection. One would have to provide grounds for an inspection. How do we have it now: suddenly someone comes, inspects, entrepreneurs are punished, and the latter cannot even react. In order to avoid this, the system is being reformed. We always seek simplification, abolition of a licensing system, i.e. identification of goods that require complex procedures. We have to work constantly on that' (PO8/Periphery).

Another reason why the state attitude holds different attitudes towards different layers of private business relates to the *ownership* of private companies. Twelve respondents, eight of whom were representatives of international organizations, said that the country of origin of a private company influences how the state treats it. Table 5.11 presents examples of respondents' opinions on company ownership and how that influences the overall attitude of the state. Example 1 shows that a private company from Kyrgyzstan may enjoy less preferential treatment than one from Australia. Example 2 backs up this point and sheds light on how foreign companies enjoy a more favourable state regime, with better security of property rights because norms of international legislation are given priority over national legislation. This situation is further explained by IOR5 (Core), who notes that negative state attitudes towards foreign business may be detrimental to the investment climate of Kazakhstan. Foreign investment plays an increasingly important role, so the state has established a regime for foreign companies that differs from the regime for domestic companies. This perception is not fully in line with the official position (as identified in subsection 2.1.7 on FDI) that the state has created an investment regime which targets domestic and foreign investors equally (Tasmagambetov 2005: 34; UNCTAD 2010).

As shown in subsection 5.1.1, there was little state involvement in the activities of big foreign companies in the years immediately after independence. This began to shift during the second period, as Example 3 demonstrates. Here, the respondent explains how, over the course of the past decade, the state has embarked on a strategy of re-assessing the contracts previously granted to large foreign companies governing extraction of natural resources. In the 1990s, the country's leadership lacked negotiating experience and know-how regarding large-scale contracts on resource extraction. The respondent himself had participated in these negotiation processes. Then, in the second decade, after the state had accumulated more experience in the ways of the market economy, and based on international practice, it decided to reconsider some of these contracts, because the government had come to see most of the provisions in these early contracts as being unfair. This state attitude can be characterized as resource nationalism policy, as discussed in subsection 2.1.7 on FDI and trade. Interestingly, one foreign head of a big international organization (IOR24/Core) holds that this change in state attitude towards large foreign business was in fact justified, in view of existing international practices and the disadvantageous conditions for Kazakhstan that were reflected in the very first contracts. He added that this view was shared by many representatives of foreign oil and gas companies operating in Kazakhstan despite numerous court cases.

However, the state has not embarked on the same strategy of reconsidering *all* contracts. Certain countries have enjoyed better treatment. For instance, IOR2 (Core) notes that most US companies were exempted from this process, and their contracts did not undergo change. This points to another important observation: we should differentiate foreign companies by country. Companies from powerful countries with a range of leverage channels may exert more influence than ones from smaller, less influential countries. Moreover, Example 4 shows that a big US company can enjoy more benefits and have more influence, whether through the FIC or the US embassy, than a small US company.

Example 5 provides a recipe for the success of joint companies: as proposed by IOR23 (Core), the bigger a company with foreign shares is, the more formalized its relations with the state will be. As a result, such a company can operate in a more predictable environment. Thus higher predictability of the operating regime is what makes the 'core' different from the 'periphery'.

Table 5.11. Company ownership as a reason for differential treatment

Ex. 1
'I guess the impact is limited. It all depends on origin (...) on citizenship: if it is Kyrgyz, it is the one thing; if it is Australian, it's another thing. I guess there is some inequality among foreign investors. I think some foreigners may resort to other levers of influence such as embassies' (IOR1/Core–Periphery).

Ex. 2
'It is one story when it is the work of a national company; another when it is the international company which is regulated by different laws, normative documents within the framework of international legislation. International legislation is prioritized in comparison with national legislation. It is backed up by the legislation of Kazakhstan and therefore, you cannot just take away or nationalize a foreign enterprise. Well, it is technically possible as it happened in Venezuela but you do not know how it may negatively influence the overall investment climate, international ranking and future opportunities. Everybody clearly understands what might happen. So, nobody is going to play around with that. Thus, on average, foreign companies enjoy better treatment from the state than local ones' (IOR5/Core).

Ex. 3
'The major problems investors face has to do with the recent tendency on contract re-consideration on the use of natural resources. In the 1990s, Kazakhstan had no experience in making contracts on the use of natural resources. I participated in this process as well. I did not have appropriate education, I did not have experience and negotiation qualifications; we had to learn all that right during the process. We had a team and the task of that team was to attract investors and have negotiations with them. We were required to apply the imperfect post-Soviet legislation to the modern international oil and gas and mining projects. We did as we could without having special education. Now, when Kazakhstan has gained enough experience with a market economy, it is quite clear that some of the things were missed then – we learned that when the contract has been signed, it is not subject to any revision and should serve as some provision. There should be a strategy; it should always be persisted that there've been oversights, and therefore, it should be reviewed with reference to international practice, similar international transactions, etc. Certain exceptions are given to certain countries' (IOR2/Core).

Ex. 4
'If you hold an American passport, you just need to contact your embassy and they will make a lot of noise if you are a large company. However, if it is a small company, even from the US, there will be more problems (...) it depends on which companies the

American embassy decides to lobby for or protect. Well, of course, the American embassy will protect the rights of any company, but it is a matter of the extent and intensity of this protection' (IOR2/Core–Periphery).

Ex. 5
'In many cases, some of the smaller companies that were formed by two partners did not survive at all. For larger companies, there is highly formalized process and it works fine' (IOR23/Core–Periphery).

Furthermore, according to PO3 (Core), foreign investments are better protected by the state than domestic investments, and that does not go down well with all domestic entrepreneurs. Some may decide to go abroad, register their business there and then return as investors – that entitles them to be treated by the state as foreign investors:

> All the problems in terms of administrative barriers, wrong tax levies, numerous inspection visits and controlling bodies are discussed to make Kazakhstan look more attractive for investors. However, domestic business complains about it: 'Why aren't these conditions created for domestic investors?' The FIC and the President discuss and work on these issues; I think foreign investments are better protected than domestic (…) Large business established their own associations (e.g. FIC, AmCham, etc.), where they accumulate all their current issues. So in practice we can even see situations when representatives of domestic business go abroad, register a company there and come back as investors. After that they joined some association and now they say that they are more protected than being alone in the domestic market (PO3/Core).

The country of origin matters a great deal in the context of state–business interaction. Foreign companies from the USA, Germany or Australia ('core') may enjoy more favourable treatment than companies from smaller and less influential countries, such as Kyrgyzstan, South Korea or Finland ('periphery').

The third important reason is the *strategic importance* of the sector cited by six respondents. The government regulates and limits access to the strategic sectors of the economy that are deemed important to the national economy. Example 1 in Table 5.12 shows the importance of the oil and gas industry, where the government sets certain restrictions. For instance, increasing opposition to the penetration of Chinese companies in the industry resulted in the adoption of a law on strategic assets. According to the head of an international organization (IOR5/Core–Periphery), this depends largely on the type of industry (see Example 2). He also argues that in industries without strategic elements there are no restrictions in terms of the origin of capital or the company, and foreign companies may purchase assets and control shares in domestic companies in Kazakhstan, also through a takeover transaction.

Table 5.12. Strategic considerations as a reason for differential treatment

Ex. 1 'Well, the government has introduced a lot of laws governing some of the strategic assets of Kazakhstan that should not be taken over wholly by foreign investors. And that includes the oil and gas sector; energy and so on. Whatever they define as being important to the economy and economic security of the country. I think the government of Kazakhstan is against the Chinese buying up all of Kazakhstan's oil. So, they brought in this law about strategic assets and there is supposed to be certain percentage that is left under the control of the government of Kazakhstan' (IOR23/Core).
Ex. 2 'It depends on the area and strategic interest. If it is the oil and gas sector, it's hard to imagine KazMunayGas being taken over by some foreign company. Or let's take big banks such as CenterCreditBank, one of the largest in the country. The Korean share in the bank is constantly increasing. These actions are not prohibited. If the bank is experiencing problems and has opportunities to attract external investments and new management systems, then it's allowed to do so. You see, the point is that this bank is not strategic – it has no strategic elements behind it. Or let's say retail chains: retailing is a purely private business and nobody is interested in them even though they have millions in turnover. Examples can be Eldorado or Euroset of Russia, which own chains of stores and have recently acquired several other stores in Kazakhstan. There are examples when Turkish communication companies were gradually taken and transformed into national companies. It was a reverse process, so to speak. But it depends on to what extent the industry is strategic' (IOR5/Core–Periphery).

Another important reason is the *merging of state interests with business interests*. Example 1 in Table 5.13 shows that it is difficult for a private company to grow large and expand its activities without having the support of the public sector.

Table 5.13. Merging of state interests with business interests

Ex. 1 '*Q: There are two models: American model where the role of the state is minimal in the economic activity and continental European model where, on the contrary, the state is trying to be more involved in coordinating the economy; so, we are trying to find out to which category we can attribute Kazakhstan.* R: In recent years there have been attempts to control through Ata-Meken. However, Ata-Meken could stay only with large businesses (…) You cannot grow large if you do not have the support of the public sector. It is much easier with small and medium-sized businesses; it is more democratic, so to speak, just like anywhere else in the world. It is more risky, of course: thousands of companies open up and close down every year; big business is more stable in this respect' (EAR1/Core–Periphery).

Example 1 also shows that some small companies prefer to stay small and operate in a more 'democratic', or in other words, a market-oriented environment ('periphery'). On the other hand, as EAR1 (Core–Periphery) argues, the rules of the game for big business are more stable than for smaller business.

As for other reasons, three public officials say that the 2010 Customs Union between Russia, Kazakhstan and Belarus has gained in importance and can also serve as an indicator of differentiated treatment of private business by the state. They explain that within the Customs Union, companies from Russia and Belarus receive more favourable treatment, as stipulated in the agreement of the Union. Here I should note a relevant point: the fact that only public officials mentioned this reason is that they were interviewed in 2010, the same year the Customs Union was established. For private companies it was too early to assess the impact and consequences, whereas public officials had already been heavily involved in establishing and administering the Union. Thus, they were aware of the possible consequences and operating conditions for private companies from Belarus and Russia.

Thus, there are many reasons for differing state attitudes towards private business, which help to shed light on the differences between the 'core' and 'periphery' parts of the economy. The next subsection examines the type of investment policies adopted by private companies, analysis of which will help in further exploring the nature of the emerging market economy and the role of the state in determining company investment policy.

5.1.5. Type of company investment policy

What types of strategy do private companies choose to pursue in their business activity? In an LME, private firms will prefer making short-term investments, due to the structure of financial markets; whereas in a CME, private firms tend to invest long-term (Hall and Soskice 2001). In the case of Kazakhstan, the term 'investment policy' should be viewed differently, given the enormous role of the state in shaping the investment regime and operating conditions for private business. This shows the weakness of the VoC approach when applied to the economy of Kazakhstan (see also subsection 3.3.7). Why is this so? In an LME or CME, the structure of a market defines the type of investment policy of private firms (either long- or short-term), and not the extent of state coordination of economic processes, as is the case in Kazakhstan. 'Long-term investment policy' in the context of Kazakhstan means that private companies are confident in their future perspectives because the security of their investments is guaranteed and appropriate conditions are provided by the state. 'Short-term investment policy' means that private companies are not confident in the security of their investment, and appropriate conditions for long-term investments are not fully provided; the investment regime set by the government is somewhat unpredictable; and the rules of the game may constantly change.

Frequency Table 5.14 indicates a clear tendency: twenty respondents said that in general private companies tend to have long-term investment strategies; ten respondents mentioned that private firms pursue mainly short-term investment strategies, given the chaotic economic environment and constantly changing investment rules and regulations.

Frequency table 5.14. Investment strategies of private companies

Type of company investment policy		
Long-term investment strategy	Short-term investment strategy	Other
20	10	5
6 POs 6 IORs 4 PDCRs 3 FCRs 1 SOCR	4 PDCRs 3 FCRs 3 IORs	2 POs 1 SOCR 1 FCR 1 PDCR

Finally, five respondents said that investment strategy depends on specific conditions, and that it is impossible to generalize to other companies and other industries. This indicates clear pattern. I first highlight the distribution of companies by size, as shown in Table 5.15.

Table 5.15. Investment strategy by company size

Long-term investment strategy (CME type of economy)		
Company	**Industry**	**Company size**
1. PDCR9 (core)	Oil and Gas	Large
'We have been running the company for ten years now and it has been successful, we have developed the business over the years, it is growing considerably. We have invested in other businesses here. We are committed to the long term here and investing where there is an opportunity' (Core).		
2. PDCR10 (mixed)	Construction	Large
3. PDCR6 (periphery)	Construction	Large
4. FCR1 (mixed)	Service	Large
5. SOCR2 (core)	Oil and gas	Large
6. FCR6 (core)	Oil and Gas	Large

'We are not worried about making long-term investments (…) with regard to the company, strategic planning is very much developed here. We have good prospects, I guess (…) we are planning to increase the Kazakh share in our purchases; we are taking steps to produce here in Kazakhstan, to avoid imports from abroad' (Core).		
7. FCR11 (core)	Financial industry	Medium
'*Q: Are you afraid of making long-term investments, i.e. are you confident in the stability of the investment regime?* R: You know our country is politically stable. The banking industry will grow anyway. Of course, I think that there will be more and more foreign banks in Kazakhstan. Definitely! They find the investment climate attractive' (Core).		
8. PDCR1 (mixed)	Financial industry	Small
Short-term investment strategy (LME type of economy)		
1. PDC12 (periphery)	IT services	Medium
2. PDCR3 (periphery)	Construction	Medium
'R: I try not to use bank loans. You see, the situation in our country is not that stable. Actually, you should take a bank loan for the things that will bring you profit. *Q: Is it difficult to make plans in the long-term perspective?* R: Yes' (Periphery).		
3. FCR7 (core)	Logistics	Small
4. FCR5 (periphery)	Construction	Small
5. PDCR8 (periphery)	Consultancy services	Small
'I prefer to work on a project-by-project basis. Today the government pays ever increasing attention to small and medium-sized business. The crisis is over, but some problems are still there (…) I work hard to promote my initiatives. However, there are many complicated procedures, and entrepreneurs do not really understand how to get through them' (Periphery).		
6. FCR4 (periphery)	Trade	Small
7. PDCR2 (mixed)	Trade	Small

The main pattern here is that most large private companies employ a strategic approach and invest long-term ('core'), whereas SMEs tend to be more concerned with short-term profit strategies ('periphery'). Importantly, in Kazakhstan, the difference stems not from the fact that the size of business and capital define the type of investment strategy, but from the conditions the government creates for large businesses and small ones. How the government shapes the investment regime for foreign and for domestic companies defines the strategies that private companies pursue in their economic operations. Concerning investment restrictions for foreign investors, all respondents say there are no formal limitations except in the uranium sector and to a lesser extent in telecommunications, where access is restricted.

PO2 (Core) says that priorities to support certain industries are defined by the state by strategic considerations such as the overall significance of a project, its export share, its break-even point, its profitability and the associated employment opportunities. Another public official (PO4/Core–Periphery) says that company investment strategies differ from sector to sector: companies in the natural resources and telecommunications sectors invest long-term, but in general, the more capital-intensive and profitable a sector is, the more interested will the state be in providing a stable investment regime ('core'). He gives examples from other sectors: in the market for electrical energy, he explains, companies do not have a strategic vision as they are 'constantly fighting for survival' due to the low levels of investment and state support in developing the industry. This respondent concludes 'whether investors make strategic decisions or whether they prefer instant profits depends on the regulatory policy of the government.' (Core–Periphery). In turn, according to all representatives of international organizations interviewed, investment policy of private companies also depends on the ability of each company to influence the government. Companies with access to the FIC or other government channels can negotiate their long-term strategies (see subsection 5.1.3). The same holds for state-owned companies. All major state-owned companies under the umbrella of Samruk-Kazyna belong to the economic 'core'. SOCR2 (Core), when asked whether national companies invest long term, noted that 'taking into consideration the fact that it is a national company, related to the state, it is more likely that it will have long-term strategic plans.'

The pattern thus is that most companies, whether private or public, that pursue long-term strategies can be classified as belonging mainly to the 'core', whereas companies with short-term strategies are located mainly in the 'periphery'.

5.1.6. Instruments for solving problems of private business with the state

This important subcategory concerns the four sets of preferred tools used by private companies in case of problems or conflict with the state. First, 'state mechanisms' means that private companies make use of existing legal mechanisms such as economic courts in order to find a solution to their problems. Second, private companies may use 'domestic business mechanisms' – negotiation mechanisms and/or communication channels, such as various forums of entrepreneurs or business associations. Third, private companies may use international platforms for solving their problems with the state, such as international economic courts or various international associations in

Kazakhstan or abroad. Fourth, depending on the particular problem, private companies may use what I have termed ‘a combination of tools’.

As shown in Frequency Table 5.16, most respondents (16) think that the best available option for dealing with public agencies in case of economic disputes or conflicts is to use *business mechanisms*, negotiating and seeking a solution through various channels as they are more effective and less costly. Interestingly, representatives of the ‘international organizations’ category are equally present across all subcategories. This can be explained by the fact that various IORs were aware of the cases when different types of instruments had been utilized.

Frequency Table 5.16. Instruments for problem resolution

Instruments for solving the problems of private business with the state				
State mechanisms	Business mechanisms	International platforms	Combination of tools	Other
3	16	2	4	1
2 IORs 1 PDCR	6 PDCRs 4 FCRs 3 IORs 1 PO 1 SCOR 1 EAR	2 IORs	2 FCRs 2 IORs	1 IOR

In explaining the ineffectiveness of state mechanisms, respondents often mentioned that court decisions tend to go in favour of state companies or public agencies. Moreover, resolving disputes through courts may prove too costly and burdensome for many private companies. Thus, private companies prefer to exhaust all other mechanisms first.

Only three respondents view the use of *state mechanisms*, such as legal means to solve economic disputes, as an effective option. Two respondents perceive international arbitration platforms or international courts as an effective solution for private companies. Four respondents say that both business and state mechanisms can be effective (the combination of state and business mechanisms), depending on the extent of the problem and the specific conditions of the particular case. Finally, one representative of an international organization saw state mechanisms as effective, but too time-consuming. Given this ambiguous response, this respondent was subsumed under the category ‘other’.

Thus, companies prefer business mechanisms such as negotiation and mediation, as they are less time-consuming, and thereby more efficient for private business in terms of time and economic costs incurred. If, however, there is no need for a quick solution, then private companies may turn to the economic courts and open a legal case, which may take longer to resolve. Table 5.17 gives several examples of respondent opinions on this subject. As can be seen, companies from the 'core' may sometimes use state mechanisms to solve their problems (PDCR 9/Core; IOR1; IOR7). However, the great majority of respondents expressed the view that using business mechanisms is preferable for solving disputes with public agencies.

Thus we can conclude that business mechanisms are most widely used by private companies to solve their conflicts and disputes with the state. Representatives of private business stress that negotiating and pre-court resolution mechanisms are important for their overall success, and so ensuring access to these mechanisms is crucial. Yet, representatives of 'periphery' companies generally find business mechanisms less effective than representatives of the 'core' companies. Why is that the case? As shown in subsection 5.1.3, SMEs are at a disadvantage in comparison to big business, with somewhat limited access to channels for effective negotiation mechanisms and channels of communication. In turn, that means that private SMEs require more time to solve their problems, and that may stifle their business activities for a certain period ('periphery'). Large companies are better off, as they have access to communication channels and can quickly and effectively deal with their problems and issues ('core'). Thus, my findings with respect to the use of business instruments for problem resolution reinforce the argument of the importance of having access to effective communication channels with the state.

Most respondents expressed the view that the legal system could be more efficient. Because of the current inefficiencies of the system, economic actors prefer to use negotiation mechanisms and pre-court dispute settlement. How the legal system can be inefficient is clearly expressed by IOR7 (Core–Periphery):

> I mean if you are willing to spend a lot of time you will find later that your case is correctly settled. But usually you require a quick settlement (…) If you don't require speedy resolution, then you go through the court system – yes, you'll get – typically you'll get the correct judgment. But it is a lengthy process. So, it is better to negotiate everything instead of going to the courts.

Businessmen tend to prefer quick resolution of disputes. Legal dispute settlement is seen as being too slow a process. However, as IOR7 notes (Core–Periphery), if there is no time pressure, then it is possible to go through the court mechanism and obtain a fair judgement.

Table 5.17. Respondents' perceptions of problem-solving instruments

State mechanisms
'Q: In the case of conflict: How do you deal with public agencies? Is it the same procedure that you follow with suppliers and clients or not? R: Normally, with a public agency, if there is a decision you are not happy with you have to go through a more formal process. Say if you are not happy with a decision or work permit or a visa being issued, then there is a formal appeal process you have to go through for that' (PDCR9/Core: Core). 'I guess it is increasing. It's not an exception anymore when an entrepreneur goes to court against public agencies and wins the case' (IOR1/Core–Periphery).
Business mechanisms
'Mutual negotiations, etc. This is what we choose. We have never had any kind of court cases and we definitely do not want to take this as an option. So, I mean, until now, we have handled our cases with discussion and negotiation' (FCR7/Core: Core). 'I would try to find a compromise…' (PDCR3/Periphery: Periphery). 'Business-related conflicts? Well, we try to resolve them without resorting to the courts (…) it is very difficult to litigate with public agencies: even when the case is known to be a winnable one, a court may make a decision in favour of some public agency' (EAR1/Core–Periphery). 'We haven't had non-payment or delay type conflicts. As far as I know, the way competitors are trying to solve the issues is they are trying not to get involved in a conflict. If there is some dependency on certain public agencies it is better to find a compromise; to your own loss, perhaps, but it is better not to enter into a conflict; you don't gain from it' (PDCR2/Mixed: Core–Periphery). 'First of all, conflict with a public agency is much worse than a conflict with a supplier or customers. We negotiate. It is hard to negotiate with the law, though. But in general the system works and I would even say that legislation is good and the level of law enforcement is quite high in the country' (PDCR12/Periphery: Periphery).
International platforms
'If companies have disputes instead of going to courts, they go to international arbitration. And that arbitration will be done under English law between external lawyers, where you can be fairly certain that you will get a fair view' (IOR17/Core–Periphery).

Combination of tools
'I think the investor community sees it as a real problem. Number one – because the judges and the lawyers are not terribly well-trained in business disputes. They do not really understand issues. It is particularly weak at the lower levels (…) the higher you go, the better it gets. That's the consensus of opinion. The supreme court is seen as really being very fair and not corrupt. But then also Kazakhstan recognizes decisions, binding decisions at international tribunals as well. So, if investors are totally unhappy even with the decision of the supreme court, they can go to the international labour or business court abroad. And whatever decision is taken or recognized by Kazakhstan it is enforced here (…) Well, maybe a big investor would go to the international courts; for small investors it is expensive. Certainly big oil companies have gone to the international courts on issues like penalties, taxation and so on. Because if they are not satisfied with the resolution they get here, they will go international' (IOR23/Core–Periphery).
Other
'I mean if you are willing to spend a lot of time you will find later that your case is correctly settled. But usually you require a quick settlement…' (IOR7/Core–Periphery).

Another example is provided by IOR23 (Core–Periphery), who expressed the view that private companies may use different tools (see 'combination of tools' in Table 5.17). First, he notes that the court level matters for greater efficiency of the court system. It means the higher the level of the court, the better the entire system works. As an option, foreign investors may appeal to international arbitration. However, small and medium-sized domestic and foreign companies find using international arbitration too costly. This points to an important observation with respect to the 'core–periphery' framework: companies with enough resources to use international arbitration belong mainly to the 'core', whereas companies which find it too expensive to use international arbitration are found mainly in the 'periphery'.

The overall conclusion is that economic actors, both in the 'core' and in the 'periphery', prefer to use business mechanisms to solve their disputes with the state. On the one hand, this points to the inefficiencies of the current legal system. On the other hand, this also indicates the importance of informal mechanisms for problem-solving, which can sometimes be part of business mechanisms. However, analysis of the influence of such informal mechanisms on state–business interaction requires further research and is beyond the scope of this work.

A detailed overview of the instruments for solving problems between private companies is presented in subsection 5.2.5. This will enable comparison of instruments of state–business dispute resolution presented here with instruments of company-to-company problem solving. This in turn will shed more light on key differences between the 'core' and the 'periphery'.

5.2. Analysing inter-firm relations

5.2.1. Type of interaction

This dimension covers interaction between firms, types of interaction, competition, regulation of competition, M&As as well as instruments for solving problems between private firms. It covers the relationships between companies and their suppliers and clients as defined by Hall and Soskice (2001: 7).

Do certain types of firms in Kazakhstan tend mainly to compete or cooperate with each other? Perhaps private or state companies use both approaches (mixed approach), depending on the particular business project or type of industry. As explained, according to the VoC approach, a high level of competition between market competitors is inherent in an LME, whereas in a CME, market competitors will exhibit a high degree of cooperative behaviour (Hall and Soskice 2001).

Frequency Table 5.18 demonstrates that representatives of all types of companies are evenly distributed across two subcategories: 'mainly competitive approach' (11 respondents) and 'mainly cooperative approach' (10 respondents).

Frequency Table 5.18. Interaction between private firms

Type of interaction			
Mainly cooperative approach between firms	Mainly competitive approach	Mixed approach	Other
10	11	2	1
3 PDCRs 4 FCRs 2 EARs 1 SCOR	5 PDCRs 4 FCRs 2 SOC	2 IORs	1 IORs

Two respondents represent the 'mixed approach' and one respondent the 'other' subcategory. Further, judging from the responses, private firms in manufacturing, services, finance, construction, agriculture, postal services prefer to cooperate with each other. By contrast, companies tend to compete with each other in the petroleum industry, logistics, trade in household products, construction (in Almaty), IT services, communications and consultancy (see Table 5.19).

As regards the two respondents who say that private companies use a mixed approach, they also note that it is hard to draw general conclusions, as companies may use various strategies and the choice of strategy depends upon many factors.

Table 5.19. Inter-firm relations by industry

More cooperative relations	More competitive relations
– Manufacturing – Services – Finance – Construction (overall) – Agriculture – Postal services	– Oil and gas – Logistics – Trade in household products – Construction (in Almaty) – IT services – Communications – Consultancy

IOR 24 (Core–Periphery) offered the example of the banking industry, arguing that banking institutions tend to cooperate with each other. However, he then went on to say that the degree of cooperation and competition in other industries would depend upon many factors. The larger and more capital-intensive the sector is, the more competitive it becomes ('core'). Moreover, the presence of large companies tends to force companies to compete with each other. As the representative of a large national oil company notes:

> R: Well, competition in the oil industry is always there, because we live by market principles. In general I guess there is both competition and cooperation.
> *Q: And where is the competition? Is it in the development of new oil fields or it is in production?*
> R: In the development of new oil fields, of course. Any oil company has a right to make an independent application to enter public tenders. This is where we have competition (SOCR2/Core: Core).

As regards SMEs ('periphery'), if an industry is shared by many small companies, there is likely to be both inter-firm cooperation and competition between firms. This indicates that in industries where several monopolies exist, they are more likely to compete with each other for a larger market share; by contrast, in industries without large monopolies, private firms also compete for a better market position, but they also tend to cooperate so as to lower their transaction costs and join efforts in case they need to push their agenda forward or solve an issue with the state. As PDCR3 (Periphery: Periphery) notes:

> From time to time we (*competitors*) meet at the office of the deputy *akim* who is responsible for utilities unit. There we discuss the common issues. Today elevators do not have owners and this is the acute issue in Kazakhstan. It is not clear who the elevators belong to. This is what causes problems (…) There are reforms being undertaken by the government. There is the special agency that deals with these issues. Thus, we cooperate with our competitors in order to find a compromise and settle the common issues more effectively.

Here it is necessary to bear in mind that competition is seen as generally low between small and medium-sized businesses, and this impacts negatively on the quality of services provided and the production of goods. The problem is especially acute with respect to small businesses:

> The quality of business services, honestly speaking, is not high enough; especially pertaining to small businesses. I mean the level of competition is not high enough so that a particular company could survive due to providing better quality services or work. There are fields where the market is saturated. However, in general, the competition level in Kazakhstan is not fierce enough, and this results in production of low-quality goods and low-quality services (EAR1/Periphery).

Thus, more competition between companies should raise the quality of goods and services provided by these companies and this is exactly what the economic theory suggests.

Assessing different types of interaction (cooperation vs. competition) between private companies, I should note that this depends on a whole range of factors. Companies may use various strategies and the choice of strategy depends upon many factors. One distinctive pattern is that companies in the 'core' tend to compete with each other. This is explained by the fact that the more capital intensive a sector is, the fiercer will be the competition between the 'core' companies. Also 'periphery' companies tend to compete with each other; but when it comes to overcoming various obstacles, these companies may join their efforts and deal collectively with various stakeholders, including the state, to solve their problems. As PDCR12 (Periphery: Periphery) notes, 'in my own understanding it is better to cooperate, negotiate and agree with each other…'

5.2.2. Key factors for interacting with competitors

What factors lead competitors to cooperate with each other? This is important to know in order to understand the market environments in the various industries in which private companies operate. Above, we saw that private companies in the 'periphery' may join in efforts to promote their interests vis-à-vis the state and solve their problems. However, what drives direct competitors in various industries to cooperate with each other?

The following criteria were applied in content analysis:

- 'market conditions matter': relations between competitors are market-driven and companies are free to choose whether or not to cooperate;
- 'size of business matters': private companies interact with each other depending on the size (turnover) of business activities;

- 'type of industry matters': competitors cooperate because the type of industry they represent requires private companies to work together closely;
- 'state regulation matters': the state requires and/or lays the foundations for cooperation/non-cooperation between private companies.

In an LME, competitors tend to compete fiercely for a better market position, whereas in a CME competitors tend to unite into large associations and share market information with each other (Hall and Soskice 2001). This helps companies both in LMEs and CMEs to 'secure access to finance' (ibid) (see also section 3.2).

Frequency Table 5.20 shows that six respondents say that market conditions matter for interaction between competitors. Six respondents see the size of the business as crucial for interaction. Another six respondents say that the type of industry is a key factor here; two respondents say that state regulation matters for cooperation or the lack thereof between competitors, and six respondents mention other factors. It is important to emphasize that all these factors are closely interconnected and the differences between them are sometimes blurred.

Frequency Table 5.20. The nature of competitor relations

Key factors for interaction with competitors				
Market conditions matter	Size of business matters	Type of industry matters	State regulation matters	Other
6	6	6	2	6
3 PDCRs 2 FCRs 1 SOCR	2 IORs 2 FCRs 1 PDCR 1 EAR	3 PDCRs 2 FCRs 1 SOCR	1 SOCR 1 FCR	3 PDCRs 2 FCRs 1 PO

As for other reasons for cooperating with competitors, companies in the 'periphery' pointed that cooperation helps companies to solve their problems; existing employer associations are not effective enough; business ethics matters and if it is more profitable to cooperate, then companies cooperate (see Table 5.21). These reasons drive competitor companies to join in their efforts and work together.

Table 5.21. Factors behind interaction between competitors

Market conditions
'Our competitors are our clients; they use our services; competing companies and our top-management systematically meet with each other. They talk about strategic contracts scheduled for several years ahead' (SOCR3/Core: Core). 'I gain much from collaborating, because for me many areas of business are new. I mean we are involved in wide range of activities. So, my outlook on this business was somehow limited; respectively, when I interact with competitors there is a great exchange of experiences' (PDCR2/Mixed: Core–Periphery).
Size of business
'R: The competition tends not to need us, they can do things themselves, there is not much cooperation at our level; though, there is cooperation when the projects get larger. Then those which we couldn't access ourselves we would cooperate with and it would sometimes come down to our level of projects. *Q: And do you think that in general it makes sense to cooperate with your competitors, or to compete instead?* R: Yes, it makes sense, because also it takes out the competition if you team up with others you are reducing the competition and also certain elements or certain competitors will have advantages that you might not have and you offer synergies collectively and might be able to do certain elements cheaper. You are more competitive and effective. So there are definitely advantages with cooperating together. And particularly if you bring in skills, which they might want to have or which they have outsourced it anyway. To do it with high technology, that German companies could obviously bring in, would be a significant advantage because there would be overall cost-savings to projects' (PDCR10/Mixed: Periphery). 'We do work together. But there are no formalized contracts necessarily but on a project-by-project basis we do work together. If a project is too large, then we often work on what's called 'revenue share' basis. So, we determine who's contributing what and then we take 30 percent of the revenue; the other company takes 70 percent or depending on the make up with the assets and personnel that you are putting in. Once we had a project, in which we had a revenue split of 70–20–10. So, that tends to be the collaboration. Ideally, you want to get the whole project yourself. But in reality, certainly, both commercially and technically that might be difficult…' (FCR1/Mixed: Core–Periphery). 'All business associations are founded to protect the interests of small and medium-sized business; it's just each organization has its own niche; (…) we protect, consult, provide paid services and this is what attracts entrepreneurs (*SMEs*) and make them cooperate' (EAR1/Periphery).

Type of industry
'We work with our competitors. With the companies we cooperate we have certain agreements with certain rates. If it is a competitor, we normally charge them certain rates. They serve their clients through us (…) So, in that particular activity area of our business we cooperate' (SOCR1/Core: Core). *'Q: Do any contacts exist between your company and other competitors?* R: Of course, they do, because the nature of our field (*construction*) is very specific. There are not so many of us who are specialized in this field in Kazakhstan. Therefore, we contact our competitors and meet them at joint orders at *akimats* (municipalities), for example. We always meet them but our relations with them are different: with some of them we cooperate; with some of them we are neutral. Business is a business and the type of relations can be different. But we do contact and talk to them, of course. It can't be otherwise' (PDCR3/Periphery: Periphery).
State regulation
'There are certain anti-monopoly laws that prohibit direct contacts and some engagements with competitors; the rules come from the US and Europe. Here in Kazakhstan everything is regulated and then explained to our employees. Therefore, we don't have direct contacts and business meetings with our competitors. Well, what can we have? 'In the field' – as we like to say – in stores we meet each other and we stay next to our product shelf, whereas they stay next to their product shelf. We tend to cooperate with companies where our products complement each other. But I can't remember any cases where we've cooperated directly with our direct competitors' (FCR4/Periphery: Periphery).
Other
Cooperation helps better in solving problems 'We cooperate with competitors in order to find a compromise and settle the common issues more effectively' (PDCR3/Periphery: Periphery). **Superficial cooperation because of ineffective business associations** 'At the top level, at the executive level – yes. But if you are asking this question with respect to creating synergy establishing some entities to transfer from industry etc., then not really (…) We have the association of freight but we are poorly represented there. The national freight-forwarding association represents only certain segments or business units we have here. We have the main pillars: freight-forwarding, warehousing, distribution and brokerage. So, this freight-forwarding is associated under the association. We are not a member there because we do not see too much progress. We do not have communication tools to develop some common strategies for the better of the industry. There is infrastructure, but it is not 100 per cent fulfilling what we need' (FCR7/Core: Core). **Business ethics and economic profitability matter** 'R: We have very different relations with them depending on the level of their business ethics. Unfortunately, the level of business ethics in companies on average is not that high. *Q: Is collaborating more fruitful?*

R: Of course. For instance, you specialize on one product; you see, our products do not overlap with all other products in our product range; some parts of our product range do overlap but in general each company has its own segment. Some specialize in water-based paints, some in stucco, some in finishing, some in glue, some in dry mix, etc. I see no point in competing with each other' (PDCR11/Periphery: Periphery).

Not all the reasons for cooperation indicated by the private sector may be viewed positively by the state: for instance, price-fixing activity between competitors is a type of illegal practice. Thus, it would be completely wrong to say that 'core' and 'periphery' private companies are always the victims of unjustified public inspections. In fact, the overall perception is that state agencies do their work as prescribed by law. Private firms often complain that there are numerous sudden and unjustified inspections by public agencies. However, it is important to note that sometimes private companies themselves participate in illegal or semi-illegal activities. Therefore, the situation is more complex than it is usually viewed by the private sector. Activities of private business often cause legally justified public inspections.

Furthermore, SMEs operate in an environment where there is little public disclosure of market information among the firms. Example 1 in Table 5.22 shows that, in contrast to big companies, small and medium-sized enterprises are not required to publicly disclose information on their operating activities (e.g. publicly available financial reporting). Moreover, as FCR4 (Periphery: Periphery) notes, there are no legally binding mechanisms for firms to do so. In Example 2 representative of a foreign logistics company (FCR7/Core: Periphery) holds that SMEs do not share their market information because they are concerned about competitors, who may use this market information for their own benefit.

Examples 3 and 4 support the view that companies do not possess market information from their competitors, as it is not available publicly. Thus, businessmen may try to estimate financial information from other companies based on various kinds of indirect observations (see Example 3). What does this mean for market economy? According to the VoC approach, in an LME companies tend not to share sensitive information with each other, preferring to operate in a more competitive environment with limited business coordination. In a CME, companies tend to cooperate in an environment, in which there is high degree of business coordination and sharing of information (Hall and Soskice 2001). Thus, here we can argue that at least as regards sharing of market information, private firms tend to operate in an LME-environment.

Table 5.22. Examples of disclosure of information among firms

Ex 1. 'About the financial situation of our competitors? I would not say that I keep track of their financial reports on a day-to-day or weekly basis. I would put it this way: I keep track of the news in the mass media both local and European – Euronews, CNN and BBC. If it is a general type of information, we try to monitor that or try to see what is there on the Internet. But we do not go too much in details. For the most part, at least in Kazakhstan, if it is not a public company and it is not listed on the stock exchange, this type of information is normally closed. Disclose of information depends on the ownership type of this particular company. If it is an open company, I mean if it is a public company with stocks listed on a stock exchange, of course, by law they have to disclose their information. If it is a small or a medium-sized closed company, then, of course not. And there are no legally binding regulations for that' (FCR4/Periphery: Periphery).
Ex. 2 'As word of mouth in most of the cases, because at the end of the day, if you are even an established mark, you cannot get this data properly unless it is a public company. This is the trade secret, again, and there is much confidential data that may be used in their own way by competitors. That's why, of course, it is not disclosed by stakeholders of the particular competitors' (FCR7/Core: Periphery).
Ex. 3 'We are not informed at all. We only have some slight idea of their situation. For instance, I know the varnish and paint market quite well. However, it is based on my personal opinion and it does not necessarily mean it is correct. I just have some approximate idea of some company's turnover based on their market share, for example. Stemming from production and market share of my company, I can get some rough idea of how many tons of paint they produce annually. This is the only way we can calculate their annual turnover' (PDCR11/Periphery: Periphery).
Ex. 4 'Our company is a limited liability one. Some people translate it as company, some translate it as partnership and there are not any financial statements which are made public anywhere. And that is the same for any LLC operating here. So it is not like for example in the UK where you can get financial statement for any company from the government or the companies' house website, but there isn't anything like that here. All financial statements of the companies are private information for the companies and they are not in the public' (PDCR9/Core: Core–Periphery).

How does this observation help in explaining the differences between 'core–periphery' economic actors and the constellation of actors in these two economies? Public companies as well as big private businesses, including companies listed on the stock exchange ('core'), must disclose their financial information and information on their activities. These companies represent the 'core' part of the economy, as the state regulates and coordinates this economic part and require from the 'core' companies to be transparent and accountable to the state and society. Thus, as regards disclosure of market information, 'core' companies tend to be transparent. Moreover, the government policy requires active promotion of the concept of corporate social responsibility (CSR) by big businesses. By this the government seeks to make the activity of big companies more transparent and accountable to the population. As Ex19 (Core) indicates:

> Over the last couple of years oil companies started to follow government's requirements to invest into social projects, such as construction of schools and kindergartens. In an attempt to avoid corruption practices, companies pay directly to suppliers and then approve the construction of these schools and only after that present these projects to the state. This is good for the employees and for companies' reputation.

At the same time, the government scrutinizes thoroughly the implementation of CSR projects by foreign companies and less so by national ones (IOR15/Core).

However, more research is needed to better understand whether companies in the 'core' tend to more cooperate or compete with each other. 'Periphery' companies are mainly represented by SMEs, which tend not to publicly disclose information on their activities. This makes 'periphery' companies operate in a more competitive environment.

Another important observation regarding competition and cooperation practices among firms relates to the fact that foreign companies also bring their own business culture with them, as indicated in Case in Point 5.3. This example shows that foreign companies may also push through their country-specific 'competition' or 'cooperation' type of behaviour, to some extent shaping inter-firm relations in Kazakhstan. For instance, companies from the USA may pursue aggressive market strategies by trying to promote M&As, as is typical of an LME (Hall and Soskice 2001). By contrast with the US companies, firms from Japan tend to unite and cooperate by supporting each other abroad, which is typical of a CME (ibid).

Case in Point 5.3. Influence of foreign companies' business culture

'*Q: Would you argue that some companies from the US try to pursue their competitive strategies as they do in the US. Or, as you mentioned, the Japanese companies join their efforts with other companies. So, would you say that companies from these countries don't really adapt to local conditions?*

R: The thing is that Japanese companies always try to stick together (…) This is much less in common with us and some American companies.

Q: For example, companies in Germany or Japan try to cooperate because this will pay off in the long run. But this is not the case with other companies in other countries where they may aggressively compete with each other and do not to share market information...

R: Yes, this happens as well. I don't want to mention the names but often this is the case with the US companies which are quite aggressive in the market; that is their policy...' (FCR2/Periphery: Core–Periphery).

Thus, market strategies of foreign firms operating in Kazakhstan may be influenced by market strategies which these firms pursue in their home countries. This is a further example of the importance of the cross-cultural dimension (see also subsection 5.1.1).

A range of factors may force various types of competitor companies to cooperate or compete with each other. Market conditions, size of business, activity of business and type of industry, state regulation, cooperation gains, and ineffective employer associations may influence companies' decision to cooperate or compete. It is difficult to draw clear-cut conclusions regarding the market strategies of the 'core' and 'periphery' companies and more research is needed in this regard. However, based on the observation that companies in the 'periphery' do not disclose the information on their activities, I can cautiously argue that 'periphery' companies tend to operate in a competitive environment. However, as discussed in subsection 5.2.1, if 'periphery' companies need to solve existing problems or push their agenda through with the government they may cooperate by joining their efforts and speaking in one voice. This can also be the result of ineffective employer associations which represent 'periphery' companies. In turn, 'core' companies are more transparent as regards public disclosure of company information and are subject to more thorough scrutiny on the part of the state (e.g. implementation of CSR projects), which is natural for big companies in any country.

5.2.3. Regulating competition

This dimension concerns the degree of state regulation of competition between private firms in various industries. It has the following four values: 'strong regulation', 'moderate regulation', 'little regulation' and 'no regulation at all'. Five respondents had the same perception on the industries which are most regulated by the state. Seven interviewees named the industries in which they felt competition was moderately regulated. 11 respondents held the same view as to which industries are least regulated in terms of competition. Finally, five respondents mentioned specific industries in which competition is not regulated at all by the state (Frequency Table 5.23).

Frequency Table 5.23. Degree of state regulation of competition

Regulation of competition			
Strong regulation	Moderate regulation	Little regulation	No regulation at all
5	7	11	5
3 SCORs 1 FCR	2 FCRs 2 POs	5 PDCRs 3 FCRs	2 PDCRs 2 FCRs

1 IOR	1 PDCR 1 EAR 1 IOR	2 IORs 1 EAR	1 EAR

From the views of respondents, I distinguish between various sectors of the economy where competition is regulated differently (see Table 5.24). Here it should be noted that competition between private companies in capital-intensive sectors ('core') is higher than in less capital-intensive industries ('periphery'). Therefore, the state appears to be an active regulator of industries where competition is high.

Table 5.24. Perceptions of competition regulation, by industry

Strong and moderate regulation	Little regulation	No regulation
– Aviation – Railroad – Energy and water allocation services – Trade (certain segments) – Finance – Oil and gas – Postal services and communications – Agriculture – Mining	– Infrastructure development – Maritime services – Construction – Trade (certain segments)	– Consultancy – Retail trade – Services (IT, HR)

The interview excerpt below sheds light on the degree of state regulation of different industries and existing problems as regards the anti-monopoly legislation and regulation in Kazakhstan. We can note an important point: in industries with active foreign competitors, domestic companies must compete in order to survive; they have to improve their services and products in order to stay competitive.

Interview excerpt, regulation of competition

'In general, the situation with competition is poor but differs from sector to sector. The most competitive, the most liberalized, the most privatized and the most deregulated sector of all is the retail and services sector. That was the fundamentals of the mass privatization during the 1990s. Everything was sold out to private hands. The retail stores were sold to private hands. Today there are no obstacles for opening a barber shop or a small store; no problems with that. Even in comparison with Germany where everything is very structured I think. In this respect, there are no problems with competition. In addition, the poor market is a serious protection for this sector from the domination by overseas players. Large foreign retailers do not enter this market if we compare to the Ukrainian or Russian markets, because on average a consumer in a store in Kazakhstan spends much less. Consumers are poorer, and therefore serious competitors do not target this market. Therefore, even low-

efficient, some small family business with old methods of trade can exist in this market (...) they are not afraid to treat customers badly because they know that they will come back anyway. This is why there is not so much competition from foreign players but much among domestic ones.
Q: What about other sectors? Are they for the most part monopolized?
R: Infrastructure sectors are monopolized, of course. Consumer goods manufacturing is localized. The competition is in free fall and paving its own way' (PO4/Core–Periphery).

Since the consumer market of Kazakhstan is smaller than those of the neighbouring countries, many foreign companies prefer to enter the Russian or Ukrainian markets. This in turn leads to the dominance of domestic companies in the sectors that are of little interest to foreign firms and capital. As a result, domestic companies in these economic sectors are less competitive than their counterparts in industries where there is greater foreign participation, as is the case in the petroleum industry. Thus, we may conclude that the higher the involvement of foreign competitors in a particular industry, the more competitive will that industry become.

Table 5.24 on perception of regulation of competition by industry also supports this argument. Foreign competitors are particularly active in energy, finance, oil and gas, postal services and telecommunications, and the mining sector, all of which are heavily regulated by the state. Thus, the higher the degree of competition in a particular sector, the more regulation the state exercises. The remaining industries in that group include aviation, railways, trade and agriculture: and these sectors have few foreign players, even though they are regulated because the state controls these sectors or is seeking to develop them. The aviation and railway sectors are monopolized by several state corporations under the umbrella of Samruk-Kazyna (see subsection 3.3.2.2), and agriculture is heavily subsidized by the state. Therefore, respondents see the state as seeking to regulate competition among firms in these sectors.

Thus we can conclude that the 'core' industries of the economy are heavily regulated by the state, whereas the 'periphery' industries are subject to little regulation. This is an important observation in terms of identifying key differences between the 'core' and 'periphery' parts of Kazakhstan's market-oriented economy.

5.2.4. Mergers and acquisitions

This subcategory focuses on merger and acquisition (M&A) transactions between private firms and between private and state companies. According to the VoC approach, takeover transactions are frequent in LMEs, whereas they are rarely implemented in CMEs (Hall and Soskice 2001; Jackson and Miyajima 2007: 3). Frequency Table 5.25 shows that 14 respondents mention that they are aware of frequent M&As; three respondents say that M&As are rare in their industries; and seven have not encountered any M&As in their industries. As all respondents noted, M&As are not usually publicized in Kazakhstan; those respondents who answered that M&As occur frequently were probably aware of them because of experience in their own industry or in an industry closely linked to their own.

Frequency Table 5.25. Frequency of M&As

Mergers and acquisitions		
Frequents M&As	**Rare M&As**	**No M&As**
14	3	7
8 IORs 3 FCRs 2 PDCRs 1 SOCR	1 PDCR 1 FCR 1 SOCR	5 PDCRs 2 FCRs

M&As occur most frequently in the petroleum industry, the financial industry, and the retail trade and manufacturing industries; they are quite rare within IT services, communications, construction and consultancy services (see Table 5.26).

Table 5.26. M&As by industry

Frequent M&As	Rare M&As
– Petroleum industry – Financial industry – Retail trade – Manufacturing	– IT services – Communications – Construction – Consultancy services

Based on the observation in the previous subsection (5.3.3) that competition between private companies in capital-intensive sectors is higher than in industries which are less capital-intensive, it is reasonable to conclude that M&As occur more frequently in highly competitive industries of the 'core' and are rare in the 'periphery'. When inter-firm competition is high, companies will seek to acquire other firms, in order to gain a more advantageous position in the market. When asked about M&As, the representative of a state-owned enterprize (SOCR2/Core: Core) notes that it is a common practice when companies, both domestic and foreign, take over or merge with other companies in the petroleum industry.

Another respondent explains why M&As are rare in the 'periphery'. He points out that 'in the recent years it has become difficult for small businesses to grow as well as it has become difficult for middle-sized businesses to grow into large ones. As soon as a small business grows into a middle-sized company, it becomes the locus of attention from large players. The same holds true when a middle-sized business becomes large…' (Ex4/Core–Periphery). Thus, the reason why M&As in the 'periphery' are rare is that 'periphery' companies may have some concerns with respect to growth and expansion. A merger is an unlikely event in the 'periphery' as say a company A by merging with a company B may grow and get bigger. As shown in Example 6 (see Table 5.10), some SMEs opt against growing and exceeding their standard capital turnover, to be able to freely operate in an environment with less involvement from 'core' actors. Otherwise, if they expand, they may be taken over by the 'core' companies. Some SMEs try to avoid this. This is also an example of interaction between the 'core' and 'periphery' actors. The two economic parts are interlinked; however, relations between the players of two economies are complex and need further in-depth research.

Another view on M&As is provided by Ex1 (Core–Periphery):

> M&As do not take place in their classical forms; they don't get implemented through capital markets because capital markets don't exist in Kazakhstan. They are not purely classical transactions because mechanisms for that do not exist. For instance, within the last years KazMunayGas has been actively buying shares of other oil companies through 'Exploration and Mining' (…) Another example is that Russian companies are entering the gold mining sector through purchasing companies. I know some cases of hostile takeovers which took place in the last years.

As can be seen from this example, the market for M&As is not fully developed. Because capital markets are underdeveloped (see subsection 3.3.1.3), M&A transactions are implemented through takeovers whereby a big company may purchase the shares of a small company. However, in strategic sectors which are part of the 'core' economy, the government appears to be an active regulator of M&As. This is not the case in the 'periphery' industries. As Ex1 puts it (Core), 'the government has made a right step by regulating company acquisition mechanisms within strategic sectors and making sales of companies only through the endorsement with government agencies. That was the right step.' Given high degree of state involvement in the 'core', it is reasonable to expect that the state will regulate M&A transactions. Thus, an acquisition can be done through the approval of relevant public agencies. Ex1 finds this role of the state in M&As justified, as he deems it to be widespread international practice.

Therefore, we may conclude that market conditions for M&As are just emerging. There are frequent M&As in the 'core' economy, because of higher competition levels between firms. M&As in the 'periphery' are rare, because competition levels are not as high there due to the fact that some domestic market segments are not fully satiated yet. Moreover, some SMEs ('periphery') decide not to grow and expand their activities, as they are concerned about being taken over by 'core' companies. The state appears to be active regulator of merger and acquisition transactions in the 'core' sectors of the economy, but exercises little regulation in the 'periphery' industries.

Given these distinct characteristics of the M&A market, it is difficult to classify M&A transactions in terms of the VoC approach. The nature of these transactions is different from the theoretical assumptions underlying the VoC approach. The 'core–periphery' framework is more suitable in this respect.

5.2.5. Instruments for solving problems between private companies

This subcategory concerns the four types of tools frequently used by private companies when problems or conflicts arise with other private companies. 'The use of state mechanisms' means that private companies employ state mechanisms, such as economic courts, in order to find a solution to their problems with other private companies. Second, they may use 'domestic business mechanisms' – negotiation instruments and/or business communication platforms like various forums of entrepreneurs or business associations. Third, private companies may use 'international platforms', such as international economic courts or various international business associations in Kazakhstan or abroad. Fourth, and depending on the problem in question, private companies may use a combination of these tools.

Frequency Table 5.27 shows that 17 respondents view that most of private companies tend to use business mechanisms for solving problems with each other.

Frequency Table 5.27. Instruments for problem resolution

Instruments for solving problems between private companies				
State mechanisms	Business mechanisms	International platforms	Combination of tools	Other
6	17	0	5	0
2 SOCRs 2 EARs 1 IOR 1 PDCR	6 FCRs 6 IORs 5 PDCRs	–	2 PDCRs 1 IOR 1 FCR 1 EAR	–

According to IOR5 (Core–Periphery), 'the standard phrase that you find in the legislation is 'through court'. These things are stipulated in any contract: *Executed in compliance with the legislation of the Republic of Kazakhstan. If the parties fail to come to an agreement, the case must be forwarded to court*. This is the standard phrase that finalizes any contract. The disputes of economic entities should be resolved through economic courts...' However, the tendency is the same both for 'private vs. state' and 'private vs. private' dimensions (see subsection 5.1.6), and indicates that pre-court resolution in the form of negotiating economic disputes is seen as preferable, because using the economic courts is usually time-consuming and not very effective. In particular, entrepreneurs tend to trust the lower-level courts less than supreme courts (see response of EAR1 in section 'combination of tools' in Table 5.28). And yet, both representatives of state-owned companies thought that the courts are effective for resolving economic disputes. Why? One of the possible reasons is that representatives of private companies tend to perceive that state-owned companies receive more privileged treatment in the economic courts. If that is so, then it is natural for representatives of state-owned companies to view the economic courts as an effective instrument for solving disputes, whether against other state-owned companies or private firms. Only one representative of a private domestic company mentioned the use of state mechanisms as being effective. However, this respondent did not have direct experience of dispute resolution, but referred to another entrepreneur from her industry who had decided to use the courts to solve an economic dispute with another private company.

At the same time, the overall situation with regard to using the legal system among 'periphery' companies is improving. As PDCR6 (Periphery: Periphery) noted (see Table 5.28), many companies view dispute resolution through courts as a standard tool. The company of this respondent represents the 'periphery' part of the economy; he states that the company has begun to use court mechanisms more frequently. This indicates that 'periphery' companies, aside from using pre-court mechanisms, may also use economic courts to resolve disputes with each other. However, it would be important to understand how dispute settlement between 'periphery' and 'core' companies takes place. That could not be covered in this study and requires further in-depth research.

Table 5.28. Tools for solving problems

State mechanisms
'We try to use legal mechanisms for conflict resolution, because we find them effective' (SOCR3/Core: Core).
Business mechanisms
'Of course, the parties prefer pre-trial examination, because they realize that once they end up in a court of law, the case may last forever' (IOR5/Core–Periphery). 'I mean, of course, we follow up the rules. First of all, we try to solve it in amicable way. Then, we go ahead with arbitration (…) as the last step' (FCR7/Core: Core). 'Any issue that comes up, related to contractual issue or anything, we always try to resolve it amicably with the client and negotiate; and again we have never been in any situation where we have got into any dispute or anything we have not been able to resolve. I don't know of any of competitors that have ended up in court with a client. Everyone has the same view as us; it is better to resolve things amicably' (PDCR9/Core: Core).
Combination of tools
'You are talking about regional or local courts, I guess? Well, of course, the lower the body, the less effective it is. We always appeal to them protesting against their decisions. We can go to the city court; if that doesn't help, we go to the Supreme Court. The company is the one that decides what kind of tools to use to solve its problems' (EAR1/Core–Periphery). 'In case of a conflict, we usually deal with the suppliers in a friendly way. Sometimes we resort to small fines. We have long-term obligations to our clients. In some cases we have already supplied the product, but they don't have the money. Then, we sue them and resort to all kinds of fines. Normally, legal proceeding is a standard process; fines are also a normal thing. We resolve our issues through court if we have to. So, we go to courts quite frequently. In recent years we have had quite many legal cases' (PDCR6/Periphery: Periphery).

5.3. Assessing the influence of other market players (labour unions and employer associations)

5.3.1. Influence of labour unions

To what extent do labour unions affect and shape state–business interrelations in Kazakhstan? This dimension concerns the impact of labour unions and employer associations on state–business interaction, in the form of protecting employees' rights and promoting private business interests vis-à-vis the state, respectively. In the following, I examine the extent of labour union influence on state–business interaction and the core–periphery constellation of actors. Influence, as perceived by respondents, is measured as 'rather strong', 'rather moderate', 'rather low' and 'no influence at all'. As explained, in an LME, the role of labour unions will be less significant than that in a CME (see section 3.2 and subsection 3.3.7).

As shown in Frequency Table 5.29, four respondents think that the influence of labour unions is rather strong, and three view their influence as rather moderate. Five respondents hold that labour unions have little influence on state–business interrelations – and 23 respondents, the vast majority say that labour unions do not influence state–business relations at all.

Frequency Table 5.29. Perceived role of labour unions

Influence of labour unions on state–business interaction			
Rather strong influence	Rather moderate influence	Rather low influence	No influence at all
4	3	5	23
2 POs 1 SOCR 1 FCR	1 SOCR 1 PO 1 IOR	2 IORs 1 PDCR 1 EAR 1 PO	7 PDCRs 6 FCRs 5 IORs 4 POs 1 SOCR

Table 5.30 provides examples of respondents' perceptions. One representative of a large state-owned company and one representative of a big foreign company see the influence of labour unions as strong. As the first company represents the state sector and the second the petroleum industry, labour unions would appear to be important and influential in the state-dominated petroleum sector. Two public officials also hold that the influence of labour unions is significant. Since both of them are involved in coordinating and developing labour unions, they have regular interaction with them, and may perceive their role as significant.

Three respondents saw the influence labour unions as rather moderate, while five held that they have fairly little influence. However, the great majority of respondents (23) saw their influence as absolutely insignificant. Importantly, this view is shared by representatives of all categories of respondents in the analysis. Therefore, labour unions play somewhat a stronger role in the natural resource industries, which belong to what we have defined as the 'core' part of the economy, but project insignificant influence in the 'periphery'. This is in line with the findings of the literature review (see subsection 3.3.3.3).

Table 5.30. Perceptions on the influence of labour unions

Rather strong influence
'We have labour unions and they are quite active, they participate at the level of a head of the state. I can give an example: we recently elaborated the programme on trade development in Kazakhstan for the period of 2010 to 2014. The Association of Trade Enterprises of Kazakhstan worked with us as well as the labour union, which represented the interests of employees in trade and service industry. We discussed with them the programme in detail' (PO8/Core–Periphery). 'There is the independent union of oil industry workers who fight for their rights. All employees are 100 percent unionized. Today, labour unions fight for better salary conditions' (FCR6/Core: Core).
Rather moderate influence
'There are labour unions, of course. We have not worked with them directly. There are also independent labour unions. However, it is hard to judge to what extent they are efficient in negotiations. Usually, the workers go out on the streets and put forward their economic requirements. In some cases they can be effective. For instance, in the petroleum industry. In other industries they are not. Assessing their role from 1 to 5 (*where 1 means no influence and 5 strong influence*), I would put around 2 or 3' (IOR3/Core–Periphery).
Rather low influence
'We do not deal with labour unions here in Almaty, but we do when we have larger pools of labour working for us, so in Atyrau, for instance. We meet with them and deal with their requests. There we have a labour union, which is typical for the oil and gas industry. There is also a system here which they call collective agreements. And again our employees can sign up there if they wish…' (PDCR9/Core: Core).
No influence at all
'I don't know if there are any such organizations in Kazakhstan. We are not involved in any and we have never been asked to get involved. Well, I am against any unions anyway; I mean the unionism in the West has become excessive…' (PDCR10/Mixed: Core–Periphery). 'There are labour unions but their role is very insignificant. They exist in the mining industries: in the coal industry. You can see and hear them, at least from the position of a regular person. However, labour unions here don't have the same role as they do in Europe' (IOR5/Core–Periphery). 'As regards wage-setting, it depends on how I negotiate it with my customer. I can pay higher if it is a good contract or I can pay lower if it is a small contract. We negotiate each salary individually. We do not have labour unions' (PDCR3/Periphery: Periphery). 'Honestly speaking, I haven't encountered labour unions and I don't see any considerable or influential power in them that could have an influence on business processes. They do exist; I've heard their names somewhere, but I have never seen them playing an active role' (IOR2/Core–Periphery).

5.3.2. Influence of employer associations

What then of the influence of employer associations on state–business interaction? Do they assist private business in solving problems and promoting business interests with the state? Also here, the measures used are ‘rather strong’, ‘rather moderate’, ‘rather low’ and ‘no influence at all’. And, as with labour unions, the role of employer associations in an LME appears as less significant than in a CME, where coordination between markets players through various networks and employer associations is high.

As the results of the content analysis indicate (see Frequency Table 5.31), seven respondents hold that employer associations play an important role and exert a rather strong influence on state–business interaction. Eleven respondents say that employer associations exert a rather moderate influence.

Frequency Table 5.31. Perceived role of employer associations

Influence of employer associations			
Rather strong influence	Rather moderate influence	Rather low influence	No influence at all
7	11	9	9
3 FCRs 1 PDCR 1 EAR 1 SOCR 1 PO	4 IORs 4 POs 2 EARs 1 SOCR	3 PDCRs 3 POs 2 IORs 1 FCR	4 PDCRs 3 FCRs 2 IORs

By contrast, nine interviewees see employer associations as rather weak, exerting only insignificant influence on state–business relations; and a further nine say that such associations have no influence over economic processes in Kazakhstan. Table 5.32 below provides examples of respondents’ perceptions.

Two important patterns should be noted in the results of the content analysis here. Respondents who see employer associations as influential represent companies in industries where employer associations do play a prominent and powerful role, including the natural resources and financial sectors. These associations are the American Chamber of Commerce, Ata-Meken, the Association of Mining and Metallurgical Enterprises, EUROBAK, FIAK, FIC, KAZENERGY (see subsection 5.1.3).

Table 5.32. Perceptions on the influence of employer associations

Rather strong influence
'We are the members of FIAK. The Association protects the interests of financial organizations such as banks, other financial organizations, credit institutions. It protects the interests when it comes to the interaction with state bodies. It also has relations with the National Bank. FIAK serves as a bridge between the government and second-tier banks. I think the role of the Association is essential' (FCR1/Mixed: Core–Periphery). 'FIAK's basic objective is to lobby for our interests. I think it has been quite successful in lobbying for our interests. They participate in law-making, make their amendments or present their proposals. All market players rely on the Association in that regard' (PDCR1/Mixed: Core–Periphery). 'We work closely with employer associations. They all have to be at our meetings. We are advocates of that. Last year we had negotiations on the formation of the Customs Union, establishment of single customs tariff. I myself talked directly to the representatives of the Associations in the regions. They are important' (PO8/Core–Periphery).
Rather moderate influence
'Yes, there is the Forum of Employers with whom we conducted joint research. On a 5-point effectiveness scale I would put 4. They are trying very hard and at least, I don't feel they are infringed or something of the sort. The fact that the authorities don't listen to them much is something different; but they are active' (IOR1/Core–Periphery). 'There are holding groups such as 'Arcelor Mittal' that owns enterprises in Karaganda – several companies are in this group. I am sure they have a special body in charge of coordinating the general policy of the corporation. I am sure there are special associations for natural-resource extraction industries or some other industries (...) These associations do unite entities within certain industries: metallurgy, oil producers. There are also associations for healthcare workers and associations for teachers, etc. According to the statistical data, there are several thousand unions that can be classified as such. However, it is totally a different story how many of them are really active and how many will disappear soon. In general, the employer associations have more resources to be more influential, as opposed to labour unions' (IOR5/Core–Periphery).
Rather low influence
'We are members of some of these organizations. I don't think they make any difference. Everyone for himself or herself, I think. In that context you do not have that kind of the grand schemes that they have in Germany, where you have an effective supervisory board of employers...' (IOR17/Periphery).
No influence at all
'Under the Soviet Union we had general meetings. Now we have friendly relationships with other employers. Once every few years we all meet and talk about work, projects. They are competing companies. Usually, we meet when some of the companies have an anniversary or some other special occasion to celebrate' (PDCR6/Periphery: Periphery).

Overall, as noted by IOR5 (Core–Periphery), employer associations are more influential than labour unions, as they have more financial resources and support from employers. Employer associations in less capital-intensive industries, like trade, construction, tourism and manufacturing, are less influential when it comes to interaction with the state and protecting and promoting the rights of companies. However, they may still prove useful for their members. For instance, EAR1/Core–Periphery describes a functioning employer association that unites SMEs in various industries: '…we cooperate and have a constant dialogue with various business associations and public organizations. We provide accounting services to SMEs. They are beneficial especially for individual entrepreneurs, since tax regulations are a big problem for them and many do not understand them, especially in the regions (…) It is obvious that, as a big company, they have their own accounting departments and can do it on their own.' Thus, SMEs find it useful to join employer associations, where they can receive qualified support as to tax policy arrangements and administration or legal matters. As literature review showed, the problem of tax administration is especially acute for SMEs, so they may opt to use the services of employer associations for dealing with tax issues. Since big companies have their own accounting departments and personnel for dealing with tax policy, they may participate in less influential associations, but only for the purposes of representation and reputation. Companies belonging to influential employer associations that represent key economic and capital-intensive industries are driven by different motivations. As employer associations in these industries are more influential in interaction with the state, their members seek to lobby and promote their interests actively.

Thus, we must distinguish between powerful employer associations which mainly serve the interests of big companies in capital-intensive industries (the 'core'), and the less influential associations which unite mainly small and medium-sized companies in less capital-intensive sectors (the 'periphery').

5.3.3. Reasons for the weak influence of other market players

As shown above, labour unions are largely seen as having insignificant influence in most sectors of the economy, with the exception of the natural resource industries. In contrast, the influence of employer associations is perceived as relatively strong – but again, not in all industries. Why, then, do some of these market players have so little influence on state–business interaction?

Prior to the content analysis, three reasons were identified. First, Soviet path-dependence limits their influence: these actors were weak during the Soviet period, and no appropriate measures have been taken or policies implemented to strengthen their role since independence. Second, private firms view them as ineffective and prefer to solve their problems by communicating directly with the state. Aside from these reasons, respondents also mentioned other points, presented below. The content analysis helped to calculate the frequency of respondents' answers for each reason.

As can be seen in Frequency Table 5.33, four respondents stress that Soviet path-dependency is particularly important when explaining the weak role of labour unions. Six respondents hold that private firms view existing institutional frameworks for labour unions and employer associations as inefficient and prefer to communicate with the state directly.

Frequency Table 5.33. Weak influence of other market players

Reasons for the weak influence of labour unions and employer associations		
Soviet path-dependency	Private firms view them as ineffective and do not cooperate	Other
4	6	11
1 EAR 1 PDCR 1 SCOR 1 IOR	2 PDCRs 2 POs 1 FCR 1 IOR	4 IORs 2 POs 3 EARs 1 PDCR 1 FCR

As private companies ignore other market players and prefer to proceed without these actors, in the end, this contributes to their low efficiency. The second reason is not so much a reason as a consequence of weak labour unions and employer associations. However, when asked, these six respondents felt that it also serves as a reason for companies that have only recently started their activities. Thus, because of the widespread perception of labour unions are being weak and ineffective, also new generations of entrepreneurs regard them as useless and do not seriously consider them as important market players.

Table 5.34 presents some examples of respondents' views on reasons for the weak role of labour unions and employer associations.

Table 5.34. Reasons for the weak influence of other market players

Soviet path-dependency
'I agree that employers should be consolidated. We should be united and move on in order to protect our common interests. Those actors in trade – be it bazaars, supermarkets, restaurants have common problems. The problems in the legislation are the same. It's the same bureaucrats who do not let them grow. Those functions that bureaucrats have to implement are farfetched. Such a unit as a Sanitary-and-Epidemiologic institution ('*Sanepidemstancia*'). It was established in 1956 or 1958 during Soviet times. It duplicates everything: State Standardization Department, Veterinary. The guys from the Sanitary-and-Epidemiologic Unit come and check all health regulations and put ban on our activity. This kind of farfetched regulations we have here. I think this is an echo of the Soviet period' (EAR4/Periphery). 'Typically the objectives have been more geared not so much towards salaries but more other employment benefits (...) I think certain benefits, not so much salaries as other things, like holiday benefits' (PDCR9/Core: Core–Periphery). 'As far as I know there are no labour unions. I mean there were a lot of labour unions in Soviet times, but there were no *real* labour unions. I don't know what they were exactly but they were not labour unions. And I think they just disappeared, and because there was no particular tradition of labour activism I think they did not emerge in any other form. I mean every country, every economy needs labour unions, but because there is no Soviet history in this, maybe this is why there is no any model for real labour unions here' (IOR23/Core–Periphery).
Private firms view them as ineffective
'Labour unions exist only on paper; besides, our company is not so large so that we would turn to them for help or collaborate with them' (PDCR2/Mixed: Core–Periphery). 'There is the Association for Entrepreneurs. However, the information they supply us with is quite outdated. It's been long since we grew out of such situation. We have passed that stage long time ago. Of course, we still maintain membership in case we can grab something useful from it. In any case, the directors of these associations are my good contacts. Therefore, we still pay membership fees to sustain their activity and for symbolic reasons we try not to spoil our relationship with them. They do not give us anything useful. You waste your time hoping to get something that does not exist' (PDCR11/Periphery: Periphery).

IOR5 (Core–Periphery) describes a widely shared perception in noting that 'formally labour unions do exist. There are a lot of industrial labour unions, municipal labour unions, but we do not see them much. Therefore, it is hard to talk about their role.' In addition, 11 respondents noted also other reasons for the weak influence of other market players on state–business interrelations, as shown in Table 5.35.

Table 5.35. Other reasons for weak influence

The weak response of the state
'As of today our labour union does not play such a big role. I am honest in that respect. But we hope we will. We are advancing with small steps. I will explain you what I mean. We try to use each round-table meeting, each sitting, each meeting to express our position to the state, etc. There is no point in sitting at home and doing nothing. Rolling stones gather no moss, as you know. At least we have some chance' (EAR3/Periphery).
The mentality of employees and improved economic situation
'I would not say labour unions are more advanced in Russia; I would just say their role is more significant than here. Probably it's the matter of social activity of the people. The people here are quieter; the majority of economic experiments undertaken by the government were perceived rather friendly and peacefully by the people in Kazakhstan. For instance, in the neighbouring countries it is all categorized as some revolutionary things (…) In particular, it all became not pertinent as soon as the economic situation became more or less stable in Kazakhstan; their role is lessening gradually' (IOR5/Core–Periphery). 'As a person employed in the educational sector, I do not feel much support rendered by a labour union in the educational field. I guess the legal culture is not perfect yet. Not all of our people know what they are supposed to do' (PO6/Core–Periphery).
Absence of big names
'As a matter of fact, who are actually the labour unions and who are their leaders? I can't recall a single name! That's an indicator of their role, by the way' (IOR5/Core–Periphery).
Different layers of business are not united
'R: Since I have been simmering in this water for many years already, I can say that several attempts have been made to unite employers regionally and nationally. While it was informal, it was rather effective; when it became formal – because anyway some things should be formalized such as paying a salary or making a decision – there is always a split. Each association has its interest; especially if we are talking about some industrial association. This kind of conflict is always there (…) It is a totally different platform – small, medium-sized and large businesses. There can be totally different interests involved. *Q: Are the rules of the game different as well?* R: Yes. Therefore, small business does not trust big business; big business does not consider the interests of small business; therefore, it is impossible to unite all the employers. It was demonstrated at some regional level – in Karaganda, in Eastern Kazakhstan, there were attempts to do so; it was inefficient. Sooner or later it breaks up' (EAR1/Core–Periphery).
Employee interests protected through other channels (e.g. labour courts)
'The law will look after you. It will protect the interest of the taxpayers or the employees, and the labour law is quite strong and enforcement is strong. There are labour courts here and they are pretty good. They are very protective of the employee. From my experience this is well documented and the labour courts are strong' (PDCR10/Mixed: Core – Periphery).

Employer associations mainly serve PR-purposes
'Honestly speaking I am not really impressed with the activity of some employer associations. We haven't really noticed serious stakeholders who could influence this sector. I mean their members are mainly interested in their image…' (IOR2/Core–Periphery).
Lack of systematic communication with the state
'Representatives of labour unions and employer associations work and communicate unsystematically with the state' (PO11/Core–Periphery).
Requirements of foreign investors in the 1990s
'Everything was created and established in conditions when the entire economy was in ruins and so, nobody would dare to set terms. For instance, foreign investors just came and said: "We are increasing our statutory fund but in exchange you have to leave us alone with your labour unions stuff." So, they set this tendency' (IOR5/Core).

As EAR1 (Core–Periphery) notes, one of the main problems which leads to low influence of employer associations in the economy is the gap and lack of trust between big businesses ('core') and SMEs ('periphery'). When it comes to labour unions, EAR1 (Core–Periphery) notes:

> All big enterprises forming a company have labour unions in the following big industries: metallurgy industry, oil and gas, mining; at the enterprises where there are 1000–3000 people there are labour unions, of course. Within small and medium-sized businesses there are no labour unions because small business comprises about 5–6 people on average which make 70–80 per cent of all enterprises. How come can there be a labour union? Especially, considering that small business is a family business; almost 60 percent is a family business; therefore, they don't have labour unions. Whatever the parents or other family members say is an order!

The observation that many SMEs in Kazakhstan are family businesses points up the importance of family ties in shaping economic processes in Kazakhstan. SMEs are often the product of family investments. There is little demand for labour unions, as industrial relations are directly regulated by family members or friends in a hierarchical manner. All issues and concerns of employees can be negotiated directly without resorting to the use of a third party such as a labour union. Moreover, as PDCR10 (Mixed: Core–Periphery) notes, some employees are protected through other mechanisms, other than labour unions. This respondent mentions that alternative channels, such as labour courts, are effective in protecting employees' rights.

These observations shed light on the reasons for the overall weak influence of other market players, important for understanding the structure of the economy and differences between the 'core' and 'periphery' parts.

5.4. Discussion of results: the essence of the emerging 'core–periphery' economy

The results of content analysis make it possible to define in detail and distinguish between two parts of the economy: the economic *core*, largely state-led; and the economic *periphery*, more market-oriented. Table 5.36 summarizes the key characteristics of the two.

This helps to clarify the type of market economy now emerging in Kazakhstan, with one part as the core, the other as the periphery. These findings are based on the literature review and the analysed interviews. I analysed three main dimensions in order to grasp the complexity of institutional development in the economy and specify the core/periphery structure as well as rules of the game in each part: *state–business interaction*, *inter-firm relations*, and *influence of other market players*. Each economic part has its own advantages and disadvantages for economic actors. The indicators presented in Table 5.36 are described in detail below.

Within the dimension *state–business interaction*, the following important indicators have emerged:

Type of business and capital-intensity of an industry. The core part of the economy involves capital-intensive industries, whereas the periphery generally consists of less capital-intensive industries. It is mainly large foreign and domestic business that belong to the core part of the economy, whereas mainly small and medium-sized domestic and foreign business tend to belong to the periphery – although some companies may be situated between the two parts. The rules of the game are subject to dynamic change, so the same company may shift quickly from the core to the periphery, or find itself between the two. Moreover, not all big companies necessarily belong to the core; and likewise with small and medium-sized companies: some SMEs in less-capital intensive sectors of the economy may belong to the core, although most SMEs in less capital-intensive sectors are found in the periphery.

Role of the state. In assessing the role of the state in the economy, most respondents saw the core part as largely regulated and coordinated by the state, and the periphery as less regulated or coordinated. The periphery was considered to have greater economic freedom than the core. Thus, the core can be described as mainly state-led but with certain elements of a market economy, or 'market economy under state supervision' as IOR1 put it, whereas the periphery part can, with certain caveats, be described as mainly market-oriented.

Table 5.36. The emerging market-oriented economy in Kazakhstan

KEY FEATURES	ECONOMIC CORE (state-led)	ECONOMIC PERIPHERY (market-oriented)
1. STATE–BUSINESS INTERACTION		
Type of business	Mainly large domestic and foreign business	Mainly domestic and foreign SMEs
Capital-intensity of industry	High	Low to medium
Role of the state	Strong regulation and coordination	Little regulation and coordination
Rules of the game	Rather stable and predictable	Less stable and predictable
Predictability in economic policy-making	Rather predictable	Rather unpredictable
Degree of vulnerability	Low	High
State–business relations	More formalized	Less formalized
Direct access to government	Yes	No
Available state mechanism for problem solution	Rather effective	Rather ineffective
Access to finance	Unrestricted	Limited
Investment policy	Rather long-term	Rather short-term
State subsidies	Relatively high	Relatively high
Control over subsidies	Strong control	Poor control
International courts/arbitration	Used rather frequently	Too costly to use
Tax regime	Rather burdensome	Attractive
2. INTER–FIRM RELATIONS		
Disclosure of information	Required	Not always required
Transparency of transactions	Rather high	Rather low
Competition	Rather high	Medium to low
Regulation of competition	Rather strong	Rather weak
Merger and acquisitions	Frequent	Rare
Regulation of M&As by the state	Strong	Little
3. INFLUENCE OF OTHER MARKET PLAYERS		
Labour unions	Relatively strong	Weak
Demand for labour unions	Little demand	Little demand
Employer associations	Strong	Weak
Demand for employer associations	Weak demand	Rising demand

Rules of the game and predictability of policy-making. The rules of the game for economic players in the core are seen as rather predictable and the operating environment as stable. The periphery part is subject to more dynamic changes, which may lead to less predictable rules of the game and a less stable operating environment. This applies also to the degree of predictability in economic policy-making. Economic players in the core perceive the economic policy of the state as fairly predictable, because of the effective communication channels and mechanisms for information exchange. By contrast, actors in the periphery view economic policy as less predictable, due not least to the fact that they lack effective channels for communication.

Degree of vulnerability. The economic periphery appears rather unsustainable and vulnerable compared to the economic core. Although the periphery economy is more market-oriented, it is also more vulnerable. Moreover, as noted, companies in the periphery may deliberately opt not to expand, in order to avoid becoming overly attractive to the core actors. This limits their growth opportunities, which serves as an indicator of vulnerability.

State–business relations. Relations between the state and private business in the core are more formalized than between the state and periphery companies. This may also help to explain why the rules of the game are more stable in the core, and why policy-making is more predictable there. Moreover, the level of informal relations is higher in the periphery and lower in the core, where actors interact within a more formalized framework.

Direct access to government for solving problems; availability of state mechanisms for problem solving. State-owned and private companies in the core enjoy direct access to the government through well-established communication channels. If a business faces a problem and needs state support, it can quickly contact a public agency and get the issue settled. Companies in the periphery face a disadvantage, as the business associations that represent their interests are not particularly effective.

Even though the state is heavily involved in the activities of large private businesses, big business still has its own ways of leveraging influence over the state, mainly through various influential communication channels. Small companies and companies from less capital-intensive sectors receive little attention from the state. On the one hand, they may operate in a more or less market environment with simplified business regulation. On the other hand, they are disadvantaged as they enjoy little institutional support from the state and have fewer ways to influence the government, as associations representing their interests are usually less powerful and influential.

Access to finance. Companies in the core have ready access to funding: bank loans, external borrowing, state subsidies and many other sources. They may rely on state support, as shown by the economic crisis of 2008. For companies in the periphery, access to finance is more limited and complicated. During the period of economic boom (2000–2008), it was basically simple for periphery companies to get bank loans. However, since the 2008 economic crisis it has become more difficult for them to gain access to financial resources. Thus, such companies may rely on their own resources or informal borrowing from relatives or friends – but not all private companies have such options at hand.

Investment policy. Economic actors in the core pursue long-term investment strategies in Kazakhstan (three or more years), as they have confidence in the investment regime and the state reiterates its commitment to create and provide all the conditions necessary to guarantee their long-term growth. By contrast, economic actors in the periphery tend to pursue short-term strategies (one to two years), as the investment regime is more dynamic and chaotic for them, and they must fend for themselves in a less predictable, constantly changing environment.

State subsidies and control over subsidies. Both the core and the periphery receive relatively high state subsidies and investments, adequate for the size and capital-intensity of the industry (e.g. the programmes 'Business Road Map – 2020' launched in 2010, and 'Productivity-2020' started in 2011, for supporting SMEs; see also subsection 3.3.6.1). This shows that the state is committed to developing and diversifying its economic development equally, and it is hard to distinguish between the two parts of the economy in terms of government subsidy policy. However, the mechanism of control over subsidies and investment indicates one important difference: the state is committed to controlling the use of investment by economic actors in the core; in practice, the state demonstrates less commitment in effectively monitoring and controlling the use of subsidies and investment in the periphery. This may be explained by the significant differences in the amount of financial support provided. For example, subsidies and investment in the energy sector (core) will generally be much higher than subsidies for the agricultural sector (periphery). With this greater commitment on the part of the state to controlling investments in the core, the distribution and use of subsidies and investment is perceived as being more effective than in the periphery. This is no less due to the weak mechanisms of control, which may result in the misuse of subsidies in the periphery. Companies in the periphery often complain that the state does not support the development of vulnerable industries. In fact the state does – but it is not very effective when it comes to implementation and monitoring of subsidy and investment projects.

International courts. Another important indicator of the differences between the two parts of the economy is the use of international courts and arbitration. As the content analysis showed, companies in both the core and the periphery generally find legal mechanisms of dispute settlement rather ineffective. Companies tend to prefer to settle disputes by using business mechanisms, e.g. negotiations and pre-court arbitration. Legal instruments may also be used, but pre-court settlement is usually seen as preferable. In cases where neither pre-court nor legal mechanisms can help to solve an issue between private companies or between the state and private companies, companies in the core have an advantage when it comes to using international arbitration and international economic courts – such companies have sufficient resources to resort to the use of international courts, unlike companies in the periphery.

Tax regime. This indicator is important for the core/periphery distinction. Companies in the core find the tax regime more burdensome and complicated, whereas the tax regime is seen as rather 'business-friendly' in terms of low tax rates for the periphery. Periphery companies have a clear advantage as regards the current tax regime.

Within the dimension *inter-firm relations*, several important indicators have emerged:

Disclosure of information. In general, companies in the core must report their activities in a transparent way. Disclosure of company information is a requirement that the state imposes and rigorously monitors. The fact that Kazakhstan became part of the Extractive Industries Transparency Initiative (EITI)[38] in 2005 and received the 'EITI Compliant' status in 2013 (EITI 2014a) shows the commitment on the part of the state to increase transparency in the management of natural resources. Today, most large companies in capital-intensive industries are required to provide information on their activities (e.g. corporations under the umbrella of Samruk-Kazyna), including the oil and gas companies. The situation is different for companies in the periphery. Whereas they may be formally obliged to disclose information, they generally do not do so in practice. As they face only limited regulatory control from the state, they find it relatively easy to limit information disclosure and avoid detailed reporting. Thus they operate in an LME-type of business environment.

Transparency of transactions. The requirement for disclosure of company information has implications for the transparency of transactions. Transactions between companies in the core are usually more transparent, subject to greater scrutiny and control, than in the periphery.

Competition. Companies in the core experience higher levels of competition than companies in the periphery. Capital-intensive industries in Kazakhstan are more attractive to various economic actors, including foreign ones, than less capital-intensive industries. In addition, the consumer market is still relatively small and unattractive for foreign investors. As most periphery industries relate mainly to the consumer market, there is less intensive competition between companies in these industries. Periphery companies compete for a better market position, but they may also unite in efforts to make the state listen to their concerns and to help in solving their problems.

---

38 'EITI is a global coalition of governments, companies and civil society working together to improve openness and accountable management of revenues from natural resources' (EITI 2014b).

Regulation of competition. Given the higher competition levels in the core, the state regulates competition between core companies more actively and heavily. Companies in the periphery face little regulatory pressure from the state.

Merger and acquisitions. M&As are more frequent between companies in the core, and rare in the periphery. Given the frequency of M&A transactions, the former resemble LMEs (high frequency), whereas the latter are closer to CMEs (low frequency). M&As serve as an example of interaction between core and periphery actors. Some SMEs try to avoid this and prefer not to take part in M&As, because otherwise they would grow and might become attractive for possible takeover by big companies in the core.

Regulation of mergers and acquisitions by the state. The state appears to be the strong regulator of M&A transactions in the core and is little involved in controlling them in the 'periphery'. This serves as an explicit indicator of higher state involvement and regulation of the core economy, with little involvement and coordination of the periphery economy.

Regarding the third dimension, *the influence of other market players (labour unions and employer associations),* several points help to characterize and define the two parts of the economy in Kazakhstan more clearly.

Labour unions. The role of labour unions in the core industries of the economy is seen as relatively strong, whereas labour unions are weak in periphery industries. This perception was found among the great majority of respondents.

Demand for labour unions. There is little demand for labour unions in the core part of the economy, mainly because relatively strong labour unions already exist. However, also in the periphery there is little demand for effective labour unions, for various reasons. First, labour unions have been rather weak in periphery industries, so employees of periphery companies do not feel that labour unions are of any use to them. This also has to do with Soviet path-dependence. Second, employees may use other mechanisms (like labour courts) to protect their rights, individually or collectively. Third, some 60 per cent of SMEs in Kazakhstan are family businesses: with these, there is little demand for labour unions, as employer-employee relations are directly – and hierarchically – regulated by family members or friends, without using a third party like a labour union.

Employer associations. Employer associations in the core have been shown to be rather strong, whereas employer associations in the periphery are weak when it comes to promoting the interests of companies. This is explained by the presence of effective communication channels for core companies which reinforce strong positions of employer associations in their dialogue with the state.

Demand for employer associations. Due to the existence of relatively strong and effective employer associations in the core, core companies evince little demand today for employer associations. By contrast, because employer associations in the periphery are relatively ineffective, there is an increasing demand for the establishment of effective business associations that could help to promote the interests of SMEs.

Figure 5.1 summarizes the main findings of this study. As explained, the economy is presented as consisting of two parts: the core and the periphery. The core part is larger in economic terms. The periphery part is smaller, but involves a much greater number of economic actors. However, the higher level of informal activities in the periphery (in contrast to the core part) makes it hard to identify the economic boundaries clearly. It is important to note that despite all difficulties in the core and the periphery, both economies are self-sustainable, and offer certain benefits and advantages for economic actors.

Figure 5.1. ‘Core–periphery’ market-oriented economy in Kazakhstan

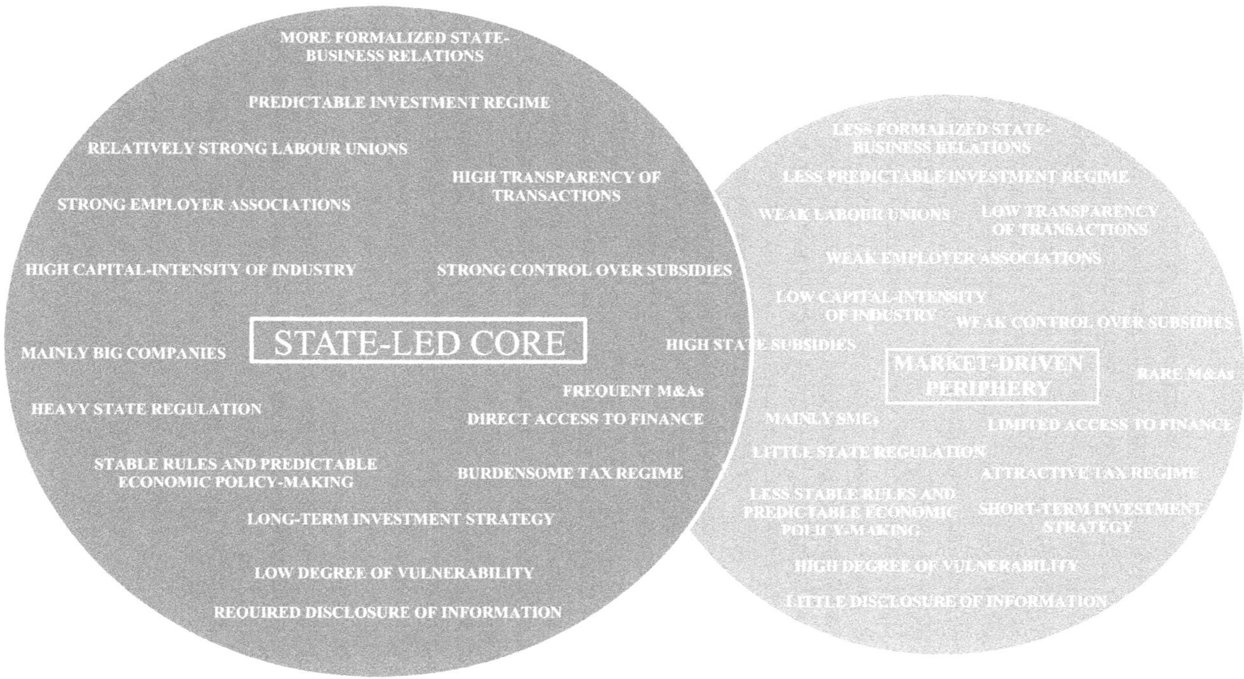

5.5. Caveats and limitations in data analysis

The interpretations and conclusions presented in previous sections are based not only on the results of the content analysis, but also draw on the author's own experience from 159 interviews, as well as observations from the field and prior knowledge of Kazakhstan's economy. That said, some limitations of the sample should be acknowledged.

First, for data analysis, only 48 interviews out of 159 were used. This decreases the degree to which the smaller sample can be considered representative. The entire sample of 159 interviews is representative of all the stratification criteria initially elaborated (see subsections 4.4.2–4.4.8 on sampling). Even though the smaller sample of 48 interviews covers all sampling levels (see sampling levels in Table 4.1), still it is less representative than the entire sample of 159 interviews. This increases the probability of error, which may negatively affect the results of content analysis. However, it should also be acknowledged that this study have not sought to achieve a representative sample in purely quantitative terms. Thus, this sample should not be viewed as representative in quantitative terms as it was not done according to the random procedure. I sought to present the views and perceptions of a great variety of economic actors and decision-makers in order to achieve an equal representation of various actors' perceptions and opinions on the type of market economy currently emerging. This goal I largely achieved by collecting the data according to my sample, covering all categories of interviewees initially identified.

Second, the results of the interview analysis should not be regarded as the 'ultimate truth' when it comes to understanding the type of market economy in the country. This work sheds light on how Kazakhstan's economy has evolved since 1991, providing an in-depth analysis and identifying specific aspects of the structure of the economy, its 'core' and 'periphery' parts. The findings are based on the perceptions and views expressed by many political actors directly involved in the decision-making and reform process, as well as economic actors in selected industries who are the drivers of economic processes in Kazakhstan. However, it was not possible to include every political and economic actor, or every industry. Moreover, respondents' perceptions are based on personal subjective judgments and observations, which may add various biases to the results obtained (see also subsection 5.1.1). Even though the content analysis helped in enabling respondents' views to be analysed systematically, thereby reducing biases of perception and interpretation, it is still important to take into account the limits of interviews as data sources. The results of the data analysis, and the interpretations offered, should be considered in the context of these limitations.

Chapter 6. Conclusions

Under the leadership of President Nursultan Nazarbayev, Kazakhstan has achieved remarkable economic progress since 1991. The country's market-oriented reform path has been distinct in many respects. This book has studied the emerging market economy in Kazakhstan and its institutional structure after 20 years of independence, in order to contribute to a better understanding of the economic development path of the country. It has provided a detailed description of market institutions and the interaction between various economic actors. The main research question sought to investigate what type of market economy has been emerging in Kazakhstan. Through qualitative data collection, an in-depth description of Kazakhstan's economy was provided. In particular, this research project has studied the role of the state in steering economic processes, and has analysed interaction between the state and private business, labour unions and employer associations.

The findings build on a literature review conducted according to the Varieties of Capitalism (VoC) approach. Moreover, 159 semi-structured interviews were conducted in Kazakhstan in 2009 and 2010. Thus, the findings also draw on the perceptions and views expressed by a large number of political actors directly involved in the decision-making and reform process, as well as economic players in selected industries who are the drivers of economic processes in Kazakhstan. Methodologically, the use of content analysis proved effective in analysing semi-structured interviews. It helped to identify respondents' perceptions and views on state–business interaction, inter-firm relations and the role and influence of other market players (labour unions and employer associations) on state–business interrelations. The coding frame for content analysis was based on the 'core–periphery' framework, which was the data-driven part of this analysis. The VoC theoretical framework played a supplementary role; some of its key assumptions were also integrated into the coding frame.

The VoC approach served as a starting point for classifying economic institutions. In this study it was assumed that Kazakhstan's economy has been gravitating towards a distinct type of a market economy which might exhibit elements of two distinct types of economies: a Liberal Market Economy (LME) and a Coordinated Market Economy (CME). The use of this analytical framework for the literature review facilitated the descriptive analysis of institutional development.

However, the literature review indicated that applying the VoC approach to the post-communist transition economy of Kazakhstan has its limits. This is in line with the findings of Mendelski (2008), Nölke and Fliegenthart (2009) and Luly (2012), who hold that the VoC approach fails to acknowledge the active role of the state in the transition context and cannot explain sudden institutional change and dynamics. Therefore, in this study the VoC approach was complemented by a 'core–periphery' analytical framework, which proved useful in accounting for the role of the state in the economy. The main problem with using the VoC approach was that the nature of coordination in Kazakhstan differs from key VoC assumptions. According to the VoC approach, business activities are coordinated via market mechanisms (LME) or strategic coordination (CME) initiated by firms (Hall and Soskice 2001). In both cases, firms are seen as the key actors of coordination. In Kazakhstan, however, the state is the main coordinator of inter-firm relations in the core, with somewhat greater presence of market coordination in the periphery. Inter-firm relations, the financial system, corporate governance, vocational education and training, the social security system as well as industrial relations – all are coordinated by the state. Thus, complementing the VoC approach with a 'core–periphery' framework enabled a better understanding of the essence of the emerging market economy.

The 'core–periphery' theoretical framework was developed after the preliminary technical analysis of 159 interviews. This framework has served as the main analytical tool of this study, facilitating analysis of the structure of the economy. The analysis of primary data indicated that the economy of Kazakhstan is in fact neither an LME nor a CME: it is more correctly classified as a 'core–periphery' economy. On the other hand, certain features of the two institutional systems of the VoC approach can be traced in the core and the periphery, with more elements of an LME found in the periphery and more elements of a CME in the core.

The key component of the core economy is that it also has market elements in its structure. Since independence, Kazakhstan has successfully pursued liberalization and market reforms. The government has implemented policy reforms that include privatization, fiscal, tax and monetary policies. The government has also been responsive to social demands, adopting measures to promote socially-oriented development. The economic crisis of 2008 led to a strengthening of the role of the state in the economy. Today, on the one hand, the state is heavily involved in the core economy by heavily monitoring and controlling economic processes. On the other hand, it also seeks to steer and coordinate the economy by market mechanisms in order to attract domestic and foreign investors – as shown by the special treatment of, and attitudes towards, large foreign investors. Successful privatization measures have attracted numerous foreign investors who entered the local market, investing heavily in the economy since the 1990s, and who are today part of the core.

The periphery economy is more market-oriented, and involves mostly small and medium-sized enterprises (SMEs). The fact that the core is mainly represented by big companies and the periphery by SMEs also reflects the effects of Soviet path-dependence in shaping institutions and institutional subsystems in Kazakhstan. As identified in the literature review by Lee et al. (2008: 80), SMEs in Kazakhstan are not Soviet path-dependent, because most of them were formed during the market era in the 1990s. By contrast, most big state-owned enterprises were formed during Soviet times, and have been controlled by the state since then. The corporate structure of these enterprises has implied active involvement of the state. These initial institutional conditions should also be taken into account when analysing why the economy of Kazakhstan has evolved into a hybrid 'core–periphery' market economy.

In the case of Kazakhstan, the 'core–periphery' distinction is especially interesting as it reflects the broader structure of the economy. The core part is substantial in economic terms. The periphery part is smaller, but involves a greater number of economic players. However, due to the higher level of informal activities in the periphery, it is hard to identify clearly its real contribution to economic output. The big companies of the core have more resources and capacities and are thus more influential in their relations with the state than the periphery companies. However, more economic opportunities may imply greater responsibilities for state and society. This study has shown that the state today is committed to strict monitoring of implementation of corporate social responsibility projects by big foreign investors and national companies in the core.

The hybrid 'core–periphery' model that has emerged in Kazakhstan is the result of dynamic changes, modified priorities, as well as the overall economic policy objectives set by the government. This structure of the economy allows the core as well as the periphery to be self-sustainable. This observation is supported by the fact that the hybrid market economy of Kazakhstan has achieved high economic growth since 2000. Thus, despite its dual structure, the economy should be characterized as successful.

How do the results and the major findings contribute to the literature, as well as cumulative knowledge-building on economic transition in the post-Soviet space? This study confirms that Kazakhstan today is in a phase of development in which most economic and political institutions have already been formed. Therefore, it appears that twenty years of independence is a sufficient period to allow for assessment of the results of economic transformation, and to identify the type of market economy which has been formed in Kazakhstan during this period.

This work contributes to the bigger picture of economic transition in the post-Soviet space and expands the existing body of literature on economic transition in Kazakhstan. By identifying and analysing the key institutions and the model of the emerging economy, this research makes theoretical and empirical contributions toward a deeper comprehension of economic developments not only in Kazakhstan but also in similar countries in transition.

This study makes also several other important contributions. First, this research provides an innovative contribution to the broader scholarly literature on the economic and institutional transition of Kazakhstan. Some scholars have tended to identify Kazakhstan as being somewhat closer to a Liberal Market Economy. Charman (2007: 180) has defined Kazakhstan as 'a state-led liberal market economy'; Spechler (2008: 33) puts it as a 'state-led' capitalist economy; Rybina et al. (2010: 93) calls it 'a government-dominated transition economy'. These authors all point to the key role of the state in the economy, while also mentioning some elements of a liberal market economy. The findings of the present study prove the key role of the state and the presence of market mechanisms in the economy. However, this study has also showed that the structure of the economy is far more complex. It makes sense to divide it into two categories – the 'core' and the 'periphery' – in which the core is more state-led and the periphery is more market-oriented. At the same time, each economic part has also elements of state coordination and market mechanisms. In light of these findings, this study contributes to the emergence of the concept of a 'hybrid capitalist economy' which may be seen as specific to transition economies, particularly those of the post-Soviet sphere.

Second, the findings of the present study can also be applied to other resource-rich countries of the former Soviet Union. In particular, the 'core–periphery' theoretical framework can be also applied to Azerbaijan, Russia and Uzbekistan. It is possible to assume that the economies of these three resource-rich nations also exhibit similar features of economic transition as those found in Kazakhstan. It would be relevant to conduct a comparative study of the four countries to identify commonalities and differences. This would help in better understanding and explaining the likely future trajectories of their institutional transition.

Third, qualitative research methods have been employed in this study. This approach has shown that the systematic analysis of perceptions may help to provide useful insights into the type of market economy that has been emerging in Kazakhstan. Collecting and analysing perceptions of market participants revealed that the country has been exposed to a range of ideas of economic development stemming from various schools of economic thought, individual background of respondents, their work experiences. In order to specify the type of the economy it was important to collect perceptions, views and assessments from various actors. Unlike the widely-adopted external approach used by international organizations (the World Bank, the IMF, etc.) to assess economic development, this approach provided a no less important 'internal' perspective on market-oriented development in Kazakhstan. The main conclusion is that the market behaviour of various actors is not shaped solely by the institutional structure provided by the state, but is also predetermined by the norms, values, previous experiences, professional and academic backgrounds of these actors.

Thus, the qualitative approach of this study makes an important contribution to the field of economic studies by revealing contrasting perspectives, shared by market actors, on the role of the state, state–business interaction and state vs. market debate. It complements the external approach in many important ways. First of all, it has identified behaviour and incentives by which market actors are driven. Furthermore, it has revealed how their behaviour and opposing perceptions contribute to the formation of a heterogeneous economic discourse. We have seen how the economy is perceived by some respondents as being highly interventionist, but is seen as liberal and market-oriented by others. This enriches and expands the definition of an *economic system*: we find that various actors co-exist and their diverging market perceptions are well accommodated in one economic system. This heterogeneous system has brought significant economic progress to Kazakhstan and established well-functioning economic institutions since 1991. It can be even argued that the existence of diverse economic actors and approaches has been one of the factors of country's economic success. Moreover, it may be assumed that this heterogeneity has contributed to the formation of the 'core–periphery' economy in Kazakhstan. Continued exposure to this diversity of ideas should have a positive effect on country's economic future.

Fourth, this book makes an important contribution to the body of knowledge on the methodology of interviewing elites in Kazakhstan and Central Asia. It indicates some of the challenges associated with doing fieldwork in Kazakhstan. It also provides useful lessons and presents successful strategies for reaching various representatives of the economic and political elites. The study has shown the overall openness and positive attitudes of elite respondents towards scientific interviewing. In particular, high-ranking public employees were one of the most accessible categories of respondents in the present study.

The second methodological contribution of this study is the creation of the grading scale for measuring the quality of interviews. It is an innovative methodological tool that was employed in this study. The grading scale was elaborated and introduced by the research team at the very beginning of the fieldwork. This tool proved useful and effective in assessing the quality of interviews, as well as classifying and selecting interviews for analysis.

And finally, this work contributes to the ongoing debate on state capitalism. By employing the VoC approach and the core–periphery framework, the study makes an innovative contribution to the debate on the varieties of state capitalism in the CIS and elsewhere in the world. The recent school of thought on state capitalism postulates that the tendency of the past ten years or so has been for countries with state capitalism to let the private sector grow and tighten its control over strategic economic industries (Musacchio and Lazzarini 2013; *The Economist* 2012a; Szamosszegi and Kyle 2011; Bremmer 2010). Indeed, that appears to have been the case in Kazakhstan and is well reflected in the found 'core-periphery' economy.

In China, for instance, the private sector has gained enormous importance in the state-capitalist economy, helping the state to adopt new innovations and technologies, improve the services industry and become more globally competitive (Szamosszegi and Kyle 2011: 92). Bremmer (2010: 5) views this type of state capitalism as a system in which the state uses market tools to achieve political goals. State-owned enterprises, sovereign wealth funds, national oil and gas companies are characterized as tools of new market-oriented state capitalism (Ostrowski 2012). Further, Guillén and Garcia-Canal (2013: 1) note that we are now observing 'the spectacular growth of globe-spanning businesses in the developing world'; they predict that corporations based in the emerging markets will 'reshape the global economic order for decades to come.'

How can we explain such progress of the emerging economies? Many emerging markets with state capitalism participate more actively in globalization presently than 10–20 years ago, which has helped them to increase their capacity to learn from the developed countries *(The Economist* 2012b; 2012d; Bremmer 2010; Guillén and Garcia-Canal 2013: 9–10; Chattopadhyay et al. 2012: 21; Ostrowski 2012: 3). Here we may note the development model of Kazakhstan, coupled with the country's openness and experience in learning from other countries (see subsection 5.1.1 and Table 5.2). Musacchio and Lazzarini (2013: 31) point out that the governments of the emerging economies have realized the need to introduce more effective corporate governance and ownership structures for their state-owned enterprises. We find the same trend in Kazakhstan. The government has invited numerous professional managers from abroad to run key state-owned corporations.[39] Highly-skilled and experienced managers are invited to manage big state-owned corporations and improve their productivity – in line with the global tendency (Guillén and Garcia-Canal 2013: 10). According to *The Economist* (2012c), 'instead of handing industries to bureaucrats or cronies, it (*state capitalism economy*) turns them into companies run by professional managers.' Moreover, Tony Blair, former British prime minister, was invited by President Nazarbayev to advise the government to pursue economic reforms in 2011. In 2012, Tony Blair extended his contract, and has been assisting the government in conducting economic and political reforms.

The state remains the key actor in emerging economies (Sharma 2013: 257). Paradoxically with respect to the 'state vs. market' debate, the state plays an active role in regulating market processes in Kazakhstan. It is thus necessary to expand and modify the VoC approach with regard to economies with state capitalism, by explicitly accounting for an active state role and state interest in using market mechanisms for implementing economic reforms. Furthermore, it

---

39 Here we may note Peter Foster, CEO of Air Astana (leading air company); Peter Howes, former Managing Director of Samruk-Kazyna; Richard Harry Evans, Member of the Board of Directors and Independent Director of Samruk-Kazyna, among others.

is necessary to elaborate new theoretical approaches which could help in analysing the complexity of emerging state capitalism and its changing nature. Guillén and Garcia-Canal (2013: 1) note that little attention has been paid to the analysis of this phenomenon.

Emerging economies with state capitalism become more sophisticated in terms of coordinating and controlling their economies *(The Economist* 2012a), shifting from direct to indirect management of economic assets, as has been recently the case in Brazil, where the state has been referred to as 'Leviathan as a minority investor' (Musacchio and Lazzarini 2013: 30). The government in Kazakhstan pursued a similar strategy with respect to the Kashagan oil field. Although the biggest state-owned oil company KazMunayGas raised its stake from 8 per cent to 16 per cent over time (see subsection 2.1.7), the state did not acquire all stakes from multinational companies, and has remained a minority stakeholder (Bremmer 2010: 64). Therefore, as state capitalism becomes innovative, we need more innovative analytical tools for analysing it.

It is also necessary to provide a critical assessment of this study. This work should help to better comprehend the type of economy which has evolved in Kazakhstan since its independence. However, it should be acknowledged that, due to the dynamic nature of economic processes and the constantly changing business environment, the results presented here may not fully reflect the specifics of the emerging economy in Kazakhstan in the future. It is important to bear in mind the dynamic pace of change of institutional processes in Kazakhstan. As one interviewed expert notes (Ex1/Core–Periphery):

> We should clearly understand that we are a young developing economy and the rules of the game haven't been fully established yet. They (*the rules of the game*) are dynamic and not static; the overall dynamics is quite high in this respect.

A first sign of possible changes in the constellation of core and periphery actors can be seen in the effects of Kazakhstan's membership in the Customs Union involving Russia, Belarus and Kazakhstan. As a result of the Customs Union, from 2011 to early 2013, more than 500 Russian SMEs had re-registered their businesses in Kazakhstan due to lower tax rates (VAT in Russia is 18 per cent, but only 12 per cent in Kazakhstan), less bureaucracy and an easier operating environment compared to Russia (Vielmini 2013; *Forbes.kz* 2011). What does this mean for the market economy in Kazakhstan? First of all, it indicates that, despite all difficulties in the periphery economy, the operating environment has many market elements and is relatively attractive for foreign investors. Second, the active inflow of foreign SMEs may change the market environment and provide stronger incentives for the government to improve conditions for doing business. Operating conditions for SMEs should be further improved and their growth should be encouraged by the state, as SMEs are likely to be the major drivers of economic development in the long run.

Providing greater economic freedom and adding more market elements into the periphery may also have spillover effects for the core economy. On the other hand, the core and the periphery may follow a diverging path, with the core being more controlled and coordinated by the state and the periphery being less regulated. Future changes will depend on many macro- and microeconomic factors. However, the direction of change will further rest with the government, and the state is likely to play the leading role in coordinating economic processes in Kazakhstan in the future.

Another critical point is that, there are certain limitations as relating to a broader empirical generalization of this study. This relates to the representativeness of the sample. This study did not seek to achieve a representative sample in quantitative terms. Instead, it was seen as more important to present the views and perceptions of the main groups of economic actors and decision-makers, industries and countries in order to achieve a fairly equal representation of various actors' perceptions on Kazakhstan's market-oriented economic development. The research design was effective in covering all stratification criteria. With certain reservations, as discussed in section 5.5, some findings and conclusions relate to the entire economy.

Finally, not all aspects of state–business interaction have been covered and not all causal mechanisms of this interaction described in this study. That would have been beyond the scope of this work. That said, it would be advantageous to conduct an explanatory study in order to better comprehend the dynamics of the emerging market economy in Kazakhstan. This could assist analysis of the causal mechanisms of interaction between the core and the periphery parts of the economy.

This study also indicates promising future areas for study. Further research is needed to identify to what extent the 'core–periphery' economy will prove sustainable in the long run. How, for example, would the dynamic relationship between the two parts of the economy change in case of external shocks? How do economic players in the core and the periphery interact with each other? It is also important to understand how the dispute settlement between periphery and core companies functions. What are the broader social and political implications of the interaction between the core and the periphery economic parts in Kazakhstan? This book has shown that these two economies co-exist, and has described what makes them different and similar, what the incentives are for companies to remain in either the core or the periphery. Economic actors in both parts interact dynamically with each other, and an actor may shift from one economy to the other. Many companies also combine the elements of the two parts, making it difficult to assign them to either the core or the periphery.

This study has shed some light on these aspects of dynamic interaction. In-depth analysis of these dynamics in a follow-up study would be necessary to fully comprehend the future transition path of Kazakhstan and the essence of its market-oriented reform strategy. Moreover, institutional complementarity has not been analysed here, but the methodology approach employed would appear well suited to achieve this goal in subsequent studies.

Indeed, answering these research questions could promote further insights into the future transition path of not only Kazakhstan, but also other states of Central Asia, as well as similar countries in transition.

References

Abusseitov, K. (2011). *Kazakhstan on the Move.* Diplomat Magazine, 11 May, available at: http://www.diplomatmagazine.com/index.php?option=com_content&view=article&id=451&Itemid=, accessed 1 March 2014.

ADB (2000). *The Role of Central Banks in Microfinance in Asia and the Pacific.* Vol. 1, Overview. Manila: Asian Development Bank.

ADB (2003). *Program Performance Audit Report on the Pension Reform Program in Kazakhstan.* PPA: KAZ 31091. Manila: Asian Development Bank.

ADB (2005). *Proposed Assistance to Private Bank in Kazakhstan.* Report and Recommendations of the President to the Board of Directors, Project No. 40908. Manila: Asian Development Bank.

ADB (2008). Social Protection Index for Committed Poverty Reduction, Vol 2: Asia. Manila: Asian Development Bank.

AFN (2012). *Insurance Organizations.* Committee for the Control and Supervision of the Financial Market and Financial Organizations of the National Bank of the Republic of Kazakhstan (AFN), available at: http://www.afn.kz/en/information-for-entities-of-financial-market/insurance-sector/2009-12-21-06-51-21/2009-12-21-06-54-00, accessed 9 March 2012.

Agency of Statistics of the Republic of Kazakhstan (2011). *Dolia Malogo i Srednego Predprinimatelstva v VVP*, available at: http://www.stat.kz/digital/mal_pred/Pages/default.aspx, accessed 29 June 2012.

Agency of Statistics of the Republic of Kazakhstan (2012a). *Main Socio-Economic Indicators*, available at: http://www.stat.kz/Pages/default.aspx, accessed 28 October 2012.

Agency of Statistics of the Republic of Kazakhstan (2012b). *Labour*, available at: http://www.eng.stat.kz/digital/Labour/Pages/default.aspx, accessed 28 October 2012.

Agency of Statistics of the Republic of Kazakhstan (2012c). *Tehnicheskoe i Professionalnoe Obrazovanie v Respublike Kazahstan na Nachalo 2011–2012 Uchebnogo Goda*, available at: http://www.stat.kz/news/Pages/n2_2_02_2012.aspx, accessed 17 March 2012.

Agency of Statistics of the Republic of Kazakhstan (2013). *Kazahstan v 2012 Godu,* Statistical Yearbook, available at: http://stat.gov.kz/getImg?id= WC16200033549, accessed 20 March 2014.

Agency of Statistics of the Republic of Kazakhstan (2014a). *Ob Inflacii v Respublike Kazahstan.* Ekspress-Informacia, available at: http://stat.gov.kz/getImg?id=ESTAT071918, accessed 19 March 2014.

Agency of Statistics of the Republic of Kazakhstan (2014b). *Osnovnye Socialno-Ekonomicheskie Pokazateli Respubliki Kazahstan*, available at: http://www.stat.gov.kz, accessed 16 April 2014.

Agrawal, P. (2008). Economic Growth and Poverty Reduction: Evidence from Kazakhstan, Asian Development Bank, *Asian Development Review,* 24 (2), 90–115.

Ahrens, J. (2002). *Governance and Economic Development. A Comparative Institutional Approach*, Chelthenham: Edward Elgar.

Ahrens, J. (2008). *Emerging Market Economies in Central Asia: The Role of Institutional Complementarities in Reform Processes.* Application for funding a research project in the realm of the funding initiative 'Between Europe and the Orient – A Focus on Research and Higher Education in/on Central Asia and the Caucasus'. Private University of Applied Sciences Göttingen.

Ahrens, J. and Platje, J. (2010). Sustainability of Institutional and Economic Change in Central Asia, Editorial, *Economic and Environmental Studies,* 10 (2), 155–60.

Aidarkhanova, B. (2010). The KAZSTEM Kazakhstan Macroeconomic Model of Forecasting in G7 Econometric Package. In R. Pocs, A. Auzina, V. Ozolina (eds), *Development and Applications of Multisectoral Macroeconomic Models*, pp. 119–34. Riga: RTU Publishing House.

Aitken, J. (2009). *Nazarbayev and the Making of Kazakhstan*. London: Continuum International.

Aitken, J. (2012). *Kazakhstan: Surprises and Stereotypes After 20 Years of Independence.* London: Continuum International.

Akimov, A. and Dollery, B. (2006). Uzbekistan's Financial System. An Evaluation of Twelve Years of Transition, *Problems of Economic Transition*, 48 (12), 6–31.

Akimov, A. and Dollery, B. (2007). An *Evaluation of Kazakhstan's Financial System Reforms in 1993–2002*, Working Paper Series in Economics, University of New England, School of Economics, available at: http://www.une.edu.au/bepp/working-papers/economics/1999-2007/econ-2007-3.pdf, accessed 27 February 2012.

Akorda (2012). *The Strategy for Development of the Republic of Kazakhstan*, Official Website of the President of the Republic of Kazakhstan, available at: http://www.akorda.kz/en/category/gos_programmi_razvitiya, accessed 19 December 2012.

Akorda (2013). *Predsedatelstvo Kazahstana v OIK*, Official Website of the President of the Republic of Kazakhstan, available at: http://akorda.kz/ru/pa ge/predsedatelstvo-kazakhstana-v-ois_1341478616, accessed 12 January 2014.

Akorda (2014). *Address by the President of the Republic of Kazakhstan, Leader of the Nation, Nursultan Nazarbayev 'Strategy Kazakhstan–2050: New Political Course of the Established State'*, available at: http://www.akorda.k z/en/page/page_poslanie-prezidenta-respubliki-kazakhstan-lidera-natsii-nursultana-nazarbaeva-narodu-kazakhstana-, accessed 24 June 2014.

Alam, A. and Banerji, A. (2000). *Kazakhstan and Uzbekistan: A Tale of Two Transition Paths*, World Bank, Policy Research Working Paper, No. 2472, Washington, DC.

Alibaev, A. (1998). *Pensionnaya Reforma v Respublike Kazahstan*, Council of Pension Funds of Kazakhstan, Almaty.

Alshanov, R. (2011). Ekonomika Kazahstana za 20 Let: Dostijenia i Puti Dalneishego Razvitia, *Kazahstanskaya Pravda*, 7 October 2011.

Amagoh, F. and Markus, U. (2010). Kazakhstan's Outward Foreign Investments: Issues and Perspectives. *Central Asia Business Journal*, 3 (November), 12–25.

Amagoh, F. (2011). New Public Management and Health Reform in Kazakhstan, *International Journal of Public Administration*, 34, 567–78.

American Chamber of Commerce (AmCham) (2004). Kazakhstan's Foreign Investment Climate. In M. Terterov (ed.), *Doing Business with Kazakhstan*, pp. 41–56. London/ Sterling, VA: Kogan Page.

American Chamber of Commerce (AmCham) (2011). *The U.S. – Kazakhstan Public – Private Economic Partnership Initiative (PPEPI)*. American Chamber of Commerce, available at: www.amcham.kz/ppepi, accessed 1 March 2012.

AMFOK (2014). *Mikrokreditovanie v RK*, Association of Microfinance Organizations of Kazakhstan (AMFOK), available at: http://www.amfok.kz/ sections, accessed 24 March 2014.

Amin, A. and Ainekova, D. (2012). The Long Run Growth Rate of the Kazakhstan's Economy, *Eurasian Journal of Business and Economics*, 5 (9), 45–56.

Anderson, K. and Heyneman, S. (2005). Education and Social Policy in Central Asia: The Next Stage of Transition, *Social Policy and Administration*, 39 (4), 361–80.

Armingeon, K. and Careja, R. (2008). Institutional Change and Stability in Post-Communist Countries, 1990–2002, *European Journal of Political Research*, 47, 436–66.

Arner, D. and Park, C.-Y. (2011). Developing Asia and the Global Financial Regulatory Agenda. *Journal of Banking Regulation*, 12 (2), 119–43.

Åslund, A. (2007). *Russia's Capitalist Revolution: Why Market Reform Succeeded and Democracy Failed*, Washington, DC: Peterson Institute for International Economics.

Baimakhanov, S. (2009). Local vs. Foreign Banks in Kazakhstan, Kazakhstan Banking, Tengry Finance, *World Finance Review*, September, available at: http://www.worldfinancereview.com/pdf/Local%20vs%20Foreign%20Banks%20in%20Kazakhstan.pdf, accessed 4 April 2014.

Ball, S. (1994). Political Interviews and the Politics of Interviewing. In G. Walford (ed.), *Researching the Powerful in Education*, London: UCL Press.

Baker&McKenzie (2009). *Doing Business in Kazakhstan.* Almaty: Baker&McKenzie.

Bank for International Settlements (2009). *Issues in the Governance of Central Banks*, A Report from the Central Bank Governance Group, Basel, available at: http://www.bis.org/publ/othp04.pdf, accessed 7 January 2014.

Barisitz, S. (2008). *Banking in Central and Eastern Europe 1980–2006.* London: Routledge.

Barisitz, S. and Lahnsteiner, M. (2010). From Stormy Expansion to Riding out the Storm: Banking Development in Kazakhstan. *Financial Stability Report* 19, Austrian National Bank, pp. 62–71.

Barsukov, A. (2004). Regulation of the Banking Sector, McGuireWoods, Kazakhstan LLP. In M. Terterov (ed.), *Doing Business with Kazakhstan*, pp. 256–63. London/ Sterling, VA: Kogan Page.

Bavdaz, M. (2009). Conducting Research on the Response Process in Business Surveys, *Statistical Journal of the IAOS*, 26 (1–2), 1–14.

Beck, T. and Laeven, L. (2006). Institution Building and Growth in Transition Economies, *Journal of Economic Growth*, 11, 157–86.

Becker, C., Marchenko, G., Khakimzhanov, S., Seitenova, A. and Ivliev, V. (2009). *Social Security System in Transition Economies: Lessons from Kazakhstan.* New York: Palgrave Macmillan, New York.

Becker, T. and Meyers, P. (1975). Empathy and Bravado: Interviewing Reluctant Bureaucrats, *Public Opinion Quarterly*, 38 (4), 605–13.

Bekbaeva, M. (2009). Problemi Strahovogo Rinka v Kazahstane, *Gak.kz*, available at: http://www.gak.kz/ru/view/press_2009/page_936_problemy-strakhovogo-rynka-v-kazakhstane-kazakhstan-tv, accessed 12 June 2014.

Belaya, V. and Mykhaylenko, M. (2010). Agrargigant Kasachstan: Probleme und Perspektiven der Landwirtschaftlichen Entwicklung, *Zentralasien-Analysen,* 27, 2–10.

Berry, J. (2002). Validity and Reliability Issues in Elite Interviewing, *Political Science and Politics*, 35 (4), 679–82.

Bertelsmann Foundation (2006). *BTI 2006 – Kazakhstan Country Report*, Gütersloh: Bertelsmann Foundation.

Bertelsmann Foundation (2010). *BTI 2010 – Kazakhstan Country Report*, Güterlsoh: Bertelsmann Foundation.

Bertelsmann Foundation (2012). *BTI 2012 – Kazakhstan Country Report*, Güterlsoh: Bertelsmann Foundation.

Bhuiyan, S. (2010). E-Government in Kazakhstan: Challenges and Its Role to Development, *Public Organization Review*, 10, 31–47.

Boehnke, K., Lietz, P., Schreier, M. and Wilhelm, A. (2011). Sampling: The Selection of Cases for Culturally Comparative Psychological Research. In D. Matsumoto and F.F. van de Vijver (eds), *Cross-Cultural Research Methods in Psychology*, pp. 101–29. Cambridge: Cambridge University Press.

Bohr, A. (2004). Regionalism in Central Asia: New Geopolitics, Old Regional Order, *International Affairs*, 80 (3), 485–502.

Bolashak (2012). *Activities*, Association of Kazakhstan President's Bolashak International Scholarship Fellows, available at: http://bolashak.kz/en/news, accessed 14 March 2012.

Borisov, V. and Clarke, S. (2006). The Rise and Fall of Social Partnership in Post-Socialist Europe: the Commonwealth of Independent States, *Industrial Relations Journal*, 37 (6), 607–29.

Bremmer, I. (2010). *The End of the Free Market. Who Wins the War Between States and Corporations?* New York: Penguin Group.

Brown, R. (1998). Culture, Chaos and Capitalism: Privatization in Kazakhstan, *Journal of International Economic Law*, 19 (4), 909–64.

Bryman, A. (2004). *Social Research Methods*, 2nd ed. Oxford: Oxford University Press.

Buchen, C. (2007). East European Antipodes: Varieties of Capitalism in Estonia and Slovenia. In D. Lane and M. Myant (eds), *Varieties of Capitalism in Post-Communist Economies*, pp. 65–89. Basingstoke: Palgrave Macmillan.

Burke, J. and Okulova, X. (2009). *The Effects of Devaluation of the Tenge upon the Kazakhstan Economy*, the KZT Project, the Kazakhstan Institute of Management, Economics and Strategic Research (KIMEP), available at: http://works.bepress.com/john_burke/4, accessed 12 December 2012.

Business Dictionary (2012a). *Financial Institution*, BusinessDictionary.com, available at: http://www.businessdictionary.com/definition/financial-instituti on.html, accessed 22 February 2014.

Business Dictionary (2012b). *Social Security System*, BusinessDictionary.com, available at: http://www.businessdictionary.com/definition/social-security-system.html, accessed 22 February 2014.

The Business Year (2011). Focus. Down at the Sukuk. The Business Year, available at: http://www.thebusinessyear.com/publication/article/5/212/kaza khstan-2011/down-at-the-sukuk, accessed 9 February 2014.

Cadbury Committee (The Committee on the Financial Aspects of Corporate Governance) (1992). *The Financial Aspects of Corporate Governance.* Report of the Committee. London: Burgess Science Press.

Carcary, M. (2009). The Research Audit Trial – Enhancing Trustworthiness in Qualitative Inquiry, *Electronic Journal of Business Research Methods*, 7 (1), 11–24.

Carlin, W. and Mayer, C. (2000). How Do Financial Systems Affect Economic Performance? In X. Vives (ed.) *Corporate Governance: Theoretical and Empirical Perspectives*, pp. 137–68. New York: Cambridge University Press.

CASE (2008). *The Economic Aspects of the Energy Sector in CIS Countries*, Centre for Social and Economic Research (CASE), Economic Papers, No. 327, Warsaw.

Caspionet.kz (2012). 'Productivity – 2020 Programme Underway in Kazakhstan',Caspionet.kz, available at: http://caspionet.kz/eng/general/Prod uctivity2020_programme_underway_in_Kazakhstan_1311220972.html, accessed 26 November 2012.

Cernat, L. (2002). Institutions and Economic Growth: Which Model of Capitalism for Central and Eastern Europe? *Journal for Institutional Innovation, Development and Transition,* 6, 18–34.

Chapman, G. (2011). Poverty in Central Asia: Kazakhstan versus Tajikistan, *Global Majority E-Journal*, 2 (1), 19–30.

Charman, K. (2007). Kazakhstan, A State-Led Liberalized Market Economy? In D. Lane and M. Myant (eds), *Varieties of Capitalism in Post-Communist Countries*, pp. 165–82. Basingstoke: Palgrave Macmillan.

Chattopadhyay, A., Batra, R. and Ozsomer, A. (2012). *The New Emerging Market Multinationals. Four Strategies for Disrupting Markets and Building Brands.* New York: McGraw-Hill.

Ciarreta, A. and Nasirov, S. (2012). Development Trends in the Azerbaijan Oil and Gas Sector: Achievements and Challenges, *Energy Policy*, 40, 282–92.

Cohen, A. (2003). Confronting Kazakhstan's Dutch Disease, *Central Asia-Caucasus Institute Analyst*, 26 March, available at: http://www.cacianalyst.o rg/?q=node/1007, accessed 25 March 2014.

Conrad, J. (2008). *Three Dimensions of the Banking Crisis in Kazakhstan.* Asian Development Bank. CWRD Discussion Paper #2, available at: http://www.adb.org/Documents/Produced-Under-TA/37318/37318-KAZ-DP TA.pdf, accessed 11 March 2014.

The Constitution of the Republic of Kazakhstan (1995), Constitutional Council of the Republic of Kazakhstan, available at: http://www.constcouncil.kz/eng /norpb/constrk/, accessed 23 March 2014.

Crowley, S. and Stanojevic, M. (2011). Varieties of Capitalism, Power Resources, and Historical Legacies: Explaining the Slovenian Exception, *Politics and Society*, 39 (2), 268–95.

Cummings, S. (2005). *Kazakhstan: Power and the Elite.* London: I.B. Tauris.

Cummings, S. and Nørgaard, O. (2004). Conceptualising State Capacity: Comparing Kazakhstan and Kyrgyzstan. *Political Studies,* 52, 685–708.

Cutler, R. (2012). Kazakhstan's 'Resource Nationalism': Its Sources and Motives, Central Asia Program, *Central Asia Economic Paper,* 2, 1–6.

Daly, J. (2008). Kazakhstan's Emerging Middle Class, Silk Road Paper, *Central Asia-Caucasus Institute*, Central Asia – Caucasus Institute and Silk Road Studies Program.

DAMU (2012). *Action Programme of Small Entrepreneurship Development Fund JSC to Develop Microcredit Organizations in the Republic of Kazakhstan for 2008–2012.* Almaty: DAMU Entrepreneurship Development Fund, available at: http://www.damu.kz, accessed 4 April 2013.

DAMU (2014). *History and Key Milestones*. Almaty: DAMU Entrepreneurship Development Fund, available at: http://www.damu.kz/239, accessed 15 May 2014.

Dave, B. (2007). *The EU and Kazakhstan. Balancing Economic Cooperation and Aiding Democratic Reforms in the Central Asian Region*, Centre for European Policy Studies (CEPS), Policy Brief No. 127, available at: www.ceeol.com, accessed 1 October 2012.

De Broeck, M., De Masi, P. and Koen, V. (1997). Inflation Dynamics in Kazakhstan, *Economics of Transition,* 5 (1), 195–213.

Decree of the President (2010). *Ukaz Presidenta Respubliki Kazahstan ob Utverjdenii Gosudarstvennoi Programmi Razvitia Obrazovania Respubliki Kazahstana na 2011–2020 Godi,* December 2010, No. 1118, Astana.

Deeg, R. (2005). *Complementarity and Institutional Change: How Useful a Concept?* Discussion Paper SP II, 2005-21, Wissenschaftszentrum Berlin.

Delegation of the European Union to Kazakhstan (2012). *Trade and Economic Relations*, available at: https://eeas.europa.eu/delegations/kazakhstan/eu_kazakhstan/eu_kazakhstan/trade_relation/index_en.htm, accessed 19 January 2014.

DeWalt, K. and DeWalt, B. (2011). *Participant Observation: A Guide for Fieldworkers.* 2nd edn., Walnut Creek, CA: AltaMira Press.

DeWalt, K., DeWalt, B. and Wayland, C. (1998). Participant Observation, in H. R. Bernard (ed.), *Handbook of Methods in Cultural Anthropology.* Walnut Creek, CA: AltaMira Press.

DiCicco-Bloom, B. and Crabtree, B. (2006). The Qualitative Research Interview, *Medical Education*, 40 (4), 314–21.

Dingwall, R., Murphy, E., Watson, P., Greatbatch, D. and Parker, S. (1998). Catching Goldfish: Quality in Qualitative Research, *Journal of Health Services Research Policy*, 3, 167–72.

Dragneva, R. (2004). Is 'Soft' Beautiful? Another Perspective on Law, Institutions, and Integration in the CIS. *Review of Central and East European Law*, 3, 279–324.

Dufrenot, G. and Sand-Zantman, A. (2004). Structural Reforms, Macroeconomic Policies and the Future of Kazakhstan Economy, *Observatoire Français des Conjonctures Économiques*, Document de Travail, 2004–11, 1–21.

Duvanova, D. (2007). *Interest Groups in Post-Communist Countries: A Comparative Analysis of Business and Employer Associations.* Doctoral dissertation, Graduate School of the Ohio State University, available at: https://etd.ohiolink.edu/!etd.send_file?accession=osu1183919779&disposition=inline, accessed 26 June 2013.

Dzharkinbayev, Z. (2011). Neftianie Dohody i Osnovnie Parametry Fiskalnoi Politiki v Respublike Kazahstan v 2001–2010 Godah, *Ekonomika i Statistika (Economy and Statistics),* 3, 51–57.

Dzhumambaev, S. (2001). Aktualnie Voprosy Issledovanij Socialno-Trudovih Otnoshenij v Kazahstane, *Vestnik KazGU*, Economic Sciences Series, No. 2–3, available at: http://lib.kaznu.kz/libr/vestnik/ECONOM%5CYEAR01%5CN2-3%5C12.HTM, accessed 30 June 2014.

Ebbinghaus, B. and Manow, P. (2001). Introduction: Studying Varieties of Welfare Capitalism. In B. Ebbinghaus and P. Manow (eds): *Comparing Welfare Capitalism: Social Policy and Political Economy in Europe, Japan and the USA,* pp. 1–24. London: Routledge.

EBRD (1998). *Financial Sector in Transition.* Transition Report 1998. London: EBRD.

EBRD (1999). *Ten Years of Transition.* Transition Report 1999. London: EBRD.

EBRD (2000). *Employment, Skills and Transition.* Transition Report 2000. London: EBRD.

EBRD (2001). *Energy in Transition.* Transition Report 2001. London: EBRD.

EBRD (2002). *Agriculture and Rural Transition.* Transition Report 2002. London: EBRD.

EBRD (2003). *Integration and Regional Cooperation.* Transition Report 2003. London: EBRD.

EBRD (2004). *Infrastructure.* Transition Report 2004. London: EBRD.

EBRD (2005). *Business in Transition.* Transition Report 2005. London: EBRD.

EBRD (2006). *Finance in Transition.* Transition Report 2006. London: EBRD.

EBRD (2007). *People in Transition.* Transition Report 2007. London: EBRD.

EBRD (2008). *Growth in Transition.* Transition Report 2008. London: EBRD.

EBRD (2009). *Transition in Crisis?* Transition Report 2009. London: EBRD.

EBRD (2010a). *Recovery and Reform.* Transition Report 2010. London: EBRD.

EBRD (2010b). *Strategy for Kazakhstan.* Document of the EBRD, Approved by the Board of Directors.

EBRD (2011). *Crisis and Transition. The People's Perspective.* Transition Report 2011. London: EBRD.

EBRD (2012). *Integration across Borders.* Transition Report 2012. London: EBRD.

The Economist (2008a). *Kazakhstan Risk: Labour Market Risk,* Economist Intelligence Unit, available at: http://www.eiu.com/index.asp?layout=RKArticleVW3&article_id=1023919487&page_title=Article&rf=0, accessed 12 March 2012.

The Economist (2008b). *Kazakhstan's 'New Silk Road'. Eyes on the Road. Becoming Central Asia's Crossroads*, available at: http://www.economist.co m/node/12604400, accessed 9 February 2014.

The Economist (2012a). State Capitalism's Global Reach. New Masters of the Universe. How State Enterprise is Spreading, Special Report: State Capitalism, available: http://www.economist.com/node/21542925, accessed 29 November 2013.

The Economist (2012b). Pros and Cons. Mixed Bag. SOEs are Good at Infrastructure Projects, not So Good at Innovation, Special Report: State Capitalism, available at: http://www.economist.com/node/21542929/print, accessed 29 November 2013.

The Economist (2012c). The Visible Hand, Special Report: State Capitalism, available at: http://www.economist.com/node/21542931/print, accessed 29 November 2013.

The Economist (2012d). A Choice of Models. Theme and Variations. State Capitalism is not All the Same, Special Report: State Capitalism, available at: http://www.economist.com/node/21542924/print, accessed 29 November 2013.

Economy Watch (2012a). *Investment (per cent of GDP) Statistics for Kazakhstan, Year 2010 – In Detail*, available at: http://www.economywatch. com/economic-statistics/Kazakhstan/Investment_Percentage_of_GDP/, accessed 17 March 2012.

Economy Watch (2012b). *Kazakhstan Trade Statistics, Export Statistics, Export Partners and Products, Import Statistics, Import Partners and Products, Year 2009* available at: http://www.economywatch.com/economic-statistics/ Kazakhstan/Trade_Statistics/, accessed 12 October 2012.

Edu.gov.kz (2010), *Socialnoe Partnerstvo*, Ministry of Education and Science of the Republic of Kazakhstan, available at: http://www.edu.gov.kz/ru/activity/ srednee_professionalnoe/socialnoe_patrnerstvo/, accessed 28 June 2011.

Egert, B. and Leonard, C. (2008). Dutch Disease Scare in Kazakhstan: Is It Real? *Open Economies Review*, 19 (2), 147–65.

Eicher, S. (2004a). *Is Kazakhstan a Market Economy Yet? Getting warmer...* William Davidson Institute Working Paper, No. 637, William Davidson Institute, University of Michigan Business School.

Eicher, S. (2004b). *What Causes Bank Asset Substitution in Kazakhstan? Explaining Dollarization in a Transition Economy*, William Davidson Institute Working Paper, No. 688, William Davidson Institute, University of Michigan Business School.

EITI (2014a). *Kazakhstan*, Extractive Industries Transparency Initiative (EITI), available at: http://eiti.org/Kazakhstan, accessed 30 April 2014.

EITI (2014b). *What is the EITI?* Extractive Industries Transparency Initiative (EITI), available at: http://eiti.org/eiti, accessed 30 April 2014.

Emerging Markets Monitor (2007). *Analysis and Market Intelligence on Fixed Income, Forex and Equities in Asia, EMEA and Latin America.* Incorporating Global Fund News, Business Monitor International Ltd, 12 (42).

Ernst and Young (2010). *Kazakhstan Investment Attractiveness. Ernst and Young's Investor Opinion Survey.* Almaty: Ernst and Young.

Esanov, A. and Kuralbayeva, K. (2010). *Ricardian Curse of the Resource Boom: The Case of Kazakhstan, 2000–2008*, OxCarre Research Paper, 43, Oxford Centre for the Analysis of Resource Rich Economies, University of Oxford, available at: www.oxcarre.ox.ac.uk, accessed 25 January 2013.

ETF (2002). *Vocational Education and Training in Kazakhstan.* European Training Foundation and National Observatory of Kazakhstan.

ETF (2003). *Review of Vocational Education and Training and Employment in Kazakhstan.* Working Paper. European Training Foundation, Torino.

ETF (2007). *Skills Development and Poverty Reduction in Kazakhstan.* European Training Foundation. ETF Working Document, Torino.

ETF (2009). *Kazakhstan. ETF Country Plan 2009*. Working Paper, European Training Foundation, Torino.

European Commission (2003). *Industrial Relations as a Key to Strengthening Innovation in Europe.* Innovation Papers No. 36, a Publication by the Innovation Directorate as Part of the Sixth Research Framework Programme, Directorate-General for Enterprise. Leuven: Katholieke Universiteit Leuven, Belgium.

European Community (2007). *Regional Strategy Paper for Assistance to Central Asia for the period 2007–2013.* European Commission's Assistance Strategy Paper, ENPI, Brussels.

Expert Kazakhstan (2012). V Skorom Vremeni Bazarov I Rinkov v Almati ne Ostanetsa, Expert Kazakhstan, Almaty, Kazakhstan, #15 (356), available at: http://expert.ru/kazakhstan/2012/15/smert-baraholki/?subscribe, accessed 12 April 2014.

Falkingham, J. (2005). The End of the Rollercoaster? Growth, Inequality and Poverty in Central Asia and the Caucasus, *Social Policy and Administration*, 39 (4), 340–60.

Fast, S. (2004). A Country Profile. In M. Terterov (ed.), *Doing Business with Kazakhstan*, pp. 3–10. London/Sterling, VA: Kogan Page.

Federal Ministry of Economics and Technology (2012). *German Mittelstand: Engine of the German Economy*, Business. Growth. Prosperity, available at: http://www.bmwi.de/English/Redaktion/Pdf/factbook-german-mittelstand,property=pdf,bereich=bmwi,sprache=en,rwb=true.pdf, accessed 24 March 2014.

Federation of Trade Unions of the Republic of Kazakhstan (2012). *About the Federation.* available at: http://www.fprk.kz/?m=article&lng=rus&cid=9&id=1&act=see, accessed 13 March 2012.

Fergus, M. (2003). A Strategy for Reducing Poverty in Kazakhstan. *Asian Affairs*, 34 (2), 109–22.

Fingramota.kz (2011). Analiz Tendencij Centralnoaziatskogo Strahovogo Rinka, Fingramota.kz, available at: http://fingramota.kz/publication/show-28468, accessed 12 March 2012.

Forbes.kz (2011). Prazdnik Obshey Bedy, Forbes.kz, No. 1, September, available at: http://forbes.kz/finances/integration/prazdnik_obschey_bedyi, accessed 15 March 2014.

Foreign Investors' Council (2012). *About Us*, available at: www.fic.kz, accessed 18 March 2012.

Foreign Investors' Council (2014). *Working Groups*, available at: www.fic.kz/eng/rabochie_ gruppy/, accessed 27 July 2014.

Forsythe, J. (1977). Obtaining Cooperation in a Survey of Business Executives, *Journal of Marketing Research,* 14 (3), 370–73.

Foster, H. (2010). *Kazakh Measures Spur Banking Recovery*. Central Asia Newswire, July 2010, available at: http://centralasianewswire.com/Kazakh-measures-spur-banking-recovery/viewstory.aspx?id=1006, accessed 12 January 2014.

Fry, M., Goodhart, C. and Almeida, A. (1996). *Central Banking in Developing Countries. Objectives, Activities, Independence.* Bank of England/Routledge.

FXTrade.kz (2011). Ekonomicheskij Krizis v Kazahstane. Finansy v Kazahstane, FXTrade.kz, 3 May, available at: http://www.fxtrade.kz/v-kazaxstane/ekonomicheskij-krizis-v-kazaxstane/, accessed 2 April 2014.

Gabdullin, K., Bek, Y. and Aldabek, N. (2012). Oil Prices Impact on Energy Policy of Kazakhstan, *World Academy of Science, Engineering and Technology*, 66, 481–84.

Gaggiotti, H., Low Kim Cheng, P. and Yunak, O. (2008). City Brand Management (CBM): The Case of Kazakhstan. *Place Branding and Public Diplomacy*, 4 (2), 115–23.

Gassmann, F. (2011). *Protecting Vulnerable Families in Central Asia: Poverty, Vulnerability and the Impact of the Economic Crisis*, Innocenti Working Paper, No. 2011-05, UNICEF Regional Office for CEE/CIS, Geneva, and UNICEF Innocenti Research Centre, Florence.

Gazeta.kz (2004). *Osnovnoi Akcent Fiskalnoi Politiki Kazahstana Doljen Bit Sdelan na Process Vivedenia Lishnih Dollarov iz Ekonomiki Strany – Prezident RK*, Gazeta.kz, available at: http://news.gazeta.kz/art.asp?aid=193 346, accessed 17 April 2014.

George, A. and Bennett, A. (2005). *Case Studies and Theory Development in the Social Sciences*. Cambridge, MA: MIT Press.

Ghosh, A. and Ramakrishnan, U. (2006). Do Current Account Deficits Matter? *Finance and Development*, A Quarterly Magazine of IMF, 43 (4), available at: http://www.imf.org/external/pubs/ft/fandd/2006/12/basics.htm, accessed 15 March 2014.

Ginsburg, V. and Troschke, M. (2005). Positioned between China and Russia: The Central Asian Countries Find their own Approach to Privatization. *Central Asia and the Caucasus*, 5 (35), 140–53.

Gleason, G. (2003). *Markets and Politics in Central Asia: Structural Reform and Political Change.* London: Routledge.

Golafshani, N. (2003). Understanding Reliability and Validity in Qualitative Research, *The Qualitative Report*, 8 (4), 597–607.

Golodniuk, I. (2005). *Financial Systems and Financial Reforms in CIS Countries*. Center for Social and Economic Research; Studies and Analyses, Warsaw.

Government of the Republic of Kazakhstan (2007). *Srednesrochnaya Fiskalnaya Politika Pravitelstva Respubliki Kazahstan na 2008–2010 Gody*, available at: http://www.minplan.gov.kz/archive_site/files/594.pdf, accessed 22 January 2013.

Government of the Republic of Kazakhstan (2012a). *Strategic Development Programmes*, available at: http://ru.government.kz/documents/govprog, accessed 10 April 2014.

Government of the Republic of Kazakhstan (2012b). *Postavlenie Pravitelstva Respubliki Kazahstan ot 30 Ijuna 2012 Goda № 898*, available at: http://adilet.zan.kz/rus/docs/P1200000898, accessed 12 April 2014.

Government of the Republic of Kazakhstan (2013). *Foreign Direct Investments in Kazakhstan,* Invest in Kazakhstan, available at: http://invest.gov.kz/?optio n=content&section=4&itemid=75, accessed 5 February 2013.

GRATA (2010). *Kazakh Law Amendments Related to Local Content,* GRATA Law Firm, available at: http://www.bksoc.org.uk/articles/Article9.pdf, accessed 16 January 2014.

Griffith, D., Zeybek, A. and O'Brien, M. (2001). Knowledge Transfer as a Means for Relationship Development: A Kazakhstan-Foreign International Joint Venture Illustration, *Journal of International Marketing*, 9 (2), 447–62.

Grodeland, A., Koshechkina, T. and Miller, W. (1998). Foolish to Give and Yet More Foolish Not to Take: In-Depth Interviews with Post-Communist Citizens on Their Everyday Use of Bribes and Contacts, *Europe–Asia Studies*, 50 (4), 651–77.

Guillén, M. and Garcia-Canal, E. (2013). *Emerging Markets Rule. Growth Strategies of the New Global Giants*. New York: McGraw-Hill.

Guion, L., Diehl, D. and McDonald, D. (2002). *Triangulation: Establishing the Validity of Qualitative Studies,* IFAS Extension, Document No. FCS6014, University of Florida.

Gumppenberg, M.-C. Von (2007). *Kazakhstan Challenges to the Booming Petro-Economy*, FAST Country Risk Profile Kazakhstan, Working Paper, No. 2, Swiss Peace Foundation.

Halal Journal (2011). Kazakhstan: Islamic Banking and Finance in Emerging Markets – Seizing Opportunities, Overcoming Challenges. Keynote Address by His Royal Highness Raja Nazrin Shah (Crown Prince of Perak, Malaysia) at the 7th World Islamic Economic Forum, Kazakhstan, available at: http://www.halaljournal.com/article/5865/kazakhstan:-islamic-banking-and-finance-in-emerging-markets-%C3%A2ae%E2%80%9C-seizing-opportunities,-overcoming-challenges, accessed 9 March 2012.

Hall, P. A. and Soskice, D. (2001). An Introduction to the Varieties of Capitalism. In A. Hall and D. Soskice (eds), *Varieties of Capitalism: The Institutional Foundations of Comparative Advantage*, pp. 1–68. Oxford: Oxford University Press.

Hall, P. and Gingerich, D. (2009). Varieties of Capitalism and Institutional Complementarities in the Political Economy: An Empirical Analysis, *British Journal of Political Science*, (39), 449–82.

Hall, T. and Elliott, J. (1999). Poland and Russia One Decade after Shock Therapy, *Journal of Economic Issues*, 33 (2), 305–14.

Hare, P. and Naumov, A. (2008). *A Study of Changing Income Distribution in Kazakhstan Using a New Social Accounting Matrix and Household Survey Data*, Centre for Economic Reform and Transformation (CERT), paper prepared for the 30th General Conference of The International Association for Research in Income and Wealth, 24–30 August 2008, Discussion Paper 2008/02, Portoroz, Slovenia.

Haritonova, N. (2008). Kashagan: Perviy Boy – On Trudnij Samij, *Ia-Centr.ru*, 17 January 2008, available at: www.ia-centr.ru/expert/240/, accessed 7 March 2014.

Hartwell, C. (2013). A Eurasian (or a Soviet) Union? Consequences of Further Economic Integration in the Commonwealth of Independent States, *Business Horizons*, 56, 411–420.

Hawley, J. (2006). *Public Private Partnerships in Vocational Education and Training: InternationalExamples and Models*. World Bank, available at: http://siteresources.worldbank.org/EXTECAREGTOPEDUCATION/Resources/444607192636551820/Public_Private_Partnerships_in_Vocational_Education_and_Training.pdf, accessed 28 March 2014.

He, J. and van de Vijver, F. (2012). Bias and Equivalence in Cross-Cultural Research, *Online Readings in Psychology and Culture*, International Association for Cross-Cultural Psychology, Unit 2, Theoretical and Methodological Issues, Subunit 2, Methodological Issues in Psychology and Culture, Article 8, The Berkeley Electronic Press, available at: http://scholarworks.gvsu.edu/cgi/viewcontent.cgi?article=1111&context=orpc, accessed 15 April 2014.

Heinrich, A. and Pleines, H. (2012). Weder Fluch noch Segen – Die Politischen Herausforderungen des Erdölbooms in Kasachstan, *Zentralasien-Analysen*, 57, 2–8.

Hendricks, V., Blanken, P. and Adriaans, N. (1992). *Snowball Sampling: A Pilot Study on Cocaine Use.* Rotterdam: IVO.

Heritage Foundation (2011). *Kazakhstan. Quick Facts.* The Index of Economic Freedom, available at: http://www.heritage.org/index/Country/Kazakhstan, accessed 29 June 2011.

Heritage Foundation (2012). *Kazakhstan. Quick Facts.* The Index of Economic Freedom, available at: http://www.heritage.org/index/Country/Kazakhstan, accessed 13 March 2012.

Herrigel, G. and Zeitlin, J. (2010). Alternatives to Varieties of Capitalism, 'Varieties of Capitalism' Roundtable, *Business History Review*, 84 (4), 667–74.

Hosman, L. (2009). Dynamic Bargaining and the Prospects for Learning in the Petroleum Industry: The Case of Kazakhstan, *Perspectives on Global Development and Technology*, 8, 1–25.

Howitt, R. and Stevens, S. (2005). Cross-Cultural Research: Ethics, Methods, and Relationships. In I. Hay (ed.), *Qualitative Research Methods in Human Geography,* 2nd ed., pp. 30–50. Melbourne: Oxford University Press.

Huiskamp, R. (1995). Regulating the Employment Relationship: an Analytical Framework. In R. Huiskamp, J. Ruysseveldt and J. Hoof (eds), *Comparative Industrial and Employment Relations*, pp. 16–36. London: Sage.

Humphreys, M., Sachs, J. and Stiglitz, J. (eds) (2007). *Escaping the Resource Curse*, New York: Columbia University Press.

IBF International Consulting (2010). *Project Recommendations.* Social Partnership in the System TiPO of Kazakhstan. Europe Aid/215181/C/SER KZ. IBF International Consulting.

IFK (2012). *Information about Investment Fund of Kazakhstan*, Investment Fund of Kazakhstan, available at: www.ifk.kz, accessed 10 March 2012.

Imam, P. and Kpodar, K. (2010). *Islamic Banking: How Has it Diffused?* IMF Working Paper, IMF African Department, Washington, DC.

Imanberdiev B., Kasimov S. and Turginbaeva A. (2011). The Influence of Technological Advantages on the Economic Development of Kazakhstan, *International Journal of Applied and Fundamental Research*, 2, 3–9.

Index Mundi (2010). *Kazakhstan – GDP Composition by Sector*, available at: www.indexmundi.com/kazakhstan/gdp_composition_by_sector.html, accessed 11 August 2011.

Index Mundi (2012a). *Kazakhstan – Market Capitalisation of Listed Companies,* available at: www.indexmundi.com/facts/kazakhstan/market-capitalization-of-listed-companies, accessed 27 February 2012.

Index Mundi (2012b). *Kazakhstan – GDP Composition by Sector*, available at: http://www.indexmundi.com/kazakhstan/gdp_composition_by_sector.html, accessed 15 February 2012.

Index Mundi (2012c). *Kazakhstan – Unemployment rate,* available at: http://www.indexmundi.com/g/g.aspx?c=kz&v=74, accessed 27 October 2012.

Index Mundi (2012d). *Kazakhstan – Inflation Rate,* available at: http://www.indexmundi.com/g/g.aspx?c=kz&v=71, accessed 28 October 2012.

Insur.kz (2012). Strahovaya Kompania 'Kommesk-Omir' Podvela Itogi po Strahovim Viplatam za 2011 God, Insur.kz, 29 February, available at: http://www.insur.kz/index.php?option=com_content&view= article&id=2028:-l-r-2011-&catid=3:news-sk&Itemid=59, accessed 9 April 2014.

Interfax (2007). Kazakh Foreign Debt Soars 24.3 per cent in H1, September 24–October 8, 2007, 21 (117), *Interfax-Kazakhstan*, available at: www.interfax.kz/index.php?lang=eng&int_id=12&function=view&news_id=1353, accessed 4 September 2012.

International Crisis Group (2010). *Central Asia: Migrants and Economic Crisis.* International Crisis Group, Working To Prevent Conflict Worldwide, Asia Report #183, Brussels, January.

International Finance Corporation (2009). *Kazakhstan: Microfinance and Financial Sector Diagnostic Study*. Final Report. MIFA. Promoting Microfinance in Asia. International Finance Corporation. Washington, DC/ Frankfurt-am-Main: WorldBankGroup/KFW Bankengruppe, available at: http://www.frankfurt-school.de/dms/ias/publications_2009/mifa_kazakhstan/ Kazakhstan%3A%20Microfinance%20and%20Financial%20Sector%20Dia gnostic%20Study.pdf, accessed 15 April 2014.

International Labour Organization (2010). *Social Security Expenditure*. available at: http://www.socialsecurityextension.org/gimi/gess/RessFileDow nload.do?ressourceId=15170, accessed 18 July 2014.

International Monetary Fund (2006). *Financial Soundness Indicators*, Compilation Guide. Washington, DC: IMF.

International Monetary Fund (2011a). *Slowing Growth, Rising Risks*, World Economic Outlook, World Economic and Financial Surveys. Washington, DC: IMF, available at: http://www.imf.org/external/pubs/ft/weo/2011/02/pdf /text.pdf, accessed 17 December 2013.

International Monetary Fund (2011b). *Republic of Kazakhstan: 2011 Article IV Consultation – Staff Report; Supplement; and Public Information Notice.* IMF Country Report No. 11/150, available at: http://www.imf.org/external/p ubs/ft/scr/2011/cr11150.pdf, accessed 17 December 2013.

International Test Commission (2010). *International Test Commission Guidelines for Translating and Adapting Tests*, available at: http://www.inte stcom.org/upload/sitefiles/40.pdf, accessed 2 April 2014.

Invest-Market.kz (2011). Nationalnij Innovacionnij Fond Zhdet Preobrazovanie, Invest-Market.kz, 1 June, available at: http://invest-market.kz/article.php?id =2844&type=news, accessed 1 April 2014.

Invest-Market.kz (2012). Pension Funds of Kazakhstan, Invest-Market.kz, 1 December, http://invest-market.kz/npf/, accessed 20 February 2014.

Iradian, G. (2009). *What Explains the Rapid Growth in Transition Economies?* International Monetary Fund, IMF Staff Papers, 56 (4).

Islamic Development Bank (2011). *Enhancing Competitiveness and Diversification of the Kazakhstani Economy,* Country Economic Work, Country Programmes Department, Muharram 1432, available at: http://www.isdb.org/irj/go/km/docs/documents/IDBDevelopments/Internet/English/IDB/CM/Publications/Parnership_Strategies/Kazakhstan_CEW.pdf, accessed 11 April 2014.

Isaacs, R. (2011). *Party System Formation in Kazakhstan: Between Formal and Informal Politics.* London: Routledge.

Isaacs, R. (2013). Nur Otan, Informal Networks and the Countering of Elite Instability in Kazakhstan: Bringing the 'Formal' Back In, *Europe-Asia Studies*, 65 (6), 1055–1079.

ISTOK-SOUYZ (2009). *Express Diagnostics of Potential for ICT R&D Collaboration with the European Union: Kazakhstan*, Information Societies Technologies to Open Knowledge for Eastern Europe and Central Asia (ISTOK-SOUYZ), available at: http://www.eeca-ict.eu/uploads/dmdocuments/ED_Kazakhstan.pdf, accessed 30 April 2014.

ISSA (2010). *Impact of the Crisis on Social Security in the Eurasia Region.* International Social Security Association (ISSA), June, available at: http://www.issa.int/ger/News-Events/News2/Impact-of-the-crisis-on-social-security-in-the-Eurasia-region, accessed 22 February 2012.

Jackson, G. and Deeg, R. (2006). *How Many Varieties of Capitalism? Comparing the Comparative Institutional Analyses of Capitalist Diversity,* Max Planck Institute for the Study of Societies, Discussion Paper 06/2, Cologne.

Jackson, G. and Miyajima, H. (2007). *Varieties of Capitalism, Varieties of Markets: Mergers and Acquisitions in Japan, Germany, France, the UK and USA*, The Research Institute of Economy, Trade and Industry (RIETI), RIETI Discussion Paper Series 07-E-054, available at: http://www.rieti.go.jp/jp/ publications/dp/07e054.pdf, accessed 21 March 2014.

James, E. (1998). The Political Economy of Social Security Reform: A Cross-Country Review. The World Bank, Policy Research Department, *Annals of Public and Cooperative Economics*, 69 (4).

Jandosov, O. (1998). *Prospects and Challenges of Financial Systems in Transition Economies. Development, Prospects and Challenges of Financial System in Kazakhstan,* IMF, Session I: Prospects and Challenges of Financial Systems in Transition Economies, available at: www.imf.org/external/np/eu2/kyrgyz/pdf/jandosov.pdf, accessed 12 April 2014.

Jeffries, I. (2003). *The Caucasus and Central Asian Republics at the Turn of the Twenty-First Century: A Guide to the Economies in Transition.* London: Routledge.

Jermakowicz, W., Kozarzewski, P. and Panków, J. (1996). *Privatization in the Republic of Kazakhstan*, Center for Social and Economic Research (CASE), Warsaw.

Jorgensen, D. (1989). *Participant Observation: A Methodology for Human Studies.* Thousand Oaks, CA: Sage.

Kairlenov, M. (2009). *The Model of Transition of a Financial Crisis to an Economic Crisis.* Working Paper, Zertteu DC Group, Almaty.

Kalyuzhnova, Y. (1998). *The Kazakhstani Economy: Independence and Transition.* London: Macmillan.

Kalyuzhnova, Y. and Trimidas, G. (1998). Policy Arena. Dilemmas of Financial Development in Kazakhstan. *Journal of International Development*, 10, 681–93.

Kalyuzhnova, Y. (2006). Overcoming the Curse of Hydrocarbon: Goals and Governance in the Oil Funds of Kazakhstan and Azerbaijan, *Comparative Economic Studies,* 48, 583–613.

Kalyuzhnova, Y. and Kambhampati, U. (2007). Education or Employment – Choices Facing Young People in Kazakhstan, *Journal of International Development*, 19, 607–26.

Kalyuzhnova, Y. and Nygaard, C. (2008). State Governance Evolution in Resource-Rich Transition Economies: An Application to Russia and Kazakhstan, *Energy Policy*, 36, 1829–42.

Kalyuzhnova, Y. and Nygaard, C. (2009). Resource Nationalism and Credit Growth in FSU Countries, *Energy Policy*, 37, 4700–10.

Kalyuzhnova, Y. (2011). The National Fund of the Republic of Kazakhstan (NFRK): From Accumulation to Stress-Test to Global Future, *Energy Policy*, 39, 6650–57.

KASE (2012). *About Membership*, available at: www.kase.kz/ru/membership, accessed 13 January 2014.

Kaukenow, A. (2009). Chinas Wachsender Wirtschaftlicher Einfluss in Kasachstan, *Zentralasien-Analysen*, 22, 2–5.

Kazakhstan Democracy (2012). Kazakhstan President, Kazakhstan Democracy, available at: http://kazakhstan-democracy.com/kazakhstan_president/, accessed 26 November 2012.

KAZINFORM (2012). Kazakh Government Elaborates Monotown Development Program, KAZINFORM, 27 February, available at: http://www.inform.kz/en g/article/2444240m, accessed 17 March 2014.

Kazkommerts Securities (1998). Kazakhstan Debt Research. External Debt, *Kazkommerts Securities*, October 1998, available at: http://s3.amazonaws.com/zanran_storage/www.emgmkts.com/ContentPages/116202759.pdf, accessed 5 April 2014.

KazMunayGas (2011). *Kashagan*, National Company KazMunayGas, available at: www.kmg.kz/manufacturing/upstream/kashagan/, accessed 19 February 2014.

Kazahstanskaya Pravda (2007). U Biznessa – Rol Vedushaya. Kazahstanskaya Pravda, 30 March, available at: http://kazpravda.softdeco.net/c/1175198745, accessed 25 January 2014.

Kazahstanskaya Pravda (2012). Ot 'Eksperta-100' k 'Ekspertu-200', Kazahstanskaya Pravda, 8 November, available at: http://www.kazpravda.kz/c/1352318858, accessed 14 November 2012.

King, L. (2007). Central European Capitalism in Comparative Perspective. In B. Hancke, M. Rhodes, and M. Thatcher (eds), *Beyond Varieties of Capitalism: Conflict, Contradictions, and Complementarities in the European Economy*, pp. 307–327. Oxford: Oxford University Press.

Klaveren, M.V., Tijdens, K., Hughie-Williams, M. and Ramos Martin, N. (2010). *An Overview of Women's Work and Employment in Kazakhstan*, Decisions for Life MDG3 Project, Country Report No. 10, University of Amsterdam, Amsterdam Institute for Advanced Labour Studies (AIAS).

Knell, M. and Srholec, M. (2007). Diverging Pathways in Central and Eastern Europe. In D. Lane and M. Myant (eds), *Varieties of Capitalism in Post-Communist Economies*, Palgrave Macmillan, Basingstoke, pp. 40–64.

Knox, C. (2008). Kazakhstan: Modernizing Government in the Context of Political Inertia. *International Review of Administrative Sciences,* 74 (3), 477–496.

Knox Thames, H. (2007). The OSCE Chairman-in-Office and the Republic of Kazakhstan. *Helsinki Monitor: Security and Human Rights*, No. 2.

Koch, L. and Chaudhary, M. (2002). Economic Transformation of Kazakhstan: Evidence from Liberalization Reforms, *Journal of Academic Studies*, 13, 135–48.

Koshanov, A. (1995). Problems of Market Transformation of the Kazakh Economy, *Problems of Economic Transition*, 37 (10), 5–23.

Kozhumov, K. (2011). Resursnoe Prokliatie. Daily Republican Social-Political Newspaper *Liter*, 21 May 2011, available at: www.liter.kz/index.php?option=com_content&task=view&id=6082&Itemid=31, accessed 3 June 2011.

Kryvoi, Y. (2006). *National Labour Law Profile: Kazakhstan,* International Labour Organization (ILO), November 2006, available at: http://www.ilo.org/public/english/dialogue/ifpdial/info/national/kazakh.htm, accessed 15 March 2012.

Kuralbayeva, K., Kutan, A. and Wyzan, M. (2001). *Is Kazakhstan Vulnerable to Dutch Disease?* ZEI Centre for European Integration Studies, University of Bonn, Working Paper, No. B 29, Bonn.

Kurmanov, A. (2010). The Current State of the Trade Union Movement in Kazakhstan, *International Viewpoint, IV Online magazine,* IV424 – May 2010, available at: http://internationalviewpoint.org/spip.php?article1862, accessed 13 March 2012.

Kursiv (2012). Effekt ot Nizkih Stavok Umenshaetsa iz-za Slozhnogo Nalogovogo Administrirovania, Kursiv, June 2012, available at: http://www.kursiv.kz/banki-i-finansy/banki-i-finansy-weekly/1195227017-y effekt-ot-nizkix-stavok-umenshaetsya-iz-za-slozhnogo-nalogovogo-adminis trirovaniya.html, accessed 2 January 2013.

Kutan, A. and Wyzan, M. (2005). Explaining the Real Exchange Rate in Kazakhstan, 1996–2003: Is Kazakhstan Vulnerable to the Dutch Disease? *Economic Systems*, 29 (2), 242–55.

Kuzmits, B. (2008). Losing My Illusions. Methodological Dreams and Reality in Local Governance Research in the Amu Darya Borderlands. In C. Wall and P. Mollinga (eds), *Fieldwork in Difficult Environments. Methodology as Boundary Work in Development Research,* pp. 19–40. Berlin: LIT Verlag.

Kvale, S. (2007). *Doing Interviews.* London: Sage.

Labour Code of the Republic of Kazakhstan (2007). Code of the Republic of Kazakhstan, 15 May 2007 No. 251, *Kazahstanskaya Pravda* No. 76, 25321, 22 May 2007.

Lambert, S. and Loiselle, C. (2008). Combining Individual Interviews and Focus Groups to Enhance Data Richness, *Journal of Advanced Nursing*, 62 (2), 228–37.

Lane, D. (2007). Post-State Socialism: A Diversity of Capitalisms? In D. Lane, and M. Myant (eds), *Varieties of Capitalism in Post-Communist Countries*, pp. 13–39. Basingstoke: Palgrave Macmillan.

Laruelle, M. (2008). Kazakhstan Challenged by the World Economic Crisis, *Central Asia-Caucasus Institute Analyst*, 12 November, available at: http://www.cacianalyst.org/?q=node/4979, accessed 11 February 2014.

Laurens, P. (2004). For Many Investors Kazakhstan's Credit Upgrades are a Mixed Blessing, *Central Asia-Caucasus Institute Analyst*, 25 August, available at: www.cacianalyst.org/?q=node/2347, accessed 11 March 2014.

Law on Collective Labour Disputes and Strikes (1996). Law of the Republic of Kazakhstan of 8 July 1996, Zakonodatelstvo Kazahstana Online, available at:http://www.pavlodar.com/zakon/?dok=00030&all=all, accessed 16 January 2013.

Law on Currency Regulation (1993). Law of the Republic of Kazakhstan of 14 April 1993, Online Zakon, available at: http://online.zakon.kz/Document/?doc_id=1051027, accessed 3 November 2012.

Law on Investments (2003). Law 373-11 of the Republic of Kazakhstan on Investments of 8 January 2003, (with amendments and additions as of 24 December 2012), available at: http://online.zakon.kz/Document/?doc_id=1035552, accessed 7 June 2013.

Law on Subsoil and Subsoil Use (2010). Law of the Republic of Kazakhstan of 24 June 2010 (with amendments as of 26 December 2012), Online Zakon, available at: http://online.zakon.kz/Document/?doc_ id=30770874, accessed 16 January 2013.

Law on Trade Unions (1993). Law of the Republic of Kazakhstan of 9 April 1993, Online Zakon, http://online.zakon.kz/Document/?doc_id=1001889, accessed 16 January 2013.

Law of the Republic of Kazakhstan on the National Bank of the Republic of Kazakhstan (1995). Law of the Republic of Kazakhstan of 30 March 1995 (with amendments as of 1 February 2012), Online Zakon, available at: http://online.zakon.kz/Document/?doc_id=1003548, accessed 16 January 2013.

Ledeneva, A. (2006). *How Russia Really Works: The Informal Practices That Shaped Post-Soviet Politics and Business.* Ithaca, NY: Cornell University Press.

Ledeneva, A. (2008). Telephone Justice in Russia, *Post-Soviet Affairs*, 24 (4), 324–50.

Lee, J.-W., Brahmasrene, T. and Tai, S. (2008). Recent Evidence of Small Business Development in CIS Transition Economies. *International Journal of Entrepreneurship*, 12, 71–85.

Leschenko, N. and Troschke, M. (2006). *Fiscal Decentralization in Centralized States: The Case of Central Asia.* Osteuropa-Institut Working Paper, No. 261, Munich.

Levine, R. (2000). *Bank-Based or Market-Based Financial Systems: Which is Better?* Working Paper, Finance Department, Carlson School of Management. Minneapolis: University of Minnesota.

Libman, A. (2008). *Government–Business Relations in Post-Soviet Space: The Case of Central Asia,* Munich Personal RePEc Archive Paper No. 11874, available at: http://mpra.ub.uni-muenchen.de/11874/, accessed 11 February 2014.

Libman, A. and Ushkalova, D. (2009). *Post-Soviet Countries in Global and Regional Institutional Competition: The Case of Kazakhstan.* Munich Personal RePEc Archive Paper No. 12595, available at: http://mpra.ub.uni-muenchen.de/12595/1/MPRA_paper_12595.pdf, accessed 5 January 2014.

Lim, J. (2005). Pension Reform in Russian and Kazakhstan, *Wharton Research Scholars Journal*, 4 (1), 2–24, available at: http://repository.upenn.edu/wharton_research_scholars/27/, accessed 17 January 2014.

Lipton, D. and Sachs, J. (1990). Creating a Market Economy in Eastern Europe: The Case of Poland, *Brookings Papers on Economic Activity*, 21 (1), 75–147.

Lücke, M. (2010). *Stabilization and Savings Funds to Manage Natural Resource Revenues: Kazakhstan and Azerbaijan vs. Norway*, Kiel Working Paper, No. 1652, Kiel Institute for the World Economy, Kiel.

Luly, T. (2012). The Varieties of Capitalism Dichotomy (and Beyond) in Post-Communist States, *Vestnik: The Journal of Russian and Asian Studies*, June 2012 Issue, available at: http://www.sras.org/the_varieties_of_capitalism_dichotomy_and_beyond_in_post-communist_states, accessed 21 March 2014.

Luong, P. and Weinthal, E. (2001). Prelude to the Resource Curse: Explaining Oil and Gas Development Strategies in the Soviet Successor States and Beyond, *Comparative Political Studies*, 34 (4), 367–99.

Luong, P. and Weinthal, E. (2010). *Oil is not a Curse: Ownership Structure and Institutions in Soviet Successor States.* Cambridge: Cambridge University Press.

Mack, N., Woodsong, C., MacQueen, K., Guest, G. and Namey, E. (2005). *Qualitative Research Methods: A Data Collector's Field Guide.* Research Triangle Park, NC: Family Health International and USAID.

McKee, M., Healy, J. and Falkingham, J. (2002). *Health Care in Central Asia*, European Observatory on Health Care Systems Series. Buckingham: Open University Press.

Maggs, P. (2011). Islamic Banking in Kazakhstan Law. *Review of Central and Eastern European Law*, 36, 369–96.

Marchenko, G. (2000). Ekonomicheskoe Razvitie Kazahstana i Politika Nacionalnogo Banka na Sovremennom Etape, *The KAZAKHSTAN International Business Magazine*, No. 2, available at: http://www.investkz.com/journals/25/416.html, accessed 4 July 2014.

Marchenko, G. (2003). V Nakopitelnuju Sistemu Nado Otchisliat Minimum 8 per cent Zarplati. Interview with Grigory Marchenko, *Business Magazine 'Finans'*, No. 41, 22–28 December, available at: http://www.finansmag.ru/4680, accessed 30 March 2014.

Martin, R. (2002). Politicized Managerial Capitalism: Enterprise Structures in Post-Socialist Central and Eastern Europe, *Journal of Management Studies*, 39 (6), 823–39.

Mashuri, D. (2010). Kazakhstan Labour Market: Current Trends in Executive Recruitment. *American Chamber of Commerce*, No. 38, 34–35, Almaty.

Matsumoto, D. and van de Vijver, F. (2011). *Cross-Cultural Research Methods in Psychology*. Cambridge: Cambridge University Press.

Mendelski, M. (2008). *The Varieties of Capitalism Approach Goes East: Institutional Complementarities and Law Enforcement during Post-Communist Transition.* Draft version, Göttingen: Private University of Applied Sciences.

Merrill, S. and Whiteley, D. (2003). Establishing Mortgage Guarantee Insurance in Transition and Emerging Markets: A Case Study of Kazakhstan. *Housing Finance International*, 9, 10–19.

Meyers, W. and Goychuk, K. (2012). The Ukraine in KRU (Kazakhstan, Russia and Ukraine): Prospects for the Ukrainian Grain Economy, *Village and Agriculture*, 4 (157), 75–89.

Mikheev, V. (2010). Prospects for Relations within the Russia–China–Kazakhstan Triangle under Conditions of Global Crisis. *Problems of Economic Transition*, 53 (5), 4–16.

Ministry of Education (2012a). *Prisoedinenie Kazahstana k Bolonskomu Processu*, Ministry of Education and Science of the Republic of Kazakhstan, available at: http://www.edu.gov.kz/ru/dejatelnost/bolonskii_process/prisoedinenie_k_bolonskomu_processu/, accessed 16 March 2012.

Ministry of Education (2012b). *Nezavisimaya Ocenka Kachestva Urovna Professionalnoi Podgotovlennosti Prisvoenia Kvalifikacii kak Osnovnoi Element Nacionalnoi Ocenki Kachestva*, Ministry of Education and Science of the Republic of Kazakhstan, available at: http://www.rnmc.kz/Default.aspx?tabid=164&language=ru-RU&grm2catid=12, accessed 23 February 2012.

Mir Finansov (2010). Osnovnie Napravlenia Denezhno-Kreditnoi Politiki na 2010 God, Mir Finansov, 4 March, available at: http://wfin.kz/node/7765, accessed 15 October 2012.

Mir Finansov (2011). Kazahstanu dlia Uspeshnoi Industrializacii Nuzhni Zakon Lobbirovanii i Novaya Kadrovaya Politika, Mir Finansov, 8 July, available at: http://www.wfin.kz/node/17058, accessed 28 January 2013.

MIX and CGAP (2011). *MIX Microfinance World: Eastern Europe and Central Asia, Microfinance Analysis and Benchmarking Report 2010.* A report from Microfinance Information Exchange (MIX) and Consultative Group to Assist the Poor (CGAP). Washington, DC: Microfinance Information Exchange, available at: http://www.themix.org/sites/default/files/PPP263%2810-11%29%20MIX_ECA%20Report_30-04-2011.pdf, accessed 18 June 2014.

Modern Analyst (2012). Interview Questions for Business Analysts and Systems Analysts, *Modern Analyst*, available at: www.modernanalyst.com/Careers/InterviewQuestions/tabid/128/articleType/ArticleView/articleId/1003/What-is-the-Herfindahl-Hirschman-Index-HHI-and-why-would-you-use-it.aspx, accessed 15 February 2014.

Mollinga, P. (2008). Field Research Methodology as Boundary Work. In C. Wall and P. Mollinga (eds), *Fieldwork in Difficult Environments. Methodology as Boundary Work in Development Research*, pp. 1–17. Berlin: LIT Verlag.

Morisset, J. and Pirnia, N. (2000). *How Tax Policy and Incentives Affect Foreign Direct Investment. A Review,* World Bank Policy Research Working Paper, No. 2509, Washington, DC.

Müller, K. (2003). *Poverty and Social Policy in the Central Asian Transition Countries*, German Development Institute, Report and Working Papers, No. 2, Bonn.

Musacchio, A. and Lazzarini, S. (2013). Reinventing State Capitalism: Leviathan in Business, Brazil and Beyond, Cambridge: Harvard University Press, forthcoming, available at: http://people.hbs.edu/amusacchio/downloads/reinventing_state_capitalism.pdf, accessed 17 December 2013.

Muzalevsky, R. (2009). Fears of Financial System Collapse in Kazakhstan, *Central Asia-Caucasus Institute Analyst*, 14 January, available at: http://www.cacianalyst.org/?q=node/5017, accessed 3 April 2014.

Mykhnenko, V. (2007). What Type of Capitalism in Eastern Europe? Institutional Structures, Revealed Comparative Advantages, and Performance of Poland and Ukraine. In D. Lane and M. Myant (eds), *Varieties of Capitalism in Post-Communist Economies*, pp. 124–45. Basingstoke: Palgrave Macmillan.

Najman, B., Pomfret, R., Raballand, G. and Sourdin, P. (2005). *How Are Oil Revenues Redistributed in an Oil Economy? The Case of Kazakhstan*, Working Paper, No. 18, School of Economics, University of Adelaide.

National Bank of Kazakhstan (2011). *Denezhno-Kreditnaya Politika Respubliki Kazahstan*, available at: http://www.nationalbank.kz/index.cfm?docid=941, accessed 2 December 2012.

National Bank of Kazakhstan (2012). *About the Bank*, available at: www.nationalbank.kz, accessed 7 March 2012.

National Innovation Fund (2011). *About Us*, National Innovation Fund (NIF), available at: www.nif.kz, accessed 25 June 2011.

National Observatory of Kazakhstan (2005). *Analiz Socialnogo Partnerstva v Professionalnom Obrazovanii I Obuchenii v Kazahstane,* National Observation Center and European Training Foundation (ETF).

Nazarbayev, N. (2003). *Strategia Nezavisimosti.* Almaty: Atamura.

Neweurasia.net (2010). Minimum Wages in Kazakhstan and Abroad, Neweurasia.net, Business and Economics, 5 January, available at: http://www.neweurasia.net/business-and-economics/minimum-wages-in-kazakhstan-and-abroad/, accessed 25 March 2014.

Newskaz (2011). Vsemirnij Bank Profinansiruet Proekt Modernisacii Professionalno-Tehnicheskogo Obrazovania v Kazahstane, Newskaz, 9 September, available at: http://www.newskaz.ru/economy/20110909/187542.html, accessed 2 February 2014.

Nichol, J. (2012). *Kazakhstan: Recent Developments and U.S. Interests*, Congressional Research Service (CRS) Report for Congress, August, 2012, available at: http://www.fas.org/sgp/crs/row/97-1058.pdf, accessed 15 January 2014.

Nölke, A. and Vliegenthart, A. (2009). Enlarging the Varieties of Capitalism. The Emergence of Dependent Market Economies in East Central Europe, *World Politics,* 61 (4), 670–702.

North, D. (1994). Economic Performance through Time. *American Economic Review*, 84 (3), 359–68.

Noy, C. (2007). Sampling Knowledge: The Hermeneutics of Snowball Sampling in Qualitative Research, *International Journal of Social Research Methodology*, 10 (5), 1–18.

NPVET (2008). *Gosudarsvennaya Programma Razvitia Tehnicheskogo I Professionalnogo Obrazovania v Respublike Kazahstan na 2008–2012 Godi*, Approved by the Decree of the President of the Republic of Kazakhstan of 2008, Astana.

Nuttall, P., Shankar, A., Beverland, M. and Stallworth, C. (2011). Mapping the Unarticulated Potential of Qualitative Research, *Journal of Advertising Research*, 51 (1), 153–66.

Obrazovanie.kz (2011). Rashirennoe Zasedanie Ministerstva Obrazovania i Nauki RK, Obrazovanie.kz, 21 January, available at: http://www.obrazovanie.kz, accessed 28 June 2011.

OECD (2004). *OECD Principles of Corporate Governance*. Paris: OECD Publication Services.

OECD (2005a). *Country Assistance Evaluation of Uzbekistan and Kazakhstan*, Summary, The Ministry of Foreign Affairs of Japan Third-Party Evaluation, available at: http://www.oecd.org/dataoecd/62/63/36495036.pdf, accessed 27 January 2014.

OECD (2005b). *Glossary of Statistical Terms. Corporate Governance*. OECD, Statistics Portal, available at: http://stats.oecd.org/glossary/detail.asp?ID=6778, accessed 11 April 2014.

OECD (2011a). *Competitiveness and Private Sector Development: Central Asia 2011,* OECD, the World Economic Forum. Competitiveness and Private Sector Development, Preliminary Version. Paris: OECD Publishing.

OECD (2011b). *Competitiveness and Private Sector Development: Kazakhstan 2010 – Sector Competitiveness Strategy.* Paris: OECD Publishing.

OECD, IBRD and World Bank (2007). *Higher Education in Kazakhstan.* Paris: OECD, the International Bank for Reconstruction and Development and the World Bank.

Okonjo-Iweala, N. (2011). Diversifying Kazakhstan's Economy and Aspirations. *World Bank News*, available at: http://web.worldbank.org/WBSITE/EXTERNAL/NEWS/0,,contentMDK:22929503~pagePK:64257043~piPK:437376~theSitePK:4607,00.html?cid=3001_4, accessed 28 March 2014.

Olcott, M. B. (2008). Kazakhstan: Will "BRIC" Be Spelled with a K? *China and Eurasia Forum Quarterly*, 6 (2), 41–53.

Omarov, N. (2008). *Central Asian States in the Era of Globalization: In Search of a Development Strategy.* Bishkek: Friedrich-Ebert Stiftung.

Ostrowski, W. (2009). The Legacy of the 'Coloured Revolutions': The Case of Kazakhstan. *Journal of Communist Studies and Transition Politics*, 25 (2–3), 347–68.

Ostrowski, W. (2010). *Politics and Oil in Kazakhstan*. London: Routledge.

Ostrowski, W. (2012). *State Capitalism: an Emerging Regime*, Polinares Working Paper, No. 51, available at: http://www.polinares.eu/docs/d4-1/polinares_wp4_chapter1.pdf, accessed 17 April 2014.

Özcan, G. (2011). Heiß Umkämpft – Der Neue Kapitalismus der Basare in Zentralasien, *Zentralasien-Analysen,* 38, 2–5.

Palazuelos, E. and Fernandes, R. (2012). Kazakhstan: Oil Endowment and Oil Empowerment, *Communist and Post-Communist Studies*, 45, 27–37.

Partlett, W. (2008). *Understanding Post-Soviet Resource Nationalism and Contractual Renegotiation: the Demand for Foreign Capital and Contractual Stability*, Working Paper, Columbia Law School, available at: http://www.units.muohio.edu/havighurstcenter/publications/documents/Partlett_ResourceNationalism.pdf, accessed 9 April 2014.

Panova, O. (2008). Komu Nuzhni Profsoyuzy, *Birzhaplus,* No. 27, 21 July, available at: http://www.birzhaplus.ru/birzha/?40813, accessed 23 January 2014.

Pasadilla, G. (2010). *Financial Crisis, Trade Finance, and SMEs: Case of Central Asia*, Asian Development Bank Institute (ADBI) Working Paper Series, No. 187, Tokyo, available at: http://www.adbi.org/working-paper/2010/01/25/3440.financial.crisis.trade.smes.central.asia/, accessed 9 February 2014.

Patton, M. (2002). *Qualitative Research and Evaluation Methods*, 3rd. ed. Thousand Oaks, CA: Sage.

Pavlova, O. and Rohozynsky, O. (2005). Labor Markets in CIS Countries, Center for Social and Economic Research, *Studies and Analysis*, 311, 1–19.

Peck, A. (2004). *Economic Development in Kazakhstan: the Role of Large Enterprises and Foreign Investment*. London/New York: Routledge/ Curzon.

Perecman E. and Curran, S. (2006). *A Handbook for Social Science Field Research,* Essays and Bibliographic Sources on Research Design and Methods. Thousand Oaks, CA: Sage.

Perlman, B. (2007). Cultural Determinism versus Administrative Logic: Asian Values and Administrative Reform in Kazakhstan and Uzbekistan. *International Journal of Public Administration*, 30, 1327–42.

Petrick, M. (2011). *Agricultural Development in Central Asia: Are There Lessons to Be Learned from Comparative Analysis?* Presentation at the Workshop for Young Researchers on Agricultural Development in Central Asia, Leibniz Institute of Agricultural Development in Central and Eastern Europe (IAMO), Halle (Saale).

Peyrouse, S. (2008). Chinese Economic Presence in Kazakhstan. China's Resolve and Central Asia's Apprehension, *China Perspectives*, 3, 34–49.

Picker, A. (2010). *Opportunities and Challenges for Foreign Banks Entering Kazakhstan, Banking and Financial Reform*, presentation at a roundtable discussion under the auspices of the US–Kazakhstan Public–Private Economic Partnership Initiative in Almaty, Kazakhstan, 14 June 2010.

Polterovich, V., Popov, V. and Tonis, A. (2010). *Resource Abundance: A Curse or Blessing?* United Nations Department of Economic and Social Affairs (DESA), Working Paper, No. 93, ST/ESA/2010/DWP/93, available at: http://www.un.org/esa/desa/papers/2010/wp93_2010.pdf, accessed 12 April 2014.

Pomfret, R. (1995). *The Economies of Central Asia.* Princeton, NJ: Princeton University Press.

Pomfret, R. (2003). *Central Asia since 1991: the Experience of the New Independent States,* OECD Development Centre, Working Paper, No. 212, Research programme on Market Access, Capacity Building and Competitiveness.

Pomfret, R. (2005). Kazakhstan's Economy since Independence: Does the Oil Boom Offer a Second Chance for Sustainable Development? *Europe-Asia Studies*, 57 (6), 859–76.

Pomfret, R (2006a). *Will Oil Be a Blessing or a Curse for Kazakhstan?* Paper presented at the British Association for Slavonic and East European Studies (BASEES) conference in Cambridge (UK), April 2006.

Pomfret, R. (2006b). *The Central Asian Economies since Independence.* Princeton, NJ: Princeton University Press.

Pomfret, R. (2009). Central Asia and the Global Economic Crisis. *EU-Central Asia Monitoring* No. 7, Center of European Policy Studies.

Pomfret, R. (2011). *Resource Management and Transition in Central Asia, Azerbaijan, and Mongolia*, Working Paper Series, Working Paper, No. 11 (8), Peterson Institute for International Economics, Washington, DC.

Pleskovic, B., Åslund, A., Bader, W. and Campbell, R. (2000). State of the Art in Economics Education and Research in Transition Economies, *Comparative Economic Studies,* 42 (2), 65–108.

President's Decree (2010). *O Konceptii Razvitia Finansovogo Sektora Respubliki Kazahstan v Post-Krizisnij Period.* Committee for the Control and Supervision of the Financial Market and Financial Organizations of the National Bank of the Republic of Kazakhstan, available at: http://www.afn.kz/attachments/12/264/publish264-1633896258.pdf, accessed 9 March 2012.

Rabionet, S. (2011). How I Learned to Design and Conduct Semi-Structured Interviews: An Ongoing and Continuous Journey, *The Qualitative Report,* 16 (2): 563–66.

Raiskhanova, R. (2000). *Corporate Governance in Kazakhstan,* OECD in Co-Operation with the World Bank and the International Finance Corporation, the United States Agency for International Development, presented at the

Eurasian Roundtable on Corporate Governance, Kiev, Ukraine, 19–20 October.

Rajshekhar G., Granot E. and Alejandro, T. (2011). Qualitative Methods in International Sales Research: Cross-Cultural Considerations. *Journal of Personal Selling and Sales Management* (PSE National Educational Foundation), 31 (2), 157–70.

Rakurs (2011). *The Institutions of Kazakhstan's Financial System,* RAKURS Center for Economic Analysis, paper written for the project *'Emerging Market Economies in Central Asia'* at Private University of Applied Sciences, Göttingen/RAKURS, Almaty.

Rivera, S., Kozyreva, P. and Sarovskii, E. (2002). Interviewing Political Elites: Lessons from Russia, *Political Science and Politics*, 35, 683–88.

Root, H. (1996). *Small Countries, Big Lessons: Governance and the Rise of East Asia.* Oxford: Oxford University Press.

Rybina, L., Reardon, J. and Humphrey, J. (2010). Patriotism, Cosmopolitanism, Consumer Ethnocentrism and Purchase Behaviour in Kazakhstan. *Organisations and Markets in Emerging Economies,* 1, No. (2), 92–107.

Sachs, J. and Warner, A. (1995). *Natural Resource Abundance and Economic Growth*, The National Bureau of Economic Research (NBER), Working Paper, No. 5398, available at: http://www.nber.org/papers/w5398.pdf?new_ window=1, accessed 11 February 2014.

Sagitova, G. (2012). Management Information System for Higher Educational Institutions during Kazakhstan Transition to Knowledge Economy, *World Applied Sciences Journal,* 18 (Special Issue on Economics), 55–60.

Sahin, O. (2011). Risk Management for Banks: Evidence from Banks of Kazakhstan. *Suleyman Demirel University Journal of Faculty of Economics and Administrative Sciences,* 16 (1), 315–32.

Samruk-Kazyna (2012a). *About the Fund*, Samruk-Kazyna, available at: http://sk.kz/page/kratko-o-fonde, accessed 2 April 2014.

Samruk-Kazyna (2012b). *Indicators of the Subsidiaries of the Fund*. Samruk-Kazyna, available at: http://sk.kz/company/indicators/?lang=en, accessed 1 April 2014.

Samruk-Kazyna (2013). *Promezhutochnaya Sokrashennaya Konsolidirovan-naya Finansovaya Otchetnost*, Samruk-Kazyna, available at: http://sk.kz/pag e/download/6066?lang=ru, accessed 15 April 2014.

Sarsenbayev, K. (2011). Kazakhstan Petroleum Industry 2008–2010: Trends of Resource Nationalism Policy? *Journal of World Energy Law and Business*, 4 (4), 369–79.

Satpaev, D. (2010). New Investment Game Rules. European Business Association of Kazakhstan (EUROBAK). *World Monitor, Oil and Gas*, 4 (25), 28–30.

Satpaev, D. and Umbetalieva, T. (2011). Die Dynamik von Machterhalt und -nachfolge. Die Politische Elite in Kasachstan und Perspektiven für den Machtwechsel, *Zentralasien-Analysen,* 39, 2–7.

Schäfer, D., Siliverstovs, B. and Terberger, E. (2010). Banking Competition, Good or Bad? The Case of Promoting Micro and Small Enterprise Finance in Kazakhstan, *Applied Economics,* 42, 701–16.

Scharff, R. (2010). Kasachstan: Aktuelle Wirtschaftslage und Wirtschaftspolitische Strategie, *Zentralasien-Analysen,* 26, 2–6.

Schatz, E. (2004). *Modern Clan Politics: The Power of 'Blood' in Kazakhstan and Beyond.* Seattle, WA: University of Washington Press.

Schatz, E. (2005). Reconceptualising Clans: Kinship Networks and Statehood in Kazakhstan. *Nationalities Papers*, 33 (2), 231–54.

Schmitz, A. (2009). Die Außenpolitik Kasachstans zwischen Regionalismus und Globalem Gestaltungsanspruch, *Zentralasien-Analysen*, 17, 2–5.

Schreier, M. (2012). *Qualitative Content Analysis in Practice.* London: Sage.

Seale, C. (1999). Quality in Qualitative Research, *Qualitative Inquiry*, 5 (4), 465–78.

Seitkasimov, G. (2009). Problemi Bankovskoi Sistemy Kazahstana, *Finansovaya Analitika*, 30 September, available at: http://finanal.ru/008-009/problemy-bankovskoi-sistemy-kazakhstana, accessed 14 March 2014.

Shalgimbayeva, G. (2001). *From Guidance to Sanctions: Powers that Securities Commissions Should Possess.* 2nd Meeting of the Eurasian Corporate Governance Roundtable, USAID, 7–8 June 2001, Tbilisi, Georgia.

Sharma, R. (2013). *Breakout Nations. In Pursuit of the Next Economic Miracles*, W. W. Norton, New York.

Simon, G. (2009). Market Reforms and 'Economic Miracle' in Kazakhstan. *Economic Annals*, 54 (182), 67–92.

Sinicina, I. (2006). *Bednost i Socialnaya Politika v Stranah SNG*, Center for Social and Economic Research (CASE), Studies and Analyses, 316, Warsaw.

Sitenko, D. (2011). National Innovation System in Kazakhstan: Analysis and Prospects. *Review of Management and Economic Engineering*, 10 (1), 107–14.

Smirnova. Y. (2014). Attitudes of Companies in Kazakhstan towards Knowledge Collaboration with Universities. *Procedia – Social and Behavioral Sciences,* 109, 639–644.

Smirnova, Y., Mustafina, A. and Aldabekova, M. (2012). Doing Business in Kazakhstan: What Can We Learn from Malaysian Experience? *Interdisciplinary Journal of Contemporary Research in Business*, 4 (4), 24–35.

Smith, M. (2012). China–Kyrgyzstan–Uzbekistan Railway Project Brings Political Risks, *Central Asia-Caucasus Institute Analyst*, 7 March, available at: http://www.cacianalyst.org/?q=node/5731, accessed 15 April 2014.

Solé, J. (2007). *Introducing Islamic Banks into Conventional Banking Systems,* IMF Working Paper, IMF Monetary and Capital Markets Department, Washington, DC.

Spechler, M. (2000). Uzbekistan: The Silk Road to Nowhere? *Contemporary Economic Policy*, 18 (3), 295–303.

Spechler, M. (2003). Crouching Dragon, Hungry Tigers: China and Central Asia, *Contemporary Economic Policy*, 21 (2), 270–80.

Spechler, M. (2004). Central Asia on the Edge of Globalization, Challenge, 47 (3), 62–77.

Spechler, M. (2008). The Economies of Central Asia: A Survey, *Comparative Economic Studies*, 50, 30–52.

Spechler, M. (2010). *Can Central Asian Countries Become Emerging Economies? Sustainable Recovery and Reform in Central Asia,* paper presented at the Euro 2010 Conference, Milas, Turkey, 16–18 July.

Spence, M. (2009). Internationalisation of Entrepreneurship in Kazakhstan, *International Journal of Globalisation and Small Business*, 3 (3), 252–62.

Spradley, J. (1980). *Participant Observation*, New York: Holt, Rinehart and Winston.

Standard and Poors (2012). *Banking Industry Country Risk Assessment: Kazakhstan*, Standard and Poors, 15 May, available at: http://www.standardandpoors.com/ratings/articles/en/us/?articleType=HTML&assetID=1245333605360, accessed 29 March 2014.

Syroezhkin, K. (2009). *Kitaicam Zemlu ne Otdaut,* Informacionno-Analiticheskij Center, Izuchenie Obshestvenno-Politicheskih Processov na Postsovetskom Prostranstve, 25 December, available at: http://www.ia-centr.ru/expert/6769/, accessed 21 March 2014.

Szamosszegi, A. and Kyle, C. (2011). *U.S.-China Economic and Security Review Commission: An Analysis of State-Owned Enterprises and State Capitalism in China*, Capital Trade, Incorporated, Washington, DC, available at: http://origin.www.uscc.gov/sites/default/files/Research/10_26_11_CapitalTradeSOEStudy.pdf, accessed 17 December 2013.

Tanzi, V. and Tsibouris, G. (1999). *Fiscal Reform over Ten Years of Transition,* Paper presented at the Fifth Dubrovnik Conference on Transition Economies, Dubrovnik, Croatia, 23–25 July.

Tasmagambetov, I. (2005). Kazakhstan: From a Strategy of Survival to a Strategy of Prosperity. *American Foreign Policy Interests*, 26, 33–38.

Tax Code (2008). The Tax Code of the Republic of Kazakhstan of 10 December 2008, 99-4, available at: http://www.salyk.kz/ru/taxcode/pages/default.aspx, accessed 26 January 2013.

Teal, E., Toxanova, A. and Izzo, M. (2011). Entrepreneurial Development in Kazakhstan. A Review and Update, *Journal of International Business and Cultural Studies*, 5, 1–10.

Teddlie, C. and Tashakkori, A. (2009). *Foundations of Mixed Methods Research. Integrating Quantitative and Qualitative Approaches in the Social and Behavioural Sciences.* London: Sage.

Tekenov, U. (2006). Teoreticheskie i Prakticheskie Aspekti Formirovania i Razvitia Klasternoi Sistemi v Kazahstane, *Analitika.org*, 2 October, available at: http://analitika.org/kazakhstan/kz-economics/1282-2006100202 5526187.html, accessed 5 April 2014.

Temasek (2012). *About Temasek. Corporate Profile*, available at: http://www.te masek.com.sg/abouttemasek/corporateprofile, accessed 19 March 2014.

Terjesen, S. and Hessels, J. (2009). Varieties of Export-Oriented Entrepreneurship in Asia. *Asia Pacific Journal of Management*, 26, 537–61.

Toft, P. and Duero, A. (2011). Reliable in the Long Run? Petroleum Policy and Long-Term Oil Supplier Reliability, *Energy Policy*, 39, 6583–94.

Toxanova, A. (2008). *Diversifikaciya Ekonomiki Kazahstana: Problemi I Perspektivi Razvitia.* Materiali Nauchno-Prakticheskoi Konferencii, Astana, KazGUY. Economic Research Institute, available at: http://www.economy.k z/public/749/4398, accessed 28 June 2011.

Toxanova A., Vasa L. and Zhakupova S. (2008). *Kazakhstan in Global Competitiveness Ranking of World Economic Forum. Economics of Sustainable Agriculture*. Scientific Book Series of Szent Istvan University, Gödöllo, 267–86.

Treacher, A. (2007). Political Evolution in Post-Soviet Central Asia, *Democratization*, 3 (3), 306–27.

Troschke, M. and Zeitler, A. (2006). *Privatisation and Corporate Governance in Kazakhstan and Uzbekistan: Insights from a Corporate Survey in Food and Light Industries*. Osteuropa-Institut Working Paper, No. 259, Munich.

Tumenbayeva, O. (2012). Kazakhstan Banking System Restructuring (2007-2010), *Procedia – Social and Behavioural Sciences*, 62, 1107–09.

Twyman, C., Morrison, J. and Sporton, D. (1999). The Final Fifth: Autobiography, Reflexivity and Interpretation in Cross-Cultural Research, *Area*, 31 (4), 313–25.

UNCTAD (2008). *World Investment Report*. New York and Geneva: UNCTAD.

UNCTAD (2010). *Foreign Direct Investment in Kazakhstan: Overview,* available at: http://www.unctad.org/templates/page.asp?intItemID=3198&lang=1, accessed 1 March 2012.

UNDP (2005). *The Great Generation of Kazakhstan: Insight into the Future*. UNDP Kazakhstan. Almaty.

UNECE (2012a). *Innovation Performance Review: Kazakhstan,* United Nations Economic Commission for Europe (UNECE), available at: http://www.unece.org/fileadmin/DAM/ceci/publications/icp5.pdf, accessed 11 April 2014.

UNECE (2012b). *Waste Classifications and Inventories in Eastern Europe, the Caucasus and Central Asia*, United Nations Economic Commission for Europe (UNECE), available at: http://staging.unece.org/env/europe/monitoring/waste_en.html, accessed 25 April 2012.

UNESCO (2005). *O Sobludenii Prav Cheloveka i Grazhdanina v Respubliki Kazahstan v 2005 Godu.* UNESCO in Kazakhstan, Almaty.

UNESCO (2012). *The Education for All Development Index*, Education for All Global Monitoring Report, available at: http://www.unesco.org/new/fileadmin/MULTIMEDIA/HQ/ED/pdf/gmr2012-report-edi.pdf, accessed 27 June 2014.

UNICEF (2002). *Bednost i Tendencii Blagosostojania v 90-e Godi v Kazahstane,* Analytical Report, Coordinator Erbolat Musabekov, Agency for Statistics of the Republic of Kazakhstan, 2002.

United Nations (2011). *Statistical Yearbook for Asia and the Pacific 2011*, United Nations Economic and Social Commission for Asia and the Pacific, available at: http://www.unescap.org/stat/data/syb2011/I-People/Income-poverty-and-inequality.asp, accessed 17 March 2014.

Ursulenko, K. (2010). *Regional Development in Kazakhstan,* Osteuropa-Institut Regensburg, Kurzanalysen und Informationen, 47, 1–10.

USAID (2005). *Evaluation of Junior Achievement/Kazakhstan's Economics/ Business Education Programs.* USAID, available at: http://pdf.usaid.gov/pdf_docs/Pdacf534.pdf, accessed 30 April 2014.

USAID (2010). *Kazakhstan Introduces Legislation that Would Restrict Communications with Government Officials and Parliamentary Deputies*. USAID. Electronic Newsletter. International Center for Not-For-Profit Law (ICNL), Issue 3, available at: http://50.6.35.158/programs/location/nis/resources/Newsletter%203%20%28English%29.pdf, accessed 1 March 2012.

US Department of State (2002). *Background note: Kazakhstan*, available at: http://www.state.gov/r/pa/ei/bgn/5487.html, accessed 27 June 2011.

US Department of State (2011). *Openness to, and Restrictions Upon, Foreign Investment, 2011 Investment Climate Statement – Kazakhstan*, Bureau of Economic, Energy and Business Affairs, available at: http:// www.state.gov/e/eb/rls/othr/ics/2011/157302.htm, accessed 11 January 2014.

Ustyantseva, N. (2010). *Preventing the Oil Curse: the Role of Government Policy in Kazakhstan: in the Period of 1991–2009*. Saarbrücken: VDM Verlag Dr. Müller.

Uzagalieva, A. (2006). Fiscal Consequences of Monetary Integration within a Common Economic Area: The Case of Belarus, Kazakhstan and Russia, *Post-Communist Economies*, 17 (4), 399–424.

Vakulchuk, R., Irnazarov, F. and Libman, A. (2012). Liberalization of Trade in Services in Kazakhstan and Uzbekistan: Analysis of Formal and Informal Barriers. In D. Tarr (ed.), *Influence of Liberalization of Services on Productivity, Export and Development: Empirical Studies in Transition Economies*, pp. 165–200. World Bank/International Bank for Reconstruction and Development, World Bank Book Series, Moscow: 'Ves Mir'.

Van de Vijver, F. and Tanzer, N. (2004). Bias and Equivalence in Cross-Cultural Assessment: an Overview, *Revue Européenne de Psychologie Appliquée*, 54, 119–35.

Veldwisch, G. (2008). Authoritarianism, Validity and Security. Researching Water Distribution in Khorezm, Uzbekistan. In C. Wall and P. Mollinga (eds), *Fieldwork in Difficult Environments. Methodology as Boundary Work in Development Research*, pp. 161–81. Berlin: LIT Verlag.

Verme, P. (1998). *Unemployment, Labour Policies, and Health in Transition: Evidence from Kazakhstan*, United Nations University/World Institute for Development Economics Research, Working Paper, No. 15, Helsinki, available at: http://wider.unu.edu/publications/working-papers/previous/en_GB/wp-151/, accessed 15 April 2014.

Vershinina, G. (2007). Stanovlenie i Razvitie Nalogovoi Sistemy, *Vestnik KASU*, 4, 17–22.

Vielmini, F. (2013). The Challenges of Eurasian Integration for Kazakhstan, *ISPI Analysis*, 151, 1–7.

Vinokurov, E. (2010). Accelerating Regional Integration: Directions for Research. In E. Vinokurov (ed.), *Eurasian Integration Yearbook 2010*, pp. 20–27. Annual publication of the Eurasian Development Bank (EDB), Almaty: Eurasian Development Bank.

Voloshin, G. (2011). Legal Battles Continue Between Kazakhstan and Major Oil Companies, *Central Asia-Caucasus Institute Analyst*, 13 (2), 16–17.

Waikar, A., Cappel, S. and Jepbarova, L. (2009). Analysis of Foreign Direct Investment in Kazakhstan. In V. Bhargava (ed.), *Proceedings of 2009 Sobie Annual Meetings,* pp. 6–11. Destin, Florida, 4–17 April.

Waikar, A., Jepbarova, L., Lee, S., Gardner, L. and Johnson, J. (2011). Impact of Foreign Direct Investment on Kazakhstan's Economy: A Boon or a Curse, *International Journal of Business and Social Science*, 2 (22), 92–98.

Wakeman-Linn, J., Mathieu, P. and Selm, B. V. (2003). Oil Funds in Transition Economies: Azerbaijan and Kazakhstan. In J.M. Davis, R. Ossowski and A. Fedelino (eds), *Fiscal Policy Formulation and Implementation in Oil-Producing Countries*, pp. 339–56. Washington, DC: International Monetary Fund.

Wall, C. (2008). Working in Fields as Fieldwork. *Khashar*, Participant Observation and the Tamorka as Ways to Access Local Knowledge in Rural Uzbekistan. In C. Wall and P. Mollinga (eds), *Fieldwork in Difficult Environments: Methodology as Boundary Work in Development Research,* pp. 137–59. Berlin: LIT Verlag.

Wall, C. and Mollinga, P. (eds) (2008). *Fieldwork in Difficult Environments: Methodology as Boundary Work in Development Research.* Berlin: LIT Verlag.

Wandel, J. (2010). *The Cluster-Based Development Strategy in Kazakhstan's Agro-Food Sector: A Critical Assessment from an 'Austrian Perspective'*, Leibniz Institute of Agricultural Development in Central and Eastern Europe, Discussion Paper No. 128, available at: http://nbn-resolving.de/urn:nbn:de:gbv:3:2-10641, accessed 9 June 2013.

Warkotsch, A. (2008). Normative Suasion and Political Change in Central Asia. *Caucasian Review of International Affairs*, 2 (4), 62–71.

Weinthal, E. and Luong, P. (2001). Energy Wealth and Tax Reform in Russia and Kazakhstan, *Resources Policy*, 27, 215–23.

Wesche, S., Nuynh, N., Nelson, E. and Ramachandran, L. (2010). Challenges and Opportunities in Cross-Cultural Geographic Inquiry, *Journal of Geography in Higher Education*, 34 (1), 59–75.

White, S., Kryshtanovskaia, O., Kukolev, I., Mawdsley, E. and Saldin, P. (1996). Interviewing the Soviet Elite, *The Russian Review*, 55 (2), 309–16.

Wilkinson, C. (2008). Positioning 'Security' and Securing One's Position. The Researcher's Role in Investigating 'Security' in Kyrgyzstan. In C. Wall and P. Mollinga (eds), *Fieldwork in Difficult Environments: Methodology as Boundary Work in Development Research,* pp. 43–54. Berlin: LIT Verlag.

World Bank (2000). *Entering the 21st Century: World Development Report 1999–2000.* World Bank, Washington, DC, available at: http://web.worldbank.org/, accessed 1 December 2012.

World Bank (2005). *Investment Climate Survey: Kazakhstan.* World Bank, Washington, DC.

World Bank (2007). *Doing Business 2007. How to Reform.* International Bank for Reconstruction and Development/World Bank, Washington, DC, available at: http://www.doingbusiness.org/reports/global-reports/doing-business-2007, accessed 15 April 2014.

World Bank (2008). *Adapting to Climate Change in Europe and Central Asia,* Background Paper on Water Supply and Sanitation, prepared by B. Evans and M. Webster, Sustainable Development Department Europe and Central Asia Region, World Bank, Washington, DC.

World Bank (2009a). *Kazakhstan Country Profile. Enterprise Surveys*, World Bank, Washington, DC, available at: http://www.enterprisesurveys.org/~/media/FPDKM/EnterpriseSurveys/Documents/Profiles/English/kazakhstan-2009.pdf, accessed 17 March 2014.

World Bank (2009b). *Republic of Tajikistan Poverty Assessment*, Report No. 51341-TJ, World Bank, Washington, DC, available at: https://openknowledge.worldbank.org/bitstream/handle/10986/3159/513410ESW0P112101Official0Use0Only1.pdf?sequence=1, accessed 12 March 2014.

World Bank (2010). *Russian Economic Report*, The World Bank in Russia, No. 22, available at: http://siteresources.worldbank.org/INTRUSSIANFEDERATION/Resources/305499-1245838520910/rer_22_eng.pdf, accessed 11 March 2014.

World Bank (2011a). *Doing Business 2011: Kazakhstan. Making a Difference for Entrepreneurs.* International Bank for Reconstruction and Development/World Bank, Washington, DC, available at: http://krefeld.ihk.de/media/upload/ihk/imap/20110106/doing_business_2011_kazakhstan.pdf, accessed 1 January 2014.

World Bank (2011b). *Kazakhstan at a Glance.* World Bank, Washington, DC, available at: http://devdata.worldbank.org/AAG/kaz_aag.pdf, accessed 11 March 2014.

World Bank (2012a). *Definition of Self-employed*, 2012, available at: http://data.worldbank.org/indicator/SL.EMP.SELF.MA.ZS, accessed 18 March 2014.

World Bank (2012b). *Kazakhstan*, available at: http://data.worldbank.org/country/kazakhstan, accessed 7 March 2012.

World Bank (2013). *Doing Business 2014. Understanding Regulations for Small and Medium-Size Enterprises. Comparing Business Regulations for Domestic Firms in 189 Economies.* International Bank for Reconstruction and Development/World Bank, Washington, DC, available at: http://www.doingbusiness.org/~/media/GIAWB/Doing%20Business/Documents/Annual-reports/English/DB14-Full-Report.pdf, accessed 15 April 2014.

World Bank (2014). *World Bank Group – Kazakhstan Partnership Program Snapshot*, World Bank, Astana, available at: http://www.worldbank.org/content/dam/Worldbank/document/Kazakhstan-Snapshot.pdf, accessed 27 June 2014.

Wu, W., Wu, Y. and Lo, Y. (2004). The Impact of Governance Mechanisms on Inter-firm Learning and Relationship Performance, *Proceedings of the Asia Pacific Management Conference*, 447–62.

Yermukanov, M. (2003). Streamlining Social Security in Kazakhstan, *Central Asia-Caucasus Institute Analyst*, 23 April, available at: http://www.cacianalyst.org/?q=node/1094, accessed 12 April 2014.

Yermukanov, M. (2005). Kazakhstan and Turkey Search for Common Ground, *Eurasia Daily Monitor*, The Jamestown Foundation, 2 (87), 4 May, available at: http://www.jamestown.org/single/?no_cache=1&tx_ttnews[tt_news]=30348, accessed 3 March 2013.

Yesdauletova, A. (2009). Kazakhstan's Energy Policy: Its Evolution and Tendencies, *Journal of US–China Public Administration*, 6 (4), 31–39.

Zakirova, G., Narenova, M., Kenshibai, T. and Usenbaeva, G. (2009). *Reformirovanie Vishego Obrazovania v Kazahstane I Bolonskij Process: Informacionnie Materiali dlia Prakticheskih Deistvij*, Association 'Education for All in Kazakhstan'. Almaty: National Office of the TEMPUS Program in Kazakhstan.

Zakon.kz (2008). V 2008 Godu Budut Pozitivnie Itogi Raboty po Stabilizacii Urovna Cen – Nazbank RK, Zakon.kz, 4 January, available at: http://www.zakon.kz/100858-v-2008-godu-budut-pozitivnye-itogi.html, accessed 20 January 2014.

Zakon.kz (2012a). Uroven Bezrabotici v Kazahstane Odin iz Samih Nizkih v SNG, Zakon.kz, 16 April, available at: http://www.zakon.kz/4485131-uroven-bezraboticy-v-kazakhstane-odin.html, accessed 15 January 2014.

Zakon.kz (2012b). Kazahstan Mozhet Prodolzhit Snizhenie Stavki Refinansirovania pri Sohranenii Nizkoi Inflacii, Zakon.kz, 7 June, available at: http://www.zakon.kz/4495431-kazakhstan-mozhet-prodolzhit-snizhenie.html, accessed 12 February 2014.

Zarakhovich, Y. (2006). Kazakhstan Comes on Strong. *Time Magazine*, 27 September, available at: http://www.time.com/time/world/article/0,8599,1539999-1,00.html, accessed 11 April 2014.

Zhatkanbaev, E. and Mukhtarova, K. (1999). Unemployment as a Factor of Reducing Living Standards of Population, *Vestnik KazGU*, Serial of Economic Sciences, No. 1, available at: http://lib.kazsu.kz/libr/Vestnik/LibrEn/Vestnik/Econom/year99/N1/2.htm, accessed 30 June 2011.

Emerging Markets Studies

Edited by Joachim Ahrens, Alexander Ebner, Herman W. Hoen, Bernhard Seliger and Ralph Michael Wrobel

The Peter Lang series *Emerging Markets Studies* includes works which address opportunities, problems, and challenges of socio-economic development and reform in so-called emerging markets. These comprise middle-income developing and transition economies which are relevant for the world economy due to a large market potential, a favorable or improving investment climate, or due to the availability of important natural resources. Emerging markets have realized or show the potential to generate sustained socio-economic development and growth processes over time.

The volumes in this series seek to address three key questions: What are the determinants of successful socio-economic development, What are appropriate reform strategies to overcome impediments to catching-up processes, and How do politico-institutional factors affect the performance of an emerging economy?

The scope of the series is comparative, institutionalist, and international. The overall focus of all titles is to enhance the understanding of socio-economic catching-up processes and their institutional foundations from a political-economy perspective. Due to the complexity of development processes and policy reform, various methodological tools and academic approaches may prove to be appropriate. Hence the series includes contributions from various disciplines such as economics, political science, or sociology.

Vol. 1 Dominik F. Schlossstein: Institutional Change in Upstream Innovation Governance. The Case of Korea. 2010.

Vol. 2 Manuel Stark: The Emergence of Developmental States from a New Institutionalist Perspective. A Comparative Analysis of East Asia and Central Asia. 2012.

Vol. 3 Bernhard Seliger: The Shrimp that Became a Tiger. Transformation Theory and Korea's Rise After the Asian Crisis. 2013.

Vol. 4 Dirk Johann: The Reconfiguration of a Latecomer Innovation System. Governing Pharmaceutical Biotechnology Innovation in South Korea. 2013.

Vol. 5 Roman Vakulchuk: Kazakhstan's Emerging Economy. Between State and Market. 2014.

www.peterlang.com

www.ingramcontent.com/pod-product-compliance
Ingram Content Group UK Ltd.
Pitfield, Milton Keynes, MK11 3LW, UK
UKHW020834290926
15470UKWH00004B/1337

9 783631 650950